LIVE ALBOM II

Editor: Tracee Hamilton

Associate editor: Gene Myers

Project co-ordinator: Dave Robinson

Copy editing: Brad Betker, Bill Collison, Owen Davis, Tom Panzenhagen, Steve Schrader and the Detroit Free Press sports copy desk

Cover design and illustrations: Jef Mallett

Cover photograph: Andy Greenwell

Photo colorization: Kathleen Thompson

Research: Chris Kucharski

Research assistant: Linda Beard

Special thanks: Janine, Mike, Ken and Elvis

© Detroit Free Press Inc., 1990
321 W. Lafayette
Detroit, Michigan 48226

ISBN 0-937247-19-7

On a professional level, I would like to dedicate this book to the people who employ me and tolerate me, namely, my bosses and my editors. In particular, Dave Robinson, who always finds something positive to say, even when I screw up, and Tracee, Gene, Owen, Tom, Toni and the rest of the staff, who endure my often funny concepts of deadline and space.

Personally, there are four people I wish could have seen this book: my grandparents, Ruth, Selma, and Frank, and my uncle, Mike. I love them and miss their company. Wherever in heaven they are, this is for them.

FOREWORD

By Ernie Harwell

T he heroes of my youth were sports writers.
    After I discovered I couldn't stop a grapefruit from rolling uphill, I
    abandoned my earlier ambition of being a big-league baseball player
and dreamed of covering sports for a metropolitan newspaper.

I lost those dreams somewhere between youth and adulthood. *But* I
never lost my admiration for the writers. They are still my heroes.

At the top of my hero list is Mitch Albom. This collection of Mitch's
columns will demonstrate why.

Mitch can make you laugh or cry. He can touch your heart. He can play
your emotions like the classy piano player he is. I'm proud to be in his vast
audience of admirers. All of us agree with those Associated Press editors
who four times have named Mitch the best sports columnist of the year —
an unprecedented run for that prestigious award.

Mitch Albom wrote these columns under pressure. It may not seem so,
but he did. A deadline was staring him in the face. Maybe his visit to the
locker rooms had been hectic. The athletic heroes and villains sometimes
wouldn't talk and were downright nasty. Maybe his word processor was
balky. Or Mitch's plane was leaving within the hour from a distant airport.

All these pressures should be pounding at our hero as he composed on
his magical keyboard.

Yet, somehow, he did it. The columns emerge smooth and readable.
You'd think Mitch had written the stuff in a peaceful library. We readers are
lucky he can continue to produce such gems with astounding consistency.

When I read a sports column, I want to be entertained or informed. If a
columnist can satisfy me on one of those counts, he has done a good job. If he
can accomplish both aims, he is outstanding. Mitch Albom's genius is
double-barrelled. He both entertains and informs.

I grew up reading Grantland Rice. Later, it was Red Smith, Westbrook
Pegler, Shirley Povich and Dick Young. They were my early heroes.

Now, I enjoy Mitch Albom. Read the columns in Mitch's collection.
Savor them. You'll appreciate a great talent, and Mitch Albom will become
your hero, too.

E.H., August 1990

TABLE OF CONTENTS

1988

1989

1990

Etc.

(Columns from the Detroit Free Press Sunday Comment section)

WITH FROZEN TEARS, PAYTON WALKS AWAY

January 11

CHICAGO — He sat there, alone, ignoring the cold, ignoring the departing crowd, ignoring the scoreboard, which read Washington 21, Chicago 17. The game was over. Both teams were already inside. A frozen wind blew over Soldier Field. Walter Payton remained on the bench.

"What's he doing?" someone whispered.

"He's just sitting there," someone said.

His eyes were barely visible beneath his dark blue helmet. His shoulders slumped beneath the pads. A yellow metal heater was blowing a few feet away, but he made no attempt to move closer.

"Is he OK?" someone whispered.

"He's just sitting there," came the answer.

In the final minute of this playoff game, on fourth down, no time-outs left, Jim McMahon, the Bears' quarterback, had seen all of his receivers covered, and, in desperation, had tossed a short pass to Payton in the flat. The Bears needed eight yards for a first down and any hope. Payton got seven.

"WAL-TER!" the fans began to yell as he sat.

"WAL-TER! WAL-TER!"

He did not move, did not respond. He just sat there as fans screamed, then fell into a respectful silence. Cameramen spotted him and ran over, recording his meditation on tape.

"Is he saying anything?" someone asked.

"No. He's just sitting there."

For a while it seemed as if he might never leave. His head was bowed, his body limp. After 13 years, and 199 games, and more yards than any other football player has ever gained, there were tears running down a grown man's cheeks. Walter Payton did not want to go home.

It'll be a long time before we see the likes of him again," said offensive lineman Mark Bortz, tearing off his jersey in the Bears' locker room.

"It's just too bad we couldn't get him one more game, you know?" said center Jay Hilgenberg, shaking his head.

These were his linemen talking, the men whose job was to clear holes so that Payton could run for glory. They were bruised and sweaty. They had just seen their season end.

They were talking about Payton.

Finally, in he came. He found a place by his locker and curled against the wall. A mob of reporters encircled him. A locker room attendant stepped in front: "Five yards! Give him five yards to breathe!"

It may have been the first time Payton, 33, had asked for five yards in his life. Here is a guy who earned every step he took, a running back who so dazzled the sport that he defied logic. Didn't he miss only one game in his career? One game? In 13 seasons? As a running back? What was he made of?

Who knew? We only knew he was durable, and never stopped pumping, moving his feet, juking, twisting, thumping and high-stepping into end zones. There were games where he raked in more than 200 yards rushing and seasons where he raked in more than 2,000 all-purpose yards and, although much of his career was spent with dismal Bears teams that worked him like a plow horse, he finally saw his mountaintop in the 1985 season, when the Bears won the Super Bowl.

"Sweetness" they called him, a sissy moniker only tough guys can carry. No one could ever keep pace with Payton's off-season routine (running sand hills behind his house in combat boots was only one part of that). No one ever crossed him. And now, after his final game, a huge crowd of reporters stood in a silent circle, waiting, not interrupting, as Payton, officially retired, sat with his helmet on and his eyes closed.

In time, after a shower, a shave, moments with his teammates, Payton spoke. He spoke in the soft, high voice that has always contradicted his playing style. He said leaving the sport hadn't really sunk in yet. Maybe later.

"I want to say these 13 years overall have been a lot of fun. When football stops being fun, you should stop doing it. That's why it's so hard to leave. . . . The fun is still there."

In his happiest year, when they were all Super Bowl winners, Payton was the superstar on a team full of crazies, so wild and offbeat that the country took them to heart. But that team was vanishing now. Gary Fencik, the erudite safety from Yale, also was retiring, and McMahon, the tobacco-spitting, can't-lose quarterback, had just lost, at home, and Mike Ditka, the barking coach, was barking about "changes that need to be made."

So maybe the time was ripe. But as we say good-bye to Walter Payton, let the tapes show that on his final play, that final swing pass, he charged right into Washington's Barry Wilburn and would not be tackled — he wrestled, struggled, twisted and resisted until both stumbled out of bounds.

The game was lost. But he had retired the way he had always played: fighting for one more yard. In the end, only the sidelines could stop him. ♦

BOXING'S BLOOD AND GUTS HAVE LOST THEIR CHARMS

January 22

T here was a time, back in college, when I laced up boxing gloves and tried to prove myself in a ring. I was not very talented; I did more ducking than hitting. But one night, while sparring with my coach, I tagged him, unsuspecting, and he straightened up and blinked. At that moment, I felt a surge of naked power, almost primitive, as if my blood had thickened and I was bloated with muscle. It was a manly thing I had done. I felt manly.

And then he pounded the hell out of me.

A far less pleasant feeling that was, like putting your head inside a metal drum and rolling down a hill. What amazed me was how quickly I lost my senses; it was less than seven seconds before I could find the corner. My jaw ached the next morning, and my shoulders felt like bricks pinning me to my bed.

That was a long time ago. Today, I will board an airplane and fly to Atlantic City to see a fight. Heavyweights. Larry Holmes vs. Mike Tyson. When I began in this business, I would arrive a week early, take notes at the workouts, talk with the fighters. This time the main event is just hours after my plane lands. And tomorrow morning, as soon as I can, I will fly out.

Boxing has dimmed; it is embarrassing now. The pre-fight remains cartoonish. The boxer says: "I'll kill him." The promoter says: "He's the greatest." It's the worst sort of theater. Everyone is full of it.

Yet I am still going to the fight.

W hy? What is it with boxing? You do what Marvin Hagler and Thomas Hearns did out in the street, they book you for assault. I sat ringside that night in Las Vegas. There was blood on my notebook by the second round. After one brutal exchange, Hearns wobbled away, grinning stupidly.

"Jesus!" screamed the guy next to me. "He's laughing after that?"

"He's not laughing," I mumbled.

Moments later, Hearns was flat on the canvas. His smile, which seemed the height of arrogance, was actually his body saying, "Good night."

Tonight Larry Holmes, 38, who once promised he would never be as foolish as Muhammad Ali, returns to the ring at the same age Ali finally sank. Soft and powerless, Ali was pounded by a younger Holmes, and Larry was almost in tears afterward, having demolished a mentor who should never have been fighting.

Yet tonight, Tyson, 21, gets to bang Holmes' old bones. And if he slaughters the ex-king, it is not likely he will cry.

Nor will anybody else.

"I like the idea of putting $3 million in the bank," Holmes admitted recently. So much for his motivation. Where is ours? Do we even have any?

Remember that once Ali left the stage, it seemed there were no worthy heavyweight champs. Holmes wore the crown against nameless blobs, until Michael Spinks gained weight and took it away. "Ah, they all stink," we would say.

We cannot say that now. Mike Tyson is a legitimate champion, all power, from his black trunks to his black shoes with no socks. He has beaten everyone. Yet we're remarkably uninterested. Why? Perhaps because, unlike Ali's, Tyson's personality is not jolting. He does not scream, does not taunt the world. He is a good fighter. So what?

Norman Mailer once wrote that we were so obsessed with Ali because of his ego. We could not ignore him. But these days the sports world has Dexter Manleys, Brian Bosworths, Reggie Jacksons. What's new about ego anymore?

So Tyson can say, "No man on the planet can beat me," and people yawn. There are no new boasts left. Personality has cheapened, and when you take personality out of boxing, all you have left is two men slugging each other.

And that, in this violent age, is no big deal.

Duk Koo Kim was killed in the ring by Ray Mancini. George Foreman tries to punch and preach. Ali mumbles, a husk of his old self. The horrors of brain damage are common news now. People cluck their tongues in disgust.

I think the cumulative effect is finally taking hold. Boxing may be great copy — Hemingway and Mailer penned majestic works — but it is brutal, repulsive, bloody and, in today's world, nearly prehistoric. There's no point anymore.

And I am still going to the fight. What is wrong with me? That same mix of compulsion and revulsion — the breathy moment when I stunned my instructor, the dizziness I felt after his pounding — still lures me. But it grows weak. I go less. I arrive late. And I imagine I will soon say: "Forget it. I can't cover this stuff anymore."

Which will be OK. Maybe I should be saying it already. This much I learned on the canvas of that ring a long time ago — there is only one good conclusion to the seductive punch of boxing: If you're lucky, you come to your senses.

When we come to ours, the sport will be gone. ♦

IN BASEBALL TODAY, MONEY TALKS – AND GIBSON WALKS

January 31

They come for money, they go for money. If you're lucky you get a few memories in between. Kirk Gibson always played baseball with the cold glint of opportunity in his eyes — he saw a chance, he took it — and today, for those same reasons, he heads west, no longer a Tiger but a Los Angeles Dodger. Like it, hate it, gone is gone. You have something to say, you can yell it at his airplane.

Wave good-bye to a native son. There is no way the Detroit clubhouse will be the same without Gibson, no replacing his harsh but contagious air of winning, or his joyous home run dashes. He grew up in Michigan, a cagey, whiskered, time bomb of a player, but always a guy you wanted on your side.

"I wanted to stay in the worst way," he said. Instead, he chose to leave in the richest: a three-year, free-agent contract worth $4.5 million — more than half of which he will earn by the end of this season.

The numbers, as they say, weigh heavily in his favor.

His departure is historic: the first time a player has been freed from a contract because of the owners' sins. Do you care? Probably not. Detroit fans feel only deprived, as if someone left the back door open and the cat ran away.

"It's kind of sad," someone said to Gibson. "Lance Parrish, Dan Petry — now you. The homegrown Tigers seem to be slowly disappearing."

"Hey," he said, "that's modern baseball."

Man, is that a mouthful.

Here is the game, America. A man gets one contract offer, he signs it, his union files a grievance because he didn't get any others, the arbitrator agrees, the man is freed from his deal, and he signs with a different team — which didn't offer him anything the first time around — for lots more money.

The feeling is that there should be someone to blame. Were the Tigers too cheap? Was it Gibson's greed? The Dodgers? Gibson's agent?

The truth is, it was simply baseball — which is so top-heavy with dollar signs and legal mumbo jumbo you almost can't recognize it. Little wonder that the final holdups on Gibson's new contract had to do with drug clauses and payment in case of a strike. Once upon a time contracts dealt with home runs and strikeouts.

But that was a long time ago. Gibson was sprung from the shackles of a $1.3 million Detroit salary — not such a horrible prison — because the owners had colluded in 1985. Gibson was unwanted then, but being a smart shopper, he checked around, and this time — although he is 30, with two unspectacular seasons behind him — he found there were takers.

"It happened real quick," he admitted. He said he gave the Tigers "every opportunity" to match the offer. The Tigers — who had offered a one-year extension with a no-trade clause — say the last they heard, LA was offering only a two-year deal. No matter. Detroit would not have matched the final Dodgers offer.

"Hey, there's gotta be a top line for the Tigers and a bottom line for me," Gibson said. "In the end that gap was just too big. . . .

"I'm not resentful. I'm not vengeful. I respect the way the Tigers handled it and I hope they respect me.

"I'm not gonna tell you I won't miss Detroit, the team, the people. I know I'm going to. But when I considered the whole picture, this was what was best for me."

What was the "whole picture"? Here was a player raised in the Tigers organization, whom a few months ago the Tigers were ready to trade. Bill Lajoie, the Tigers' general manager, maintains he never shopped Gibson, but rather "other teams asked for him" when Lajoie was looking for right-handed hitters. Gibson admits that the trading idea stung him at first.

"I'll go so far as to say (the trade talk) happened," he said. "And leave it at that."

So what? Should the Tigers have tried not to trade Gibson out of fear for hurting his feelings? Come on. Baseball has never worked that way. It just so happens that, in this case, Gibson was suddenly put in a rare position: master of his own fate. With the Dodgers, he'll earn $2.5 million this season in salary and bonus — $1.2 million more than he would have gotten as a Tiger.

Would you turn that down?

"If I could rewrite the script none of this would have happened," he said. But none of us can rewrite scripts. Gibson will go to La-La Land, where he could become an endorsement-ad star — and the Tigers are left with a hole in their lineup in the crucial No. 3 spot. It's amazing to think had the Tigers completed that deal with LA last year, Gibson would be free from the Dodgers now, without ever having played a game. He could have even signed back with the Tigers.

Modern baseball.

So wave good-bye. Many people hated Gibson, but many more swooned over him. He was almost perversely charismatic, crass, boorish, fiercely independent. But there was always something about that grizzled face, a nagging belief that as long as he was on the team, it could never really sink too far from winning. He'd beat everybody up, right?

Gone now. Just an empty locker.

"Where do you think your departure leaves the Tigers?" he was asked.

"I don't think that's a concern of mine," he said, an outsider now. "That question is better suited to Bill Lajoie."

At the Free Press, we have photo files of all the Tigers, pictures from when they had more hair and less mileage: Lance Parrish, with his almost hippie-ish young looks, Dan Petry in his fresh-scrubbed early 20s, Gibson when he was a campus monster back at Michigan State, his eyes wide, his hair a Prince Valiant wild. They are thick files. We label them under other cities now.

They come for money, they go for money. Gibson's nine years in Detroit, his home runs, his World Series leap, his antics with Dave Rozema, his impish grin, his churlish behavior — "the total package," as he might put it — will be stored away in the cabinet of our memories. Sunday will turn to Monday, winter to spring, and everybody will survive, a little bit colder. Money has a way of spitting on passion.

"I may be gone, but I'm not forgotten," Gibson joked about himself.

Give it time, Kirk. ♦

LAKE PLACID, 1980:
THE REST OF THE STORY

February 17

C ALGARY, Alberta — I walked down the corridor of press offices and knocked softly on the door marked "TASS." It was opened by an older man in a gray coat.

"Hello," I said quickly, extending a hand. The man shook his head, pointed at the floor and began babbling in Russian.

Trouble, I figured. But I figured wrong. What he was saying, I would learn, was: "We Russians don't shake hands through a doorway; come inside and shake like friends."

Which only proves there are two ways to look at everything. Tonight, at these Winter Olympics, the Americans and the Soviets will meet again in ice hockey, a rivalry now and forever glossed with the words "1980, Lake Placid." Remember? When a team of fresh-faced U.S. kids defeated the mighty Soviets and went on to the gold medal?

For America, it was a snapshot of glory. Fans cried. Even journalists were cheering. But a stern-looking, 48-year-old man named Vladimir Dvortsov also was in that Lake Placid, N.Y., press box, and when the game ended he was the only one to go into the losers' locker room.

He was the TASS reporter.

And now he was standing in front of me.

"Yes, of course, I remember that game," he said through an interpreter. "Afterwards, the Soviet players were all sitting quietly by their lockers. They were in shock. I said to them, 'What is the reason for this defeat? You have such a great team, and you lost to students.'

"They said, 'We lost? We lost?' They could not believe it. This was a titanic failure."

A s he spoke, it dawned on me how much of this story had never been told. After all, losers are normally interviewed at sports events, too. But the Soviets, impenetrable under good conditions, were off limits after the 1980 defeat. And back at home, Dvortsov said, the whole game was viewed as "a mistake." The lifting of famed Soviet goalie Vladislav Tretiak after the first period — with the score tied 2-2 — was seen as a crucial blow, a move decried by Russian fans, the way Pistons fans might now lament: "Why did Isiah throw that pass?"

"It never should have happened," Dvortsov said, waving his hands.

"The American students were too encouraged when Tretiak left. They scored two goals on (Vladimir) Myshkin, the replacement. It was a mistake by the Soviet coach. It was nonsense."

Dvortsov said most people in Russia felt that way. He said the Soviet players told him afterward that his questions in the locker room would be the only ones they would ever answer about that game.

"Really?" I said. "And have you never talked to them about it again?"

"Ninety-nine percent," he said.

We want to remember. They want to forget.

It was strange to hear such a new account of such a familiar game. We are so used to wonderful stories — who doesn't shiver at the words "Do you believe in miracles?" — that we forget there were losers in that affair, Olympians who went home with dreams disappointed. "I know in the U.S. the game was seen as something wonderful," Dvortsov said, breaking into a grin. "Journalists wrote the mighty USSR had finally been defeated!"

"And what did you write?" I asked.

"I wrote the U.S. team had a very good performance and they deserved the victory. And for the Soviet team, it was a tragedy."

The translator paused.

"Perhaps not tragedy. Uh . . . disappointment?"

He told other stories about that night, like how he entered the U.S. locker room and was shocked to see that the guards were celebrating. ("The players were on the telephone with President Carter. There was no security! I could have taken the uniforms!")

And then, suddenly, he stopped, and began talking quickly to the translator. This is what he said:

"You must consider the time this game happened, yes? It was quite different from now. There was no talk of a summit, for example, like we signed last year. . . .

"Today it would be different. If it happened, it might be unexpected, but we would congratulate the U.S. team."

He paused. "You know, Monday night, when the Czechs played the U.S., some of us rooted for the Czechs, and some for the U.S.? Not because one is the Soviet bloc and one is not. But because we like their hockey. A team is a team, not a bloc. Do you understand?"

I nodded, and said I did.

It grew late. He had to go. We shook hands — inside the office — and I left. To be honest, I never figured on this interview happening. I was lucky I had a few sheets of paper in my pocket. I am reading them now, crinkled and sloppy, new notes on a game that is eight years old. And I'm glad I have them. Funny, no? Sometimes we think we've got the whole picture. The truth is, we're only a part of it. ◆

IT'S CHAMP VERSUS CHUMP FOR KING OF THE SKI HILL

February 24

CALGARY, Alberta — Finally, ladies and gentlemen, we bring you the Olympic 90-meter ski jump, where the burning question remains: Can a man they call "The Flying Finn" be upstaged by a clumsy, bespectacled Brit who once bit off his tongue?

Strange but true. Remember, this is an event where grown men ski off a huge ramp and fly into the wild blue yonder — without a pole, much less a parachute. No wonder the Canadian winds kept postponing this thing: Chinooks are attracted to schnooks.

Which brings us to our stars. There were only two jumpers who mattered in this competition.

Let's meet them:

ATHLETE NO. 1: Matti Nykanen, 24, Finland. The best in the world, the gold medal favorite, the guy who says to Sly Stone, "No, sucker, I want to take you higher." So outstanding is Nykanen (NU-kah-nen) that fellow athletes call him "Matti Nukes." Which pretty much sums up his personality. Aloof? Nasty? Spoiled? Keep going. He already has been thrown off the Finnish team once for alcohol problems (which, when he really gets wild, have earned him the nickname "Matti Pukes" — but that is another story).

ATHLETE NO. 2: Michael (Eddie) Edwards, 24, Great Britain. The worst ski jumper in the world.

Now, you might not consider this much of a competition. Well. Maybe not for the gold medal. But hey. We all knew Nykanen would win that. We're talking applause. Attention. Endorsement contracts!

Let's go to the hill.

There's Eddie, short, big-jawed, Coke-bottle glasses — he looks like a squashed Buddy Holly — about to take his second and final jump. He smiles at the crowd. The crowd goes nuts. He waves at the crowd. The crowd goes nuts. "ED-DIE! ED-DIE!" it screams. Wait. Didn't we say he was the worst jumper here? Yes, we did. That's why they love him. Behind those pink goggles is the most dangerous of mixes: eccentricity (his) plus boredom (ours). What do hundreds of reporters write about when they don't understand a single winter sport, and along comes a nerd-do-well ski jumper who admits he once slept in an insane asylum to save money? As a child of 7, he fell from a seesaw and bit off his tongue. They sewed it back on. Sewed it on? Whoa. Look out. Give us a week. We'll make this guy a star.

And so we did. Although he can't jump to save his life (which, come to think of it, is exactly how he jumps), Eddie now gets mobbed at restaurants. Eddie now poses with pinup girls. Eddie has an agent.

When officials here threatened to keep Eddie (nicknamed "The Eagle") from jumping the 90 meters for fear he would break every bone in his body, it was front-page news. The fans roared. Eddie was allowed to jump.

And here he comes.

"ED-DIE! ED-DIE! ED-DIE!" . . . Now some of us thought the most fitting exit for old Ed would be to fly off that 90-meter jump and impale himself on a ski — splat! — sort of sticking up right in the middle of the hill, and then folks could come by and say, "Yeah, well, you know. He wasn't very good anyhow."

But that may seem cruel.

No matter. Spurred by the cheering crowd, Eddie came off the run the way ketchup comes out of a bottle, stayed in the air long enough for one snap of the Instamatic, then plopped to earth. The Eagle had landed. His distance: 67 meters. That is not very far. If ski jumping were football, 67 meters would be a fumble.

He was dead last.

No matter. Edwards looked happy to be alive. Which, no doubt, he was. He held his skis high and waved.

"How did you like it?" the mob of reporters yelled.

"I loved it! This has been the greatest day of my life!"

"Will you celebrate with a drink?"

"No. I don't drink. I got drunk once and never drank again."

"How old were you?"

"Thirteen."

"What next, Eddie?"

"Oh, I'll go home for a week."

"No! After that!"

"Well, I've only been at this for two years," he said, poking at his glasses. "Who knows? Maybe in four years I'll be the best."

The best?

Speaking of the best, the best was soon at the top of the ramp. Matti Nukes. On the first of his two jumps, he broke the hill record. He came off the ramp and flew. And flew. He stayed up so long, his coffee got cold. The only thing bringing him back to earth was the need to collect his gold medal, which he would surely have if he hit this second jump as he hit the first.

And down he came.

We should pause to describe the difference between Eddie the Eagle's jumping style and that of Nykanen:

Everything.

OK. Back to the jump. Nykanen lifted off the end of the run, head out over the tips of his skis, and rode the wind better than Christopher Cross ever did. As the crowd gasped, he touched down near the farthest measuring line, the end of the rainbow, where, of course, you find gold. One-hundred and seven meters. Add that to his first jump of 118.5 meters and you've got a Northwest Airlines route.

"Congratulations, Matti!" a TV reporter screamed at him. "You've won the gold medal. How do you feel?"

"The second jump wasn't as good as the first jump," he droned.

And he waddled away.

So much for Matti.

The officials promised he would come back. They were still promising two hours later. Finally, Nykanen, the gold medalist in the 90- and 70-meter jumps, a guy whose coach says he is the "best ever," consented to five minutes.

"Can you describe your feelings at winning the gold?"

"I am very happy," he said, bleakly.

"How long will you keep jumping?"

"I have plans to compete until 1992."

"What do you think of Eddie Edwards?"

He paused.

"We need a few clowns in this business," he said.

And then he left.

And there you have it. The competition that took three days to pull off was history. Who won? Well. Hard to say. Nykanen goes home with the gold. But last time I looked, a mob of reporters was racing toward the bus area. They were looking for Eddie. ♦

IN A WATERSHED MOMENT, WILLIE PROVES HE'S A JERK

March 3

L AKELAND, Fla. — The good news is, Willie Hernandez has rediscovered the strike zone.

The bad news is he was standing only six inches away and it wasn't a baseball.

It was a bucket of ice water. A large bucket of ice water. He threw it on my head.

I should explain.

I had just arrived at the Tigers' spring training camp from the Winter Olympics in Calgary. I was talking in the clubhouse with pitcher Frank Tanana. And the next thing I know, I am drenched. All over. And Willie is walking away, saying, "Take that, bleeper-bleeper!"

I kept my cool. That wasn't hard to do, because ice cubes were running down my neck. But I did have a few questions.

Like: Why did Willie do it? It could be because he heard me talking about the Winter Olympics and wanted to create the proper atmosphere.

It could be because I was sweating, and a concerned Willie wanted to cool me off.

Or it could be because Willie Hernandez is an immature hothead who is carrying a grudge over a column that is 11 months old and figures he doesn't have to account for his actions when he's in the clubhouse.

Any one of those three. But back to the story.

I continued my conversation with Tanana, who, understandably, had moved a few steps back. And then I left to get a dry shirt. When I returned, several reporters asked me what happened and I told them: I had not said a word to Willie in five months. I had not laid eyes on Willie in five months. Perhaps this was a new way of saying hello.

I s he mad at you?" the question came.

"I don't know," I said. I do know that last year, Hernandez was upset with a column in which he said: "Bleep the fans. I don't give a bleep about the fans. ... I don't care if you write it. The way they treat me? Bleep them."

Now. Willie knows he said this. He admits he said it. Besides, I have it on tape. I even asked him three or four times whether he was sure he wanted to be quoted that way. He said he didn't care. When the column came out,

27

suddenly he cared.

Anyhow, in the months that followed, Willie's pitching went sour. Fans at Tiger Stadium, who already jeered him, began booing his very entrance. By October, he was useless.

And all during that time, I barely wrote a word! Other writers ripped him up and down. Yet, for some reason, he would curse when he saw me, and I would ask him what's wrong, and he'd curse again, and when I asked whether he wanted to talk about it, he would curse again. Then one afternoon, he whacked the stereo system with a baseball bat, and I figured, OK, fine, talking isn't that important.

And now, suddenly, I had wet underwear.

But wait. Later, I am in the clubhouse hall, and Willie walks past me. And I'm thinking, maybe he'll say: "I'm sorry." Or: "I lost my head."

Instead, he said: "I had to do it."

Now, on the list of all-time apologies, "I had to do it" doesn't rank really high. Willie then yelled how I was the cause of all his problems last year. Not the home runs he gave up. Not the walks or the mushballs he threw. Me.

"You turned the fans against me!"

"Don't you think your performances had anything to do with it?" I asked.

"No. You did it! Look at my performances!"

I wanted to tell him I would, but they kept going over the rightfield wall. But I did not say this. What I did say was, listen, if you have something to say to me, come up and say it, like a man. Dumping a bucket of ice water on my head might get my attention, but then I'd have to leave to get dry clothes.

"I hear another bleep out of you, we're gonna go at it!" he yelled, threatening me.

"You'll go at it alone, Willie," I said. And I meant it. I've never seen punches solve a thing.

And so Willie took off, cursing. I still don't know his problem. I still can't believe one column 11 months ago, for which he has only himself to blame — after all, those were his words, not mine — can still upset him.

Since this happened, I have been asked many questions. A common one is: "Why did you keep talking with Tanana?" Because we hadn't finished our conversation. I'm not going to let a little shower ruin a nice chat.

"Why didn't you go after Willie?" Because that would be just as childish.

"What have you learned from this incident?" Well. I would have to say this: 1) Always carry shampoo. 2) Never talk near a sink.

Frankly, I can only feel sorry for Willie. My biggest concern is not physical harm, or embarrassment. To be honest, given his history, when I think of Willie tossing that bucket over my head, I have but one worry:

That might be his best pitch all year. ◆

Rumeal Robinson's Tale: Love Over Everything

March 19

S ALT LAKE CITY, Utah — The boy had been sleeping in an apartment building hallway. His mother didn't want him anymore.
"When was the last time you ate a meal?" Helen Ford asked him.
"Three weeks ago," he said.

She took a breath. As a volunteer at the Cambridge (Mass.) Community Center, she had seen lots of kids. Lots of sad stories. But three weeks? Sleeping in the hallways? In December? He was only 12.

"Young man," she said, "you are coming home with me."

That evening the boy ate pork chops, string beans and mashed potatoes, portion after portion, and the next morning he came downstairs and said, "Good morning, Mom," and that was that. Helen and Louis Ford made him one of their own.

We marvel at sports, we celebrate the athletes, and yet today, when Rumeal Robinson takes the floor for Michigan in the second round of the NCAA basketball tournament, we will be watching something truly remarkable. His is a tale about love over everything. It is the kind of thing you don't hear much anymore.

"What did your husband say when you brought home a strange boy and said you wanted to adopt him?" Helen Ford, 44, is asked.

"He said, 'No problem,' " she answers.

See what we mean?

H ow can we ever complain? How can we moan about the cost of designer jeans for our kids, or the high tuition for gymnastics lessons? Helen and Louis Ford, already parents of four, were just surviving on Mr. Ford's postal worker's salary when Rumeal Robinson came into their lives. He was a quiet, Jamaican-born kid who had never known his father.

"His mother just put him out one day," says Mrs. Ford. "I don't know why. But children didn't ask to come into this world. Why should they suffer?"

So the Fords decided to adopt him. His mother was notified. She came to the courtroom, asked where to sign, and walked out. No struggle. No resistance. That young Rumeal was not scarred forever by that rejection is testament to the warm embrace of his new home.

Suddenly he had new brothers, and a sister, and family dinners. He spent afternoons behind the house, playing basketball on a makeshift hoop that hung from a tree. There wasn't a lot of money, but nobody seemed to notice that. And when Rumeal grew into a star player at Rindge & Latin High School in Cambridge, and the recruiters came after him and tried to turn his head, he told them all he wasn't signing anything until his mother approved.

"He was at the McDonald's tournament in Detroit, I remember, in the hotel lobby, and I came in and he yelled, 'MOM!' and then he said to the men from Michigan, 'OK. I'm ready now. My mom's here,'" Mrs. Ford says.

What would have happened to Rumeal Robinson if not for the kindness of strangers? A dropout? A bitter adult? Here were two people who could easily have said, sorry, we have enough problems. Yet they took him in, sent him to school, fed him, clothed him, encouraged his dreams, and never even asked that he change his last name.

Even today, as Rumeal travels, seeing places his parents never will, the Ford house remains so loaded with neighborhood kids that Cambridge people teasingly call it "the high school annex." Mrs. Ford, who adopted another son — in addition to now five children of her own — laughs that she doesn't remember how to cook for two anymore, only crowds.

"When was the last time you and your husband had a night alone?"

"Oh, we don't have any," she says. "But my husband doesn't like too much quiet. We like the doorbell ringing and the sounds of feet running around."

When Rumeal Robinson came to Michigan, there was a problem with his test scores, and under the new Proposition 48, he had to sit out his freshman year. People immediately whispered, "Great. Another pampered athlete with no education."

And yet Robinson, who suffers a learning disability, didn't listen to that. He went to class, taped the lectures and played them back in his room, over and over, until he got the words. Today his grades are fine. He is a starting sophomore guard for the Wolverines, and an excellent player. By everyone's account, he is also a warm, caring young man, this lonely kid who once slept in a hallway.

You never can tell.

As for Helen and Louis Ford? Well, they'll be watching the Michigan-Florida game on TV today. They don't get to travel much. See, there are these twin boys, Ernie and Tyrone, 5-year-olds, and they've been in foster homes since birth, and the Fords have decided to . . . well, you know.

"I was raised to believe there's always room for one more at the table," says Mrs. Ford, who'll give Rumeal two new brothers this summer. "We're not rich, by no means, but we have plenty of love. And I figure I've been blessed with the children in my life."

Truth is, it's the other way around. ◆

GRETZKY, STEFAN AGREE ON ONE THING – FRIENDSHIP

May 5

E DMONTON, Alberta — Once upon a time, before we ever heard of them, they were best friends, two blond-haired boys skating on frozen lawns in Brantford, Ontario. Wayne Gretzky says they were 7. Greg Stefan says they were 5. Whatever.

"We used to call Wayne 'Weener,'" Stefan says. "He was dominant even then. He'd score seven or eight goals a game."

"We met when Stef joined our local tyke team," Gretzky says. "He was the best goalie around. One time, he lost his stick and dove to the ice and stopped a puck with his face mask. I'll never forget that."

Back then, they were all tousled hair and lace-up skates. There were many early morning rides in the station wagon. When Wayne's dad couldn't drive to games, Greg's dad would. When Wayne slept at Greg's house, Mrs. Stefan made him breakfast.

When summer came, hockey was traded in for baseball: Stefan says he played third and Gretzky pitched; Gretzky says he played shortstop and Stefan pitched. Whatever.

Gretzky: "He batted cleanup, so he was always knocking me in."

Stefan: "He batted third, and usually hit a homer before I came up."

What are the odds that two kids who giggled themselves to sleep in the same basement 20 years ago would wind up on opposite sides of a Campbell Conference final in the NHL? It's happening now. For the remainder of this Red Wings-Oilers playoff series, Stefan and Gretzky, both 27, will try to best each other in a brutally focused fashion — one shoots the puck, the other tries to stop it — and yet with every slap shot, with every kick save, there is a memory that binds them together.

O ne time we were driving to a peewee game a long way from home," Stefan says. "Wayne's dad would always ask before we left, 'Wayne, do you have everything? Wayne, did you forget anything?' So we were halfway there, and suddenly, Wayne says uh-oh, he forgot something, I don't know, his mouth guard or whatever. And his father went off the wall! He's screaming and yelling and Wayne's mom is telling him to calm down and Wayne looks at me and I look at him and we're trying not to laugh. . . . "

"I remember I used to sleep over at Stef's house all the time 'cause he had this great setup down in the basement," Gretzky says. "It was a big

31

room, and we'd play down there for hours, floor hockey with those plastic pucks, you know? Geez, sometimes there'd be like 14 kids sleeping there. Poor Mrs. Stefan. She was running a community center. . . . "

There was the time Wayne cried after losing a big game, and people mocked him but Greg understood. And there was a time, when Wayne's dad, their coach, teased Greg, calling him a "sieve," but Wayne told him, hey, he's not serious.

There was the time when their midget team won championship after championship and the two of them, too young to really understand celebrity, switched jackets as a practical joke. Suddenly Stefan was besieged by kids wanting Gretzky's autograph. "It was weird," Stefan said. "At first I felt kind of important. I was signing all these autographs as Wayne Gretzky and Wayne was over there getting a hot dog and a pop."

But in time, the novelty wore off and the distance between the two grew. Stefan was a fine young goaltender, but Gretzky, well, he was being hailed as the Second Coming. People drove from miles around to watch him skate. At 14, he left Brantford for Toronto and Junior-B level hockey. No more nights in the basement, or afternoons in the frozen back yards.

"It happens to most kids at age 17 or 18, when they leave high school," Gretzky says. "It just happened a little earlier for me and Stef. The funny thing is, I got a lot of attention but I remember whenever we traveled with those old teams, my father used to say, 'We're gonna win today because we have the best goalie, Greg Stefan.' I can still hear him say that."

Can you imagine? Wayne Gretzky's father? We're gonna win because of the goalie?

Time has a way of pulling us all apart. These days, Gretzky is the NHL's premier attraction, a superstar, a hero to millions. He is getting married soon, to a Hollywood actress named Janet Jones.

Stefan, meanwhile, the top goaltender with Detroit, is already married and is expecting his first child about the time of Gretzky's wedding.

They get together during the summers, they say, at Gretzky's tennis tournament, here or there, now and then. A few years ago they went out to dinner in Edmonton and, according to Stefan, "laughed so hard we couldn't get any food down."

"I see Stef out there during a game now and I'll think about how many years we've been doing this," Gretzky says. "I'll always say, 'Hey, Stef,' or 'Nice save,' when I pass him. I don't do that with other goalies but, you know, he's my friend. That's what it's all about."

And indeed it is. All those years. And tonight, in front of thousands of viewers, one shoots and the other tries to stop it. Funny, no? Sometimes the world is as big as a dream, and sometimes it's so small you could sleep two inside it, down in the basement. ♦

IN EDMONTON, WINGS LOSE MUCH MORE THAN A GAME

May 12

EDMONTON, Alberta — Long before the puck was dropped, before the Detroit hockey season saw its sad and bitter conclusion with that final 8-4 loss to Edmonton, there was a crack in the heart of this Red Wings team. It may take a long, long time to mend.

We are talking about an incident that left half the team angry and its coach almost numb with disbelief. It is not a story I want to write. It is not a story you want to read — not this morning, when we should be paying tribute to the fine effort of the Wings all year.

On the night before the biggest game of their season, at least seven Red Wings players went out drinking. Not all together. Not all with the intent of getting drunk. But they stayed out late, well past curfew — a curfew that wasn't being checked because, as coach Jacques Demers would say: "We never ever thought we'd need to enforce curfew when our team reached the final four of hockey."

And one of the culprits was Bob Probert.

This will break your heart. It already broke Demers'. Probert has been battling alcoholism for years. It has tackled him, trashed him, landed him in jail. Yet recently, with the help of medication, he seemed to have it under control. He was playing his best hockey of the year and was Detroit's top performer against Edmonton.

Yet there he was, less than 24 hours before Game 5 of the Campbell Conference final, at a nightclub called Goose Loonies. He came with Petr Klima (who was out of the lineup with a broken thumb). By all accounts, it was Klima who encouraged Probert to go out, and if that is true, Klima should be so ashamed he should turn in his uniform right now.

"My god, Petr Klima could be ready to play if we reach the finals," Demers said a few hours before the game, his face red with anger and disappointment. "If he keeps the big guy eating ice cream, he might get a chance at it. Instead they do this. . . . "

He sighed. He looked as if he was going to cry. He talked about how Probert and Darren Veitch returned to the hotel drunk, after an assistant coach found them at the bar. I have never seen news affect Demers like this. He looked as if the police had just knocked on his door and told him his children had been arrested.

"Klima and Bobby could have spent the most wonderful summer of their lives this summer," Demers said. "People thought so much of them. The way they played this year. All the adulation. Now, they'll hear about this instead. For one night. One night. It's not worth it. . . .

"It's just not worth it."

Probert, who was allowed to play by Demers, looked awful on the ice ("godawful," Demers said afterward). Probert was sluggish. The fire from the earlier games was gone. By the second period, Demers had moved him off the first line and onto the second. What happened? Was it the night before? Was it the knowledge that he had let down his coach, perhaps for the last time?

"It definitely had an effect on our whole team," said a weary Demers. "We came out flat in the first period. There was a loss of respect going on.

"My first thought when this happened was to send them all home, but I felt I owed it to the fans to put the best team I could out on the ice."

OK. Let's be clear about what happened here. First, remember this was not all the Red Wings, just a handful — reportedly, Klima, Probert, Veitch, John Chabot, Joe Kocur and Darren Eliot were caught.

Having said that, let us say this: Anyone on this team who encourages, accompanies or allows Bob Probert near alcohol is committing an unforgivable crime. The guy has already been junk-heaped by booze. As a fellow human being, you keep him away from the stuff. Then you can worry about the Stanley Cup playoffs. Going out there with a hangover sure isn't going to help your team's chances.

Which doesn't absolve Probert. "Hey, he's 22," Demers said, sighing. "He's an adult. Nobody had to twist his arm."

One night. The night before a game they had played all year to reach. Why do this? For what? Aren't there dozens of other nights, summer nights, when you can have a few beers and safely enjoy yourself? Demers and the rest of the Wings have worked so hard to build a team that may have lacked superstars but always had heart — a heart that never seemed to beat louder than at Joe Louis Arena in Game 4, a breathtaking 4-3 overtime loss to the Oilers.

Just two nights later, the heart was slashed, the character wounded.

"Do you think the players involved in this incident just said, 'Well, we can't win this series,' after Monday?" Demers was asked. "Is that why they did it?"

He bit his lip.

"If they did, then I don't want players like that on my team."

When contacted about this, Klima and Probert denied they were out that night. This, despite the fact that Demers had addressed the situation in a team meeting. He told his team the press might find out. He told them he would not shield the players involved.

Now. All right. This is not a witch-hunt. No doubt some teams make a practice of drinking the night before games. Fine. But the Wings had rules, an agreement among themselves that they would do whatever it took to be at their very best against Edmonton. They certainly were not in Game 5.

"It put a black cloud over what we accomplished," said Steve Yzerman, the Wings' captain, in the locker room after the game. "It's not a big thing, but in some ways it is a big thing. I don't agree with what they did, but we're all adults. I'm not going to be their baby-sitter."

How sad. These were their rules. Demers' rules. All the coach has done for these players is treat them with respect, with dignity, with love. He has stuck with Probert longer than most other people would, simply because Demers' father died an alcoholic, and the coach sympathizes. But this was not the first rule-break by the kid. It was not the second. It was not the third or the fifth or the seventh.

"It's my biggest disappointment since coming to Detroit," said Demers, before a game that would only confirm those fears. "It's totally unprofessional. It hurt me more than anything."

In the coming days, we may see the repercussions. Demers vowed to "take some action right away, like tomorrow." He said he let Probert play only because of the innocent guys on the team who wanted nothing more than to win. Guys such as Yzerman, who fought all the odds to overcome knee surgery to play again in this series, and Glen Hanlon, who has killed himself emotionally defending against the Oilers, and Brent Ashton, Gerard Gallant, Harold Snepsts, Shawn Burr. Run down the list. Veterans. Young kids. They deserve better than a betrayal from their own ranks. And that is what it was. If you had seen the faces of some of the Red Wings, you'd know it was true.

Not the story I wanted to write. Not the one you wanted to read. This Detroit team played gallantly all year, and it should be coming home knowing that everyone gave his best to the end. Instead, the Wings lost the game, they lost the playoff series — and a handful of them lost something more important. They lost trust. They lost spirit. They broke their coach's heart, and there's no excusing that. ♦

MOVE OVER, GREEN MEN! IT'S PISTONS' TURN NOW

June 4

A t the buzzer, they hugged each other. Isn't that the right reaction? You're happy, you hug. You're grateful, you hug. Joe Dumars was hugging John Salley and Chuck Daly was hugging Dick Versace and Isiah Thomas was hugging Adrian Dantley at midcourt — as the crowd mobbed them in celebration — hugging as if they would never let each other go.

"Have you ever hugged another man that tightly?" someone would ask Thomas after the Pistons captured the Eastern Conference title with a 95-90 victory over the Boston Celtics.

"Never," he said, breaking into a smile. "Never."

Gloryoski! Somebody up there finally heard us. Whatever magic power decides what's fair is fair, what's due is due, was surely pressing that final buzzer at the Silverdome, the one that sent a dozen Detroit basketball players into a heavenly leap, and an entire state into unbridled ecstasy.

Move over, green men.

Our turn now.

"YEEEAAAH!" yelled the Pistons. Over and in. How about that? They will play for the NBA championship; they are sliding down the rainbow, and the Boston Celtics are finally — count the seconds, one to 10, check for breath, take a pulse, poke their eyes, it's true, it's true — dead. And if it feels like the final seconds of a monster movie, when the sun rises and the monster is history and your heart can finally come out of your throat, well, that's because that's what this series was like.

Everybody . . .

. . . breathe!

Our turn now.

"I'm more excited about beating the Celtics than winning the Eastern Conference," said Vinnie Johnson, whose 24 points did the most to make that happen. "It feels great!"

What a series! What a war! Did you ever believe the Pistons were home free until that final buzzer? Have you ever lost more sleep, endured more goose bumps, suffered more stomachaches over any other dumb old sporting event? This thing took on dimensions beyond the court, it became an obsession. "Beat the Celtics!" "Kill the Celtics!"

So fervent was the wish that Bill Laimbeer brought an iron sickle in his gym bag, and he showed it to his team upon arrival.

"Chuck said the Celtics are like a snake; you have to cut their head off to kill them," Laimbeer said. "Well. . . . "

Well. That'll do it.

H ere was the nightmare put to rest. Here was Detroit, reaching championship status. And here are the scenes that linger: Johnson hitting jumper after jumper, from inside, from outside, from New Jersey, from Paris, from Peking. And Dantley, driving, spinning, going to the hoop with the determination of 12 NBA years and a million NBA miles. And Thomas pushing the ball upcourt, running, running, as if his youth and exuberance alone could carry him to glory. And Salley, in the best game of his career, soaring to block Kevin McHale, to block Danny Ainge, to block Larry Bird, twice.

"Have you ever jumped higher than that in your life?" he was asked.

"Not since some guys were chasing me back in Brooklyn," he said.

He grinned. All around, the Pistons' locker room was stuffed, high-fives and low-fives and hugs, always hugs.

People in Boston may not understand why this victory meant so much. But then, as they say, people in Boston don't live around here.

Try 31 years without a basketball champion. Try four years since any major Detroit team has reached a final in anything. Try the sting of defeat by a stolen pass, by a pair of banged heads, by a little green leprechaun. How much of that can one team take?

This time, it was the Celtics — minus center Robert Parish, out with a knee injury — falling apart in the clutch. They looked old, they shot poorly (38 percent), they missed open baskets. (Bird actually missed a lay-up and two consecutive free throws; does that tell you something?) As the minutes wore down, it was the Boston players making faces of defeat, brows creased, mouths hanging open in disbelief. They haven't missed the NBA Finals in four seasons.

Losing hurts, huh, fellas?

Your turn now.

And the Pistons? They waited until the appropriate time against Boston. The last 10 seconds. And then Laimbeer raised his arms, and Dantley raised his arms (Dantley raised his arms?), and even Dumars, Mr. Quiet and Private, raised an arm and chanted, "John! John! John!" at Salley, probably because he didn't know what else to say.

"Is that the most you've ever celebrated after a game?" he was asked.

"That's the most," he said. "I even raised a fist. One fist."

"How'd it feel?"

He smiled and shrugged.

37

"It felt good."

Our turn now.

Think of all the stories that marched triumphantly into that locker room. There was Daly, 57, the coach without a contract, his voice shot, his eyes baggy, but finally, after a lifetime of finishing second, a smile on his face. "This is the hardest thing I've done as a coach," he admitted. And maybe the hardest anyone has ever worked for free.

There was Dantley, the "old man," the quiet superstar who discovered that sometimes playing co-star can take you farther than all the statistics in the world. And alongside him, slapping his back, his best friend, Dumars. "A.D. said he's buying me a deep-dish apple cobbler tonight," Dumars said. "We never eat dessert all year. Tonight, it's everything."

There was Rickey Mahorn, who hurt so bad he had to lie down whenever he was taken out of the game, and James Edwards, the sleepy-eyed giant who never thought he would see this celebration in his career. There was Salley and Dennis Rodman, "Spider" and "Worm," the kids of the team who are kids no longer, and may they never forget how good this feels, because they will be the ones to help do it again.

"Slap me four!" Salley yelled to a friend. "One, two, three, four! That's how many we need for the championship."

There was Vinnie Johnson, the streak shooter, who had a magnificent game (10-for-15), and Laimbeer, the nation's villain, who has the reputation of the class bully, but, deep down, the personality of a mischievous kid. So what if everybody out there hates his guts? He's home. Pop the corks.

"I'm gonna go home and drink a few beers and play some cards," he said, laughing. "And I'll probably win."

And finally, Thomas. This has been his team; for better or worse, his play has swayed it. You could make a case that the angel-faced guard really wasn't ready for a title before this; but the events of the past year — the loss last season to Boston, the Bird incident, the criticism from the media — have seasoned him, matured him and, yes, hardened him. You may need that to become champion. He had the look of one this night.

"Is this the way you always imagined it?" he was asked.

He smiled. There was lipstick all over his face.

"Yeah . . . " he said slowly. "Exactly. I guess when your dreams meet your reality, it's what? Fantasy?"

Why not?

Our turn now.

So the series that would not end finally ends, to the delicious noise of 38,912 fans singing and dancing and stomping their feet. It was rainbows and lollipops and sunshine for Detroit. A happy ending. Like a Dorothy in sneakers, the Pistons may have had the power to do what they needed to do all along; they just had to believe in themselves. And click their heels three times. And say there's no place like Dome.

"To beat the Celtics you need to beat three things," Thomas explained. "The mind-set, the team and the five great players. Through determination, effort and never giving up, we finally did that."

And more than that. They have crossed a bridge now, these Pistons, jumped over the broom of expectations. Simply put, they have grown up. Give them long pants and a corsage and send them to the prom. They beat the Celtics because they beat the demons inside themselves. They believed.

Whatever happens next, never forget the sweetness of that sentence. Have a hug. Have an apple cobbler. Have a sickle and chase a snake. Green is gone, blue goes on.

Our turn now.

Over and in. ♦

A LETTER TO ISIAH'S BABY: YOUR DAD'S A REAL WINNER

June 16

T his column caught me by surprise, much the way, well, much the way a baby catches you by surprise. I was having dinner with some friends for the first time since these crazy NBA playoffs began. I excused myself to call the office. It's a habit I should learn to break.

"Did you hear about Isiah?" the voice asked.

"No. What?"

"His baby was born. A boy."

Well, good, I figured. That's nice. I hung up and went back to dinner. But the sentence stayed in my mind. And an hour later I found myself driving home, early, and now I'm sitting at a typewriter about to throw out the column that was in the earlier editions and write this — because I think that little Joshua Isiah Thomas, who came out, like his father, small, quick and early, should know a few things about what he's getting into.

Kid, I can't claim to know your dad the way some people do. I can't claim to have watched every game he has ever played. I can't claim to have seen him in high school or to have been there when his mother, your grandmother (wait till you meet her, she's a pistol), took on the neighborhood thugs at her doorstep and said, "You touch my son and I'll kill you."

But I know him a little. I have seen him laugh, I have seen him cry, I have seen him dance as if God were moving his feet. I have seen him amused by people, and stunned when people turned on him. I have seen him work his body when his body said, "Don't do it." In fact, just the other night, I saw him unwrap a bandage, slip on a jersey and play one of the gutsiest basketball games of his life.

A few years ago, your father told me his fantasy about the moment his team won an NBA championship: "We win the game, all the people are going crazy, I congratulate my teammates, go running out the door, jump in my car and drive off to a park. And I just sit there, watching the kids play."

Does that surprise you? Well, of course. Everything probably surprises you. But you should know that there's a lot of kid in your father, even today. You see it first in his face, in his smile, you hear it in his voice when his heart is light and he is not worried about being everybody's hero.

He sometimes sees the world the way you are seeing it now. And he

40

sometimes sees the world as a much older man. Your father has been around. What stories he'll tell you! Stories about growing up in Chicago, in a way that you will never have to grow up, dark and poor and dangerous. Stories about college, a wicked coach who scared him. Stories about his professional life, where he has become a star, a hero, a rich man.

He'll tell you about success. And he'll tell you about failure. About a night in Boston when he let a ball go from his hands that he has wished back 100,000 times. He'll tell you about a comment he made there that got him in trouble, and how he learned that life doesn't always provide you with a safety net. Even heroes can fall.

He'll tell you a little about your grandfather, who died just last year. And about your uncles, some of whom are still on the slippery end of life, struggling, falling. He'll take you down to the basement of your new house, where he goes to be alone, late at night, when everything is dark and quiet. It's a basketball court. You'll probably learn how to play his game there. Keep your eye on the rim. Keep you head up when you drib–.

Well, there's time for all that.

L isten, kid. I haven't always gotten along with your dad. He and I have, well, it's hard to explain really simply, but my job and his job sometimes butt heads. I need to know things and sometimes he doesn't want to tell me. Sometimes he has been silent, and once or twice even rude. But I never doubted he had his reasons. And I don't think we ever lost respect for each other.

Besides, for every one of those times there have been five times where he has shown insight, patience and a sense of humor. What a laugh he has! Deep and robust — it'll wake you up, for sure. I've heard that laugh 1,000 times. I've also seen your father serious, like when he tried to lead this city to a safer place on No Crime Day. A whole city. No kidding.

And do you know where he is now? Do you know on what day you decided to make your entrance? The eve of the fifth game of the NBA Finals against the Lakers, something your father has dreamed about for as long as he has dreamed about you. It's a huge game. The biggest in Detroit's basketball history. Normally, on a day like this, your father wants to be left alone. But I bet if the Pistons win the game, he'll dedicate it to you.

So you might as well have this newspaper. One day, when you can read, you'll see just how grand an entrance you made. Like I say, kid, I can't claim to know your dad as well as some folks. But I know him a little bit. And I know this. You have already, in your few hours on earth, done what probably nothing or no one else could have done. On the eve of the most important basketball game of his life, you have diverted his attention. You have captured his heart.

Nice steal. You'll probably be a point guard. ♦

41

GUTSY PISTONS: BEST TEAM THAT DIDN'T WIN IT ALL

June 22

INGLEWOOD, Calif. — They lost? They lost. Those are all the words needed. There was only one team in the world for Detroit, and all night long — in this breathtaking Game 7 of the NBA Finals — that team, the Pistons, fought off defeat like some Atlas in sneakers, the weight of the world on their shoulders. Until finally, with just moments left in the longest season in basketball history, their shoulders buckled and the world caved in.

They lost. It's over. The most magical of all Detroit basketball seasons ended one victory short of glory, final score 108-105, Los Angeles, a heartbreaking, heart-stopping final show that wasn't over until A.C. Green beat the Detroit defense for a lay-up with two seconds left.

"We came within a hair's breadth," said Pistons coach Chuck Daly. "A hair's breadth. . . . "

"Does that give you any consolation?" someone asked.

"No," he said.

They lost.

Oh, but what a war! Weeks from now, when the bitterness has subsided, these pictures will remain: Here was LA rocking and rolling in its home arena — and here was Detroit, miles from home, refusing to die. Here was LA, playing champion, saying, "Had enough? Ready to quit?" And here was Detroit saying, "Never! Never quit!"

Here was LA's James Worthy — the series MVP — spinning and hooking and seemingly toying with the Pistons, 36 points, 16 rebounds. And here were the Detroit kids — Dennis Rodman and John Salley — growing up before our eyes, refusing to let anybody intimidate them, playing the game of their lives.

It was all the Pistons had, all the courage, all the strength oozing from their pores. Their captain, Isiah Thomas, had an ankle injury; he was on the bench down the stretch. Their toughest scoring threat, Adrian Dantley, was on the bench as well. Youthful enthusiasm was carrying them, but youthful enthusiasm would do them in. With 39 seconds left and the Pistons trailing, 103-100, Rodman came downcourt on a fast break, he had a lane to the hoop, and suddenly, he pulled up for a jumper. A jumper?

"I don't know what I was thinking," he said later. "I don't know why I did that. I can't explain it."

His shot was long, it bounded off the back of the rim, Daly buried his head in his hands, and moments later the Lakers buried the Pistons, although not before Bill Laimbeer had cut the lead to 106-105 with a three-point bomb with six seconds left. What a finish! What a final act!

"I left everything I had out on that floor," said a weary Joe Dumars, who scored a team-high 25 points. That close. That scary.

But when that buzzer sounded, the Pistons walked off with that empty feeling, like the last day of school. Out of gas. Out of games. Out of time.

They lost.

How sad. How tragic for these gutsy Detroit heroes. How many times did they come back? The third quarter seemed like the worst kind of basketball burial, the Lakers dropping in fast-break lay-ups the way you drop pennies into a piggy bank. The Forum thumped and roared, rock music blared, it was ugly and insane and awful for anyone who didn't wear purple and gold.

Here was Byron Scott streaking past a wounded Thomas, burying a jumper, dropping in a lay-up. Here was Michael Cooper — cold all series — suddenly heating up his three-point jumper. Here was Worthy — oh, lord — we need a whole chapter for him.

Surely the Pistons will be seeing this bearded man with goggles in their sleep this summer. Nobody could stop him. He tossed in one short hook after another, one lay-up after another, one driving bank shot after another.

"It looked like they were going to bury us," Dumars said. But how many times have you seen this? The Pistons came back. They whittled, they chipped — Vinnie Johnson lit up like a Roman candle — and suddenly, a 15-point third-quarter lead was two points with 2:48 to go.

How did they do it? With defense. With unlikely heroes. With everything they had.

And it wasn't enough.

Unfair? Unacceptable? No doubt most Pistons fans feel that way. Nobody likes to lose, but it's the way the Pistons went down — a bounce here, a twisted ankle there, one missed shot — well, it's enough to drive you mad.

"It always seems to happen to us," Rodman said, "one pass, one mistake, one something."

Why them? Why us? There is no answer, except perhaps this compliment: That is how close the Pistons were to winning. Had they been blown out by the Lakers game after game, a final defeat would have been almost kind. But Detroit proved it not only belonged with the elite, it yelled to the world that NBA crowns come in its size as well. No longer the thugs, no longer a warm-up act for the men in purple and gold.

The 1988 Pistons might be the best team that never won it all.

And that will have to be enough. That and the memories of this final gutsy effort, which began with Thomas. How quickly did your heart go straight to your throat when you saw him hobble out to start this game? Two days earlier, after spraining his right ankle in three places, he was in such pain he seemed to be weeping as he answered questions.

And yet there he was, in the first half, diving into the stands and chasing passes and making steals — until his body gave out.

"What was it like for you, the captain, to have to watch from the bench during that final period?" someone asked.

"I was very proud," he said. "The guys out there played well. They played great defense. It was a joy and a pleasure to be a part of that."

But it was not enough.

How sad for these Pistons: for Thomas, who braved more pain than any man should; for Dantley, who thought, after 12 years, he was finally going to see his reward; for Laimbeer, who had his bad games at the worst times; for Daly, a second banana his whole life, and a second banana once again. Theirs will be a summer of what-ifs.

What if Rickey Mahorn had been healthy, a dominating force, as he had been all season?

What if Dumars had hit that running bank shot in the closing pandemonium of Game 6?

What if Thomas had never turned that ankle? What if Rodman hadn't taken that ill-advised jumper? What if Laimbeer had been able to save that ball from going out of bounds in the final minute?

What if? What does it matter? Life goes on. The Pistons stop here. You can remember the heartbreak or you can remember the near-glory, and everything that brought them to this oh-so-close finish.

This was more than a season for these guys, it was a sweet moment in time, a clean and well-lighted place in the history books. They won more games than any Pistons team before them. They went further than any Pistons team before them. They came onto the stage as brutes and left with an entire nation's respect — for their courage, for their determination, for their talent. They played and they fought and they sweated and they laughed and they shook the world. They took on all comers, the Bullets, the Bulls, the Celtics, the Lakers. They could beat any team in the league.

They just couldn't beat them all.

So this is where it ends: with 108 for the Lakers and 105 for the Pistons, three points. Three lousy points. While the Forum was rocking and dancing and singing its happy tune, the gamest athletes ever to play basketball for Detroit trudged slowly into their locker room and peeled off their uniforms for the last time this season. They lost? They lost.

But, man, what a ride. ♦

A BREATH FROM DEATH: THE BULLS OF PAMPLONA

July 17

PAMPLONA, Spain — They were running toward us, hundreds of men, their faces filled with horror because the bulls were right behind them. I looked anxiously at Pablo, my Spanish guide, whom I had met just hours before in the drunken streets of Pamplona. He had promised me, in broken English: "You run with me, you no die."

It was a comforting thought.

And suddenly we took off. Somebody screamed. A man next to me went down and was trampled. I glanced to my right and saw a black bull just three feet away. "This is it, this is it, this is it," I heard myself say. . . .

Nobody seems to know how it started, this tradition of running with the bulls through the streets of Pamplona. It has been going on 400 years, give or take a few. Hemingway gave it a literary kiss in "The Sun Also Rises," and since then people have been coming here summer after summer. Thousands come now, to test themselves, to look death in the eye, to measure their courage against the mighty bull — and to do it all while they're so drunk that even standing up is an accomplishment.

Maybe we shouldn't call this a sport. After all, the whole run — beginning in narrow cobblestone streets and ending in Plaza de Toros, or the bull ring — is only half a mile. Then again, I don't care if it's only 100 yards. Does Carl Lewis run with a bull behind him?

That is what brought me here in the first place. I wanted a different kind of sport. No cheerleaders. No money. Here, sometimes, people die. And the game goes on anyhow, eight mornings in a row, during the annual festival of San Fermin. Only it's really not a morning affair, it's an end-of-the-night affair — nights in which you drink and dance and sing and refuse to go to sleep. Then, finally, at 8 a.m. you hop into Santo Domingo street on the wrong side of the wooden barricades and realize, with that terrible thunder of hoofs, that there are no exits, no way out, and you had better run like hell and hope a bull doesn't find your rear end too attractive.

So why did I want to do it? I don't know. Romance? Adventure? Besides, I was a sports writer on vacation. Where was I supposed to go? Club Med? I wanted action. I wanted to see this colorful tradition up close. I also didn't want to die. Which is where Pablo came in.

I met him about 2 a.m. in the Plaza Del Castillo, a huge open area where tourists sleep when they can't find a hotel. I had a hotel. Unfortunately, it was 70 miles away, in the city of San Sebastian. I had driven my rented car into Pamplona, parked on the sidewalk (everyone did it) and figured to sleep in the backseat until the sun woke me.

Pablo negated that idea. A tall, dark-haired fellow with dangerous eyes, he had lived in Pamplona all his life, and he knew this was his one week a year to grab some foreign intrigue. I was hanging out with some Americans from Illinois, two of whom were women who just had graduated from college, and I'm sure Pablo was more interested in them than he was in showing me the secrets of the Encierro de toros. But I persisted.

"How long have you been running with the bulls?" I asked through a friend. My Spanish isn't so hot.

"Thirteen years."

"That's a long time."

"My father ran before me. My grandfather ran before him."

And what happened to them? I wanted to ask. I didn't. Eventually, Pablo agreed to take me on — provided I and my friends (and I think the emphasis here was on the friends) stayed out drinking and singing and dancing with him all night.

He drove a tough bargain.

Now I confess a certain fascination with Spanish culture and bullfighting literature. Although bullfights are truly disgusting, there is a passage about a matador (I think it's either Hemingway or Jack Kerouac) that I always loved: "A young man leaned back in his chair. No bulls would die today."

It is a strong image. No bulls would die today. I expected strong images in Pamplona. And I found them. Unfortunately, many were throwing up.

There is social drinking. There is recreational drinking. And then there is festival drinking. Take all the alcoholic consumption at your average Super Bowl, Kentucky Derby and Mardi Gras, and you've got an average night during the festival of San Fermin. The bars do not close until the sun comes up, and the natives don't worry about going to work the next day.

Into this fray we fell, behind Pablo, who seemed to know every joint in town. On one thin cobblestone alley named Calle San Nicolas (I called it "Hell Street"), there seemed to be a bar every three feet. People were hanging out the doors, out the windows, falling on top of each other. Music blared, traditional Spanish songs mixed with Bruce Springsteen's "Tunnel of Love." They danced on the bar. They danced on each other. They passed bottles of sangria and beer and wine from mouth to mouth to mouth until, I was convinced, whatever disease anyone had in Pamplona, all had it now. The streets were curb-high in bodies and smashed glass. I saw a British girl cut her foot on a broken bottle, then dip it, bleeding, into a large cup of beer.

The alcohol, she figured, would sterilize the wound. They call that the emergency ward in Pamplona.

By 4 a.m. I was beginning to drag. But Pablo wanted to go on. He was dressed in the traditional festival outfit: white shirt and pants with a red sash belt and red scarf around his neck. And he kept curling his thumb and forefinger together, then bringing it to his lips. This, loosely translated, meant: "Let's drink to your Uncle Morty."

Which we did. Past 5 a.m. Past 6 a.m. What was I thinking during all this? Don't lose your car keys. That's what I was thinking. At 7 a.m. the sky turned a hazy blue. I pointed at my watch and Pablo finally nodded. He ordered a coffee from the barman (as if that would sober him up) and spoke to me of the bulls we were about to face.

"Stay near me," Pablo said.

"Yes."

"But do not push me."

"No."

"Mucho men is drunk," he said, making two fists and slapping them together. "Bang, bang! They push you into bull. Very bad."

Let's be clear just how dangerous this is. We're talking perhaps 3,000 people in a street barely wide enough for a car, chased by six loose bulls and four more tied together. The worst thing, Pablo said, was if one bull lost sight of the others, because then he had no idea where to go, and it was likely he'd go after whoever attracted his attention.

"The solo bull," he said, shaking his head, which was sticky with champagne, "*muy malo.* Very bad."

It was 7:30. We left the bar and began walking to where the bulls would be set loose. Spectators were already six deep behind the wooden barricades.

"Momento," Pablo said. He ran off to buy a newspaper. Now? A newspaper?

"Take it," he said, handing me half, then rolling it into a baton.

"For what?" I asked.

He thrust his paper at an imaginary animal. He grinned. This, I learned, was to be our sole weapon. A rolled-up newspaper. The bull gets too wild, you jab him with the sports section.

And to think I went into journalism for the writing.

We gathered at the bottom of Santo Domingo street, beneath a high brick wall. Above us it seemed as if the entire town had come to the windows. People stood atop buildings, on ledges. They were smart. Height meant safety. When was the last time you saw a bull jump?

In the middle of that brick wall was a small statue of St. Fermin, the patron saint of Pamplona, surrounded by candles. At five minutes to 8,

Pablo and several dozen Spaniards began to sing to the statue. I guess it was a prayer. I tried to follow. St. Fermin is not part of my religion, but if it kept me from two horns in my butt, I'd say anything.

"SAN FERMIN DAH DOO DOO," they sang, or something like that. My Spanish isn't so hot.

"SAN FERMIN AH DOO HOO."

After the final verse, they waved their newspapers three times and yelled, "Hoy! Hoy! Hoy!" Then the mood shifted. You could hear a nervous rumble among the spectators. I would guess there were 10,000 people watching this thing, along the Plaza Consistorial and Estafeta street and, of course, inside the Plaza de Toros, where it all ended. And we were in the thick of it.

Pablo signaled that I should follow him, and we darted through the crowd, past the wooden barricades and the police, who, I discovered, do not let you out once the run is about to begin. Something about too much confusion. Besides, what if a bull is on your tail? You want to bring him into the crowd? No way. Those people waited hours for those seats.

We reached Pablo's favorite spot, about 200 meters from the gate. He froze. A cannon shot exploded. Then another. A woman screamed.

The bulls were loose.

I would like to explain what happened next in flowing, lyrical prose. I really would. However, I can best sum up the emotions this way: AH! MY GOD! OUT OF MY WAY!

Smack! Someone went down. Smack! Someone else went down. Pablo had bolted into the street the moment we heard hoofs on the cobblestone, and already he was 20 feet ahead. I charged to catch up with him, passing men who were already being trampled. Just then the bulls, big and angry, were right on my heels. I leaped to the side, then pulled even alongside a black one, his eyes, thank God, focused straight ahead. Then a brown one, then a spotted one. Then a body, then a foot. Colors and shapes. Helter-skelter. It was kind of like running between giant trucks on the interstate. "Don't push!" I kept reminding myself. "Watch out for stray bulls!"

My heart was pounding. I saw feet and more feet, some alongside me, some dangling above me, feet everywhere, and screams, yelps, and always the undercurrent of the hooves on the cobblestone, a devilish thunder. Two bulls began to pull ahead of me and I saw Pablo with his newspaper on one of their horns, taunting the animal, rubbing his sports section right on the deadly point. "Hay! Ha-eyy!" he screamed, as if to say, "What kind of bull are you? Fight me! Gore me!" I realized right then that Pablo and I would probably not keep in touch.

And then, just as suddenly, it was over. The bulls charged into the stadium, where one of them wheeled on a Norwegian named Thomas

Fraser and stuck its horns in his guts, lifted him and tossed him 10 feet in the air. Fraser landed in the hospital, the first casualty of this year's encierro. But it was a good run. No one died. You had to be happy with that.

I found Pablo a few minutes later, among the dazed mob that was already heading home. He shrugged and said it wasn't his best effort, tomorrow would be better. We slapped each other's back, glad to be alive, and he clasped two hands beside his head and made a sleeping face. I nodded. The night, indeed, was over.

And that was that. I found my car, eventually, and drove back toward San Sebastian. I lasted 20 miles before pulling off the road, too tired to continue. Killing the engine, I yanked down the visor and let my eyes close, happy in the knowledge that I had survived both the bulls and the sangria, although the bulls would not be giving me a headache in a few hours.

The sun was hot. I reached between my legs, found the seat release, and pulled. A young man leaned back in his chair. No journalists would die today. ◆

ARENABOWL '88 LEAVES PLENTY TO BE DESIRED

July 31

ROSEMONT, Ill. — All right. Quit laughing. So I swore I'd never attend another arena football game. So what? This was the championship, for Pete's sake. And a Detroit team was in it. Where's your spirit?

Not that it was my idea. I want to be clear on that. My boss called and said, "You're going, right?" and I said, "Where?" and he said, "The ArenaBowl," and I said, "What?" and he said, "Drive vs. Bruisers," and I said, "Who?" and he said, "Come on. It's the Big One. You wouldn't miss a Super Bowl, would you? It's your professional duty to 'observe the pageantry, patriotism and drunken insanity of all major sporting events.' You told me so, remember? When you turned in your expense account."

And I said, "Well. . . . "

And there I was, on United Airlines Flight 9, touching down at O'Hare. Now I am no expert on arena football. Basically, according to my boss, I was sent to the Illinois heartland on a hot and sticky July afternoon to see just what kind of party this league could throw. Here is my report:

First of all, let's get something straight. The Arena Football League is not the NFL. It does not pretend to be the NFL. A good reporter will spot this.

For example, at a Super Bowl, you can always tell the headquarters hotel because the entrance is packed with drunken fans, scalpers, mariachi bands, women in tight skirts, balloons, banners, sirens, ambulances and at least one stretch limo with a huge bodyguard leaning on the hood. And that's at 5 a.m.

When we pulled up to the Ramada Inn in Rosemont, $37 a night, six hours before the Big Game, there were no mariachi bands. None of the other stuff, either. I did see the commissioner of the league, Jim Foster. He was walking across the parking lot, carrying a box of T-shirts.

We checked in. The bar was empty (a clear sign, I noted, that media attendance was low). The Detroit players were scattered around the lobby, their legs up on the couches. At least I think they were the Detroit players. I'm not sure. Neither were some of the fans.

"NOVO!" a tall man screamed, grabbing my hand. "How ya doin', Novo?"

"What the. . . . ?"

50

"You're Novo Bojovic, the placekicker, right?"

Money? Let's talk money. As opposed to NFL stars, who make ungodly sums for eating tacos on television, the ArenaBowl players, many of whom play offense *and* defense, collect $2,000 apiece if they win the Big One. Which, no doubt, goes immediately toward that next insurance bill, considering there are no fair catches in this league.

This may seem low. Then again, the whole thing is sort of a low-budget affair. I know this because two hours before the game my phone rang.

"This is Leon. You don't know me."

"Yeah?" I said.

"What airport did you fly into?"

"Uh . . . O'Hare. Why?"

"Oh. . . . We flew into Midway. We were hoping you could give us a lift back out there."

But about the game. . . .

It was sold out, just like the Super Bowl. Although the top ticket cost just $18, as opposed to, say, $7 million for the NFL version. And most of these were sold an hour before the game.

Here is something I liked. They let a TV crew into the Detroit locker room just minutes before the game. One crew. Actually, they might have let in more, but only one asked. Anyhow, it was nice. The Drive coach, Tim Marcum, said: "Nobody expects us to win this game. Let's have some fun." And out they charged, all 21 players, into the steamy confines of the Rosemont Horizon, a building that has witnessed such sports history as the DePaul-Gonzaga basketball game.

Did I mention halftime?

Sorry. I didn't mean to skip over the whole first half. But with all those guys bouncing off the walls, it was kind of hard to follow.

Halftime, on the other hand, was easy to follow. Unlike the NFL, which, for an average Super Bowl halftime show, carts in six major orchestras, and half the grand pianos made in the western hemisphere, the ArenaBowl featured a "Tribute To Motown." It was great. It was superb. Actually, it was the Detroit cheerleaders dancing to "Do You Love Me?" by the Contours. But I always liked that song.

Here is my summation of the game: We won. The end.

Oh, there were a few more details, but that's the basic story. And, to be honest, it wasn't as bad as it seems. At least there was no Brent Musburger. Besides, Detroit now has another championship team. And that's nice.

So may I suggest you make it out to City Airport this morning and welcome the Drive back home. They're flying in on Southwest, the airline with the $29 fares. Cheer. Wave banners.

And if you see Leon, give him a lift, OK? ◆

TENNIS CAMP EARNED MY BACKHAND COMPLIMENTS

August 28

S T. GEORGE, Utah — Here is what I believe about tennis: In the beginning, God created the forehand. And He saw that it was good. So, on the second day, He created the backhand, in order to have something to laugh at.

That pretty much described my game. While my opponents laughed, I would race to the ball, whack it, then watch it clear the fence and land on a passing Buick, never to be seen again.

Until last week. My life changed last week. Actually it changed a few months ago, after my 30th birthday, an event I greeted with a calm and steady reserve that went like this: ARRRRGH. MY GOD. I'M 30! I'M GOING TO DIE TOMORROW!

This was followed by a trip to England to cover Wimbledon, where, in my suddenly reflective state, I realized I had never really learned to play tennis. Resolved to make up for lost time, I picked up Tennis magazine and searched for one of those faraway places that exchanges your hard-earned money for a week's worth of tennis torture, after which you can beat Jimmy Connors in three sets.

There were many to choose from. Naturally, I selected mine in a careful, scientific fashion:

"What do you offer?" I asked.

"We have 19 courts, small groups, six hours of daily instruction, high-speed videotape, special hitting lanes, ball machi–.

"Do you have cable TV?"

"Uh-huh."

"Book me."

One week. Nothing but tennis. I realized I had never done any one thing for a whole week. This would be great. I would return as a tennis machine, able to destroy those who had once condescended to play me. I was so excited I immediately rushed to the store and spent $179 on a new racket, then dragged a friend to a nearby court to test it.

"Hey, this grip keeps slipping out of my hand," I complained, after 10 minutes of hitting. "Maybe it's too big? No. It's the graphite, right? I knew it. I never should have bought gr–."

"Take the plastic off," he suggested.

"Oh."

The next day I was on a plane heading west. I leafed through the brochure from the Vic Braden Tennis College in St. George (about 100 miles northeast of Las Vegas, Nev.). I had chosen this place because 1) Vic Braden, a famous tennis coach and sports researcher, was from Michigan, my state; and 2) his ad featured two notable expressions: One was "Laugh and win." The other was: "You'll be famous by Friday!" I had checked the calendar. The U.S. Open began the following week. The wild-card draws were Saturday and Sunday. So, if I was famous by Friday . . .

I leaned back in my seat. In the bag at my feet were sneakers, shorts, sweatbands and lots of underwear. I was chewing gum and wearing a baseball cap. As we began to descend, I suddenly realized an embarrassing truth of my 30-year-old life:

I was going to summer camp.

Now, some folks choose wonderful resort locations for their tennis adventures. I chose the desert. In mid-August. Very smart. Of course, it's not the heat, it's the humidity. Unless it's 109 degrees, in which case, I promise you, it's the heat.

But let's get to camp. . . .

Day 1. Monday morning, 7:45. Our group — 10 adults — met in a green-carpeted classroom. We were introduced to our instructors, Dave Nostrant and Mark Jacques, two fine, athletic-looking men with deep tans and strong thighs.

(IMPORTANT SAFETY TIP: You will never, ever — no matter how long you play — look like one of these tennis pros. Do not try it. Do not even dream it. These men are bred on a secret farm in the high country of Northern California, next to the farm where they breed lifeguards.)

Anyhow, they greeted us, and asked us to assess our games on one-page questionnaires. Best stroke? Worst stroke? Under "Goals?" I put "Qualify for the U.S. Open." I'll bet they had a good laugh over that one.

Then we marched out to the courts. Mark The Instructor announced we would begin with volleys.

"Two lines, please, each rushing the net."

Now, I had figured we would start with something easy, such as "Opening The Can Of Tennis Balls." Rushing the net is not my strong point. I rush the net the way I would rush, say, the East German border. So I began my week by tiptoeing in, holding up my racket, and watching the ball go . . . flubpht.

And I slunk to the end of the line.

The others in my group — who were all older than I — glided through the drill with apparent ease. I tried to remember their names, in case I needed to notify their next of kin. There was David, an options broker from

Vancouver, and Lamont, a psychologist from California, and Menlo, a fire chief from Las Vegas, and, my favorite, Mike Wong from Hong Kong. There were also five women in a second group. They all shared one trait: They were all better than I was.

"What brought you here?" I asked Wong, between puffs of breath.

"I want to be the best in Hong Kong," he said. "How about you?"

"I came for the food."

After 40 minutes of rushing the net, we moved to forehands. I had listed this as my "best shot." Everyone says his forehand is his best shot. The fact is, if you think your forehand is good, it probably stinks.

And I never thought mine was good.

INSTRUCTOR: OK. Keep your racket down. Turn your shoulders. Don't lift your head. Make sure your grip is right. Lean into it. Hit up. Go for the topspin.

ME: Uh-huh.

Flubpht.

Somewhere around the three-hour mark, with the Utah sun now high in the sky, we broke for lunch. I returned to my room and stuck my head under the faucet.

In the afternoon, we worked on the backhand — but there was an added twist. Unbeknownst to us, we were being . . . filmed. Yes. Dave The Instructor took us into a little room with a TV monitor where we watched our strokes and analyzed them. I will sum up my few seconds on the screen with the following review: HAHAHAHA! . . . NO. YOU'VE GOT TO BE KIDDING ME.

This was not our only video experience. We saw film clips every time we took a break: Vic Braden on the forehand, Vic Braden on the approach shot, Vic Braden on the volley.

"How are you feeling? Tired? OK?" the instructors would ask.

"Fine," I would say.

Flubpht.

When I finally reached my room that night, after seven hours of tennis, I pulled off my shoes and saw my socks were spotted with blood. I lay on the pillow. I had lasted one day. I felt proud and content. Also, the temperature had dropped to a comfortable 94 degrees.

Of course, the problem with feeling proud the first night is how you feel the following morning. Stiff? You could say I was stiff. I don't usually take 40 minutes to walk to the bathroom.

Then came . . . The Serve.

Here is The Serve the way I always practiced it: Toss the ball up lightly and poke it with your racket and hope it lollipops over the net.

Here is The Serve According To Tennis Camp: Toss the ball halfway to the moon, swing the racket in a whippet motion behind the head, uncoil the body, corkscrew the arm and smash the ball with an explosion that rivals Mt. St. Helens on a bad day.

"Got that?" they said.

"Uh-huh," I said.

Flubpht.

I was not bad at the serve; I was nonexistent. I was the guy they put in the corner and said, "Just try not to hit anyone, OK?"

And we went for an orange break.

And some more film.

By the way, I should say right here that the instructors at this place were marvelous; they never once hit me; they never even raised their voices. They were patient, good-natured, consistent, and I am going to nominate them both for sainthood, as soon as they track down all the balls I hit into the sand dunes.

The machine.

Let's talk about the machine.

The machine is neither kind nor good-natured. The machine is a firing squad. Serious players love the way it coughs out balls on a perfect arch. Serious players refer to the machine as "the ideal practice partner."

I refer to it as Freddy Krueger.

We took on the machine at least two times a day. There was one indoors and a number of them outdoors (on specially constructed tennis "lanes" that simulate real courts). These things spit out something like 900 balls an hour. I never beat the machine. But I now see yellow tennis balls coming at me in my sleep.

"Do you ever get people here who just are so horrible they don't improve at all?" I asked Dave, hoping he wouldn't point at me and say, "Yeah. You. Heh-heh."

"No," he said, "you're gonna improve if you stay here. You'd be amazed. We've had a 76-year-old man, a beginner. He was great. We had this couple once who won a weekend here as an office prize. They had never played tennis before. They showed up for their first lesson in street clothes. But they got better."

I wondered where those people were now. I wondered whether their feet still hurt.

Naturally, as with any good camp, camaraderie plays a big part. And our group developed camaraderie. We became comrades in arms. Then comrades in shoulders. Then comrades in sore wrists and sore elbows and shots into the net.

We had lunch together. We hung around the pool. We learned each other's secret tennis desires, which, in their cases, was to beat the best guys at the office and in my case was to keep the ball off the highway. One night, the instructors took us all to Zion National Park — an area of majestic cliffs and yellow-red sandstone, which, I must admit, was breathtaking — and then we ate outdoors at a tiny Mexican restaurant and we were laughing and having a great time and the food came and it was the first good, fattening food I had seen all week. And as I lifted my fork, a grasshopper came out of nowhere and landed in my rice.

I am not making this up.

And then it leaped away.

Another critic.

By the third and fourth days, we were into the heavy stuff, such as approach shots and doubles strategy. I had learned to stay away from my serve, as had my co-campers. Actually, Mike Wong was fond of yelling, "INCOMING!" whenever I hit one, which I thought was kind of funny.

But here is the thing. Slowly, painfully, I got better. I really did. I developed a backhand. I discovered the volley. There was a certain pop to the ball off my racket — not all the time, but some of the time — and once, I rushed the net and whipped that ball into the corner and Dave The Instructor lunged for it and missed and he cheered, "Nice shot."

It was as satisfying as pumpkin pie.

And that about ended it. The last day was filled with drills and more drills and reviews and taping and happy talk, the kind you always get on the last day of school. We were not famous. And I guess I'm not going to the U.S. Open.

But the question is how good do you get by spending a whole week on one thing? And the answer is . . . flubpht.

No. Ha. The answer is you get a lot better than you think. Which only makes me angry that I didn't start this when I was 9 years old.

Anyhow, we shook hands and exchanged addresses. We had a little ceremony where we all sang the tune from the Vic Videos, then marched up and received our "diplomas" — which certified that we had "Learned to Laugh and Win."

Well, laugh, anyhow.

And now I sit with scabbed toes and tape around my fingers and a steady throb in my wrist, as I stare out my window across the desert mesa and into the big Utah night. I don't know whether tennis camp is the cure for growing up. I do know this: For the first time in 30 years of staring at the moon, I realize it looks like a tennis ball. And I have this strange urge to whack that sucker with topspin. I really do. ◆

MIGHTY SWING HITS TIGERS WITH GRIM DOSE OF REALITY

September 12

NEW YORK — The skies were dark now, and Sparky Anderson had slipped on his jacket to fight the chill. It was the longest moment of the longest game of the season. It was the bottom of the 18th, and after what had seemed like a lifetime, the Tigers were finally ahead of the Yankees by a run.

And that made it worse.

Better to have loved and lost, Shakespeare said, but he wasn't talking about baseball. It hurts twice as much when you have it and blow it.

Which brings us to Guillermo Hernandez, the focus of Anderson's gaze. Hernandez had already committed the cardinal sin — walking the leadoff man, Rickey Henderson — and now he was facing Claudell Washington, who had beaten the Tigers Friday night with a home run in the bottom of the ninth. Half of Yankee Stadium was empty by this point, unfilled seats whose patrons had bailed out for dinner, for traffic, for work the next morning. Geez. Why not? The game was already six hours old. Only the bloodthirsty would stay for this.

Hernandez got a strike on Washington. 0-1. In the dugout, Anderson did not move. His breath was coming faster. His hands shook. "I've been around too long to celebrate anything," he would say later. Especially a one-run lead against a team that had beaten his three straight, all from behind.

Hernandez set, looked and delivered a fastball — and there went the season. From the press box, you could almost hear Washington smack his lips. Crack! The ball lifted off toward the bleacher fans and did not descend until it was safely in their warm caress — a two-run homer, a game-winner, a firecracker across the New York skyline. The Yankees were alive again in the pennant race. They had swept Detroit four straight. Washington was met at home plate by a mob of his teammates. They sang his praises and slapped his hands and the die-hard fans were jumping up and down.

Anderson never saw any of it. He was already deep in the stadium tunnel, heading for the longest night of a manager's season, the one in which he sleeps with the voices that whisper, "It's over."

"Did you know that ball was gone as soon as he hit it?" someone asked the manager in his small office, after the 5-4 Yankees victory.

"I knew," he mumbled, barely audible. He was staring at the floor and he did not look up. Outside his door, the clubhouse was a morgue. Something more than a victory had died in this endless afternoon and evening. "We gave it everything we had," Mike Henneman whispered. Indeed. Eighteen innings? Six hours? Countless pinch-hitters and relief pitchers? What more could they give? There were four stolen bases by Gary Pettis. There were seven scoreless innings of relief by Henneman. There was a miracle throw by Chet Lemon from the farthest rightfield corner, a throw that flew high and long and with the hopes of an entire city, and bounced magically in the glove of Tom Brookens in time to tag Gary Ward at third base and kill a rally.

How could they lose after that? How could they lose with all that effort, from a solo homer by Alan Trammell in the seventh to an RBI single by some kid name Torey Lovullo in the top of the 18th? That should have been the game-winner, right? Some rookie from California massages the heartbeat of Detroit, gives it life? Perfect ending, right?

Perfect, perhaps. But not for this day. When you lose the ones you can't lose, the game is saying something to you. It's saying: Move over. We're kissing someone else this year.

"I thought we had it," Henneman said. But they did not. They trail the Red Sox now by 3½ games — same as the Yankees — but these are two teams heading in opposite directions. The Tigers have lost 17 of 20 games, and even the staunchest of supporters would have a hard time saying they deserve the pennant now.

W hat has happened? Why has a first-place team that was always on the fat side of close games fallen horribly flat? Here is my theory: It's not so much that bad luck has caught up with the Tigers as the Tigers have caught up with themselves.

Remember, this was never a good hitting team — "We knew that this spring," Anderson admits — and so its only hope was spectacular pitching, which it had for a while but has no longer. Jeff Robinson was snatched away by the weirdest of injuries. Frank Tanana got hurt, Eric King got hurt, Doyle Alexander slumped and Hernandez returned to his old woes. The pitching became good, not great, and good is not good enough.

This is reality: Detroit has the worst offense in the league, except for Chicago and Baltimore — and you see where those teams are. Only one Tigers hitter, Trammell, gives pitchers any concern. It tells you something about your offense when Torey Lovullo has to save you after 18 innings.

And so it goes. If the Tigers finish as also-rans come October, then this game, that pitch, that gloriously awful home run, may be circled in red.

Anderson shrugged. He had nothing to say. Outside, players packed silently. Hernandez sat by himself, shirtless, staring at the wall. Suddenly he slapped his shoulder, as if there were a fly, but when he looked at his hand it was empty and he shook his head and it was quiet again, as quiet as death. ◆

IF IT'S TOMORROW, THIS MUST BE KOREA

September 15

SEOUL, South Korea — So let me tell you what happened yesterday at the Olympics. Oops. I mean today. I mean tomorrow. No. Wait. Forget it. It wasn't that good a story.

Welcome to Korea, where you never really know what time it is, but if you ask enough people, you definitely won't know what time it is. You will, however, collect hundreds of business cards, which you can then give to other people, and maybe one of them will have a watch.

(Personally, I like this Korean tradition of handing out business cards as soon as you meet somebody because you can collect a whole series, then trade with friends. Some even come with bubble gum.)

But I am getting away from the point. Which is . . . I forgot. Hahahahaha. No. That is the point. After several hours at these Summer Olympics, the greatest assignment a sports writer can have, provided he is willing to walk around in utter confusion for 21 straight days, I cannot tell whether it is morning here and evening back home or morning back home and evening here. But I can tell you this: I have figured out the language problem.

There is no language here.

There is only laughter.

YOU: Hello. I am an American journalist.

OFFICIAL: Hahahaha. Hello. I am sorry.

YOU: Can you tell me where to go?

OFFICIAL: Yes. Hello. Hahahaha.

YOU: Where should I . . . go?

OFFICIAL: Oh . . . hahahahahah.

YOU: Hahahahaha.

OFFICIAL: Hahahahaha . . . haha. . . .

But back to this time thing. . . .

LET's get this straight: The Olympics begin on Saturday morning. Here. They begin on Friday night back home. This means that NBC — which could have saved the money it paid for broadcast rights and bought Finland instead — has declared: "LET THE GAMES BEGIN . . . EARLY!"

And here is how it works: Ten o'clock in the morning here is 8 o'clock the night before back home. Just about the time you, the TV viewer, are ready for some good, old-fashioned Olympic drama.

So they juggled the schedule just a teensy-weensy bit. And now highly developed athletes from around the world who have spent years preparing for this single moment, will roll out of bed in the Olympic village, and the starting pistol will go off. Bang! First one to the bathroom wins the 100 meters. Can this be right? Finals at 10 a.m.? Medals at noon? These may be the first Olympics in which an athlete misses his gold medal because he overslept. Korea has long been known as "The Land Of The Morning Calm." This month we call it "The Land Of The Morning Basketball Final."

Why am I telling you this? Because it is 7 a.m. here. What else should I be telling you? Oh, yes. We, the Olympic journalists, work under the same conditions as the athletes. That means that at sunrise, when most good sports writers are just crawling home, the phone in the room will ring and some crispy-clean editor from home will scream: "WHERE THE BLEEP IS YOUR STORY? DO YOU KNOW WHAT TIME IT IS?!"

Whereupon the sports writer will immediately drop dead from a heart attack, and the newspaper will have to use a wire story instead.

Did I tell you about the trip over? Golly. Where can I begin? It was the most wonderful 14 hours I have ever spent in a single seat on an airplane on which the sun never set. Really. I am not making this up. We left at 11 a.m. and the sun was out and at 5 p.m. the sun was out and at midnight the sun was out and at 3 a.m. the sun was still out and when we landed in Seoul at 6 p.m. the sun was still out. I asked the flight attendant what was going on, and she said something about flying into the sun and air speed and lift and drag, or drag and lift. I don't know. I don't really understand, but it has something to do with why Carl Lewis must long-jump before breakfast.

But what the heck? These are the Olympic Games, which begin in two days or five minutes, depending on where you are standing. So far, this looks like a swell country; the locals seem remarkably nice. And if you are thinking about going into stand-up comedy and are not having much luck, you should come here because these people are the greatest audience in the world.

YOU: Help! I lost my passport and all my money.

OFFICIAL: Hahahahahaha. Hello.

Personally, my philosophy at the Olympics has always been pretty simple: RULE NO 1: NO SYNCHRONIZED SWIMMING. RULE NO. 2: STAY AWAY FROM PIN PEOPLE.

As for the time thing, who knows? I can only say if you're awake and I'm awake, then one of us has been out drinking. But that is the charm of the Olympics, where the world's greatest athletes gather to put their souls on the line for a few glorious moments, then relax with a nice dish of bacon and eggs. And we are here to serve. We are here to send you the news. I will wash up. I will collect my business cards. I will set my alarm clock for 6 a.m.

And we'll see what yesterday brings. ♦

WHAT'S IN A NAME? ASK TURKISH GOLD MEDALIST

September 22

SEOUL, South Korea — The huge interview room was nearly empty when the little man walked in. It was 2 in the afternoon. In one hour Carl Lewis, the Olympic superstar, was due to speak about his greatness and the place would be packed. But now there were just a few of us with nothing better to do and we were drinking Cokes with our feet up.

The little man sat down alongside his interpreter, and he tapped the microphone and it squeaked. "May I introduce Naim Suleymanoglu," the interpreter said, in Turkish-tinted English.

"He is the Olympic gold medalist weight lifter in the 132-pound category. We will take your questions. . . . "

The Americans rolled their eyes and tried not to laugh. Finally, a Turkish reporter in the front of the room stood and asked a question about the athlete's defecting from Bulgaria. And the little man, who, the night before, had grabbed a weighted bar of more than 400 pounds and heaved it over his head, began to speak in a soft and sometimes trembling voice. And after two minutes we put down our Cokes and began writing what is the best story of these Olympic Games so far.

What's in a name? Naim Suleymanoglu may not be an easy name to pronounce, but if it were yours, the name your parents gave you, would you fight to keep it? In Bulgaria four years ago you had to, if you were of Turkish descent, because the government had decided to rub out your heritage — no more speaking in Turkish, no visiting Turkish mosques, no Turkish cultural displays. One day they came around and told the Suleymanoglu family it would now be called Chlamanov, a good Bulgarian name. And the son, not even 5 feet, with more muscle than skin, said no.

"I have a name. A man should have one name. If you steal his name against his will, you make him a nobody."

And from that day on, he vowed to escape.

It took him nearly two years. He was, after all, a champion weight lifter, a national hero; he'd broken countless world records — they called him "Pocket Hercules" — and Bulgaria wasn't about to surrender one of its few sports stars.

"They had control over me," recalled Suleymanoglu, 20. "After every international competition, I had to return immediately to Bulgaria. They

61

listened to my phone calls. They watched me always. They knew I was trying to defect and they wanted to stop me."

He never told his parents; just knowing could get them in trouble. So he dreamed silently of freedom until finally, in 1986, he met some Turks who agreed to help him. The rest is like a Robert Ludlum novel. He was in Melbourne, Australia; he had just won a major competition and, at the banquet that evening, he stood up and "made the image of going to the bathroom." He ducked out a door into a car and hid in a house for three days.

"All during that competition I was thinking of freedom," he said. "I had hoped to break the world record that night, but I could not concentrate."

"Were you scared?" he was asked.

"In Bulgaria," he said, "you are scared every day."

When his absence was discovered, the Bulgarians immediately accused the Turks of smuggling their athlete against his will. The defector was flown to London, where he told reporters it was his idea all along. He then declared his name, proudly, loudly, his real name. Thus began the quick burning of Naim Suleymanoglu's family ties.

"They do not let me see my parents," he said now, his voice cracking. "It has been two years. For the first five months, I could not even speak on the phone. Now I can talk sometimes on the phone, but they listen to everything.

"The gold medal is very important. But the most important thing to me right now is to be together with my family. I would like to do this."

He paused as his words were translated and his boyish face was sad and unblinking. By this point, many reporters had begun to filter into the room, trying to get a good seat for the Carl Lewis show. They listened to this story and soon the pads were out and everybody was writing.

"Do your parents know you won?" he was asked.

"I am certain it was not allowed on Bulgarian TV," came the answer.

"Then they don't know about your gold medal?"

"Unless they listened to Turkish radio, no."

"How did you feel on the medals stand when you saw the Turkish flag raised?"

He sighed. "All the time I live in Bulgaria, I have always felt something going on in my heart. . . . This is my history, to be Turkish. I wanted to . . . I knew that. . . . "

He choked up and said he could not finish the answer, he was sorry. The translator had begun to cry.

When Suleymanoglu hoisted that bar and locked it over his head and smiled even as he grimaced — victory! glory! a world record! — the entire Turkish Olympic team was in the audience. They began waving and swaying in celebration. They were mostly men with black hair and mustaches and Suleymanoglu is brown-haired and light-skinned but he is theirs, a national hero, and he had just won three gold medals (the snatch, the clean and jerk, and total lifts) — his new country's first Olympic gold in 20 years. They did not come cheaply. There is talk that in order to allow him to compete, the Turkish government had to pay $1.5 million to Bulgaria to waive a ban on his Olympic eligibility. Cash for gold.

No such payoff would free his family. Tomorrow, a plane will arrive for Suleymanoglu — the prime minister's private jet — and he will be whisked back to Turkey for a national celebration. One little man, with the strength of three, inside a big airplane, all alone.

He talked about the two million other Bulgarian Turks. He talked about his brothers and how he wishes he knew where they were. He talked about being a scrawny kid and getting into weight lifting "because I wanted to be powerful," yet he could now lift three times his body weight and still could not pull the sadness from his voice.

By the end, the room was half-full. And when the translator said, "Thank you for coming," the journalists — and I had never seen this happen — stood and applauded.

We forget about the world. We take our privileges for granted. Who fights for their name anymore?

He did. Turkey, from what people tell me, is no haven of human rights itself, but this is not a contest of countries. This is about individuality, the right to be addressed as you wish, the right to your religion and expression, which, correct me if I'm wrong, is pretty much what gave birth to America.

The room began to fill with TV cameras and lights. The buzz of conversation grew louder as news came that Lewis and his entourage were about to arrive.

Suleymanoglu followed his translator off the podium and walked toward the door. And, suddenly, first one, then three, then 10, then 20 reporters began to follow him. An hour earlier they had never heard of the guy, and they certainly were supposed to cover Lewis, who was about to enter in striped pants and a black muscle T-shirt, but the hell with it.

"Who is that little man?" someone asked me.

"I think he's the Olympics," I said. And as I watched him disappear, it seemed as if giving him a gold medal was the least the world could do. ♦

BEN JOHNSON GOT CAUGHT; EVERYONE NOW A SUSPECT

September 27

SEOUL, South Korea — Willie Banks, who has been in track and field a long time, was crammed in a phone booth in the middle of the athletes' village, dropping coins at a furious pace. "I just heard," he said. "And I'm aghast! And when the rest of the guys wake up, they'll be aghast, too."

The news had sneaked in during the night and had stabbed the Olympics right in the heart. Canada's Ben Johnson, the Olympic 100 meters champion, had failed his drug test, an anabolic steroid had been found, he had handed over his gold medal, fled the country, and the greatest performance of these Summer Games had become its greatest shame.

Did you see Johnson run that race? Did you see him set that world record of 9.79 seconds and beat his arch-rival, Carl Lewis? Weren't you moved, inspired, chilled by the very sight of what human beings can do when they are at their best? And now, we learn, he was at more than his best. Superman was using a battery pack.

Ben Johnson. Steroids. The words will frame the XXIV Olympics now and forever; it is awful, horrible and, some say, only fitting. "Maybe now people will stop denying that this is a serious problem," said James Puffer, a doctor with the U.S. Olympic team.

"Were you surprised?" he was asked.

"No," he said.

No. The shock that rippled through the athletes' village and left Banks and other athletes "aghast" was less the fact that Johnson had used steroids than the fact that he had gotten caught. Already six other athletes in these Games had been expelled for drug violations. But none as famous. None as big. This — Ben Johnson, the so-called "fastest man on Earth," whose event was watched by one billion people worldwide — was the siren that would stir the giant called International News.

And here is the story: It begins simply, with moving a checkers piece or kicking a golf ball, and it swells and grows as the stakes get higher and now, as you see, it can lead to someone's swallowing chemical substances.

It's called cheating. That's what this is about. Ben Johnson was not some misguided man who fell into a nasty drug habit. He was — assuming there was no monkey business in the testing process — looking for an edge.

Winning.

It's all about winning.

H ow far will we go for it? What is the limit? Where will we draw the line and say: "I am doing the best I can. I am satisfied."? It really doesn't matter whether Johnson was a victim of sabotage — he claims someone may have drugged his drinking water — or anything else. These are the facts: Steroids and blood doping are rampant in sports, particularly amateur sports, and it stems from pressure and pride and the glorious pedestal upon which we place the word "Victory."

Think of what Johnson had to gain with that 100-meter victory: Forget the medal, forget the history. Financially, he would be set for life. That's how big the Olympic stage really is. One race. Ten seconds. And no worries forever.

Could you resist that? And yet Johnson found himself just a few months before the race less than 100 percent. An injury. Perhaps he felt that this opportunity was too big to lose. Against the wishes of his coach, he went to St. Kitts, a Caribbean island, to rehabilitate. There is talk about a doctor. Who knows?

But remember that he had been tested countless times in the past two years — since he emerged as the best 100-meter man in the world — and he always passed. Was he masking the steroid then, or was there something about the Olympic stage that made him dip into the dark athletic makeup?

Whatever. His gold medal now goes to Lewis. When informed of the test results, Johnson, sitting alongside his mother and his coach, reportedly "could not speak," according to a Canadian official who was present. And despite the army of reporters in his hotel lobby and the battalion of photographers waiting at the airport, he left without a word.

So the news spoke for him; stanozolol, a muscle-building steroid that is difficult to detect. The village buzzed with whispers of "You're kidding!" and "My god," in French and German and Swahili. And athletes were grilled over the issue and some were chuckling ironically that it took the shortest event in track and field to open the biggest can of worms.

"It's a problem that's been going on for years," said Billy Olson, a longtime pole vaulter for the U.S. team. "And it's going to continue. As long as there are drug tests, there will be people who are trying to beat it. . . .

"There's so much pressure to do well here. From your team, from your families. I always thought Ben was just an awesome stud guy. Maybe this was a desperation ploy."

He sighed.

"God, I hope people won't always look back on the 1988 Olympic Games and say, 'Those were the ones where Ben Johnson messed with drugs.' "

How can they help it?

And here is the real victim of this ugly affair: the Games themselves. For once, we finally had just about everybody gathered for a competition. The world tuned in. Things were going well.

And now, because of this — and because of the inexhaustible news that will surely follow on how athletes can mask their steroids from doping tests — no one will be able to watch a winning Olympic performance without wondering: "Does he, or doesn't he?"

There are thousands of athletes who do things the old-fashioned way — hard work, dedication and dreams. And there are probably thousands who have a little help — drugs, steroids, blood doping. One got caught. The big one. And now everybody is a bloodhound, and everybody is a cynic and this is what one man's actions led to: As divers and archers and fencers and basketball players sweated and strained and tried their Olympic best, most of the world's media were gathered in news conferences or on the long-distance phones.

Sad. As Johnson crossed the finish line with his right hand raised in victory, broadcasters around the world were screaming in disbelief. "It's a miraculous performance!" yelled one. "Just miraculous."

Oh, if that were only true. But the grim news came during the night, and breakfast was served with cold reality in Seoul. And nobody believes much in miracles anymore. ♦

SHE'S FLO WITH THE GO, A REAL-LIFE SUPER HERO

September 30

SEOUL, South Korea — Oh, Florence, be for real! Tell us that blazing world record in the 200 meters was yours and yours alone, that your magnificent sprinter's body is all hard work and dedication, that when you crossed the finish line and waved your hands and beckoned to your husband, Al, to join you in glory, and he lifted you and swung you in his loving arms and the stadium roared with delight — tell us all that was genuine, real hero stuff, because the Olympics need that right now. In the worst way.

Here was a track victory that would have stunned any other Summer Games — a world-record 21.56 seconds in the semifinals, followed two hours later by another world record — 21.34 — in the final. How about platinum? What a race! But these, suddenly, are the Ben Johnson Games, where every fan is cynical and every athlete is suspect, and nasty steroid rumors popped up before Florence Griffith Joyner had even finished her victory lap.

"I don't use drugs, I don't know anybody who does and I think cheating should not be allowed," the ever-forthright Griffith Joyner said when asked about accusations by Brazilian runner Joaquim Cruz that she and sister-in-law Jackie Joyner-Kersee used steroids. "We're investigating that charge. I don't know why anyone would say that. I don't even know him well.

"It hurt me, but I couldn't let it bother me when I was running."

What could bother her then? She runs faster than gossip, faster than evil thoughts; she runs, quite frankly, faster than any other female on the planet. The 200, combined with her 100-meter victory last weekend, makes her the only woman besides Wilma Rudolph ever to pull off that Olympic double. She came out of the curve as if teaching a clinic — "Follow me, girls. Do what I do. Legs high. That's it!" — and she beat silver medalist Grace Jackson of Jamaica by nearly four-tenths of a second, which, in track and field, might as well be another neighborhood.

"I can't tell you how happy I am with this world record," she said. "I knew in the semifinals that I still had something left, even after setting the record. So in the final I just let it all out. . . .

"As for the drug charges, I don't know why anyone would say that about me and Jackie. But I feel I am a true champion."

Be for real. Please.

I sn't this a better story than a steroid witch hunt? Florence Griffith Joyner, 28 — "FloJo" they're calling her — one of 11 children who grew up in a housing project in Watts. A working woman, who labored days in a bank last year and trained on her lunch breaks and evening hours. An independent woman, whose self-designed track suits — colorful, one-legged, lacy or see-through — make even non-track aficionados blink. A headstrong woman, who would not cut her six-inch-long fingernails and was consequently left off an Olympic relay team in 1984. An independent woman, who split from long-time coach Bobby Kersee (Jackie's husband) just months before the Games. A famous woman, whose world records and flashy dress landed her on the cover of Newsweek and dozens of other magazines just as all the world was peaking for the Olympics.

And a successful woman, perhaps too successful for some. After a silver medal in the 200 meters in 1984, she slipped, she gained weight; she was admittedly in semi-retirement as late as the fall of 1986. Yet within two years she is beating the world and, indeed, looking like a world-beater, with well-defined arms and legs that ripple when she runs.

"Wait a minute," skeptics say. Were this another Olympics, she might be hailed as a magnificent physical specimen. But since Ben Johnson broke a world record, then broke the world's heart — steroids, disqualified, his 100-meter gold medal taken away — the world is suspect. People look at photos of Johnson and say, "He never used to be that muscular. Look at that definition! We should have seen the steroids coming."

And then they look at Griffith Joyner and say, "Ah, ha! Let's not be fooled again."

Cruz, in a televised report, claimed Griffith Joyner was built like a man, and Joyner-Kersee resembled "an ape." He credited steroids. Now, hold on. It is true that Griffith Joyner has burst to the forefront and smashed world records much the way Johnson did the last two years. It is also true that Johnson failed his drug test, but Griffith Joyner — and her sister-in-law — so far, have passed all of theirs. Shouldn't that count for something?

"I feel sorry for Ben," Griffith Joyner said, "but cheating can't be allowed. I'm glad they have more scientific methods to detect people who cheat."

Does that sound like a steroid user?

H ere is a better scene: Al Joyner, a triple jumper who missed the Olympic team this time, screaming to his wife: "DEE DEE! YOU DID IT, DEE DEE!" and charging out to the track for an embrace that was captured worldwide.

And another better scene: Al Joyner telling the TV cameras: "I knew she had the world record when she came around the turn."

And another better scene: Al Joyner, hours after the race, sitting next to his wife, wearing her gold medal around his neck.

Is this the '80s couple, or what?

"When I made the Olympics, Al made the Olympics as far as I'm concerned," Griffith Joyner said. "He's my trainer, my coach, my inspiration. I need that support.

"I run against him. He's 6-foot-1, taller than any other runner I would have to face. So I tried to measure my strides against him. My goal is to beat him in training. Then I know I can beat anyone in a race."

What about her sudden success? A lucky discovery, she says, that she was a short-distance sprinter, after thinking, as late as two years ago, that she was a 400-meter runner. Training at longer distances — she sprinted 700-meter runs constantly from November of '87 until this summer — gave her strength in the shorter distances that seemed inexhaustible.

What about that physique? Credit her weight lifting, she says; some close to her describe it as "fanatic." Which is certainly better than "chemical."

And what about her inspiration?

He was sitting right next to her.

"Al gave me his gold medal in 1984," she said, looking over at him as he played with the gold around his neck. "When we go back home, I'll have to give it back."

Any more questions?

Go with the Flo. Flo with the Go. She is golden twice now — she might be golden twice more; in the 4-by-100 and 4-by-400 relays — and if she inspires skepticism then she also inspires working women, married women, older women and forward-thinking women. What she has done on this Olympic Stadium track is simply eat it up and spit it out, and it shouldn't have to be tainted with drug shadows. But these are the Ben Johnson Games, they always will be, and everything is up for question now.

Be for real, Florence. Tell us that smile, that spirit and that speed — oh, Lord, that speed! — is something special within the human soul and it got there not from ingestion but from dedication. Give us that moment in your husband's arms, as happy as Christmas. Be honest, victorious and ungodly talented. Say it's all so, Flo. Your timing, as usual, would be perfect. ◆

COLUMBIA'S SONG: HAIL TO THE LOSERS VALIANT

October 14

I am empty. I am brokenhearted. All around me, college football fans are gearing up for the weekend. They wave Michigan banners. They wave Iowa banners. They talk of how Miami (Fla.) will beat Notre Dame, or how Notre Dame will beat Miami. They stock up on pretzels and hot chocolate.

I sit by the window.

"What's wrong?" asks a voice.

"Alone," I say, waving a blue and white pompon. "All revved up and nowhere to go."

I am the man without a country, the lonely soldier on a college football battlefield. I have no team. Not anymore. I used to have a team. My team made me proud. It was not a great team. Not a good team. Some say my team did not deserve to wear cleats. But my team had a specialty. My team did one thing better than any other team in the country.

My team lost.

Over and over. By six touchdowns. Sometimes seven. To schools you never heard of. You gave us the lead, we gave it back. You punted, we fumbled. My team, my alma mater, was the Columbia Lions, the school with the longest college football losing streak in the country.

Until last week. Last week Columbia won. After 44 straight losses.

My weekends are ruined.

"Don't they know this spoils everything?" I ask, peeling the Columbia posters off the wall. "We had something unique going. We were leading the nation. We were way out in front. ..."

"You were the worst," says the voice.

"Exactly," I answer.

Better to be the worst than the next-to-worst. Nobody remembers the next-to-worst. It is as bad as being next-to-best. With the nation's longest losing streak, we were at the forefront of the news.

People loved us. We were a raindrop of reality. A reminder that all in sports was not gravy and glory. You would watch UCLA nip USC, or Michigan squeak past Ohio State, and then you'd see, aha, look at that, Columbia got blown out by Colgate, a toothpaste. And all was well.

We had the perfect record. Winless. When our band played "We're

70

BAD!" they meant it. That is, when we had a band. Usually, they were studying. Which is OK. As long as we were losing I was sure my school was concentrating on academics. In fact, the way we played, I figured our quarterback was writing his physics paper in the huddle.

But now what? I must wonder whether our little tailback is skipping classes to hit the weight room. I must wonder whether our linemen are passing up "Intro to 19th Century Literature" in favor of Gatorade fights.

"Steroids," I say, packing away my blue and white ski cap. "I bet we have to worry about steroids now, too."

"Aren't you overreacting?" asks the voice.

"I think not," I say. I open the newspaper. "Did you see this? It's a picture after last week's 16-13 victory over Princeton. Look. Our fans tore down the goalposts. Can you believe that? We never tear down the goalposts. We can't even kick a ball through the goalposts."

"Well . . . " says the voice.

Well nothing. I can see it now. Our star players will soon be living in condominiums on 96th Street. Our coach will be driving a Corvette. Norby Walters and Lloyd Bloom, the sleazeball agents, will be calling.

"And what about the stadium?" I ask, packing away the miniature Columbia footballs. "We always played in a stadium that was so far uptown, you had to take the subway through Harlem to get there. Now what? I bet they build a new one, smack dead center of campus, next to the library."

"Oh, come on," says the voice.

"Probably have a dome on it," I mumble.

This is my problem. How can I root for my team anymore? It is pointless to root for Columbia to lose. I mean, 44 games is five years' worth of losing. That was a special effort, even for us.

It is also pointless to root for Columbia to win. After all, we beat Princeton, not Penn State. Sooner or later, we will return to our old ways. What's the fun in losing to Lehigh if it isn't historic?

So I must find a new team. I suppose I could root for Princeton; its players must be awfully bad. But do they have another 43 losses in them? Then again, I could hop on the Michigan bandwagon. Or Miami's. Or Notre Dame's. But where's the fun in that? You can't get a ticket. You can't find parking. And every December, you have to fly someplace for a bowl.

I sigh. Once we had identity. Once you could find us on the college football map — right at the bottom. Once we had a team. A beautiful team. It just couldn't leave bad enough alone.

"Come on," says the voice. "Maybe they'll start another streak."

I lift the megaphone. I close my eyes. I try to envision the good old days, two weeks ago, when we still led the nation in something.

"Boolah, boolah," I say, but I do not mean it. ♦

DIAL-A-HERO DODGERS PAINT THE SERIES BLUE

October 21

OAKLAND, Calif. — It was the biggest moment of his baseball life, he was about to pitch the bottom of the ninth, lead his teammates to the promised land of the World Series, and there he was — sitting in the dugout, his head back, his eyes closed.

"What were you doing?" someone asked Orel Hershiser.

"I was singing hymns," he said.

Oh.

Singing hymns? Well. Why not? A few minutes later, he struck out Oakland's Tony Phillips — Game over! Dodgers win the World Series! DODGERS WIN THE WORLD SERIES! — and his teammates were singing him. They rushed the mound in unbridled celebration, buried themselves in history, and somewhere the baseball gods nudged each other and said, "Hey, who are these guys?"

Paint it blue. Dodgers win. The team that had nothing suddenly had it all. With a roster full of also-rans, a bench full of casualties, and one baby-faced pitcher who sang hymns (no doubt, "Amazing Grace"), they had done the unthinkable. Beat the winningest team in baseball this year, four times in five games.

Paint it blue.

"This team should be an influence on everybody in the WORLD!" bellowed Dodgers manager Tommy Lasorda, his hair soaked with champagne, after the Dodgers upset the Athletics, 5-2, capturing the Fall Classic. "I'm gonna go to LA tomorrow and dance in the STREETS! AND I'M GONNA–."

Back in a minute, Tommy.

First, your players. Oh, what they did to the Oakland Athletics. Stole their glory. Stole their thunder. In the end, they even stole their game plan. Hit with power. Take a home run trot.

So here was Mickey Hatcher, a castoff nobody wanted last year (and a man who should definitely cut down on his caffeine intake), slapping high-fives after his two-run homer in the first inning that set the tone for the Oakland decapitation.

Here was Mike Davis, another free agent, another former Athletic, another bit player, getting the green light on a 3-0 pitch and cranking a two-run homer over the wall in the fourth. A 3-0 pitch? Mike Davis?

Here was Rick Dempsey, 39, now starting at catcher and slashing a double deep to right to drive in a run. Rick Dempsey? Who had to call the Dodgers and ask for a tryout? What's next? Woody Allen as designated hitter?

Maybe so. Woody. Frank. Sammy. The Dodgers will have all the celebrities out when they land in LA. If they land. The way they played, capturing this World Series in one game over the minimum, with a cast of human Band-Aids and a heart as big as their dugout, well, they just might stay up in the sky forever.

Paint it blue.

S ay something for your old fans in Puerto Rico!" a radio guy demanded of Hatcher in the steamy, champagne-soaked clubhouse afterward.

"Puerto Rico?" Hatcher said. "They cut me in Puerto Rico. Here's what I say. Pffft!"

Perfect. Was that perfect? Here was a team that nobody wanted, a team that nobody even liked last year — after it finished under .500 and fourth in the National League West. What a remarkable comeback! Even the baseball experts who figured Oakland would win this thing easily had to applaud their mistake. The Dodgers captured baseball's most precious prize with more bandages than "M*A*S*H" and more extras than "Ben Hur."

Oh, yeah. And Orel.

"LET ME TELL YOU ABOUT OREL HERSHISER!" Lasorda barked. "I HAVE NEVER SEEN ANYBODY PITCH LIKE–."

Back in a minute, Tommy.

Hershiser can speak for himself. Just by raising his pitching arm. "You put 10 names in a hat to pitch this game," teammate Kirk Gibson said, "you want to pick Orel's."

Unless, of course, you're Oakland. Hershiser is so deadly, he should come with a childproof cap. MVP? They should let him have it for two years. You could stick him out there with the cast of "Godspell," and he'd win. Did you catch that moment in the bottom of the eighth, when Hershiser faced mighty Jose Canseco with two runners on and the entire city of Oakland taunting, "OOOO-RRELL! OOOO-RRELL!" He worked the count to two strikes, calmly, masterfully, then jammed Canseco on the fists. The slugger popped up innocently, and the World Series and the MVP award had just been decided.

The rest was merely an epilogue.

Never mind that the Dodgers were the walking wounded. Apparently the loss of Gibson (bum legs), Mike Marshall (bum back), John Tudor (bum elbow) and Mike Scioscia (bum knee) wasn't going to affect Tommy Use-em and The Tonight Show Orchestra.

LA used Dempseys, Hamiltons, Gonzalezes. Not exactly Reggie and Mickey. So what? Here was the final indignity. The Dodgers were hitting home runs. In Oakland's park. Where Don Baylor had once said the Dodger Stadium dingers would "be nothing but long fly balls."

Yeah. Long fly balls out of the park. And look who was hitting them! Mickey Hatcher? Mike Davis? Let's face it here. The A's lost to the B's.

"I haven't slept since this series started," Hatcher said. "When we got that last out, and I realized we had won it, I left the ground!"

Paint it blue.

And what of the Athletics? Try as you will to be kind, it is hard not to conclude that, simply put, they stank. OK. Maybe that's harsh. But we're judging them by their own standards. After all, it was the Athletics players — such as Baylor, Canseco and Dave Parker — who spoke so confidently before this series. It was the Athletics who won 104 games during the season and who arm-wrestled the entire American League to the ground. Power? Runs? Bulging biceps? The Athletics had it all — right up to the first game of the series.

"I just want to say one thing," manager Tony La Russa said. "We missed the biggest piece we were chasing. But we did not choke. We got beat because the Dodgers did more than we did."

Yes. Which sometimes wasn't saying much. Oakland hit .177 in the series. Its motto could have been, "When the going gets tough, the tough pop out." How many times did we see Canseco and Mark McGwire and Parker fizzle in crucial situations? The "Oakland Bashers" managed two home runs all series — or the same number as Hatcher, who was unemployed and waiting for the phone to ring last year.

The Oakland pitching wasn't much better. Dave Stewart, the ace, came up empty twice. Storm Davis got two starts and didn't pitch nine innings.

"We have nothing to be ashamed of," said Stewart, who nonetheless felt bad losing in front of the sold-out home crowd. But this was simply not meant to be for Oakland. In the sixth inning, Canseco ran to his position in rightfield, only to discover he had no glove. He thought someone else had brought it out.

Apparently someone was already packing up.

So it's the Dodgers, World Series champions, and now we get an entire winter of Tommy Lasorda on the talk show circuit, and Kirk Gibson recollecting that one swing, that one home run and that 1.000 World Series batting average.

"You can't compare this to 1984," Gibson said. "My goal coming out of spring training was to be world champions. It was all I thought about. Not the All-Star Game, not winning the MVP. Just being the world champions."

He did his part. From Gibby's shot-heard-around-the-world in Game 1, to Hershiser in Game 2, to Jay Howell's clutch relief job in Game 4, to Hatcher-Dempsey-Davis in Game 5, the Dodgers played dial-a-hero and somebody always answered.

So be it. If there's anyone out there who can say LA didn't deserve to win this thing, let him speak now.

Didn't think so.

Go ahead, Tommy.

"THIS IS THE GREATEST BUNCH OF GUYS IN THE WORLD BECAUSE–."

We know the because. Because they did it with subs, because they did it with scrubs. Because they did it with heart, soul, pasta and prayer. Because they did it with a mean-faced slugger playing "The Natural," and a baby-faced, miracle pitcher who framed his biggest baseball moment with a quiet hymn.

Because they did it in five games — no questions, no doubts, no problem.

What do you say to the team that has nothing? Happy World Series. The trophy is yours.

Paint it blue. ♦

ROGERS' INNOCENCE ENDS WITH LIVES OF THREE TEENS

October 30

When they told him three people were dead — that when he was finally released from the Pontiac, Mich., hospital where he now lay, his head in a brace, his thumb sewn to his hand, he would be charged with manslaughter — this is what Reggie Rogers said: "Why? What did I do?"

He was, for that moment, a child again, the same child who once bullied kids for lunches, then played baseball with them; the same child who once shook hands with high school football rivals and wound up in a racial brawl; the same child who once fell in love and was charged with assaulting his girlfriend. Why? What did I do? Trouble would buzz around Reggie Rogers his whole life, and he would swat as if it were a friendly fly, and he would go on.

This is the story of a little boy in a man's body. It is hard to find anyone who doesn't blame Reggie Rogers for what happened that cold morning 10 days ago, when he ran a red light, allegedly under the influence of alcohol, and plowed his Jeep Cherokee into the side of a Dodge Omni, snuffing out three teenage lives. And yet it is hard to find anyone who doesn't like him. "Reggie is not a bad person," they all insist. He is simply a person to whom things happen.

"When I first came to the hospital he said, 'Mama, I don't understand. . . . What does God want from me?' " says his mother, Loretha Rogers, 46, who sits with him each day at Pontiac Osteopathic, holding his hand, praying for forgiveness. "He said, 'My foot is tingling. My hand is numb. I can't feel my toes. I don't want to be a cripple, Mama. I don't want to die.'

"I told him we have to be strong. We are survivors. God has a plan for us, son. We don't know what it is, but God has a plan."

It is a sad sentence, saddest because, in the end, it might not be true; there might be no plan. It might be this simple: Reggie Rogers, like countless athletes in this land of athletic worship, has lived his life ricocheting from one near-miss to another, someone always there to catch him, excuse him, forgive him. Until that night, at a barren intersection, in the early morning cold of autumn, when two vehicles collided, a car burst into flames, and the days of innocence were over.

For everybody.

I *could always beat up the other kids because I was bigger. But I never had to. They just gave me what I wanted."*
— **Reggie Rogers on his childhood, during a 1987 interview.**

Life was a game to young Reggie Rogers. The middle child of an athletic family — his brother, Don, was one year older; his sister, Jackie, exactly one year younger — he was the biggest, and he loped around his Sacramento, Calif., neighborhood laughing, entertaining and getting what he wanted. Reggie would take, and smile, and take some more. Toys. Books. He had a penchant for pulling apart radios to see what was inside, or for grabbing his classmates' food or pencils. It was never malicious or mean. It was just Reggie. Big Reggie. No one argued.

It became a pattern. You are big. Get what you want. No one will mind. Once, as an eighth-grader, he scored 49 points in a basketball game. The next day, in English class, the teacher asked for his homework. He was taken aback. He scored 49 points — why should he do homework? "I don't care if you ever pick up another basketball, Reggie," the teacher had scolded. "When you get out of this class, you will know English."

Loretha Rogers says that made a big impression on her son. But so, apparently, did the fact that other teachers overlooked his transgressions. Throughout high school and college, Rogers would squeak past the standards. "He was not the best of students," admits Don James, his football coach at the University of Washington. "But neither were a lot of athletes."

Nor was Rogers the most coachable of athletes. Lateness was a regular occurrence. Missed practices were not uncommon, beginning in high school — the moment he discovered how talented he was. Rogers was recruited to play basketball at Washington, but early in his freshman year, he was late for a 3 p.m. meeting. Coach Marv Harshman had his uniform and shoes removed from his locker.

"Hey, Coach, where's my gear?" Reggie asked, when he finally arrived.

"You're late," Harshman said. "You're not practicing today."

Once again, the athlete was taken aback. Why? What did I do? He asked to stay and watch practice from the stands. Harshman said no. "I don't know if he always resented that," says Harshman, now retired, "but he didn't do it again. Reggie is Reggie. He had a hard time growing up and facing reality. Like so many athletes, things came too easily for him. And like a lot of athletes who are talented, he would challenge authority because he thought he was indispensable."

By his junior year, Rogers had quit the basketball team and said good-bye to Harshman (who was benching him anyhow). He had taken up football, in which he quickly became a star defensive lineman. This was more like it. He had been second-string on the hardwood, but in football, he could rush the line and tackle the quarterback. He would hear them chanting his name, and he was back on top, center of attention. He made All-Pacific 10. He led his team with 112 tackles as a junior. He had found his sport.

Besides, it was Don's idea. Don, his older brother, his hero, had been a football star at UCLA, and now he was the starting free safety for the Cleveland Browns. Don gave him a new car. Don bought the family a house. It was Don's idea. "Reggie, go out for football."

And whatever Don did was always good, right?

M *Y SON IS DEAD! MY SON IS DEAD!"*
— **Loretha Rogers as she ran into the street upon learning her son, Don, had died of a cocaine overdose, June 27, 1986.**

He began to die on the living room couch. That's how crazy it was. They had been out the night before at his bachelor party, the friends, the relatives. They had come home, gone to sleep, and now, on a bright, sunny morning, Don Rogers was talking to his family about the upcoming wedding. Suddenly his body began to convulse in chills. Pain gnawed at his chest, tightening around him, causing him to scream in agony. "It sounded like someone was banging on the walls and floors and somebody was screaming, 'Help me!' at the top of his lungs," a neighbor told the Sacramento Bee. Paramedics rushed him to the hospital.

He never regained consciousness.

Dead.

Cocaine.

To this day, people shake their heads at the death of Don Rogers. Cocaine? A lethal dose? The day before his wedding? Why? He had everything going for him. He was never known as a cocaine user. Where did he get it? When did he ingest it? His death occurred just eight days after the similar death of basketball star Len Bias, and America erupted in a disgusted roar against drugs.

Reggie Rogers heard none of it. Reality had just chomped into his world with a bloody bite. Don was dead. The next day, Loretha Rogers collapsed in Reggie's arms — a heart attack — and had to be rushed to the hospital. His whole world was crumbling. Why? What did I do?

It is unlikely Reggie Rogers has ever truly recovered from that tragedy. Talk to 50 people about him, and each will tell you it was the turning point.

Chris Chandler, a former Huskies quarterback now with the Indianapolis Colts: "He was definitely different after that. Before he was always the center of attention, really funny, cracking everybody up. He was more quiet after Don died."

Kevin Gogan, a former Huskies lineman now with the Dallas Cowboys: "Reggie was definitely quieter after Don's death. He didn't know if he would even play football anymore."

Loretha Rogers: "It was a year before I saw Reggie cry over Donald.

That bothered me. He felt like he had to be strong for everybody else. . . .

"One day we went to the graveyard just before the draft. He started to cry and then he looked at me and he tried to take it back. I said, 'Cry, son, cry. It's all right. You'll still be a man. Get it out.' "

But crying did not make it go away. The death haunted Rogers throughout his senior year at Washington. Wherever he went, people asked him questions. Many assumed he, too, used cocaine. He volunteered to take drug tests throughout the season. He admitted to his mother that yes, he knew people who used drugs, but swore he did not. Loretha Rogers, who herself would have troubles with alcohol, prayed he was telling the truth.

Still the memories would not cease. The bachelor party. The ambulance. Rogers would tune in and out of conversations, daydreaming about Don. He would hear him talking. In a better world, Reggie Rogers would have received counseling then and there, because the hurt was obviously seeping in and it needed to be cured. But there were games to be played and a pro career to think about and money suddenly became critical, because Don's death had caused financial problems. So when people asked, "Reggie, are you OK?" the big kid inside him would smile and say, "Yeah," and people figured great, he's OK.

This is how it goes with star athletes. And yet there were signs that Rogers was OK on the outside but mixed up on the inside. Once, during a preseason meeting of the captains, coach James spoke of the dangers of substance abuse: drugs, marijuana and alcohol.Reggie raised his hand.

"Coach," he said, earnestly, "I understand about cocaine and the drugs. But what's so bad about alcohol?"

I *'m not saying drafting Reggie Rogers has made us the best team in the NFL, but it'll help."*

— Wayne Fontes, Lions defensive coordinator, on draft day, 1987.

In April 1987, Rogers, 6-feet-6, 272 pounds, was taken by Detroit in the first round of the NFL draft, the seventh pick overall, which ensured him a multimillion-dollar contract. But from the moment he became a Lion, there was trouble.

He slept past his first meeting with the team; a missed wake-up call, he said. Next he was charged with assault by his former girlfriend, Alicia Wright of Seattle. Then, on the last day of mini-camp, he was served papers for a $1 million lawsuit brought against him by sports agents Norby Walters and Lloyd Bloom. Right on the sidelines. He walked off the field, took the papers and disappeared into the locker room.

All of that took place during a single week. And yet the Lions — as others had done before them — maintained these were manageable affairs, and that the young man would straighten them out.

In fact, had they checked more carefully, they might have recognized a behavior pattern that had haunted Rogers for years:

1) The missed practices were commonplace; they went back to high school.

2) The agent problems were predictable; Rogers, at one point, had signed with three lawyers. Pat Healy, a Tacoma, Wash.-based attorney who handled Rogers for several months before the draft, claims, "Not long after he signed with me, for a fee of four percent, Reggie met Steve Zucker (a well-known sports agent), who said he'd take Reggie for three percent. Reggie comes back to me and says, 'This guy will do it for three.' So I say, 'OK, I'll do it for three.' He says, 'OK, I'll stay with you.' Then two months later, I get a letter from Zucker saying my services are no longer required." (Zucker did not return several phone calls for this story.)

3) Reggie's girlfriend woes were nothing new. He had fathered a child with Shannon Williams in 1985. According to several sources, Rogers' problems with Wright — which led to the fight that led to the assault charge — stemmed from the fact that he wanted her with him when he visited the child, a baby girl named Brittany Elizabeth Ann.

Rogers saw no real wrong in all this. Why? What did I do? A year and half later, on the tragic morning that would end the lives of three teenagers, Rogers — who is expecting twins next month with his current girlfriend, Sheila Dorsey — was riding with 18-year-old Robin Reece. She escaped the crash with a severed finger and bruises.

"When he awoke in the hospital, he asked whether Robin was dead," recalls Loretha Rogers. "I told him no. He said, 'Thank God.'"

"Did Reggie tell you who Robin Reece was to him?" the mother was asked.

"He said she was a friend. That's all."

R*eggie is a damn good person. But he's California, he's flashy; there's nothing wrong with that. He's been through a lot of trauma. And he's had bad luck. Reggie has the same kind of luck as Mike Tyson. Buzzard's luck."*

— Jerry Ball, Lions nose tackle.

The problems continued. Rogers did not practice hard. When he messed up a play, he would often get up laughing, which irritated some of his teammates. A No. 1 draft pick, they thought, should be pulling more weight. All that money. Then, in late October, Rogers left the Lions briefly when his sister, Jackie, mysteriously disappeared with his truck. (She showed up four days later, after Reggie had searched everywhere, including the morgue, checking dead bodies. She blamed "personal problems.") Two weeks later, Reggie entered a rehabilitation facility for his own emotional problems; he stayed for a month.

Could the Lions have seen all this coming? Perhaps, had they looked harder. Before the 1987 draft, Detroit coach Darryl Rogers made a phone call to James, whom he knew from his years in the Pac-10. He asked whether there was any reason the Lions should not take Rogers. "No," James said, "Reggie wants to do well." Defensive line coach Rex Norris was sent to Seattle to watch Rogers work out. They were satisfied. He was drafted.

That can hardly be called thorough — at least when compared with the Green Bay Packers, who had also considered drafting Rogers.

From the start, the Packers wondered whether Rogers was a risky draft pick. And they had reason to be suspicious. Healy says Rogers missed "four to seven meetings" with Green Bay personnel. He was crossed off their list.

A few weeks after the draft, when the assault charge made headlines, Tom Braatz, the Packers' head of scouting, told the Madison (Wis.) Capital Times: "I can't tell you how many times we flew to Seattle for meetings that Reggie missed. We had people face up to him, we talked to the coach, we even went underground almost to find out about the guy. And you wouldn't believe what we found out. . . . Let's say it was enough to convince us we shouldn't draft him."

What did they find? How did they find it? Healy says the Packers hired someone to follow Rogers to see how he spent his free time: "They employed a local guy, like a private investigator. He trailed Reggie. It's easy to do. These athletes go to the same two or three clubs all the time. The Packers found out what anyone could have found out. . . . Reggie is a nice guy, but he still suffers from the effects of his brother's death. He has a hard time coping with problems and stress. And he is vulnerable to alcohol."

Why did the Packers go to such extremes while the Lions settled for a workout and a phone call? Says Darryl Rogers: "I have never heard of hiring a private investigator and I don't believe it is true."

Healy: "I was shocked when they drafted Reggie. It was total, absolute incompetence! They never even called me. I could not believe it. . . . Every team has its own investigators. If you're talking about a top 10 pick in the first round, you better be sure. . . .

"I'll tell you this. If they had checked Reggie out, they never would have drafted him. Never."

I *just can't win. It's like coming back home. I might run into a guy I haven't seen in years and he might be the biggest dope dealer in town. I don't know that, but if he comes up and shakes my hand, people are going to say, 'Look at Reggie Rogers with that dope dealer.' "*

— **Rogers, the day before the 1987 draft.**

Having said all this, let us point out that in talking to dozens of Rogers' friends and former teammates, not one claims that Reggie was a heavy drinker or a drug user. The portrait that emerges is that of an overgrown child who loved to be the center of attention, meant no one any harm but was saddled with an irresponsible streak that sooner or later landed him in trouble. He was playing better and working harder before an ankle injury sidelined him Oct. 2 at San Francisco.

But who really knows what is inside Reggie Rogers? Words were never reliable. After all, this is a guy who once said, "My money is going to be safe until I'm 60; I don't want it in the bank where I can spend it," then bought himself a new Mercedes and a classic 1953 Cadillac; a guy who once said, "Don't worry, I was raised on pressure," yet found it necessary to check into a clinic before his rookie season was out.

The patterns of Reggie Rogers' life go around and around. When he fails to excel (college basketball, his rookie year with the Lions), his explanation is, "They're not giving me a chance." When he does excel (high school, his last two years in college), he seems to say, "I can't get in any real trouble. They'll let me slide."

Why me? What did I do? He is guilty of naivete, foolishness and trusting the wrong people. He is guilty of irresponsibility, a lack of concentration and a love of the spotlight. But Reggie Rogers — who can be so childlike, the kids in his neighborhood come to his house and ask, "Can Reggie come out to play?" — might not be the evil force that many around the country now imagine. "If you ask me," says Bob Graswich, a reporter for the Sacramento Bee who has covered Rogers since high school, "the guy is just doomed to screw up."

Doomed? Perhaps. Bad news had followed happiness since Reggie was big enough to mow down quarterbacks. His love life led to an assault charge; a bachelor party was the last time he saw his brother alive.

And finally, on that cold morning, bad news leapt from the shadows and pierced his flesh.

He was no longer the victim.

He was the cause.

What happened that night is still a mystery. Rogers was socializing at Big Art's Paradise Lounge in Pontiac. He met teammate Devon Mitchell there. "I said hi, he said hi," Mitchell recalls. "That was about it." They stayed until after 1 a.m. and left in separate cars, although Rogers was supposed to follow Mitchell. Reports of how much Rogers drank were varied. Witnesses claim he was not drunk. But blood alcohol tests at the scene registered .14, well above the .10 level considered legally drunk in Michigan.

It was sometime around 1:50 a.m. when the world came crashing down. Rogers allegedly ran a red light at the intersection of University and Wide Track Drive at what police later claimed was "excessive speed." His Jeep smashed into the Dodge Omni on the passenger side. The Dodge burst into flames. Rogers was pulled from his vehicle, stunned, bleeding. Reece fled the scene, heading for a nearby hospital, her ring finger severed. And the lives of Kenneth Willet, 19, of Waterford Township, Mich., and his two cousins, Kelly Ess, 18, and Dale Ess, 17, both of Versailles, Mo., were suddenly, horribly, over.

What sense can be made of all this? For months, perhaps years to come, people will say the name Reggie Rogers with disdain. They will assume he was a careless, hard-partying athlete, a bad guy who was destined to take somebody down someday. Perhaps. But he is also a product of a system that coddles the star and winks at his off-field shortcomings. Call him a sadly classic American sports hero — the overgrown adolescent who figured he had lots of childhood left.

Loretha Rogers sighs. She says she and Reggie "pray every day for the families of those children. I know what it is like to lose a son. If I spoke to those families today, I would say, 'I'm so sorry. But the Reggie you hear about is not the real Reggie Rogers. He is a good-hearted person who would never do anyone intentional harm.'

"The people of Detroit have never really known Reggie Rogers. . . . He loves children. He means well. . . .

"When he was in the hospital bed, he said, 'Mama, I don't want to be a cripple for my children. . . . Mama, I don't want to die.' "

And yet he is responsible for three deaths. Why? What did I do? It goes over and over. Reggie Rogers has a fractured neck, a lacerated thumb and a future that probably will be without football and that could hold as much as 15 years in prison.

Where is the rhyme and reason in this, you ask? Nowhere. Except maybe someone should have seen this coming. The biggest crime might not be that Reggie Rogers ran a red light, but that, until the tragic moment, he thought the lights always would turn green for him.

He lies there now, in his hospital bed, a brace screwed around his head, his hand bandaged, his face scarred. And his feet hang over the edge of the bed — a grim reminder of the child who had always been too big for his own good. "We pray, that's all," says his mother, and what else can anybody do? Mothers are crying and sons are dead. And there is no childhood left for Reggie Rogers. Not anymore. ◆

FONTES RESTORES ROAR, AT LEAST FOR THE INTERIM

November 21

MILWAUKEE — He kept yanking off the headphones to go hug a lineman, or to pat a tackle on the butt, and then he had to search for the headphones and quickly yank them back on. It was that kind of day. His heart kept cutting in on his work.

But Wayne Fontes was in heaven. He was a head coach, at last, at last, and his team was winning. It was not a pretty game. And the opponent was weak. But so what? Victory is a cleansing wash, and when the gun sounded, the Lions had 19 points and the Green Bay Packers had nine, and the new coach was hugging everybody in sight as they led him across the field to talk to network television.

Suddenly, Fontes pinched at his eyes. He'd had six days to prepare for this new career. He had asked his players for support, to rally behind him, and they had done it. Now he was standing on the cold, windy field at County Stadium and he looked down and sniffed. Someone put an earphone on him, and handed him a microphone. He wiped his eyes.

"Are you OK?" the network guy asked.

"Yeah, fine," he whispered.

Was he crying? A head coach? Crying? Later he would say he just had something in his eye, but he would wink when he said it, and it's quite possible he was that overcome with emotion. Wayne Fontes is the kind of guy who gets overwhelmed with emotion, who hugs players and assistants, who wants them all to eat together and ride the bus together, and who sits in coach class with them on the plane and laughs and cuts up.

And now his men had won his first game.

"How do you feel?" the network guy asked.

"Overwhelmed . . . " he said into the mike and he stopped, choked up.

One game. It was only one game. It improved the Lions' record to 3-9. "Big deal," you say. Wayne Fontes still may not be running this team when it returns next fall. He is, after all, the interim head coach. But for one blustery Sunday afternoon, it was nice to see a Lions team play with emotion, with purpose. It was nice to see the players up on the sidelines, watching every play, well into the game.

"We were like a person dying of a bad heart," said defensive lineman Eric Williams, "and somebody comes along and transplants a new one. We felt like we were 20 years old again."

The bad heart, of course, was the Darryl Rogers regime, which officially ended one week ago, with very little complaint from the players. The new heart was ex-defensive coordinator Fontes — not just the man, but the system he installed. Everything. From more organized practices, to more constructive criticism. From a dress code, to a Saturday night team meal (instead of Rogers' tradition, which was to give the players money and let them eat out by themselves).

And, of course, the hugging.

"Hey, that's just Wayne," said safety Bennie Blades, who made his first NFL interception — which earned him several hugs. "Personally, I like it. I like being congratulated as well as criticized, which is definitely not the way it was around here before."

Throughout the locker room, the attitude was the same. Nice change. Happy to have it. We're sick of losing. Nobody was fooled. Nobody was talking Super Bowl. But players were slapping hands and someone would yell, "We're 1-0!" and the wish was if only this were the first Sunday of the season instead of the 12th, we might really have something here.

"Do you realize, the first thing Darryl would do after a game was come in and make himself a sandwich?" Williams said. "No matter what. Win or lose. He'd be first in the food line."

He nodded toward the new coach. "Look at Wayne. The first thing he does is hug the players and thank them. It's a little thing, but it matters."

Indeed, not only did Fontes thank his troops, but he invited the media into the locker room to listen. He also gave the game ball to team owner William Clay Ford. ("He's waited a long time, too.") The cynics will say Fontes is staging a great PR campaign to keep the job for next year. But the cynics will say anything.

"It's one game, I know that, just one game," Fontes said over and over. "We have to keep this in perspective."

He smiled and shook his head, his cheeky face a mix of relief and joy. Never mind that Green Bay outgained Detroit in total yardage. Never mind that the game was soaked in penalties. Never mind that on three chances on first-and-goal from the 1, the Lions couldn't score. They got the touchdown when they needed it, didn't they? They got the defense when they needed it. And Fontes kept yanking off those headphones to congratulate somebody.

It was a victory. He was smiling. The players filed out in their suits and ties. Finally, the head coach, his eyes dry now, lit up a cigar and reached for his jacket. On his way out, someone offered him a statistical summary of the game. He shook his head.

"Statistics," he said, "are for assistant coaches and losers." And on this cold Sunday evening, he was neither one. ◆

25¢ WORTH OF JUSTICE ON THE MEAN STREETS

November 27

Kenyatta Jefferson did not see the gun until it was a few inches away. Then the man shot him in the head. He fell to the ground, and landed at the feet of his friend, Willie Tucker. He remembers his blood dripping on Willie's Nike sneakers. Then Willie ran.

The man shot Willie, too. In the shoulder. Derrick, Kenyatta's older brother, heard the shots and came running back toward the store. "You shot Kenyatta! You shot Kenyatta!" he screamed.

The man said, "Here's what you get for Kenyatta."

He shot Derrick in the leg. Then he fled.

It was Friday night. The kids managed to drag Kenyatta to the curb on Kercheval — Derrick, who was bleeding, and Willie, who was bleeding, and Raymond Brown and Anthony Hall, together, just as they once had played together on their high school team. They tried to flag a car or a bus. Kenyatta was barely conscious. Already his right side was limp and his speech was gone.

Willie yelled, "C'mon, Derrick!"

Derrick yelled, "No, we gotta get Kenyatta to a hospital. The man shot him in the head!"

When the police came, there was more yelling, and soon kids from the neighborhood had gathered around the variety store, pointing at the blood. The owner grabbed a mop and swabbed it up. Lights were flashing. Sirens sounded. Back at college, on the Virginia Union football team where Kenyatta played, they had an expression for a player's toughness. "You gotta cross the desert to be a Panther." Now, riding in the back of the police car, Derrick held Kenyatta in his arms, the life oozing from his brother's skull, and whispered, "You crossed the desert, Kenyatta. You crossed the desert. Hang on. Please hang on."

This is a story about 25 cents' worth of violence and we tell it here because this has to stop, the guns, the anger, the blood of children. This weekend, college football draws to close, players peel off their helmets, flushed with accomplishment — and Kenyatta Jefferson, who represents the most important currency in Detroit, a poor kid with a chance to make it, is a cripple who must teach himself to walk.

You can believe his account of Friday, May 20, or you can believe the account of the man who fired the bullets, a drifter named John Shelton, who claimed he was threatened by five college athletes because they were big and wearing sweat suits and talking trash when they entered Honey Baby's variety store on Kercheval.

Kenyatta, who was only 18 when he took the bullet, has no doubts. Only questions.

"Why?" he says, his words still slow and slurred. "Every day I ask myself that. Why did he have to shoot us? What did we do?"

He sighs. He is sitting next to his mother in the house on East Outer Drive, dressed in an adidas T-shirt and blue jeans. His face is still smooth and handsome, but his body has changed. He is 6-feet-3, and the definition is there in his arms and shoulders, yet it has softened, the muscles melting with neglect. His right arm is stiff and he walks with a limp and there is a surgical scar that begins on his forehead and traces around his skull.

The night of the shooting, doctors said he would never walk or talk again — if he made it through the night. They operated for six hours and still could not remove all of the bullet. A fragment remains, lodged in his brain tissue, a forget-me-not of the city where he lives.

How could it happen? Why did it happen? "We had all come home from college and we were going downtown to the festival," he says. "We stopped in Honey Baby's for some candy. We've been going there since we were kids. I ordered five taffies, Laffy Taffy. They cost five cents apiece. The guy behind the counter was a skinny man, with Jheri curls and a brown sweater. I had never seen him before. He acted like 'Why did you guys have to come in here now?' Like he was mad to even be there. I gave him the quarter. He gave me the taffies.

"After that, Willie ordered 75 Big Blow candies. A penny apiece. Then the guy said, 'Wait a minute. You didn't pay me for the taffies.' And I said, 'I had to pay you for the taffies or you wouldn't have given them to me.' He said, 'Aww, bleep that. You gonna pay me for those taffies.'

"He went back to ask Honey Baby, the lady who owns the store. She knows us since we were kids. But she was behind the ice cream freezer so she couldn't see. She said, 'Let 'em go. It ain't worth it.' We were gonna give him another quarter, but he said, 'Naw, forget it.' So we went out of the store.

"I saw him walking to the door behind the counter but I didn't pay no attention. Then I looked to my left and I saw his arm sticking out the door and the gun in his hand. I never seen a gun that close. I tried to duck."

He pauses. He swallows.

"And then he shot you?"

"Yes," he says flatly.

"For 25 cents?"

"For 25 cents."

B ack at Martin Luther King High, Jefferson had been a star linebacker
and running back, one of those natural football players who liked to hit
and didn't care where or when. In a game that sent his school to the city
championship, Jefferson was everywhere — inside linebacker, outside
linebacker, fullback. "I remember it was pouring rain and we were covered
with mud," says his former coach, Jim Reynolds. "But he was on the field
almost the entire game, making key plays. We won in overtime."

Jefferson made first-team all-city. He was recruited by several major
colleges, including Clemson and Alabama. But his grades were not good and
he wound up at Virginia Union, where last year he became a starter at
linebacker. Still. An athlete on scholarship. Not bad for a kid from the 'hood.

"When I played football," he says, "I was on top of the world."

Today, he is merely a victim of it. The bullet left him paralyzed on his
right side, and although he has come much further than doctors expected,
he still limps down the steps, he still shakes hands with the left. He has been
in rehab for months. Tedious exercise. Wiggling fingers. Bending arms. "If I
concentrate on walking, then I can walk normal, but I have to think, 'One
leg, then the other,' " he says. "They say I'm like a baby that has to learn
everything over again."

He dreams of running, of tackling, of somehow returning to football. But
the days are long now because Derrick, Willie, Raymond and Anthony are all
back at college, playing sports. So he spends a lot of time with his mother, or
with his girlfriend, Scherriel Neeley.

"Watch, I'll show you something," he says. He leans over, grabs a
shoelace with his good hand, and weaves it in a loop, pinching, squeezing. It
takes 40 seconds, maybe longer.

"There," he says, finally. "I taught myself."

Kenyatta Jefferson has just tied his shoe.

T he trial took two days. The defense attorney, Arthur Bowman Jr.,
argued that his client, John Shelton, 41, had acted in self-defense. His
story was markedly different from that of the five teenagers. Although the
counter in Honey Baby's is enveloped by bulletproof glass, Shelton claimed
he was drawn out to the middle of the store, and that Derrick was pushing
him and threatening him and he pulled the gun and meant to shoot Derrick
but fell backward and accidentally shot Kenyatta, then shot the others
because he feared retaliation.

"It was my job to put the jury in the shoes of my client," Bowman said
last week. Meaning: fear. What would you think, he suggested, if five black
kids of large height and weight came into your store talking loudly and
wearing sweat suits and sneakers — the popular costume of drug dealers
these days? Never mind that these kids had been on their way from the gym.
Never mind that they had no criminal records. Never mind that they had

been coming to this store for years and had never tried to rob it, to damage it or to shoplift merchandise. Never mind that none of them had a weapon.

Under Michigan law, there can be no appeal.

Never mind that Shelton — who rode his bicycle to the store and lived in a single room in Honey Baby's house and wasn't even an employee but rather a guy who hung around and occasionally helped out for $3.50 an hour and admitted later that he was having a "bad day" — was carrying a gun in his waistband that no one knew about.

Fear. We are talking about fear — and supply exceeds demand in Detroit. So Bowman argued that fear and self-preservation motivated the trigger finger of John Shelton.

And all Kenyatta Jefferson could do was listen. At times he had to leave the courtroom, limping out, because the proceedings upset him so much. His own attorney, provided by the court, had been given the case only that day. The regular prosecutor — to whom the Jeffersons had been talking — left town suddenly on business. According to Doris Jefferson, Kenyatta's mother, the family had "five minutes with the new man" before the trial began. This is how justice works for the poor.

"He didn't even have time to see what kind of kids my kids were," she said. "This other lawyer is making them out like they're gangsters or crack dealers. These are college athletes. They are good kids. They were making their way out of the ghetto. But he never talked about that."

The jurors did not take long. At the end of the second day, the 12 of them, mostly older people, two white, the rest black, found John Shelton guilty of assault on Willie Tucker and Derrick Jefferson.

For the shooting of Kenyatta Jefferson, they found Shelton not guilty. Self-defense.

"NO! NO! NO!" screamed Doris Jefferson, when the verdict was announced. "It can't be! He shot my son! It can't be!"

It was. There is no appeal.

Last week, Judge Michael Talbot, who sentenced Shelton to the strictest penalty for the assault charge — six to 10 years in prison, versus 20 or more were he convicted on intent to murder — was asked to explain the jury's decision.

"The lawyer painted a picture of 'You know how Detroit is,' " he said. "He played on the fear. And I think folks just have such experiences with young men in this city that the good ones get tarred with the same brush as the bad ones. . . . My heart went out to that young man (Kenyatta). What bothers me most is that (Shelton) showed no remorse. None. I'm sure if you asked him today, he'd say he did the right thing. How many more people are out there like this? That's what scares me."

"What would you have ruled?" he was asked.

"Me? I would have found him guilty of intent to murder," he said. "But it was the jury's decision."

Twenty-five cents' worth of violence.

Twenty-five cents' worth of justice.

And here is where the story ends. Two days before Thanksgiving. People are racing through supermarkets, booking plane reservations, gearing up for the holiday. Kenyatta Jefferson, for the first time since that night in May, pulls on the rotted door and steps inside Honey Baby's.

The floor is covered with cardboard boxes. Windows are held together with tape. The candy jars sit behind bulletproof glass, one filled with Laffy Taffy, five cents apiece. "He shot me right here," Kenyatta begins, ignoring the customers, his voice flat. "And I fell there, and he shot Willie there. . . ."

Honey Baby, the thin, chain-smoking 59-year-old owner (whose real name is LueEthel Wright) walks over without a hello and joins the conversation. She says she didn't know John Shelton had a gun.

"Earlier that day, he said he didn't want to be here. I said, 'Fine, then. Go on home.' But he stayed. Then I heard those shots. . . . I ain't seen John Shelton since. He still got some stuff at my house. Old stuff. Junk. His bicycle."

"Do you believe the kids were trying to rob the store and hurt him?" she is asked.

"They never ripped me off for nothing. They been comin' here for years. . . . No. I don't believe they did nothing wrong."

Kenyatta Jefferson stares at her blankly. There is no sense of relief. He waits until she's finished talking, then limps outside to show a visitor the curb where he lay until the police came.

In the suburbs, this story might mobilize a community. On the national sports scene, it would be mourned as a tragedy. But Kenyatta Jefferson is not a national sports star and he does not live in the suburbs.

That should not make him less valid.

He is a Detroit kid, and when he was crippled, a piece of us was crippled, too. This is our city. These are our children. We are shooting each other and blaming fear, and now, for a handful of candy, a college kid must tie his shoes one-handed and there's something terribly wrong here.

"Man shoot that boy for 25 cents?" Honey Baby says, dragging on her cigarette. "I wouldn't get that mad for no 25 cents. I wouldn't get that mad for 25 dollars."

But Kenyatta Jefferson cannot hear her. He is standing outside in the cold November breeze, holding his old football helmet for a photographer. He grips it in his good hand and freezes, a piece of bullet still inside his head. Thanksgiving is just around the corner and he must wonder what the whole thing is all about. ◆

FAME AND FORTUNE? NOT FOR FIRST HEISMAN WINNER

December 2

H e didn't have room for the trophy at his fraternity house. So he gave it to his Aunt Gussie. She used it as a doorstop.

"It worked really well," recalls Jay Berwanger, 74, the first Heisman Trophy winner. "Later on, she used it as a hat rack. You know, with the arm sticking out, you could just hang your hat right on it."

The year was 1935. Nobody knew what a Heisman was. Nobody cared. People were more excited about a job. Or a 25-cent movie. An airplane ride? That was big. So when Berwanger, a halfback and linebacker at the University of Chicago, received the telegram saying he had been chosen by something called the Downtown Athletic Club as the best college football player east of the Rocky Mountains — well, it was the plane trip to New York that got him most excited.

"I had never been on an airplane. All the guys at the frat asked about it. What was it like? How fast? They didn't give a hoot about the award."

The flight from Chicago took five hours, two stops. In the Big Apple, Berwanger and his coach were taken to the Empire State Building. To Radio City. Even lunch at the 21 Club. Two years later, he would try to get back into that restaurant.

"I was with a date. She said, 'We need reservations.' I said, 'Oh, don't worry. Last time I was here, they treated me royally.'

"So I introduced myself to the doorman, said I was Jay Berwanger, and I had won the Heisman Trophy, remember? He said, 'The what? Jay who?' "

He laughs. "Never saw the girl again, either."

Tomorrow, they will give out the 54th Heisman Trophy. The winner — if it is, as most people suspect, Barry Sanders of Oklahoma State — will be playing a game in Tokyo. They plan to interview him via satellite. He'll be in line for fame, glory, maybe millions in salary and endorsements.

"How much did it get you?" Berwanger is asked.

"Oh, no money or anything. I think the Chicago Tribune ran a small story in the sports section. Inside. It wasn't front-page material."

T hings change. The statue is still cast in bronze, still a football player carrying the ball in his left hand, his right arm outstretched, perfect for a hat. But in the 53 years since Berwanger collected it, the significance of the Heisman has grown to almost comical proportions. Schools now plan public-relations campaigns a year in advance. Posters, buttons, bumper stickers. The best college football player in the nation? You would think we were electing a president.

And Jay Berwanger just laughs. His trophy — which was taken back from Aunt Gussie — now sits in a glass case in a University of Chicago gym. You ask yourself, "Jay Berwanger? Why didn't I ever hear of him?" Because he never played professionally. Here is how much football has changed since 1935: Berwanger turned down chances with the Philadelphia Eagles and the Chicago Bears because the money was better . . . as a sports writer.

Ha!

"I worked for the old Chicago Daily News covering football," he says. "Paid $100 a week. Ballplayers barely made that. I once ran into George Halas, the owner of the Bears. I was with a date, going to a dance. He said, 'What would it take to sign you?' I made a joke: '$25,000 for two years.' Halas said, 'Nice meeting you. Have a good time at the dance.'"

Berwanger, who still lives outside Chicago, doesn't complain. He has made a nice living in sales (journalism was short-lived). He has 16 grandchildren and two great-grandchildren. He goes to New York for the Heisman ceremonies whenever he can. And when Doug Flutie won the 50th award, Berwanger made a speech. Flutie, he notes, is the same size as the guys he played with.

"What do you think when you see how much money Heisman winners make now?" he is asked.

"I think," he says, "I had lousy timing."

Things change. Today, the University of Chicago is hardly a football powerhouse. And the stadium where Berwanger played is gone — destroyed because it was radioactive. In 1942, scientists working on the Manhattan Project created a fission chain-reaction under the west stands of Stagg Field. "Near the squash courts," says Berwanger.

Not everyone can say that about his alma mater.

But then, not everyone has a Heisman Trophy. It is funny to think how much that little statue has evolved, how overblown it has become. Considering it was once a doorstop.

"Someone once asked me what the difference was between when I won it and today," Berwanger says. "I told him, 'About $1 million.' Today, I'd say $10 million."

But no matter. He has the first, and they can't take that away. It has not made him wealthy, it has not made him famous. But it has given him something, as he says, "to hang my hat on."

Aunt Gussie can vouch for that. ♦

ST. CECILIA'S REMEMBERS A HERO OF THE INNER CITY

December 4

I have been to many funerals in my life. I had never been to one like they had for Sam Washington. People came from all over — white, black, old, young, basketball players, kids in sneakers, mothers, fathers, coaches.

They filled the pews at St. Cecilia Church, there, ostensibly, to say good-bye to a man they loved. It was a sad moment, yet there seemed to be little sadness, and when they spoke of him, one by one, loved ones rising to tell stories about "Sammy," well, there were actually ripples of laughter, and tears mixed with smiles.

A funeral.

The way he'd have wanted it.

He was that rarest of individuals, a hero of kindness. Given his wit and energy, Samuel Lee Washington could have done almost anything. Yet he devoted his life to kids. Not the well-scrubbed kids from TV sitcoms but street kids, kids without alternatives, kids for whom the choice was sometimes a basketball or a gun. Why did he do it? Why ask? He lived in Detroit and he saw a need and he went to work.

St. Cecilia's was his office, a church gymnasium just off Livernois, behind the Tuffy Muffler shop. Not a common place for miracles, but, then, there was little common about Sam Washington. For years he ran those legendary summer leagues, started them in 1968, an alternative to the racial strife that was ripping apart Detroit. They grew into perhaps the best recreational basketball in the country because he nurtured them, he believed in them, he swung his weight for them.

And Sam was pretty big.

"Hey, Dave," he once said to Dave Bing, a star then with the mediocre Pistons of the '70s, "I need some exposure. Why don't you get your teammates to come down and play at St. Cecilia's?"

"Why would they want to play there?" Bing asked.

"Because it's the only full house they'll get," Sam said.

They came.

A few years later, when Bing was holding out on his Pistons contract, Sam approached him again. Said he needed money for a new gym floor. Bing shrugged. "I'm getting fined $500 a day for holding out, Sam," he said.

"What can I do?" Bing said.

A light went on in Sam's head. He dragged Bing down to the Pistons' offices.

"What are you guys doing with the $500 a day you're taking from Dave?" he demanded.

The Pistons' people didn't really have an answer.

"Well," the big man said with a smile, "I have a very good suggestion."

He got his floor.

That was Sam.

That was Sam. People uttered the sentence all day, people such as Bing and Terry Tyler and Terry Duerod, former NBA players who stood in the church and sang prayers for him. And people such as Magic Johnson, Spencer Haywood, George Gervin, Campy Russell, famous men now scattered across the nation who owe a lot to Washington because he gave them a place to play, a clean and well-lighted place, and, more than that, he gave them his encouragement, his love and his time. All of it.

"He used to take us to places like Boston and New York to play teams there," Duerod recalled. "Those were the best days of my childhood. I never would have seen those cities if not for him."

Players gravitated to him. Black or white — made no difference. He was a heavy-set man, the kind of guy whose collars were always stretched wide open, his second chin folding under his first, huge smile, cap on his head. If we're being honest, he was fat, but that never bothered him, being honest.

"You're doing the work of two men," his co-workers would carp at him when, in addition to his duties at St. Cecilia's, he took the general manager job with the now-defunct Detroit Spirits of the Continental Basketball Association.

"I'm big enough to be two men," he would answer.

And everybody would laugh.

Laughter. That's what people remembered most. The way he would listen to a joke and begin to laugh before it was over, and take out a hanky and wipe his eyes, and bellyache, and finally, when the punch line was delivered, he would absolutely explode, and then, wheezing, he would say, "That was a terrible joke, man. Terrible."

How can you not love that? Sam Washington was gentle, yet no pushover. A former professional football player who could outshoot his future NBA stars in a game of H-O-R-S-E. He was the perfect recipe for the inner city — one part teacher, one part parent, one part Big Daddy. Because of his efforts and his lightning-rod personality, the level of basketball at St. Cecilia's grew to legendary proportions, until, among college recruiters and NBA front offices, this became common knowledge: If you wanted talent, you found it in the gym behind the muffler shop.

Go see Sam.

"We call our place 'Broadway,'" he used to say, "because when you play here, you play at the top." Indeed. People still talk about the game when a group of high schoolers from New York came to town, featuring two guys named King, Bernard and Albert, and they played the Detroiters, and an unknown named Earvin Johnson ate them up. "Best game I ever saw," people whisper.

King? Johnson? Haywood? Russell?

Broadway.

The service was called "Celebrating the Life of Samuel Lee Washington." He was 54 when he left this Earth, the victim of a stroke suffered in his office at the gym (which was where he always said he wanted to go, if he had to go). "Celebration" was an appropriate word. Bing told some funny stories, and fellow coaches told some funny stories, and then Sam's son David climbed the altar. Loved ones knew how grief-stricken he was, and yet he, too, told the story of how his father was so busy at St. Cecilia's and with the Spirits that he often lacked the time other fathers spent with their own children.

"But we could never get in trouble, because everywhere we went, there were people who knew him," David said. "They kept an eye on us. He had eyes everywhere!"

And hearts. He had hearts all over Detroit. If there can be a man who deserves the phrase "of the city, by the city, for the city," then it was Sam Washington. He can be appreciated, remembered, cherished. He will never be replaced. "I can't even imagine what it'll be like this summer," said Duerod, who still plays in the leagues when the hot weather comes. "It won't be the same without Sam."

It can't be. And yet, if we are to serve his memory well, the leagues will go on, St. Cecilia's and all that it stands for, because that is what he would have wanted, kids playing ball, in the city, black and white, rich and poor, off the streets and safe within the loving grasp of a sweaty gymnasium.

Let us hope it happens. For Sam's sake. As they were singing the final hymns, a few kids wiggled out the front door, tired of the long service. Off came the sports coats. Up went the sleeves. And one of them had a basketball. He began to dribble it on the concrete, a steady bounce that harmonized with the voices from the church. Bomp. Bomp. It sounded like a heartbeat.

In a certain way, maybe it was. ◆

STEVIE WONDERFUL'S FAME HASN'T GONE TO HIS HEAD

December 9

Y ou want to know my biggest fear about Steve Yzerman? That success will one day grab him by the neck and say, "Look, kid, wake up. You're a star. Stop treating people so nicely!"

It could happen. Plenty of athletes begin humble and wind up haughty. It's easy when the whole city is fawning over you.

And yet it is tough to fawn over Yzerman. He likes to hide in the woods of normality. Last week I called him up. I said, "What are you doing?" He said, "Nothing. My fiancee is at a Tupperware party."

A Tupperware party?

He made a commercial for Ford recently. Didn't use an agent. Just went in, heard the offer and accepted it. ("Well, it's not like I'd won any Oscars," Yzerman says. "I couldn't really demand anything.")

He has eclipsed a Detroit hockey record held by the great Gordie Howe — most consecutive games with at least one goal. Yzerman is at nine and counting.

I ask whether he has ever met Howe.

"A couple of times," he says. "He'll come over and say hi."

"Couldn't you just say hello first?"

His eyes bulge.

"No way! I would never just go up to Gordie Howe out of the blue."

"Why not?"

"Because he's Gordie Howe. What am I gonna say, 'Hey, Gordie. How's it goin'?' "

"Well, don't you think you've reached that point?"

He shakes his head.

"I'll never reach that point."

Now. Whoa. This is not Butch Deadmarsh talking. This is a guy who many believe is the third-best player in the NHL, behind only Wayne Gretzky and Mario Lemieux. This is the captain of the Red Wings, an All-Star, a skating wizard who is hockey's answer to the deer: graceful, elusive and smart. He has 28 goals in the first 27 games this season, mountains of assists, his passing is deft, his aim is true, he is arguably the most popular athlete in Detroit — Yzerman, Isiah or Trammell, toss it up — and is certainly the most widely liked. The other night he went to a Stevie Wonder concert. They could have called it: "Stevie Wonder meets Stevie Wonderful."

And he's embarrassed to say hello to Gordie Howe?

Oh, Yzerman.

You'll never last.

A nd yet . . . well, who knows? Maybe we tapped into the real thing here — humility and talent in one handsome package. For years, Yzerman has been referred to as "Detroit's rising star." But he is the hottest scorer in hockey right now. He was NHL player of the month in November. He breaks a Gordie Howe record. Perhaps we should take a hint.

Perhaps he has arrived for good. Top of the heap — Gretzky, Lemieux, Yzerman.

Just don't tell him that.

"There's no comparison between Wayne Gretzky and me," Yzerman says, sitting in his West Bloomfield apartment, his voice, as always, soft and unassuming. "He's done it all. Won Stanley Cups, won scoring championships. . . . These people who compare us, or say he and Mario and I are 1-2-3, it's so unfair to guys like Mark Messier, Dale Hawerchuk, Ray Bourque. You can't compare. . . .

"And Gordie Howe? No way. I was looking at some of his records the other day. He's got marks that will last forever. He played with a dynasty. If we ever become a dynasty, a lot of other guys will be breaking records, too."

He crosses his legs and folds his hands — and he looks as if he's 15 years old. Amazing. Most people see Yzerman only on the ice, when he's sweaty and his hair is wet and his sparse whiskers suggest at least a little ruggedness.

See him at home sometime.

I bet he gets carded at PG movies.

All of which makes his maturity a surprise. And know this: He is as mature as they come. Not just in hockey. In business. In life. And he's only 23. You look at him and you say, "Geez, the guy belongs in high school." You listen to him and you say, "Geez, the guy belongs in an office."

Did you know that Steve Yzerman is studying to be a financial analyst? Yep. He's taking a course with Shearson Lehman Brothers. "I don't want to be the typical dumb athlete," he says. "I mean, I'd like to have something to talk about other than hockey."

He also plans to be married next year to his longtime girlfriend, Lisa Brennan. They have a date all set. Now. I don't want to say he's passing up opportunities here. But if you put Steve Yzerman in a nightclub and told Detroit women he was there, we might never see him again.

"I know what I want from life," he says, shrugging, when asked about

97

his adoring female fans. "Lisa was with me long before things got going good. And she'll be with me long after.

"Usually when we go out, I try to let it be known that I'm with her. Sometimes people will come over anyhow."

He laughs.

"If I forget to introduce her, she kicks me in the shins."

Like most captains, Yzerman has learned to straddle the team's needs with the needs of the public. That is not surprising. What is surprising is that he learned it so fast. What can rattle Steve Yzerman now? When a horrible knee injury ended his regular season last winter, there were whispers; some said he would never be the same.

"I'll be back," he promised, and he delivered.

During the recent escapades of Bob Probert and Petr Klima, he was not shy with criticism of his teammates. Nor did he play St. Steven in the media. "I think we've all talked enough about it," he said, when it seemed, indeed, we had.

Most athletes treat responsibility the way a vampire treats a cross. Yet in the four years I have known him, I have seen Yzerman agree to do one of those silly playoff diaries for our newspaper — then insist that he write it himself. I have seen him wandering around the Windsor, Ontario, airport parking lot in the wee hours of the morning, making sure his teammates all had rides home.

The other night on WLLZ-FM, hockey analyst Don Cherry rated Yzerman up there with Gretzky and Lemieux in talent. "But you know," Cherry added, "if you ask players around the league, Yzerman is the one they'd most like to sit and have beer with. He's the most regular guy of the three."

And then there is this story. I heard it from Mary Schroeder, a photographer for the Detroit Free Press, who sits near the penalty box at Joe Louis Arena. Whenever Yzerman gets called for a penalty, he enters the box, cursing like a sailor.

Then he sees her.

"Sorry, Mary," he always says.

And he sits down.

Manners.

Now, OK. Before we put a halo around his head, let us point out that, yes, Yzerman is sometimes so low-key, he sounds like part of SCTV's "Great White North" show. ("Have a sandwich, eh? OK, eh? Good, eh?") And he is not without his moods, his temper, his pet peeves. He is mortal. The knee injury still bothers him, he can't sprint without pain and squatting is pretty much out; it hurts too much.

But we are talking about a guy here who could become legendary. He could become (gulp) this era's Gordie Howe. He is already the star on a team that is on the lip of excellence. And he is only 23. Detroit is a hockey town. When the team goes good, the good are canonized.

And he is on his way. Quietly. Humbly. His contract has become an issue lately because he earns only $385,000 annually, while Lemieux and Gretzky earn about $2 million. His response? It will be taken care of. Why debate it in the press? "It seems like so many contracts become controversial. I don't see why they can't be harmonious, all parties getting along."

What planet did this guy come from?

And are there any more like him? I keep worrying that one day soon I'll walk into the Wings' locker room and Yzerman will be wearing sunglasses, flanked by a bodyguard and a personal secretary. "No time to talk today, babe," he'll say, checking his hair in the mirror. "Maybe next week."

Who knows? It could be that the Bobby Knights and Joaquin Andujars and Jim McMahons have ruined us. Maybe you get a humble guy who just wants to play and do well and marry his high school sweetheart, and you immediately grow suspicious. Write something complimentary about an athlete these days. Next thing you know, the guy gets arrested.

But I don't think that will happen with Steve Yzerman. Call it a hunch. Call it blind faith. There is now at least one part of the Red Wings' history book that reads: 1. Yzerman; 2. Howe. . . . And I suspect it won't be the last.

Still, I could be wrong. . . .

"Are you comfortable with your image now?" I ask.

"Um . . . I don't know what it is," he says.

I'm not wrong. ◆

SLAPSTICK AND SLAP SHOT: SALLEY LOVES WINGS' WAYS

December 16

H e is 24 years old. This is his first hockey game. He hands his ticket to the attendant at Joe Louis Arena, who hands it back and looks up, and up, and up.

"Aren't you . . . ?" the attendant asks.

"Wayne Gretzky?" says John Salley.

And so we begin. A basketball player in hockeyland. Slam dunk meets slap shot. I am keeping a promise I made to Salley, the Pistons' 6-foot-11 forward, who has never seen a hockey game, does not understand the rules and hasn't been on skates since he was 12 years old. The promise was that one night we would all go to a Red Wings game — Salley, I and our friend, George Baier — and teach him the game firsthand.

Not that I know anything about hockey.

"These guys hit each other and everything?" Salley asks.

"Yep."

"Right out there on the ice?"

"Yep."

"And they don't get fined $5,000?"

"Nope."

He grins. "Rick Mahorn would love this game."

N ow, taking an NBA player to an NHL game is confusing enough. Taking John Salley is a whole other experience. John Salley is not exactly shy. John Salley is more like Eddie Murphy on a stepladder. He is wearing a floppy don jacket, a Raiders cap and glasses. He comes from Brooklyn. Went to college in Georgia. He should feel right at home in a Detroit hockey game, right?

And he wants some pizza.

So we order from a stand in the hallway. It takes five minutes. Seven minutes. Nine minutes. The game starts without us.

"HEY, YO!" Salley yells. "YOU FLYIN' THIS PIZZA IN FROM NEW JERSEY?"

The pizza people laugh and ask for his autograph. In fact, everyone who passes asks for his autograph. I mean *everyone*. You'd think he was the only 6-11 basketball player in the . . .

Well, OK, maybe he is.

100

Pizza in hand, we go to our seats. They are upstairs and in the corner. Salley doesn't mind. He squeezes his long legs in front. "SIT DOWN!" somebody yells.

"I AM!" he answers.

And we watch. The Red Wings and the North Stars race up and down the ice. A new line comes in, leaps over the boards. Then another, over the boards.

"I don't get it," Salley says. "You mean they don't have to check in at the desk?"

"What desk?" I say.

He watches Gilbert Delorme check his opponent into the boards. Thud. Crunch. He watches Jim Pavese check an opponent into the boards. Thud. Crunch.

"Holy bleep," he mumbles.

Hard to argue with that.

George tries to explain icing. He tries to explain offsides. Salley nods.

And a fight breaks out. Joey Kocur is going at it with some Minnesota player. The gloves are off. Fists are flying. Salley rises to his feet, mesmerized.

"LOOK AT THAT! CAN HE DO THAT?"

Finally, the linesmen step in, break it up and send the fighters off the ice — for five minutes.

"Unbelievable," Salley says, taking his seat. "I gotta tell Rickey about this stuff."

In between periods we move down to closer seats, so that Salley can witness the game from a different angle. Now we are seven rows from the ice. Salley appears nervous.

"What if the puck comes and hits me in the face?" he says. "I need my face, man. . . . . Couldn't they raise the glass a little? Maybe 20 feet?"

(By the way, all the time this is going on, people are still asking Salley for autographs. They stick tickets in front of his face, programs, caps, pictures of Petr Klima, you name it. He signs them all, and is never at a loss for words:

"Hey, John, you remember that Georgia Tech game where you guys won, 130-66? I was there, man."

"Yeah, I think I remember you. Fourteenth row?")

Anyhow, the game goes on. Salley is getting the hang of it. He comments on the pace ("It's 20 minutes on ice, 20 minutes to talk to women, 20 minutes on ice . . . "), the boisterous crowd ("We should tape these people and play it up at the Palace") and Dave Barr ("He's gotta be good. He wears my number — 22.").

And Dave Barr scores a goal.

"Told you," Salley says.

The Red Wings win, 5-4. Not long before the final horn, Salley reaches to retrieve his jacket from under the seat.

It is covered in beer.

"What the . . . ?" he says.

"Welcome to hockey," I say, shrugging.

When the game ends, we go into the Wings' locker room. Salley meets coach Jacques Demers. ("How come you wear those dark glasses, Jacques? You sleepin' out there and don't want people to know?") He meets Steve Yzerman, the captain. ("You're baaad, man. How much they paying you?") He meets Dave Barr, toothless in front. ("Hey, Barr. I used to have a smile like you — when I was three years old.")

Barr gives him his hockey stick. The equipment man gives him a puck. Salley marvels at the size of these players, and, more impressive, the size of their bruises. Shawn Burr says hello. His calf is swollen like a softball, red and purple.

"Aw, some idiot stepped on me," Burr says.

Salley watches him walk away. "These guys," he whispers, "are some crazy bleeps. . . . "

And we leave. Slam dunk meets slap shot. As we walk down the corridor, we pass a goalie net. Salley drops the puck and tries a few shots. They roll. They bounce. Hey. At least he doesn't swing and miss.

"Hockey is great, man," he declares, passing more fans, who yell for autographs. "I'm coming back. Is the crowd like this all the time? . . . Yo, baby, what's your name?"

Well. No one ever accused John Salley of being shy. Still, it is nice to see a big-name athlete go to a game and sit among the fans, expecting no free food, no executive suite. We get outside, reach the car, and Salley leans over, taps my knee, and whispers, in typical disarming fashion: "Hey, thanks for taking me."

And off he drives, with his new stick and puck — all dressed up and no place to goal. I don't know how much Salley understands hockey now. I do know he's got some interesting things to tell Rick Mahorn. And if I were Mahorn's next opponent?

I'd wear a helmet. ♦

HARK, THE HERALD ATHLETES SING . . .

December 25

G ood morning. Merry Christmas. Hear those voices outside your door? Look, it's . . .

Kirk Gibson singing "Winter Wonderland":

Watch me swing, it's a dinger,
World Seee-ries, what a dinger!
I'm hobblin' along, singing my song,
A hero now in laid-back La-La Land
It's outta here! What's my hurry?
Injured knee, I can't scurry,
But TV is neat, they repeat and repeat,
Every night in laid-back La-La Land
People say I'm now like Robert Redford,
Natural as a natural can be,
I say shucks, I'm not like Robert Redford,
I doubt that he can swing as hard as me
Tommy L., what a tummy!
Tommy M., what a dummy!
I could quit and get fat,
From just one at-bat
A hero now in laid-back La-La Land.

Mike Tyson singing "Jingle Bells":

Dashing through the snow, smack into a tree,
What a year I've had
I made history,
Knocked out Larry Holmes,
Michael Spinks was cake,
But every day my greedy wife
Gives me a bellyache, ohhh,
Jingle bells, my marriage smells,
Forty miles away,
All she wants, is all my cash,
Maybe I should punch her face

103

Jingle bells, my marriage smells,
Let's go tell the press,
Was it Barbara Walters
Who got me in this mess?

The City of Edmonton singing "Blue Christmas":

We'll have a Blue Christmas, without Wayne,
We'll be so blue, just thinking about Wayne,
Oiler nights, Oiler days,
Oiler hockey so fine,
Just ain't the same now,
Without old ninety-nine,
We'll have a blue Christmas, without Wayne,
Sure makes us wish, we'd bought tickets, when we had Wayne,
He'll be doin' OK, with his dudes in LA,
But we'll have a blue, blue, blue Christmas.

Jimmy Devellano: "God Rest Ye Merry, Gentlemen":

God rest you Stevie Yzerman,
For you are on a blaze,
Don't you need to save your strength
For April and for May?
Another goal, another goal,
New contract you'll demand,
This is gonna cost me seven hundred grand,
In one hand,
This is gonna cost me seven hundred grand.

Sugar Ray Leonard and Thomas Hearns singing "The Little Drummer Boy":

I have five titles now,
a bum-bum-bum-bum
Big deal, Ray, so do I,
a bum-bum-bum-bum
My five are better, see,
a bum-bum-bum-bum
You got 'em same as me with a
bum-bum-bum-bum, bum-bum-bum-bum, bum-bum-bum-bum
We both made history and here's how it comes
We're fighting bums.

Ben Johnson singing "Frosty the Snowman":

I'm Johnson the sprinter
I'm as fast as I can be

104

With my muscle bulge and my pigeon toes
I could outrun history,
I'm Johnson the sprinter
The winner of the race,
But they took away my Olympic day
And I flew home in disgrace
It must have been that bottle that I drank and then I dumped
Or could it be those needles that they stuck into my rump?
I'm Johnson the sprinter
Was it steroids? I won't tell
Just flex my pecs, say what the heck
Guess I'll join the NFL.

Jacques Demers singing "Deck the Halls":

Deck the halls with clothes in smolly
Falalalala, lalalala,
Tis the reason yes, lake, dolly, falalalala,
I'm still working, on my English
Don't know yet, all the word, la-la-la
Hockey, lockey, do the trolly
Falalalala, da doo run run.

Isiah Thomas, singing "Rockin' Around the Christmas Tree":

Dribblin' around the Christmas tree
Have a happy holiday,
Everyone's talking about our team
Thinking we'll go all the way,
Dribblin' around the Christmas tree
Gonna kiss Magic in June
Anyone steps on my ankle this time
... I'll kill em.

Wayne Fontes singing "Joy to the World":

Joy to the world, now I'm head coach
I'm happy as can beeeee
So what I got no quarterback?
So what I got no running back?
And receivers that are slow,
And linemen who don't show,
And no coaching staff or fan support and ... and ... hey wait a minute. ◆

EX-SPARTAN FEARLESSLY FIGHTS GEHRIG'S DISEASE

December 26

L OS GATOS, Calif. — His body is limp and covered with a blanket. His mouth moves, but there is no sound. His wife sits next to the bed, reading his lips.

"It began . . . when I was playing basketball . . . and I kept dropping the ball. . . . Then in the classroom . . . I would drop the . . . what was that, honey? Oh. . . . I would drop the chalk. . . . "

The words come slowly through her voice, just as the disease came slowly to Charlie Wedemeyer, robbing him of the marvelous athletic body he once possessed. A football star (1966-68) at Michigan State, a quarterback, a flanker, a guy voted best prep athlete of the decade in Hawaii, a lean, handsome man who resembled an island version of Joe Namath. Cheerleader wife. Two great kids. At age 31? This couldn't happen to him.

It happened.

Amyotrophic lateral sclerosis. Lou Gehrig's disease.

It is perhaps the cruelest way to die — slowly, moment by moment. No cure. And yet, somewhere in the months that followed, when he could no longer lift his arms to shave, and his students had to walk him, and soon his head needed constant support, lest it fall into his chest — somewhere in the middle of this horror, Charlie Wedemeyer decided to live.

And to live happily.

Which meant doing his job: coaching football at Los Gatos High School. At first he limped. Then he rode in a golf cart, which Lucy, his wife, drove. When speech deserted him, Lucy read his lips, passing on the plays to the offensive coordinator.

They lived. They got by.

"One time he called a play 'Max!' for maximum," Lucy says. "And I said, 'Max? Who's Max? We don't have a Max!' "

She laughs. In the bed, Charlie makes a clicking sound.

"Yeah . . . " he adds, through her voice. "I fired her after that. . . . "

H ow can we ever complain about anything? How can we moan about traffic or a lousy boss? Charlie Wedemeyer, 42, whom MSU legend Duffy Daugherty once called "my best blocker," can hear and think as well as you and I, yet he cannot move a muscle, cannot speak, cannot even

106

breathe without a ventilator. The doctors gave him one year to live. That was 11 years ago.

And in that time, his one life has touched another — and another, and another. Do you remember that Christmas movie, "It's a Wonderful Life," in which Jimmy Stewart gets to see the world had he never lived in it? What would this town be like, without this brave, now-withered man? Wedemeyer did not ask for notoriety. He kept his disease secret for several years before a newspaper story came out.

And yet all the kids he coached! All those he touched! How hard it must be for a proud man to be shaved, to be washed, to be lifted by others. Not once did he ask for sympathy. Not once from that golf cart, unable to turn his head to follow a pass or a touchdown run, did he ask his players to "win one for me."

They won anyhow. Won their division. Won their playoffs. And in 1985, on a cool December evening, Los Gatos went to the California Central Coast championships, with their coach in his golf cart on the sidelines. Smaller than their opponents, they hung in anyway, and in the final seconds, they blocked a field goal for a 14-12 upset victory. The stadium began to tremble. Then to roar. A chant of "CHAR-LIE! . . . CHAR-LIE! . . . CHAR-LIE! . . . "

It would be his last game, although no one knew it. The players mobbed his golf cart; they dropped to their knees. He whispered the words to his wife: "You guys . . . played like champions. . . . You will remember this . . . for the rest of your lives. . . . "

Not surprisingly, Hollywood has made a TV movie about the Wedemeyers, a project that has brought mixed feelings. For while the message comes across, a film can never capture the subtle courage: how friends donated money for the $60,000-a-year medical costs; how Charlie's son, Kale, would help clean the tubes in his throat; how Lucy, an attractive blonde woman who might have selfishly thought she deserved better, would sleep alongside Charlie's bed, her hand on his foot, so if he wiggled it, she could wake and attend to him.

One life touches another and another. And eventually, fate went from something that led them, to something that followed.

This is truly what is meant by "human potential."

Eventually, the disease worsened. Charlie lost his job. His assistant coaches had grown weary of the burden. Eight years? The problem was — to put it bluntly — he had lasted longer than anyone figured.

So in 1986, the principal delivered the bad news. Told him to retire, said it was for the best. True to form, an angry Charlie mouthed his response from the wheelchair.

"He says," Lucy told his boss, "you're . . . a . . . bleep."

And they pressed on. Today his son plays college football, his daughter is in school, and Charlie and Lucy cope as best they can in their warm, ranch-style home. There is no morbid talk. No over-sentimentality. When he needs to be lifted, he is lifted. When he needs to be washed, Lucy holds him up in the shower. They talk. They laugh.

They live.

"I used to be . . . so afraid of death," he says. "I would stay awake . . . for three or four nights . . . because I was afraid to . . . choke in my sleep. . . . But now I know . . . I have a purpose . . . to inspire people to . . . see their difficulties as a challenge . . . rather than a barrier. . . . "

He lifts an eyebrow at his nurse. She pulls back the blanket, disconnects the tubing, attaches an air bag to his throat, and, with the help of Lucy and a friend, lifts his limp flesh into a wheelchair.

"Where are you going?" he is asked.

He smiles.

"Christmas . . . shopping," he says.

About a year ago, the Wedemeyers received a letter. It came from a man in Canada who had lost his business, fought with his wife, and, in a fit of desperation, flown to Seattle and checked into a hotel. He planned to kill himself. In the room of his intended death, he absentmindedly flipped on the television. And there, in low-volume color, he saw a documentary on Charlie. Saw him lifted from his bed, limp as a rag, somehow still smiling.

The man went back home. He is alive today.

One life touches another — and another and another.

This column is being written on Christmas Day, and I keep stalling because I can't find a happy ending. Barring a miracle, Charlie Wedemeyer will die, far too soon, and where is the sense, where is the justice?

I have no answer. Except that maybe the ending isn't always what counts in a story. Maybe, sometimes, it's just the courage you show along the way. ◆

MICHIGAN CAN WAKE UP AND SMELL THE ROSES

January 3

P ASADENA, Calif. — He was running for all of them, for this Michigan team, and for every Michigan team that has ever come out here and had its face smeared with California egg. Someone grabbed his feet. He broke free. Someone wrapped around his thigh. He yanked loose. He ran through the linemen and through the linebackers and through the hands and arms and bodies, breaking free as the ghosts of Wolverines past screamed in a collective voice: "GO! GO! NEVER STOP!"

Leroy Hoard was charging downfield, and he was taking Michigan with him. A 61-yard run that would ensure a Michigan victory in this traditionally haunted stadium. And when he sprinted over the goal line on a gutsy fourth-and-goal call for the winning touchdown, and the Michigan fans showered the field with plastic seat cushions — "SIT ON IT, USC!" — well, you could hear the sigh of relief all the way out here.

"I can hardly even remember, it happened so fast!" gushed Hoard after Michigan beat Southern California, 22-14, in the 75th Rose Bowl. "They say when worst comes to worst take the ball and run — and that's what I did!"

Wake up and smell the roses, U-M. This was not only a great Michigan victory, a great comeback and a tribute to the spirit of a team that had to come back from the very first game of the season — but it was also long overdue. Bo Schembechler has brought too many good teams out here too many times and gone home empty.

Not this time. Here, against the No. 5 team in the country, which featured Mr. Charisma, Rodney Peete, at quarterback, the Wolverines did it the way they have all season, as a team — a suddenly choking defense, a suddenly gambling offense.

And when the gun sounded, they banded together for one final team effort: carrying Schembechler off on their shoulders.

Happy New Year, Bo.

Smell the roses.

O N BEHALF OF SOME GREAT WOLVERINES, I ACCEPT THIS TROPHY!" yelled Schembechler when they handed him the victor's trophy. And why not? In his 20 years as U-M coach, he had suffered through seven Rose Bowl defeats and gained only one victory before this one.

Finally, in the dying sunlight of Pasadena, a Schembechler dream came true.

And it was just the way he likes it. Who says this wasn't better than the "national championship" Fiesta Bowl across the TV dial? Here was a game that ran the gamut of emotion.

Pick it up at halftime, the score Trojans 14, Wolverines 3. The Michigan offense had fallen asleep. Receivers were dropping passes. The Wolverines failed to gain a first down in the second quarter. They were getting beaten up and beaten down, and Peete had scrambled through their defense twice for touchdowns. The jokes were hatching again. Good ol' Michigan. Nice team. Just can't beat the Pac-10.

And then, the second half.

"Bo told us to forget the score at halftime, just forget it," said defensive tackle Mark Messner. "He said if we stopped beating ourselves, then we could beat this team."

And he was right. In that second half, it seemed as if the voices from Wolverines past joined in a singular chorus that screamed, "No more! Enough of this embarrassment!" And suddenly the 1988 Wolverines began to rise, from the mountain of dirt on their Rose Bowl reputation, from their traditional size deficiency against Pac-10 teams, from the unforgivable errors they had committed earlier in the game — a fumble, overthrown passes, a missed 34-yard field goal.

And they rolled. A touchdown drive to close it to 14-9. A suffocating defense. Another drive featuring Hoard's running and a clutch pass from Demetrius Brown to tight end Derrick Walker. Another touchdown. More defense. And that final drive, the undying legs of Hoard carrying them to Pasadena heaven.

"HAIL TO THE VICTORS VALIANT . . ." the outnumbered U-M fans sang in the stands. For here was a comeback performance led by comeback kids. Remember Brown, the shy quarterback who was demoted in preseason because of iffy grades and a lackadaisical attitude? All he did was rifle a touchdown pass, direct the offense, scramble when necessary and, yes, not throw a single interception, thank you.

"I want to clear something up," he said afterward, looking around the locker room. "Earlier in the week I was quoted as saying my best friend on the team was myself. I shouldn't have said that. These guys are all my friends, my family, sort of. I want to give them credit."

Talk about a turnaround.

And how about Hoard? He had been suspended at midseason because he cut two classes. Schembechler doesn't bend the rules. Not for walk-ons. Not for stars.

"Sometimes it gets a little frustrating when (the coaches) get on you and get on you," Hoard said, sitting behind the Rose Bowl MVP trophy he had justifiably won with 19 carries, 142 yards and two touchdowns. "But then, at moments like this, you realize why they were doing it."

If that isn't what college football is all about, what is?

A nd what of Schembechler, the coach who refuses to bend, keeps his team under the same strict principles as always — and had to lug around that lousy bowl record year after year?

How long had he been at this? Long enough that one of his assistants in his first Rose Bowl (1970) was now coaching against him across the sidelines. Larry Smith, USC's head man, once baby-sat for Schembechler's kids. Now he was trying to do unto him what the other Pac-10 coaches had done seven of eight times.

Sorry, Larry.

"There is a world of difference between winning and losing," admitted Schembechler. "Losing tears the heart out of you."

He grinned. "And I don't have a real good heart to begin with."

His cardiologist might agree; his team might object. They end the 1988 season with only two defeats — to the No. 1 and No. 2 teams in the country, Notre Dame and Miami (Fla.), by a combined three points. And they played this last game as much for their coach as for themselves. With 50 seconds left, when John Milligan stepped in front of a Peete pass in USC's final desperation drive, intercepted it, fell on the ground and was smothered by wildly cheering teammates, well, they had delivered.

"A dream come true," said Messner.

"A dream come true," said Hoard.

What else can you say at a moment like that?

An hour after the victory, with the stadium empty and the sky dark and cold, Schembechler sat in the yellow coaches' room, reclining in a chair, his fingers wrapped around an empty Diet Pepsi can.

"That how you celebrate?" he was asked.

"Nope." He smiled. "Look here. I wanna show you something."

He got up, reached for his sports coat and pulled out a long, plastic-wrapped cigar.

"See this?" he said. "I quit smoking how long ago? But I promised myself I'm gonna smoke one of these after every Rose Bowl we win."

He broke into a howling laugh.

"And that probably ain't gonna be too many!"

Light 'em if you got 'em. Michigan wins — in January. On the feet of a once-suspended fullback, the arm of a once-demoted quarterback, the hits of a once-defeated defense and the resiliency of a team that believes in its coach, and therefore, believes in itself. Happy New Year, Michigan. Wake up and smell the roses.

Or in Bo's case, the smoke. ◆

HARSH REALITY CRASHES FOOTBALL'S BIGGEST PARTY

January 22

MIAMI — You expect, now and then, to run smack into your conscience. You just don't expect it to happen at the Super Bowl. A game. A gunshot. And today we must ask ourselves what America is all about.

This was a week of confrontation. Funny, because this is usually a week for escape, the biggest of parties, stories about football players dancing and talking crazy and living it up while awaiting the Big Game. It was to be a salsa celebration in this sun-baked city, a chance to put on the glitz for the NFL and millions of its closest friends.

And instead, tragedy. People died, just a few miles from the headquarters hotel, unnatural deaths, deaths by bullet. In sections called Overtown and Liberty City, people were beaten, robbed, stoned, cars were burned and stores looted, there were police cars at every highway exit, nobody in, nobody out, it was a riot, a racial explosion, but it took place during Super Bowl week, a party that, for some reason, must go on.

So it was that in the morning we boarded the buses for the team news conferences, prune danishes and coffee in silver pitchers, and cliched quotes about "respecting the opponent" — and by afternoon the blood was flowing in the streets. So it was that concerts and parties were held in splendor — while police raced through Overtown in full riot gear, helmets and tear gas and rifles.

What do you cover in an event such as this? Assigned to write about sports, do you close your eyes to reality? There were thousands of reporters in Miami for the game between the San Francisco 49ers and the Cincinnati Bengals, and from the moment the horror began — the moment a black man named Clement Lloyd was shot to death by a Hispanic police officer named William Lozano — the buzz was always: "Are you going out there? In the thick of it? Or are you sticking with football?"

What a question. Didn't it seem that somehow the game should have been put on hold until this was taken care of — until the cries of the poor blacks in the poverty-ridden sections were heard? Of course it did. And yet, the truth is, other Super Bowls have been held while poverty and frustration boiled in nearby streets. What made this unique was that suddenly the problem splashed out of the water and bit the nation's biggest sports celebration right in the behind.

"Lemme ask you somethin'," a black youth said to me as we stood along Northeast 20th Street, a few hundred yards from the burnt skeleton of an auto parts store. "Don't you think that game means nothing now? A man's been killed here. What's that game gonna mean to us here?"

I could give no answer. We laugh at the image of Nero fiddling while Rome burned. And yet nearly 3,000 of us attended an NFL party that featured unlimited shrimp, lobster, steak tartare, salsa bands, rock 'n' roll groups — while on the highways, the police cars still flashed their blue lights, cutting off the exits to the danger zone. Fiddling while she burns? How far off are we really?

I don't know how all the other reporters reacted to this. I know it bothered many. It bothered me. I had stayed safely inside the hotel the night of the initial violence, when Lloyd's body lay in the street, and the gathering black crowd began to tremble, then shake, then explode. Instead of running out and reporting — as I would were it a star receiver's injury, or a quarterback's mooning a helicopter — I watched the news on a TV in the Hyatt Regency lobby. The violent pictures mixed with cocktail music from the lounge. I felt somehow weak and ashamed.

The next morning, the buses rolled out to Joe Robbie Stadium for a giant news conference with the Super Bowl teams. Players laughed. Reporters swarmed them. Ickey Woods, the Cincinnati fullback, did his Ickey Shuffle dance for the cameras. Besides a few brief "sorry it happened" and "what can we do?" you would never know anything was wrong.

And just hours later, in Overtown, a group of black youths was throwing stones at passing cars. Finally, one car that was pelted slowed down, stopped, and out stepped a white man wielding a gun. He fired wildly into the crowd, four shots, five shots, six shots, seven shots, he hit a teenager in the leg, then got back in his car and hit the gas. It was 2 p.m. The sun was bright and tropical. Blood in the afternoon. He drove away.

I was on those streets by then. I had dragged myself there, scared, unsure, but feeling somehow that I needed to see this. And I had wandered clumsily into the shooting.

"Didn't anybody catch the guy?" I asked, incredulous.

"Nope," said a young black woman named Selma.

"He just drove out of Overtown?"

"Who was gonna stop him?" she said.

H ere are the scenes that linger from the week of fun and gun: Joe Montana, the 49ers' quarterback, jogging through the hotel lobby, with people turning their heads as he passed; Woods and his Bengals teammates, waving and doing the Shuffle at midcourt of a Miami Heat game; 49ers owner Eddie DeBartolo Jr., greeting his team dressed as a bellhop; Bengals linebacker Reggie Williams, who also serves as a Cincinnati city councilman, holding reporters spellbound with his daily thoughts.

And these images as well: Miami Mayor Xavier Suarez walking down a dark Overtown street, his hands up, pleading with the seething crowd to stop the violence; half a dozen jeering youths, running madly from a vandalized meat truck, their arms filled with stolen food; the hospital spokesperson who announced that Allan Blanchard, who had been riding the motorcycle with Lloyd when the policeman shot him, and who had flown off and smashed into a windshield, had died of his wounds; a black man in dreadlocks pleading to a TV camera: "Don't you understand? In a city like Miami, there should be no Overtown. That is the problem."

How do you balance these images? Which tell the real story of this week? Both. Here was pomp and unfortunate circumstance. A multimillion-dollar celebration in the shadow of a black community that has suffered police harassment and has watched other ethnic groups leapfrog them on Miami's socioeconomic ladder.

"You know, I want you to come back here in three days, when all this dies down," a man named Colanel told me. He wore a cap and an open shirt and had lived in Overtown all his life. "If you come back then, you'll see how it is here normally, and why this kind of stuff happens over and over."

And perhaps he was right. "It was the worst thing that could have happened," the writers wrote, and yet, in a way, it was sadly perfect. Had this happened the next week, how much would America have noticed? Where else can the plight of the poor draw such good light as in the shadow of a party?

And now today they play the football game. The violence has subsided. The asphalt has cooled. The halftime show will go on as planned, Billy Joel will sing the national anthem, two teams will battle it out, and in the end, when one of them wins, a player will gaze into a humming camera, and declare, "I'm going to Disney World!"

And if that doesn't spin your head with hypocrisy, I don't know what will.

This was a week for conscience, for realizing that life is more than a football game and a good crowd to have a beer with. This was a week for tears, the death of defenseless people, of schoolchildren in Stockton, Calif., of motorcycle riders in Overtown. This was a week for hope, a new president installed, promising visions of a "kinder and gentler America." This was a week for reflections, our own reflections. America had to look in the mirror and see herself in all her triumph and failure.

And we play the game today. But somewhere in the decaying streets sits the man in the cap, knowing full well that we're not coming back. Who listens to the helpless when the party is over? That, more than anything else, is the haunting question of the week. ◆

PISTONS BID FAREWELL TO A.D., THE TEACHER

February 16

F arewell to the Teacher. Farewell to that body, hard and strong, and that face, which always seemed halfway between amusement and anger. Adrian Dantley came in with a bad reputation, and, ironically, he leaves in exchange for one. Known as selfish, moody and a ball hog when he arrived in Detroit, he proved critics wrong, leading the Pistons to the NBA Finals, playing a role, muscling against giants, spinning and whirling and *desiring* his way to the hoop. He even sent himself to the hospital once diving for a basketball.

Diving? Adrian Dantley? And now, suddenly, he has been traded to Dallas for a guy named Mark Aguirre, who has a reputation for being . . . selfish, moody and a ball hog.

Go figure.

There will be those who say this is a smart trade in the long run but foolish in the short. There will be those who say it will never work. There will be those who say the Pistons just secured an NBA championship.

And nobody — to borrow some baseball vernacular — knows nuthin'. What really went on behind the scenes during Dantley's 2½ years was rarely printed. It was mumbled. It was whispered. Like an uneasy marriage, Dantley Does Detroit was encouraging in the good times and stormy in the bad, so no one would give it the kiss of death until the very end.

Why would the Pistons make this trade? Why would they cut loose last year's playoff star, their mentor to developing players, a guy who had proved his talents? Why? Here's why. Because Dantley's years were advancing and his skills were not. Because his attitude was quiet at best, aloof at worst. Because Aguirre, nearly four years younger, was available. And because the Pistons seem convinced that other people's problems — William Bedford, Darryl Dawkins, even Dantley himself — can be rehabilitated in the waters of Camp Isiah.

And yes, let us not forget Isiah Thomas in this picture. If this trade proves anything, it is that the Pistons are Isiah's team — a sentence Dantley himself used to utter with regularity. That does not mean Thomas orchestrated this trade (despite what Dantley thinks). It does mean that Isiah stays and everybody else learns to work around him. Dantley was never much of a dance partner; Aguirre, abhorred by many of his Dallas

117

teammates, was quoted after first learning of the deal, "Great. It'll be great to join Isiah."

Interesting choice of words. There are 11 other guys here, remember?

B ut let us leave the analysis of the new guy for days to come. There will be time. Aguirre is certainly capable of brilliant basketball — when he wants to play. James Donaldson, his Mavericks teammate, said, "I'll look forward to having a new guy here who is willing to play hard every night."

Hard? You never had to worry about hard with Dantley. Hard was the only game he knew to play. At his height (6-feet-5) and his position (small forward), what choice did he have? Guts. Confidence. He had them. And when push comes to shove, that is what other players look for.

"Bleep!" said John Salley, when informed of the news. "How could they trade the Teacher? He was my mentor. A lot of the guys felt that way. I like Mark. He's OK. But A.D. did a lot for us."

Never more than in last year's playoffs. He seemed invaluable then, everyone was singing his praises — including coach Chuck Daly and general manager Jack McCloskey, the very men who traded him. How could that be? Well. Nothing binds a team like the whiff of a championship. It's like Christmas morning. Who fights then? The fact is, the Pistons — like most NBA teams — are a bickering bunch, with several distinct and opposing personalities. In the tedium of the regular season, that stuff will rise like bile.

So this year, the Pistons hit some rough spots, they fell behind Cleveland — and personalities clashed. Dantley's game sagged. Coaches blamed his age; Dantley blamed the coaches. Trade rumors started, guys took sides, and you might as well pour hemlock in the water bucket when that happens.

Here is the way Dantley saw it: "It's Isiah's team. He calls the shots. That guy (Aguirre) is his friend and he wants to play with his friend. If Chuck has to make a call, who do you think he's gonna side with?

"I didn't have any problem with Isiah. But Chuck wasn't playing me for a while. He sat me down one game for the whole second quarter, then I sit through halftime, and then he puts me in the third quarter and when I can't get going, he starts yelling at me. I said, 'How do you expect me to just heat up after I've been sitting so long?' "

Because of such differences, Dantley said he went through a period with Daly in which they barely spoke. He felt as if the coach was trying to get him to change his personality. "Shoot, I've been quiet my whole life," Dantley said. "That's just the way I am."

Dantley's trust in Daly was already thin, because he saw Isiah and Daly as a tandem; what the former wanted, the latter delivered. And because Dantley never completely believed Isiah was willing to share this team, well, you get the picture. . . .

That, of course, is one man's opinion.

118

Here is the way management saw it: Dantley's best years were behind him. His moves were being anticipated by opposing teams and referees alike. He was getting double-teamed every night, and, besides, Dennis Rodman had matured into such a force that sitting him on the bench had become a mortal sin.

And then there were the personality conflicts. Daly will say of Dantley, "We got along fine," but they didn't. Daly found A.D. selfish and greedy and infatuated with money. Dantley was almost laughable in his private criticism of Bill Laimbeer, whom he does not respect at all. So when Aguirre's name came up, and his personality was questioned, no doubt management said: "Hey, how much worse can it be than what we've got now? The guy's younger. His talent is there. He already likes Isiah. Why not?"

The trade was made.

Farewell to the Teacher.

A shame. Not the trade itself, which could work out fine, who knows? But that the whole thing has to be shrouded in bad feelings. Dantley, visibly upset, his last chance at that precious championship ring probably gone, told reporters: "This has nothing to do with basketball."

"Does it have to do with personalities?" he was asked.

"No comment," he said.

Was it a smart trade? Maybe not. Was it risky? Of course. Was it inevitable? More than likely. And now comes the tough part. Making Aguirre fit. You're asking a lot of a coach to blend a new soloist into a jazz quintet — right in the middle of the show. The Pistons have taken a great risk with that fragile package called chemistry.

We will see. For now, a memory pause, because the average fan does not know — or care — about locker room feuds. For 2½ seasons, Detroit saw a marvelous effort from a marvelous talent. There was a time when Adrian Dantley rolled his shoulders and mumbled, "I want that ring." Then he went out and gave us the playoffs of his life. There was a time when he took an elbow in the jaw (from Mark Aguirre, of all people) and had to have his mouth stitched back together. There was a time when they stopped the game to give him the basketball for scoring his 20,000th point in the league. And there was a time when he celebrated a valiant effort in the NBA Finals with his best friend, Joe Dumars; they treated their health-crazed bodies to deep-dish apple cobbler. "With ice cream," he liked to tell you.

He spun, he twisted, he taught and now he's gone. Very few people really knew Adrian Dantley. Very few will. Basketball, he always said, was played "for the money, anyway. Always has been. Always will be. They can send you anywhere they want."

Farewell to the Teacher.

They just did. ♦

119

BOB PROBERT ARRESTED, YET NO ONE LOOKS CLEAN

March 3

H e finally hit bottom in the cold dawn, when a U.S. customs agent made him drop his pants and watched a packet of cocaine fall out of his underwear. Standing there, in a windowless room at the American border, alone, about to be charged with drug smuggling, Bob Probert was no longer a hockey player. He was no longer a Detroit Red Wing. He was no longer some tragic hero to the faithful at Joe Louis Arena, who all along have continued to chant, "Hey, leave Probert alone!"

He was a criminal suspect.

Arrested. Cuffed. And led away.

What did we expect? A happy ending? Bob Probert has been in trouble since he was a teenager. He would get stupidly drunk, he would wrap a car around a telephone pole, he would party the night before a playoff game. He was addicted to alcohol and apparently had developed at least a taste for cocaine, maybe more. He would follow the devils at night and lie to the angels in the morning.

"Probie, have you been drinking?" the Wings' brass would ask him, looking at his eyes. "Probie, have you been using drugs?"

"No way. Nuh-uh. No."

What is that expression? You can run but you cannot hide. There is no hiding what the Wings knew for some time now — that Probert was more than just a big kid who enjoyed his beer. That there were numerous reports of his drug involvement. That the only reason he was back on the ice was to dust him off so maybe some other team would trade for him, any team, take him, please. No more hiding. When 14 grams of cocaine are found in your shorts, you have a hard time pleading ignorance.

"I knew about the alcohol, and I heard rumors about this other stuff," admitted an anguished Jacques Demers, the Wings' coach. "But rumors are rumors. We never saw him do anything. We never caught him. Nobody ever brought Bob Probert in to me with his arm twisted behind his back and said, 'Hey, we just found this guy with a couple grams of cocaine.'"

Until now.

And now it's too late. Probert was marched before a magistrate, dressed in the same gray suit he had peeled off in front of the customs agents at the Canada-U.S. border. He was charged with a crime that is punishable by up

120

to 20 years in prison. He posted bond, and left.

"He has given this team some black eyes in the past," said Demers, shaking his head, "but this time, he split the eye right open."

In recent weeks, the Wings tried desperately to trade Probert. That, Demers said, was the only reason they brought him back. "We weren't asking for the moon, either," he said. "We would have taken very little. We tried. We honestly tried."

Yes. Everybody tried. No one succeeded. And no one is completely innocent in this story. The Wings probably should have traded Probert after the Edmonton drinking incident last April, when his market value was high but his credibility was shot. They kept him because they wanted a Stanley Cup, fast and glorious, they were so close! And a healthy Probert could help them get it. In his one good season, he was a hockey rarity: a scorer and a fighter. Blinded by his good light, the Wings held on, overlooking, excusing, until slowly, in their too-forgiving grasp, Probert turned to dust.

Maybe if they had traded him he would have straightened up. Maybe he would have realized he gets only so many chances. Maybe not. Somewhere in the process, the whole thing soured, Probert lost sight of hockey and career. By the time he came to the Wings last November, demanding that he at least get his paycheck even if he didn't play, they should have known. An athlete with rumored drug problems who is satisfied to get paid and not work? What do you think he wants the money for? Canned goods?

Probert's locker was already empty by the time reporters stormed the dressing room. His teammates seemed both remorseful and, in a weird way, relieved. Probert's shadow has hung over this team like a bad childhood. Wherever they went, the players were asked about him — his drinking, his arrests, his walking out of rehab centers — him, and not hockey. Now, with the shadow in handcuffs, no one knew what to say. Some made jokes. Some made judgments. Some just shrugged.

"What would you tell Probert right now?" someone asked Steve Yzerman, the captain, who, like his fallen teammate, is 23.

"I wouldn't know what to say," he answered. "I haven't known what to say to him for a long time. . . . "

That, in the end, was pretty much the problem. The Wings could not talk to Probert, they could not reason with him, they could not reach him. Pro sports are usually a tight fraternity, players protect players. But it is not coincidental that Probert was arrested in the company of two women and one man who had nothing to do with hockey. What Red Wing would run with Probert anymore? Whom could he trust with his secrets?

"We did everything we could for Bob," said Jimmy Devellano, the general manager, "rehab centers, counseling, doctors, dealing with the family. If we are guilty of anything, it may be too many efforts to prop him up, prop him up. He has a sickness, but he never reached rock bottom where he said, 'I need help.' "

Is he saying it today?

Who is to blame for Bob Probert? First and foremost, Bob Probert. No one pushed that cocaine in his underwear, and no one forced him out until 5 in the morning after a game. Like most too-forgiven athletes, he thought he could beat the system. He had squirmed his way out of discipline, trade talk, media. Why not a border crossing?

Still, the Wings must share some guilt. They treated the situation like a yo-yo, they never played the trump card — a trade — mostly for fear of somehow being less successful and losing fans. Instead they lost team unity, team direction and, in the end, lost Probert as well. The Wings now face the same future as they would had Probert been traded for a box of sticks.

And what about the fans? When Probert's beer drinking problems first surfaced, there was a wave of sympathy that washed over the criticism. Leave Probert alone. Stop picking on him. "I think the fans are behind me," Probert had said more than once upon his return. Did that somehow encourage him toward more trouble?

"Personally, I feel sadness," said Mike O'Connell, the defenseman who sat next to Probert in the locker room and found himself suddenly sitting next to nothing. "Think back to when you were 23. Now think of how old you are today. And imagine if all those years were lost, thrown away on cocaine. It's the big lie, isn't it? Just like they say. It's sad."

It is sad. There were no doubt days when Probert meant to turn his life around. And nights when he forgot all about it. He is sadly guilty, yes, a nice guy, yes, but it is hard to see him as a helpless victim. He has a disease, alcoholism, but he has been handed countless chances to treat it. How many alcoholics out there are offered a steady paycheck, airfare to California, treatment at the Betty Ford Center and a job whenever they return? And since when done does alcoholism excuse cocaine? At some point, you figure, a man is responsible for himself. That doesn't mean you can't feel sorry for Bob Probert. It does mean that sneaking drugs across a border is a crime, any way you slice it.

"I guess this ends our Bob Probert problem," Yzerman said, shrugging, "in the wrong way."

Sadly, and neatly, put.

There is no satisfaction in all this. And there is no outrage. How can there be? This week's stories have included a baseball hero being sued by his mistress, an Olympic gold medalist who built his body from a chemistry set. Outrage? What did we expect? We live in a nation where the rich and foolish seem destined to get caught, sooner or later, with their pants down. And there are few happy endings anymore. ♦

TIGERS, FOR FUN'S SAKE, PLEASE SAVE THE WALES

March 13

LAKELAND, Fla. — "The weirdest thing," says Jim Walewander, ripping open a miniature box of Cheerios, "was when one of these guys asked me for an autograph. What should I write? 'Good luck in taking my job.'?"

We are sitting in the dimly lit cafeteria of the Tigers' minor league complex, surrounded by lanky, young baseball players. We are eating breakfast. Actually, Walewander is eating. I am watching.

"Milk," he says, pouring some onto his cereal. "You got to conserve this stuff down here. You're only allowed one glass per breakfast."

"What happens if you ask for more?"

He shrugs. "I don't know. No one ever tried."

Yesterday — or at least, it seems like yesterday — Jim Walewander was in the major leagues, the only Tiger ever to introduce Sparky Anderson to a punk rock group. You remember? The Dead Milkmen?

SPARKY: Hello, boys.

DEAD MILKMEN: Satan rules!

SPARKY: Well, gotta go, boys.

And today Walewander, 27, is back here, in the minors, sleeping in a dormitory, eating in a cafeteria. He seems unfazed. He looks the same, little boy face, hair sticking out in all directions. Of course, he is the only guy in the room wearing a denim jacket and a button that blinks, "Kennedy: A Man For The 60s."

Wait. News flash. During the off-season, Walewander attended a Dead Milkmen concert in Chicago. They spotted him. Brought him on stage. Wanted him to sing.

"Which song?" he yelled over the crowd.

"It's a new one," they said. "Sing it."

"What? But how does it g–"

DA-DA-DA-DA-DADADA-DA-DA-DA.

I don't know the Tigers' plans for Walewander this year. Personally, I think he should be back with the club, because baseball needs guys like him to keep it from falling asleep. Here is a free spirit who kept his first major league home run ball — in his glove compartment. A guy who surfs, wears Army boots and once sent Christmas cards to the media with a picture of a cow: "MOOOO-RY CHRISTMAS."

This is how Walewander met his girlfriend last summer. He went to St. Andrews Hall, Detroit's downtown punk joint. She asked where he worked.

"Tiger Stadium," he said.

Oh. Was he a hot dog vendor?

"I showed her my baseball card," he said. "She still didn't believe me. She thought it was one of those things you get made at Disneyland."

OK. True. As a player, Walewander is a specialty guy. Small. Fast. Utility infielder. But he impressed Anderson enough in September 1987 to earn an invitation to camp last spring. For the first time, he had a locker in the big clubhouse, stayed at a hotel, per diem money, no curfews. But this year, he's back across the parking lot, in the minors — where he had spent the four previous springs — 100 yards and a lifetime away from the Show.

"Shoes," he says. "That's a big difference. Up there, you get as many as you want. Down here, they take all the shoes the big-league guys don't want and put them in a bin on the first day. You grab what fits. I saw a guy with Lou Whitaker's shoes yesterday."

"Do they go after certain names?" I ask.

"No," he says, "certain sizes."

H e finishes breakfast. We walk to his room. The hallways are sparse. The decor is early 1950s. The windows, he says, are screwed shut, to keep players from sneaking in past curfew. The room itself is tiny — a lamp, two beds (he has a roommate) and nothing on the walls. Nothing is allowed. Tigers' rules. Jim Walewander seems to belong here the way Frank Zappa belongs on "The Patty Duke Show."

"Clean or dirty?" I say, pointing to the pile of clothes against the wall.

"I just sort of recycle," he says.

A sudden voice blares over the loudspeaker, warning players that the maids are coming through. I rub my ears.

"That's nothing," he says. "When I first got here, that's how you found out you were cut. Around 8 a.m., that voice would come on and say, 'WILL THE FOLLOWING PLAYERS PLEASE REPORT TO THE CENTRAL OFFICE. . . .' "

How quickly you can come and go. Just yesterday, he was a spark plug in the big leagues. Today, he is warming up Double-A pitchers. The thing that makes Jim Walewander really rare is that, for all his punkishness, he loves baseball. And I find myself wishing the Tigers would call him up. I really do.

"It's a bit of a drag not being with the big club again," he says. He looks at the stadium across the parking lot and shrugs.

"I just hope I haven't used up my Andy Warhol 15 minutes yet."

You know what I think? I think Andy would have given him a half-hour. That's what I think. ◆

HEY, COACH FRIEDER!
WHAT ABOUT THE KIDS?

March 16

T he Michigan basketball players walked slowly to the airport gate, some talking, some joking, some, such as Rumeal Robinson, wearing headphones to tune out the world. If you expected anger, grief — well, there was none. They had lost their coach to a better offer, they had been stiffed two days before the NCAA tournament, but if they had learned anything from Bill Frieder, Papa Hoops, who kissed them good-bye on the late night news, it was take care of yourself first, baby.

So they were going to Atlanta to play. And they would not let the hurt show. Not here. Not in an airport. A half-dozen TV cameras rose like condors and flicked on their lights, ready to film the new orphans.

No tears. Sorry.

"Yeah, it was complete surprise," said Loy Vaught, the junior center, shrugging, "but I guess I understand. He called me late last night and said he had no choice; he had to take this job or lose his chance."

"It was a career move," said Terry Mills, the junior forward, digging his hands into his very high pockets. "If you're only making $96,000," which is Frieder's base salary at U-M, "and you're a great recruiter, why not take $300,000 and be a great recruiter someplace else?"

Betrayed? Yes and no, they said. Angered? Yes and no, they said. Just business. Isn't that how you're supposed to answer these questions? In the last 24 hours, they had (1) learned their coach was on a flight to Arizona when he was supposed to be watching film with them; (2) been called by their coach after midnight to be told he had taken another job; (3) been visited by Bo Schembechler, the football coach/athletic director, who said the interim coach would be Steve Fisher, the former assistant; (4) been told by Fisher that things should stay the same.

And now they were flying away to play basketball. Look out for yourself, baby. The theme was repeated all day long. But in the whirlwind of Bill Frieder's shocking split from Michigan, the one question not asked enough was the one question usually overlooked in messy divorces:

What about the kids?

B ill Frieder had coached Michigan for nine years. He accepted his new position after 20 minutes of deliberation. Charles Harris, the athletic director at Arizona State, "offered me the job. He said, 'I want to go to my people and tell them I've got a basketball coach. Do you want this job or do you want me to give it to someone else?' I said, 'I need some time to think about it.' He said, 'You've got 20 minutes.' So I made a decision."

What kind of school gives its future coach 20 minutes? How much could Arizona State really have wanted Frieder if the school was willing to drop him should he have asked to coach U-M through the NCAA tournament — which is the right thing to do, isn't it? Aren't you supposed to admire a man like that? Aren't you supposed to respect a guy who says, "I can't desert my boys. If you want me, please wait a few weeks"?

Instead, this is what Harris said: "The most important thing is to get a coach so we can start recruiting."

What about the people Frieder recruited last year and the year before and the year before that? Stuff them, Harris figured. He had a job to do. Find a coach. Get him in before the start of the tournament. Why? Because he had set that up as a deadline and he was tired of waiting.

Look out for yourself, baby.

But what about the kids?

Here is how they found out. Rumors began swirling in late afternoon. Vaught told some teammates, "If Coach isn't there at the meeting tonight, I think he's gone." The players gathered for a meeting shortly before 9 p.m. But instead of concentrating on their film, they were eyeballing the door. Ten minutes. Twenty minutes. No Frieder. A collective whistle of doom blew through the room. Two hours later, they watched the news and heard their coach's name. The man who had written them countless letters in high school, phoned them, wooed them, promised them great things if they came to Michigan — and here he was, being announced as the new coach of the Sun Devils, 2,000 miles and a world of trust away.

Hours later, in the dead of night, phones would ring, one at a time, stirring the players from sleep. It was Frieder, calling from out west. Hi, guys. Let me explain what happened here. They made me a great offer and I had to accept it immediately. Sorry. I don't want this to affect you in the tournament. . . .

Great way to teach "responsibility."

Look out for yourself.

A nd that, sadly, is what will be taken from all this. Michigan began to look out for itself as well. After waiting until the morning to call Schembechler — he claimed he didn't have Bo's home phone number, which should tell you something about their relationship — Frieder offered to continue coaching the team through the tournament. Bo refused.

"A Michigan man will coach Michigan," Bo declared.

He then made plans to fly to Atlanta himself, to boost the team and to search for head-coaching candidates. Already he has visited with Robinson,

Mills, Glen Rice and the rest. He urged them to concentrate only on the future. He called upon tradition, Wolverines pride; he marched back and forth like the football coach he is and inspired them with personal promises that he, Bo, would take care of things. Bill Frieder, it was implied, would not be missed.

"We understand Frieder will be in Atlanta," a reporter asked Bo. "If you see him down there, what will you say to him?"

Schembechler thought for a moment, then raised a hand in a friendly wave.

"Hi, Bill," he said.

Bye, Bill.

And that brings us back to the players, standing at that airport gate, their old head coach gone, their new head coach, for the time being, handing out tickets. "I got some aisle seats, and a few windows," said Fisher.

"Coach Frieder used to get us in first class," joked a player.

"Yeah," said another, "what about that?"

They were kidding. Blowing off steam. The cameras were whirring all around them, the whole scene was unnatural. Robinson said nothing. Rice said nothing. Others chatted with reporters and signed autographs.

What about the kids? Above all else, that is Bill Frieder's shame. And Arizona State's. College sports are supposed to be a little less devious than professional, aren't they? You're supposed to teach as well as coach. But what are we teaching by stealing away in the middle of the night? Oddly enough, Vaught, Mills, Mark Hughes and Mike Griffin all said they wouldn't have minded if Frieder coached them in this tournament. "It's a business thing," Griffin said.

That might be the saddest tribute of all. Gone, apparently, are the days when school spirit and team pride were the glue for a college basketball team. Gone are the days when a coach would say, "My players first, my personal fortunes next." Maybe it was foolish ever to think that. Maybe Frieder was doing the best thing for his career. You look out for yourself, you take what you can get, and remember to close the door behind you. Or don't. Doesn't matter. Everybody's doing it.

As the Michigan players boarded the plane for Atlanta, their tournament, their future, a middle-aged woman with a shopping bag sidled up to a reporter near the gate.

"Did that coach, what's his name, leave?" she asked.

Yes, she was told, what's his name was gone.

"Hmmm," she said, and walked away. ◆

127

BASEBALL IN THE '90S: PETE & MARGO, WADE & DI

April 3

C OOPERSTOWN, N.Y., Jan. 31, 1999 — Ladies and gentlemen, before I introduce the commissioner of baseball, Pete Rose, and his lovely wife, Margo, I think we should take a moment to look back on the decade we are about to complete. Weren't the '90s something? Those of you who agree, press "yes" on your armchair sensors.

Just think of the wonderful changes we've seen these last 10 years! Ten years ago, baseball was still played outdoors. Ten years ago, the Russians weren't even in the major leagues. Ten years ago, Sen. Kirk Gibson was still a leftfielder. Let's reminisce, shall we? We've prepared this little highlight video. Just punch it up on your screens, slip in your 3-D contact lenses, and let's reflect back on a kinder, gentler decade, when they actually thought chewing tobacco was bad for you. Achhh-ptuuuey!

Roll 'em.

1990: Tigers manager Sparky Anderson finally achieves his goal of a team with no player under 35. "If you ain't losing your hair, you ain't no ballplayer," Sparky declares. His team leads the American League East until the last week of the season, when the entire pitching staff departs for a shuffleboard tournament in Miami Beach. Meanwhile, Wade Boggs, no longer popular in Boston, is traded to San Diego. He is rumored to be involved with six cocktail waitresses and half the staff of the Naval Hospital. He hits .390 and wins the batting title. George Steinbrenner fires Dallas Green as Yankees manager, hires Billy Martin, fires Billy Martin, and hires Steve Fisher as interim coach. The New York Mets clinch the NL East in June and take the rest of the season off. Willie (Guillermo) Hernandez, suffering through a terrible slump, changes his name to Keith. His pitching does not improve, but he has a strange desire to kiss Darryl Strawberry. Brent Musburger takes over as the voice of baseball's Game of the Week. "Did you see that!" he exclaims in his opening broadcast. "That was absolutely marvelous! I mean, it was marvelous! Wow. Talk about marvelous!" "Brent," says his co-host, "it's batting practice."

1991: Oakland's Jose Canseco becomes the first player to hit 60 homers and steal 60 bases. "I . . . do . . . not . . . use . . . steroids," he insists. He is, however, offered the role of Lurch in the new "Addams Family." Meanwhile, a shake-up in the front office: A. Bartlett Giamatti resigns as

128

commissioner because, during his three years in office, no one understood a word he said. "His last name was Italian, his first name was a letter, and his middle name was a pear," complains Angels owner Gene Autry. "He ain't no cowboy, I tell you that." Steve Garvey takes over the job and declares every Tuesday Ladies Day; wives get in free, limit three to a customer. The Orioles win their 60th game — in two seasons. Boggs, no longer popular in San Diego, is traded to Texas, where he is rumored to be involved with six Cowboy cheerleaders. He hits .410 and wins the batting title. And in Los Angeles, the inevitable finally happens when Tommy Lasorda eats one last plate of lasagna and explodes. He is buried at Pizza Hut.

1992: Pitcher Tommy John, age 48, starts Opening Day for the Yankees. He wins, 5-0. Afterward, he falls asleep during the interviews. The doctors tuck him in and ask everyone to come back in the morning. Rose, forced out of baseball for gambling, comes up on the ballot for the Hall of Fame. Odds in Rose's new Atlantic City casino are 3-1 he gets it. When the big day comes, however, he misses by two votes. "FIX!" yell the critics. Rose is last seen boarding a plane for Switzerland with a large sack. Meanwhile, Sony invents a tiny radio transmitter to ease signal-calling between catcher and pitcher. With the Pitchman, the catcher need only whisper into the tiny cellular microphone inside his mask. Unfortunately, a problem develops when San Diego's Benito Santiago accidentally crosses the frequency and lands a Northwest jet at second base.

1993: Strike year.

1994: George Bell takes over as manager of the Toronto Blue Jays, replacing longtime rival Jimy Williams, who goes home in search of his other "m." The Blue Jays, meanwhile, are still waiting to make their first trade since 1987. "Something will come up," says GM Pat Gillick. The first fuel-injected bullpen cart is introduced in Oakland. Canseco is arrested for going 115 m.p.h. across rightfield. Boggs, no longer popular in Texas, is traded to the expansion London Bobbies, where he is rumored to be involved with Princess Diana and the royal scone maker. He hits .453 and wins the batting title. Major changes in Detroit, where the new Tiger Stadium is finally opened by Tom Monaghan. Critics note that it is the first ballpark built in the shape of a pizza. Actually, two pizzas. You enter the second stadium free. Monaghan also orders new dough-colored Tigers uniforms, complete with cheese stains. Says a smiling Anderson: "Cheese don't hurt. Now, tomato sauce . . . " Willie (Guillermo, Keith) Hernandez, suffering through a terrible slump, changes his name to Julio Iglesias. The Mariners and Padres meet in the World Series. CBS ratings are just slightly behind those of ABC's "Wild Kingdom."

1995: Strike year.

1996: Former Tiger Jack Morris buys the Pittsburgh Pirates for an undisclosed sum, becoming the first ex-player to own a major league franchise. "We're finally gonna run a team right," Morris promises. He raises the minimum player salary to $650,000. The manager makes $4.25 an hour, plus tips. Atlanta Braves owner Ted Turner, frustrated with 20 years of losing, de-colorizes his team and makes it play in black and white. Texas Ranger Nolan Ryan is moved to the bullpen when his fastball slows to 91 m.p.h. "Hey," he says, shrugging, "you know how it is when you turn 50." And in October, the Chicago Cubs finally win the World Series, prompting new club owner Bill Murray to say, "It's a Cinderella story . . . former greenskeeper. . . . "

1997: Garvey is ousted as commissioner when he admits he is actually the father of Ricky Schroder, Tiffany and Pete Rose Jr. "I expect to live up to my obligations," he says. "I'm buying a bigger house. . . . " The jet pack is introduced, increasing stolen-base statistics and prompting Musburger to say: "Boy, that Bo Jackson can really fly! Marvelous!" Orel Hershiser, one of the great pitchers of the '80s, finally retires, turning down the Dodgers' offer of a one-year contract worth $26 million. "It's not worth it for that little money," he says. "I can make more as a TV analyst." CBS proves Hershiser correct by hiring him for three years at $99 million, a standard contract. Newspaper writers also get a raise, to $23,000 a year.

1998: Strike year.

1999: Anderson comes out of spring training saying, "You know, this is the best team I've ever had." The Yankees make fashion history with the combination pinstripe suit/pinstripe uniform. "It makes a statement," says designer Halston. "You can negotiate your contract in the morning and pitch a shutout in the afternoon." Boggs, unpopular in London, is traded to the new expansion Moscow Red Sox, where he is rumored to be involved with six Kirov ballerinas and a babushka vendor. He hits .534, wins the batting title, then drops dead with a smile on his face. In a Little League game, Darryl Strawberry Jr. picks a fight with Keith Hernandez Jr. The two have to be separated.

"Why don't you grow up?" says Hernandez.

"Why should I?" says Strawberry. "I'm 10 years old."

Pete Rose returns from Switzerland with a French accent, a university degree, and a new bride, Margo Adams, who had been working in a Zurich coat factory until the inventory was mysteriously depleted. The over-under on the marriage is six months; Rose takes the under. He is voted in as new commissioner after promising expansion teams in Nassau, Monaco and Lake Tahoe. The Indians win the World Series. Bob Uecker, their manager, is given a five-year deal. And Willie (Guillermo, Keith, Julio Iglesias) Hernandez, in a terrible slump, changes his name to Mitch.

He goes 17-2 and wins the Cy Young Award. ◆

A-MAIZING BLUE! MICHIGAN SNARES BASKETBALL TITLE

April 4

SEATTLE — He stood at the free throw line, the loneliest man in the world. All around him was the enemy, hooting and hollering, the demons in Seton Hall uniforms talking trash, the crowd suddenly an army of "MISS IT! MISS IT!" The referee bounced the ball twice, slowly, like an executioner, and tossed it to him. Life came to a standstill. A school and a nation and a glorious destiny held their breath.

Dribble. Shoot. Swish.

Tie game.

"All right, baby!" yelled Glen Rice to Rumeal Robinson. "One more. One more."

Robinson licked his lips. What was riding on this shot? Only an entire season. Only a fairy-tale ending. Only the championship of the world in college basketball. Pressure?

Dribble. Shoot. Swish.

Champions.

"WOOOOH! WOOOH! WOOH!" screamed Rice, hugging Robinson three seconds later, crying in his arms, after Michigan had hung on to win the national championship in overtime, 80-79, in the most fantastic finish to a basketball season you could ever imagine. "WOOH! WOOH!"

Were there any other words? How else could you describe it? A game that had everything, classic theater, wonderful drama — the first overtime game in a tournament final since 1963. It had heroes and villains and magnificent plays and bonehead plays and moments when you could cut the pressure with a buzz saw, and moments when all the players, good and bad, succumbed to it.

It had Rice, the tournament's MVP, keeping his team alive all game long with miracle shots, scoring from every angle, yet missing a jumper at the buzzer that could have sealed it. It had Sean Higgins, the young, free-spirited guard, who three weeks ago you wouldn't trust with his own sneakers, sinking two clutch free throws in the final moments of regulation. It had Steve Fisher, the interim coach, calming his players when it seemed as if the world was coming down around them, when the Seton Hall Pirates were stealing everything they touched.

And finally it had Rumeal, a kid who has overcome everything you can imagine, a lost childhood, academic woes, a natural shyness, to become a sterling example of what college basketball should be — and there he was, where he belonged, at the free throw line, proving once again that you can't write off any team that believes in itself.

"What were you thinking when you were standing there with the championship on the line?" he was asked in the locker room afterward.

"I was thinking, 'Man, I wish the referee would stop stalling and give me the ball,'" he said.

Dribble. Shoot. Swish.

Champions.

Nobody believed us," said Higgins, clutching his little brown box with the championship ring inside. "The people were all saying, 'Seton Hall, Seton Hall.' Just like at the beginning they were saying, 'Xavier, Xavier.' They didn't know how many nights we sat up talking about a national championship. I think it was all that doubting by everyone else that enabled us to win tonight."

Well, there was certainly enough of that. What a story! Who would ever believe this? A team that three weeks ago had no coach and seemingly no chance? National champions? Not only national champions, but the first Michigan team to win that title. Not only national champions, but come-from-behind national champions.

"There were moments when it got a little scary," said Rice, who finished with 31 points. "Their defense was really good, and they kept getting me out of my type of offense."

The final minutes were enough to make you lose your hair, misplace your heartbeat. Michigan had squandered a 12-point lead in the second half and missed a chance to win at the regulation buzzer, when Rice's 20-footer thumped the rim once, twice and out. Overtime? Overtime. The Wolverines fell behind, 79-76. The Seton Hall fans seemed to own the Kingdome. Each Michigan miss brought a roar and fans leaping from their seats, smelling the kill. Wasn't this supposed to be a neutral court? Where did all this blue and white come from?

But Michigan fought back. Robinson brought the ball upcourt against a chorus of jeers — "Terry, it's your shot," he yelled at Terry Mills — and Mills made that shot, a leaping banker, to cut it to 79-78. Seton Hall came back downcourt, dripping the time off the clock, 20 seconds left, 10 seconds left, finally the Pirates took a shot, it missed badly, and Rice caught the ball and dished to Robinson.

"From that point, I wanted the shot," said Robinson, who raced upcourt, drove the lane and was fouled by Gerald Greene. "I didn't want to put the burden on anyone else's shoulders."

Can you believe that? Why not? Didn't you see him at that free throw line? Wasn't he the picture of calm — even as your heart pounded in your throat?

"I told him, 'I made mine, now you make yours,' " said Higgins.

"I told him God helps those who helps themselves," said Mike Griffin.

Everyone had a word of encouragement. Everyone had a piece of heavenly advice. But the ball was in Robinson's hands, his alone. Pressure?

"I looked at (Seton Hall's) John Morton and he was grinning at me, trying to unnerve me," Robinson said. "But I just grinned back at him. Because I had the ball and he didn't."

Dribble. Shoot. Swish.

Champions.

Wow. What a story! The only sadness is that it has to end. Didn't everyone feel a little younger these past three weeks, a little more sprightly, a little bit like we had an 8 a.m. class and a date at the student union? And, of course, the game to go to.

Basketball did that. Michigan basketball: Rice, shooting from the heavens, breaking the NCAA tournament record for points. God, what a tournament. There are rims in Atlanta and Lexington, Ky., that are still too hot to touch. And Robinson, always with the ball, dictating the creative flow, holding in midair then flicking in those two-footers. And Higgins, the baby of the group, with that goofy expression and that flexible-flier body all over the court. And Mills, with a wing span like a pterodactyl, rising toward the hoop for a rebound or a jumper. And Loy Vaught, sucking in the rebounds, and Griffin, the unappreciated guy — there's always one, right? — making the steals or the invisible defensive maneuver. Or Mark Hughes. Or Demetrius Calip. Look at them out there now, cutting down the nets.

Champions.

And Fisher, the interim coach. Here is the story to end all stories. The hero of second-fiddles everywhere. He took over for the departed Bill Frieder the day before the tournament and never looked back. Six victories later, he is the coach of the national champions. There still might be debate as to whether Fisher earned a five-year contract with this miracle run. There is no doubt he proved himself tournament tough. Tough? He took a wild tornado of talent and harnessed it into a thinking, synchronized unit. In three weeks!

"I am the happiest man in the world right now," he said. "I couldn't be prouder of this team and what they did."

Well, take a bow yourself, Coach. Fisher ran this team, not with whips or threats. He did it with kindness, a soothing word, a deep breath, a reminder of all the players had done to get here. Admit it. He surprised you, didn't he? Hey. Steve. Why worry? If you don't get the job, you can retire a legend. Six victories and a national championship. Let 'em try to beat that.

For now, however, let's not worry about jobs and futures. Savor these scenes: Michigan clamping on Seton Hall star Andrew Gaze, holding him to five points. Higgins stepping away from the free throw line at the end of regulation, having made the biggest shot of his life, then stepping up and making another. Robinson, standing at the line, waiting for that ball — "C'mon ref, I'm ready." And finally, when the buzzer sounded, Robinson and Rice locked in that eternal embrace, a hug that would never end, crying, laughing, screaming, doing everything we all would do at a moment like that, all at once.

"WOOH WOOH WOOH!"

There is a famous sign in the football building that Bo Schembechler put up 20 years ago to encourage his players through that tough first season: "Those Who Stay Will Be Champions," it reads.

Paint another one and hang it over Crisler Arena.

Those who stayed are. ♦

FINAL HORN PLAYS TAPS FOR WINGS' SAD SEASON

April 14

CHICAGO — They died slowly, inevitably, much to the delight of the howling Chicago crowd. The magic was deserting Greg Stefan; the magic was deserting Steve Yzerman; the magic was deserting Jacques Demers. The Red Wings were losing badly in the first round of the playoffs, and suddenly trying hard was not enough, believing was not enough. The deafening foghorn that is the signature of this rickety stadium blew strong and loud after every wild Chicago goal and finally, at 11:29 p.m., it sounded the good-bye moan, almost mercifully, for this most difficult Detroit hockey season.

They go home now? They go home.

"What day is it, April 15 or something?" Yzerman said after the Wings lost, 7-1, surrendering this playoff in six games. "Last year we were still playing on May 15. I don't think we're going to realize what happened here for a few days."

When they do, they will not forget it. It was sad, and perhaps an unavoidable end to a season that was star-crossed from Day 1. They had come to this city clinging to their confidence, reminding themselves who they were and what they had once done. But three goals in the second period suddenly choked their last hope, threw dirt on them, left them gasping for air. Chicago? They were being blown out by Chicago? In the first round? Really? Chicago?

Yes. Chicago. And the snapshots of defeat were all over the place. Here was Steve Chiasson lying flat on the ice, injured, after a vicious check to the boards. Here was Yzerman giving his stick to Gilbert Delorme (who had broken his) and trying desperately to play naked, slapping the puck away with his hand, only to see Chicago come back moments later and score anyhow. Here was the Blackhawks' Steve Larmer flipping a goal between Stefan's legs — 2-1 Chicago — and then, just 26 agonizing seconds later, Wayne Presley, who grew up in the Detroit suburbs, for Pete's sake, backhanding the puck past Stefan, 3-1. Before the night was over, Presley would have three goals, the hat trick, and the Wings would be buried in black hats, flying onto the ice like bullets.

"It's going to be a long summer," Stefan said afterward, "and not very much fun."

They go home now?

They go home.

In a way, this is a stunning upset — the full effect might not be realized for days, maybe weeks. Yet in other ways you could almost feel it coming. Wasn't this a dark-side season from the start for Detroit? Didn't you hear whispers and mumbles about this team all winter long: "I don't know about them. . . . They're not the same. . . . All that off-ice controversy. . . ."

Demers had been worried about this team early. Two months ago, two weeks ago, he repeated the same theme: "We're not playing defense the way we should. I am concerned." He tried to give the appropriate pep talks. He rallied the players before the final period of Game 5, telling them, "You don't want to go home and play golf now. . . . Nobody in Detroit will want to talk to you anyhow." It worked.

Once.

"Are you surprised with this defeat?" Demers was asked.

"No," he said. "Disappointed, yes. Surprised, no. We never had the right chemistry, not from the very start. This was a team that was never at peace with itself."

It has five months to rest now. And so be it, because the truth is, this was a season that needed to be completely erased to be overcome. Sure, the Bob Probert and Petr Klima problems had been wrapped up by the playoffs. But their effects lingered. The unhappiness of the regular season — "There were times when you really didn't feel like coming down to the arena," Stefan admitted — had slowed the Wings like a sore hamstring, and they were trying to run anyway.

"There are a lot of guys in here," Chiasson said, glancing around the locker room, "who are going 'Whew!' right now. We can use the summer to regroup."

Still, how sad for the guys on this team, who tried so hard all season to overcome the bad news, to rise above the antics of Probert, whose arrest at the border for alleged cocaine smuggling in March ended a sordid saga that had hung around the Wings' necks, as heavy as a tombstone. How sad for the likes of Yzerman, who had a career-best season, bouncing back from a knee injury. And for Adam Oates, who stepped out of Yzerman's shadow to play superb hockey. And for Chiasson, who has developed into a bright young star. And for Rick Zombo and Dave Barr and Gerard Gallant and for Stefan and Glen Hanlon, who had to handle the onslaught of offense without a strong defense — or a Probert — to protect them.

They deserved better, if only for effort, if only for the fact they did win the Norris Division regular-season title. Instead, here is what they got: Klima ejected in the third period for high sticking. Stefan benched for the third period, with Hanlon unable to deliver any miracles. A Chicago defense that limited them to 19 shots on goal. The Chicago fans were unmerciful; they tossed hats, trash, even a big, black balloon was tossed onto the ice. At one point, a Chicago fan knocked a beer over into the open press box — dousing Mike Ilitch, the Wings' owner.

We go home now.

W hat will come of all this? Changes, for sure. "Certain players will be traded," Demers admitted. "Certain guys have gotten complacent here in Detroit. It's a great place to work. But we need to start from the beginning next year. We need to open training camp on a different note with some different people."

Exit finesse and one-dimensional players. Enter tougher players with better defense.

Here to stay: the memories of a first-round defeat.

How did it happen, people will ask? How could they lose to Chicago, a team with only 66 points during the regular season? People will point to the loss of Probert and, yes, the lack of toughness helped take the Wings down in this series. Chicago played as if the class bully was suddenly absent from school. The Wings played, at times, like the kid who realized he was outnumbered and a long way from home. Combine that with a hot goalie (Alain Chevrier), one overtime heartache (Game 2), two bad games (3 and 6) and presto. You've got a series.

"Chicago reminded me," Oates added glumly, "a little bit of us two years ago."

That about says it all.

Thus ends the season of our discontent, a tumble off the rainbow for this once-Cinderella team that began, really, with a drinking incident last May in Edmonton and ended with that deathly horn. In between have been disillusion, disfavor, discord and disgust. Good guys were ignored, bad guys were overplayed, and it seemed the lights were always glaring on this team. It could never escape the shadows.

And in the end, that was all the Wings had left to look at as time ran out on the Chicago Stadium scoreboard. Three. Two. One. The announcer talked about Chicago playoff tickets. The fans were singing, "NA-NA-NA-NA. . . ." And here came that sound, no doubts, no questions. We go home now.

That foghorn means someone else's ship has just come in. ♦

MAYBE IT'S BEST TO LET THESE DRAFT SLEEPERS LIE

April 23

Well, once again, it's NFL draft day, and everyone knows which player should go where. The big names. The big picks.

As per tradition, however, I have combed the country looking for sleeper selections who might have escaped the NFL's watchful eye. These guys might not get the same money as Troy Aikman or Tony Mandarich, but some team out there might take a chance on them. Depends on how desperate they are:

Goober (Joe) Theismann, RB, Florida Union: Part of the famous "Run and Shoot-Off-Your-Mouth" offense, Goober, a skinny tailback, was known for his chatter across the line of scrimmage. "Hey, you, ugly, don't come in here," he would taunt the defense. "Don't come in here. You'll be dead if you come in here. Yo, ugly, don't come in here. I'm warning ya, ugly. I'm telling ya, hear me talkin' to ya?" Goober is in traction at the moment.

Biff Richards III, QB, Yale: Famous throughout the Ivy League for never soiling his uniform. A medical student, should be helpful on the bench. Low completion percentage; he tended to throw immediately to avoid injury. Once accidentally bounced ball off lineman's pads into the arms of receiver for a touchdown. "Smashing," he said. "Let's wash up, shall we?"

Larry Neon Sanders, RB, Oklahoma Correctional Institute: Not to be confused with Barry or Deion Sanders, although, as Larry says, "I think one of those guys is my cousin. What'da they look like? You got their phone number?" Ran a 4.3 in college. Unfortunately, the police were chasing him at the time. Should be available for the 1992 season, pending parole.

Hot Fudge Sanders, OL, Detroit: A local product, not to be confused with Barry, Deion or Larry Neon. Never played organized ball. Used to work in a chocolate factory. Considered a sleeper because, well, he sleeps a lot. Also because of his size — 7-feet-2, 560 pounds. "We could just roll him out and let him lie there," says Mike Hickey, personnel director of the Jets. "It would give the quarterback at least a minute and a half to throw."

Elwood (Huh?) Judson, DT, Rice: Considered a first-round pick when he came out of high school in rural Idaho. Great size. Exceptional strength. Scouts began to back off, however, when someone asked why he chose Rice as his school. "Oh, cuz I like Rice, I reckon," he said. "Especially with gravy. May I have some, ma'am?"

Bless You Williams, TE, Arkansas Theological Seminary: As a sophomore, Bless You led the nation in receiving. Unfortunately, his faith requires him to check the Bible before running his routes. His team had 3,700 yards in delay-of-game penalties.

Adolpho Jenean Bubiza, K, Tahiti: Already a legend in the South Seas. The good news is Adolpho regularly kicks from 75 yards; the bad news is he kicks only coconuts. When given a football, Adolpho smiled and cut it open, looking for milk.

Jeremy (Pumpin') Irons, LB, Nebraska State: A superb athlete at 6-feet-6, 300 pounds. Only fear of steroid use kept Irons from No. 1 status. Scouts say nothing has been proved, but at age 14 Jeremy was bald and talked like the low guy in the Temptations.

Jose (The Big) Enchilada, DT, New Mexico: A legend in Albuquerque, Jose The Big once made 28 unassisted tackles, then lifted the opposing bench and shook the others to the ground. Once won a game by tackling the opposing team's bus. Unfortunately, Jose just signed a five-year deal with the World Wrestling Federation.

Harassment Jones, DB, Institute For Driver Training: Once the most feared man in the Southeastern Conference. Fast. Strong. Brutal defense. Lost favor when he failed drug test, then said, "I shoulda studied."

Tony (Little Anthony) Mandarich, OT, Hogson College: Like his more famous cousin, Little Anthony also weighs 315 pounds. Unfortunately, he stands 4-feet-10. Used primarily in the kicking game as the tee. "I don't expect to get paid as much as Tony," he says, "but I don't eat as much, either."

Jimmy Joe (Bob) Morton, LB, Texas A&P: Gritty linebacker known for taunting opponents with endless Texas talk. "Son," he'd say to an oncoming running back, "you're dumber than a barrel full of hair. UNH! You swapped your brain for a tree stump. UNH! You're flatter than a snake. UNH!" His dream for today's draft? "To get richer than two orthodontists."

Satch Sanders, WR, Boston College: Not to be confused with Barry, Deion, Larry Neon or Hot Fudge, Satch is a wide receiver with a degree in Celtic studies. Acts mature. Looks mature. Actually, he looks 50 years old. Hell of a jump shot, though.

Pharaoh Sanders, DB, Birdland State: Not to be confused with Barry, Deion, Larry Neon, Hot Fudge or Satch. Only man in college football history to intercept two passes and play the national anthem on the saxophone in the same game.

Colonel Sanders, T, Kentucky: Comes with potatoes.

David Lewis, TE, U Cal: No speed. No hands. No apparent talent. "Hey," he says, "the Lions were stupid enough to draft me once. Maybe someone else will do it again." ♦

PISTONS' BADDEST BOYS BECOME BEST BUDDIES

B adges? They don't need no stinking badges. They will grab you, slam you, elbow you and steal your basketball. Kindness? They have no use for kindness. They will ignore you, insult you, whack your notebook and poke your microphone. Taste? They have no taste. They will curse, burp, crack filthy jokes and interrupt a teammate's TV interview by jumping in front of the camera and saying, "Excuse me, did you know this guy is a BLEEEEEP? Heh-heh."

Rickey and Bill.

Happy at last.

This is a story of the most unlikely of friendships, Rick Mahorn and Bill Laimbeer, The Beef Brothers, Partners In Crime, Murder One and Murder Two. Imagine if Capone and Dillinger decided to hang out together. Imagine if The Hulk and Lex Luthor took joint vacations. Imagine if Mahorn, one of the roughest and most disliked power forwards in the NBA, and Laimbeer, perhaps the most unpopular brute ever to jump center, got together and went . . . clothes shopping.

Clothes shopping?

"That's right," Mahorn says. "I taught him to stop dressing like a man who drives a tractor."

"Yeah," Laimbeer adds, "now I have pleats in my pants."

Imagine no more. The union has been consummated. They talk alike. They laugh alike. They go clothes shopping together. The NBA playoffs are in full swing, and lock your doors — for suddenly, we have Laimbeer & Mahorn Inc. If you visit your nearest poster shop today, you will find a new, giant-sized portrait of the two of them, dressed like Hell's Angels, Bill squeezing a deflated basketball, Rick chewing on a net and rim like a ravished grizzly bear. "Bad Boys," it reads. It is the kind of picture you send home to mother. If your mother is in prison.

"Yo, Rick. Lam. Sign one for me, OK?" asks Mike Abdenour, the Pistons' trainer, as a stack arrives in the locker room.

"Yeah, sure," says Laimbeer. He grabs a pen. Beneath his image he writes: "To Mike; this is instead of a playoff share. Enjoy. Bill Laimbeer."

He hands the pen over.

"Let's see . . . " Mahorn says, his mouth curling into that alligator grin. He scribbles a message. Laimbeer reads it. He breaks up, laughing.

"Oooh, that's nasty. You can't write that."

"Yes, I can."

"Oooh."

"Oooh."

BILL ON RICK: *"He's taught me a lot. Like rap music. And perch sandwiches. I never would have eaten one of those if not for him."*

RICK ON BILL: *"He's all right. For a Caucasian."*

Surely this is somebody's idea of a cruel joke. Mahorn and Laimbeer? Together? Buddies? Isn't that a little much? Isn't that like Mt. Everest on top of Mt. Fuji? And talk about a media nightmare! No sports writer in his right mind volunteers to do a story on either of these guys. Together? Why not just take the gas pipe?

REPORTER: Bill, can I have a minute?

BILL: What for? (Smile.) You just write crap. (Smile.) Not now. (Frown.) Don't bother me. (Snarl.)

REPORTER: Excuse me, Rick, can I –

RICK: No, you can't, you big, fat pile of bleep. (Smile.) Now leave me alone, you ugly, raisin-head bleepity bleep. (Grin and walk away.)

Are they serious? Yeah. Sure. Sometimes. Maybe. You could take all the kindness these two have shown the media, slip it in a baby's shoe and still have room in the toes. Of course, they aren't any nicer to opposing players. On offense, Laimbeer is outside, Mahorn is inside. On defense, they combine to make one ugly tollbooth to the hoop. It is their animated bulk — particularly the elbows, shoulders, knees and fists — that has made them the most feared and disliked tandem in the NBA.

And the most punished. Both players have contributed more than five figures in NBA fines this season alone.

But it is this union of intimidation that has actually pulled them together. "To be honest, the NBA can only blame itself for our friendship," says Laimbeer. "They started the whole thing with the Pistons video. The marketing people said, 'Hey, we've got a great concept. The Bad Boys.' And they kind of lumped me and Rickey in as the baddest ones. We became closer on account of that."

And now, not only do they terrorize the lane, they actually hang out. Friends. They eat together. They go to clubs together on the road. "Rick is single; I'm married," says Laimbeer, 31. "So I always ask him first, 'Is this the kind of place I'm gonna like or you're gonna like?' "

Mahorn, 30, grins and turns up his portable boom box. "You should hear Lam do some rap. He's learning. . . . When nobody's listening, he'll walk around singing, 'I don't like no Oscar Mayer Wiener!' He's into it. Especially that song 'Funky Cold Medina.' "

Bill Laimbeer? The Funky Cold Medina?

BILL ON RICK: *"When I first met him, I thought he was fat and not interested in contributing to this team."*

RICK ON BILL: *"When I first met him, I thought he was the biggest lummox on Earth."*

Can we be blunt? What are these guys doing on the same page? Here, in Laimbeer, we have the son of a wealthy white businessman, a kid who grew up along the gorgeous cliffs of the Pacific Ocean. He had a brand new car when he was 16, once flunked out of Notre Dame because of laziness and lasted just two weeks on the only summer job he ever held. ("Factory work. Too hard. I quit.")

And then there is Mahorn, who grew up on the opposite coast (Hartford, Conn.) and on the opposite side of privilege. Inner city. His dad split. Mom raised him. Family had little money — and Rickey didn't quit any job he could get. Went to Hampton Institute, got into the NBA and has been surviving ever since with whatever it takes — elbows, shoulders, a bump of the rump. ("I'm lucky to have a chance to earn this kind of money. I never forget it.")

Laimbeer jokes that he wants Mahorn to move to West Bloomfield, Mich., and learn how to sail. Mahorn claims he is teaching Laimbeer how to dance. Friends. Well, not at first. When Mahorn was traded to Detroit in 1985 from the Washington Bullets, he was an outcast. He was heavy — more than 20 pounds heavier than his playing weight of 255. He was also far less enthusiastic. And that bothered Laimbeer.

"You have to earn your way onto this team," Laimbeer says, stretching his long, pale legs. "Rick missed Washington so much (and his close friend there, Jeff Ruland), he didn't have the right attitude to play here at first. I ignore guys like that."

Which was just fine with Mahorn. After all, he had come to know Laimbeer as an opposing player — which is like coming to know Joan Crawford as a baby-sitter. Respect? Friendship? Try disgust, repulsion.

"Bill Laimbeer," Mahorn says. "Everyone knew him as a jerk. He was blunt with me from Day 1. I didn't want to hear it back then. Sometimes I still don't. I tell him, 'You're the stupidest, big, old, dumb yuppie I've ever seen.' "

And Laimbeer says, "What do you know?"

And Mahorn says, "You can't run or jump."

And Laimbeer says, "So what? You're ugly."

And they both crack up.

You can hear these debates daily inside the Detroit locker room. Mahorn's attitude has blossomed, his weight has dropped and he has been embraced by his teammates as Guardian Devil, King Muscle, pride of the Bad Boy image. He and Laimbeer are now locker to locker, 6-foot-10 next

142

to 6-foot-11, the way buddies like it. Visitors dub it the Abuse Corner.

And with good reason. No one is safe. Laimbeer will sting the media. ("What's the matter? Tigers not playing tonight? No Red Wings? Huh?") Mahorn will rag on whatever player is closest. ("Fennis Dembo, you ugly, bald-headed, lizard-faced bleep, pick out some good music for that stereo!") They will play gags. Practical jokes. No subject is too off-color. No personal effects are off-limits. "Rickey used to go around filling your drawer with water," recalls forward John Salley. "You'd come back from the shower, and you'd open your drawer, and all your junk would be floating around, your brush and letters and stuff. And you'd look up and see Rickey over there, looking down, trying to hide that smile."

But, for all the abuse they dish out, Mahorn and Laimbeer are not only the most-fined duo in the league, they are the most publicly flogged. People see them together on the road and begin screaming. Opposing announcers slime them every chance they can.

"People see Rick as the violent player and me as the cheap-shot artist," says Laimbeer, shrugging. "But they always lump us together."

And here is the most interesting kernel of this relationship. Beneath all the muscle flexing and dirty jokes and tough-guy posture, Rick Mahorn and Bill Laimbeer, believe it or not, are worried about one another.

BILL ON RICK: *"I won't start fights. But if someone is after Rick, I'll be after him."*

RICK ON BILL: *"If I see players out there taking shots at Lam, I say to him, 'Don't worry about it. You just play. I'll take care of them.'"*

G iants need love, too. Or so it seems. Laimbeer and Mahorn swear each other protection, against critics — and against opposing NBAers.

"Remember a few years ago, in Boston, when Robert Parish started doing that stuff to Laimbeer?" Mahorn says. "I told Bill I'd get him. And I did. I won't let anyone hit him or hurt him. If it means me getting thrown out, so be it. I say, 'Lam, you're more valuable out here than I am, anyway.'"

Adds Laimbeer: "We protect each other."

Strange? Yes. But in a weird way, sort of admirable. Not the fighting, or any cheap shots. But here are two guys seen around the league as selfish, boorish, the ultimate bullies, yet they are willing to be the other's bodyguard. They will defend each other publicly. And the truth is, much of their frightening image is exactly that: image. A smoke screen. Something that wins games. Really, now, as Michael Jackson asks, who's bad? "Off the court, Rick is so different from his image, people would be shocked," Laimbeer says. "I swear, he is the most polite, professional athlete I've ever met who is not a Jesus freak."

Indeed, Mahorn is painfully kind to children, old people, women. (One of his teammates describes him as "shy" around the opposite sex.) As for Laimbeer, few people remember he is married with a family. Even fewer know that six years ago, he and wife, Chris, lost their first child. A baby boy. He was born prematurely and died two days later. Laimbeer never asks for sympathy, never brings it up, never lets that side show.

"Yo! Lam!" yells Mark Aguirre, holding up a crisp new Bad Boys poster, the proceeds from which go to charity. "Sign one for me, will ya?"

"Awright!" Laimbeer says, grabbing the marker and flashing a sinister grin. He pauses. Surely he has a doozy in mind. But when he finally brings pen to paper, this is what he writes: "To Mark — Thanks for sacrificing your game so we can win a championship. Your friend. Bill Laimbeer."

Don't you just hate him when he's nice?

BILL ON RICK: *"I'm going to teach him how to golf. Get him out to the suburbs more."*

RICK ON BILL: *"He's trying hard to become a brother. I tell him he's still got a ways to go."*

And on they go. Mercy? They show no mercy. You'll get an elbow, a wrist, a shoulder blade — and then they'll want a foul called on you. Sweetness? You'll get no sweetness. Not if there are other players around, or other reporters, and they have their image to uphold. Good taste? Are you kidding? Nothing is off-limits; fat jokes, money jokes, even race jokes, which is fine, it's good, because it shows that color really doesn't matter between these two, it is insignificant enough to laugh about, and that is the ground floor of acceptance.

"Theirs really is a unique relationship," says coach Chuck Daly, smiling. "I've never quite seen anything like it. They're lumped together wherever they go, by opposing fans and media. What's the expression? Misery loves company? Maybe that's part of it."

Maybe it is. But they are enhanced by the association, the same way the Minnesota Vikings' Fearsome Foursome was once enhanced. People see one and it's an individual thing. People see two and it's a concept. Bad Boys. Thugs-R-Us. Mahorn and Laimbeer.

So what if they could build a new house with all their NBA fines? So what if they have every referee watching them? This is a friendship that has not only sprouted from the most unlikely of unions, but actually has a kind of — dare we say it? — nice side to it. White learns from black. Rich learns from not-so-rich. Perch sandwiches learn from pitching wedges.

Who'da thunk it? These two? One day soon, if the Pistons win the NBA title, they might get around to signing their Bad Boys posters to one another.

"To Lam — Rick (Par Four) Mahorn."

"To Rick — Bill (Funky Cold) Laimbeer."

Unbelievable. ♦

PLENTY TO TELL ABOUT THE JOE NOBODY KNOWS

June 4

H e stepped inside the hospital room and took a deep breath. There lay his father, a strapping truck driver who had always been the image of strength. The sheets were pulled up to his waist.

"Come here, son. I want you to see this."

Joe Dumars walked slowly to the edge of the bed.

"It won't do any good to feel sorry for me, you know. I don't need that now. Just look and get it over with."

He pulled back the sheets. The left leg was gone, amputated at the knee. Diabetes. Dumars looked down and fought back the tears.

"Hey, hey," said the father. "It's done. We just go on with life. No feeling sorry for me, OK?"

"OK, Dad," whispered his son, and nothing more was said.

This is a story about The Joe Nobody Knows, the good man behind the basketball star who has suddenly become nationally famous. The Pistons have beaten Chicago, capturing the Eastern Conference championship, and are heading, once again, to the NBA Finals. The locker room was a playground of noise.

"AWWRIGHT, BABY!"

"GOIN' TO LA!"

"OWWWW-EEEE!"

Dumars emerged from the shower, pulled a towel around his waist and made his way to a quiet corner. If anyone had a right to celebrate, it was he. He had weathered a hurricane named Michael Jordan — for six grueling games — defensed him, shadowed him, lived inside his skin. And at a crucial moment in the fourth quarter, with the Chicago Stadium crowd screaming and the Bulls surging to within two points, he stripped Jordan of the ball, raced downcourt and dished to John Salley, who drew a foul.

The play seemed to break the Chicago spirit. It silenced the crowd. He stole the ball? From the Great One? Jordan came running up behind him, stared at his back, as if to say, "How dare you? I am King here." But Dumars was already miles away, thinking about the next play, unflappable. That is the way he is. On the street. On the court. In that hospital room. People stare as he goes by and wonder, "What makes that guy so steady?"

But did you know Joe Dumars is also a "Sanford and Son" nut? Did you know he is part Creole? Did you know that he can sing Zydeco music and that he can gorge on crawfish etouffee and jambalaya and boudin? Did you know that he is mobbed wherever he goes in his hometown in Louisiana, that he need never pay for a meal, that women there, according to his best friend, John Wesley, "nearly rip his clothes off"?

Did you know that he loves to go to the library, and that he reads novels right up to game time? Did you know that he is getting married this September to his longtime girlfriend? Did you know that his father suffered three heart attacks during this NBA season — each time Joe received a phone call in the middle of the night — yet Joe never complained, never made it an excuse for poor play?

Did you know that, back home, they don't even call him Joe, they call him "Boopie," a name he has had since birth? Boopie? Even his teammates are unaware of that.

"Why are you so quiet?" people ask him over and over in Detroit. "Why are you so quiet?"

He shrugs. "I guess I don't have much to say."

This is a story of the Pistons' youngest starter and oldest soul, their MVP — most valuable and most vanished player. In the days to come, Dumars will be center stage, the man who must stop the Lakers' Magic Johnson if the Pistons hope to win an NBA championship. He will be interviewed nonstop. He will answer questions, softly, politely, patiently.

And nobody will learn one important thing about him. Quiet Joe. Shy old Joe. Nothing to say, right? Wrong. The first thing you discover about The Joe Nobody Knows is that he has plenty to say. It's just that, in many ways, he has the whole world fooled.

H e was born in the heat, in the hot, sticky Louisiana air that hangs on your body like a wet rag. It was hot in the house. It was hot outside. It was hot in church. "You never stopped sweating," he recalls now, sitting in his apartment in West Bloomfield, Mich. "My childhood was like the opening scenes of that movie, 'Body Heat.' People fanning themselves. People dripping perspiration. I can relate to that so much."

When he was 4 years old, he had to be taken to a Shreveport hospital, where they operated on him for a hernia. A kid there had lost an arm in a car accident. Before he left, young Joe asked his mother to give the kid his toy truck "because he should have something to play with." It was the beginning of a childhood that would always be a few years ahead of its time.

Joseph and Ophelia Dumars lived on Lee Street in Natchitoches, a small working-class town about 100 miles from Lake Charles, where young Joe went to college. Their house was across from the liquor store, and they had seven children, six boys and a girl, and all the boys played football. Then, one day, Joseph built a basketball court in the yard — the backboard was a sawed-off door, the hoop an old bicycle rim — and young Joe discovered a whole new world. "I was better in football, but all my brothers had done that. Basketball was a challenge.

"Besides, you needed other guys to play football. Basketball I could play alone."

In the heat of the bayou sun, he would stay for hours, making up games, shooting 50 free throws, shooting 100 lay-ups, shooting left-handed, just to see whether he could do it. By the time he was in the eighth grade, he was good enough to play with the college guys from nearby Northwestern State. They would sneak him into the gym, play for three hours every day. Boopie and the Big Boys. When the workouts were over, the college kids would slap each other, talk about girls and booze, and walk out to their cars. Joe got back on his bicycle and rode home.

"I learned a lot about college life," says Dumars, now 26. "I couldn't wait until I grew up." That was obvious. One day, when he was 11, his mother came home to find a sign on the door of the bedroom where Joe and his five older brothers slept. It read: "NO GIRLS ADMITTED WITHOUT EXPERIENCE."

"All right now," she said, laughing, "who put that sign up there?"

"Boopie did, Ma," the brothers said.

"Boopie?"

What did he know about girls? Nothing. What did he know about history? Nothing. But that didn't stop him from sneaking off to the library four or five times a week, finding a cool corner in the back and lowering himself into a book. "I never told anybody where I was. It was like my secret place, the one place I didn't have to be a tough kid. I read about famous people. John Kennedy. George Washington Carver."

Today he reads "Presumed Innocent," "Mob Boss," "Paris Trout"; he reads Robert Ludlum and Elmore Leonard; he reads a host of biographies; he reads nonfiction and fiction. He sits by his locker, bent over a book, even as his teammates are flicking towels and throwing jockstraps across the room.

"Yo, Joe," one of them once said, "what the hell you reading, man?"

"I'm reading about the Iran-contra thing."

"Oh."

End of conversation.

Not that he need worry about being accepted. For one thing, he's too nice a guy. And then, there's his home. "Joe Dumars," says Salley, "has got the most unbelievable deal of all of us. You ever been to Lake Charles, Louisiana? The man is king down there. I'm telling you, he's king."

Dumars laughs, but the description is true. Not many small-town Louisiana kids get to star in professional basketball, and because the closest NBA franchise is probably Houston or Atlanta, it's a big deal when Joey comes marching home.

"I can't wait till he gets back here every summer," admits Wesley, Joe's best friend since their college days on the McNeese State basketball team, where the Dumars legend grew. "We get an apartment together and hang out from July to October. Wherever we go, people stop him. Everybody wants to talk. Last year they gave him the key to the city. I tell you, if we stopped the car every time someone honked at us, we'd wreck the thing. Just going out to the store is an adventure."

It is not, however, expensive. According to Wesley, the hometown hero never has to pay for anything. A movie? An ice cream cone? Dinner? Gratis. "There are even people down here who offer Joe Cadillacs to drive around if he needs them," Wesley says. "I save so much money when he's back home, it's unbelievable."

When the Pistons played an exhibition game in Lake Charles last season, the crowd erupted every time Dumars touched the ball. Superstars such as Isiah Thomas and Adrian Dantley walked away shaking their heads. Wait a minute. Our Joe Dumars? King of the Bayou? Yes. And yet, typical of his personality, he seems to let it wash over him like tide. He remains friendly to every hometown soul, never haughty, never too busy. He expects nothing, is gracious when something is given, and speaks always in the throaty whisper of a voice that, from the moment you meet him, suggests a humbleness that is warm and soothing. Elvis in a sweat suit. Except that Joe has never been much for big parties, booze or drugs; you are more likely to find him at a barbecue than at a late-night saloon. Back when he turned 18, his brothers brought him before his mother.

"Ma, Boopie's old enough to drink now. We want to take him to the club. Is it OK?"

"Well, I suppose," she said. "But you all stick together and keep an eye on him."

Off they went. It was around 10 p.m. An hour later, Mrs. Dumars came down to the kitchen. There was Joe, sitting at the table, eating potato chips and drinking a Coke.

"Boopie, why are you back so soon?"

He shrugged. "Didn't seem like there was anything to do there except drink. And if you didn't drink, you just stood around watching other people drink. Who wants to do that?"

As we said, slightly ahead of his time.

Father to father, son to son, come and tell me what you've done. That was the rhyme Dumars' dad always sang, and it always worked; the boy came running and told him everything. Joseph Dumars was a husky, physical man, a truck driver, delivered produce, and his youngest boy was crazy about him. For a while the old man had Mondays off, and his kids would search for any excuse to stay home with him, to sit with him on the porch, to talk, to eat his cooking.

One day, Ophelia Dumars came home from work, and her husband said, "You know, Boopie didn't go to school today."

"Why not?"

He smiled. "I think you better ask him."

She found him out in the yard, playing. "Why didn't you go to school today?"

"The teacher told us it was a holiday," Joe said. "She said we didn't have to come."

"What holiday?"

"Mary Poppins' birthday."

"Mary Poppins' birthday?"

OK. So it wasn't a really good excuse. But, you know, father to father, son to son. "I wanted to be with my dad," Joe says, impishly. When he got older, he actually went out on the truck for a delivery route. He was giddy with excitement, sitting up front, feeling the powerful engines beneath his seat. "Then I started lifting all those crates. By the end of the day, I couldn't even move my arms. I never knew how hard my father worked until then."

The work ethic is only one thing he inherited. There is the calm. The strong principles. Mostly, however, there is the belief that you should never complain about anything. After all, Dad doesn't. And lord knows he could.

The diabetes struck in the mid-'80s. It robbed him first of his left leg. When they scraped to fit a prosthesis, they found the infection had worsened, and they had to amputate more. The following year, he lost a toe off his right foot, and eventually the foot itself. Suddenly he went from a vibrant, working father to a handicapped man. "You know the amazing thing," Dumars says, a faraway look in his eye. "He was more upbeat than any of us. He kept saying, 'There's no point in acting sorrowful. That won't help.'

"That's why, this past year, when he had the heart attacks (also brought on by diabetes), I didn't say anything to my teammates. What's the point? I still had to go out and do my job. What would be accomplished by hanging my head?

"I don't feel any less about my father because I don't act grief-stricken on the bench. I play the game, and the minute the game is over, I'm back on the phone home. I don't like a lot of emotion swings, not in front of people. He taught me to deal with anything life throws you, and deal with it privately."

Today, Joseph Dumars, 64, is pretty much confined to bed or a wheelchair. He watches tapes of his son's games with the Pistons, over and over. When young Joe visits, he sits on the edge of the bed, like the other brothers, listening, talking. One time his dad looked at him, in all sincerity, and said, "You know, that's a pretty good job you got there. Hang onto it."

"OK, Pop," Dumars said, "I will."

He has.

Which brings us to Joe Dumars' basketball — brilliant defense, steady shooting, the ability to play point guard or shooting guard — and one of the great myths going in the NBA, that somehow, because of his stoic, silent-movie actor face, Joe Dumars does not have a burning competitive flame inside.

Ha!

"They call me and Mahorn the Bad Boys," Bill Laimbeer says, shaking his head, "but I'll tell you something. Joe Dumars gets away with more than us. He bangs like crazy. He's vicious out there. He just doesn't call attention to himself."

It's true. Dumars, at 6-feet-3, 200 pounds, has more than enough size, strength and moxie to be nicknamed the Quiet Bad Boy. And competitive? This is a kid who, whenever he lost a one-on-one game to his older brother Mark, would immediately challenge him to a fight. ("He'd hold me in a hammerlock while I screamed and wiggled until I tired myself out," Joe says, laughing.) This is a kid who was such a big Dallas Cowboys fan, he used to cry when they lost. This is the man who puts himself through five hours a day of basketball and tennis — in the off-season. A man who, according to his mother, sat in a dark room all night after last week's loss to Chicago in Game 3 of the Eastern Conference finals. "He called to tell me he was just sitting there thinking about it," she says. "It bothered him so much."

Last year, in Game 6 of the NBA Finals, Dumars had the winning shot in his hands. It was an awkward try, a running banker that he put too hard off the glass. It ricocheted away, so did the game, and of course, two days later, so did the championship. The morning after the miss, Dumars came early to the Forum for practice. He lined up the shot again, same position, same basket. "I made it that time," he says, leaning back in the couch. "Then again, there was no James Worthy or Michael Cooper there."

And no Magic Johnson. This week, once again, Dumars will be called on for a defensive miracle. Air Jordan and Magic Johnson within five days? Sure. Why not give the guy a rope and tell him to lasso the moon? "It's like going from playing point guard to playing center," Dumars says of the switch. "Michael is right in front of you, but Magic tries to wear you down with his size and strength; he keeps backing in, backing in. I'm giving up six inches and a lot of pounds to him. You can wear yourself out pretty quick that way."

Then again, there's that competitiveness. Before Dumars' first professional game against the Lakers, he spoke to his father on the phone.

150

"I know you're a good player, son," Mr. Dumars said, "but I don't think you can hang with a Magic Johnson. I don't think you're ready for that."

"Yes, I am," Dumars said matter-of-factly.

He played a great game, he held Johnson in check, and 10 minutes after it was over, a phone rang in Natchitoches.

"See?"

"I'm sorry, son."

"That's OK."

If the Pistons should win this NBA championship, there will be only one hole in Joe Dumars' glory: Adrian Dantley won't be there to share it. Perhaps because they are both serious on the outside and semi-comical on the inside, perhaps because neither is fond of extra words, perhaps because their lockers were next to each other — whatever the reason, Dumars and Dantley became fast friends during Dantley's two years in Detroit. That was broken up with the trade of Dantley to Dallas 3½ months ago.

"It would definitely be a void winning without A.D.," Dumars says, nodding. "We used to talk so much about what it would be like to finally get that ring, you know, that ring that everybody's talking about.

"He used to say that if we won it, he would stand up on the table in the middle of the locker room and do something crazy. You know, start singing and dancing, scream and holler, something he'd never do any other time.

"I said, 'No, you wouldn't.'

"He said, 'Yes, I will.'

"I said, 'Bet me, so I'll be sure you'll back it up.'

"And he did. He bet me part of his playoff share — like $1,000. And with A.D., if you know him, well, you know he was serious if he did that."

There will be no dancing. Not from Dantley. The ex-Piston might come up to watch the NBA Finals. He might stay at Joe's apartment. But the post-championship celebration — if there is one — would be up to Dumars.

"Would you ever jump on the table and sing and dance?" he is asked.

"I don't think so," he says, breaking into a grin, "but then, you never know."

And that about sums it up. You never know. With Dumars, you never know anything. Those who think they have a fix on him are probably not even close. Quiet Joe, they say. Shy Joe. It is true, Dumars' basketball heroes are low-key defensive stars such as Maurice Cheeks and Bobby Jones.

It is also true that he drives a Jaguar.

Yes, Dumars is all business on the court, a professional's professional; he also once worked at Church's Fried Chicken.

True, he speaks softly and will never be accused of taking over a team meeting. Then again, he absolutely explodes in laughter at Redd Foxx playing Fred Sanford. "I don't know why that guy cracks me up so much, but he does," he says. On a radio talk show last winter, Dumars was presented with a surprise test: audio clips from the TV series. He was asked to identify the episode.

"Oh, man," he said, surprised, "well, all right, let's try it."

Not only did he get the episode, but he recited the lines word for word. With no preparation.

That is serious Sanford.

And this is serious business. An NBA title. Another chance at the glory rainbow. Joe Dumars does not dream of making the last shot, but he wouldn't mind making the final steal. And he sure would like a ring. "Let's face it, I don't figure to win a whole lot of individual awards in the NBA," he says. "A team championship would be the ultimate thing."

You almost have to hope he gets it. Here, in a league full of jammers and slammers, is a soft touch off the glass, a man without jewelry, a guy who values silence, proud and real. A guy true to his father, loyal to his friends, sweet on his hometown. Give him the parade. Let him ride in the limo. And when it's all over, he'll head right back to the Louisiana heat, peel off the long pants, grab a plate of crawfish and a dish of ice cream. Boopie, King of the Bayou, can celebrate like Mary Poppins' birthday. "Yeah," he says, smiling at the thought. The Joe Nobody Knows thinks that's just fine. ♦

LAKERS' MAGIC VANISHES AS PISTONS PULL AHEAD

June 9

James Worthy stood at the free throw line and dribbled the ball as if the world hung in the balance. Two seconds left. Two points down. The Pistons clenched their fists and mumbled silent prayers beneath the explosion of crowd noise. Suddenly, it was heart against heart; this series was more than basketball, it was character warfare. The Lakers already had lost Magic Johnson to a hamstring injury, and the Pistons had lost their last excuse. There could be no defeat now. Not with this advantage. Not with these circumstances. The basketball left Worthy's hands and arched toward the rim . . .

"I was saying, 'Miss it, miss it, miss it,'" admitted a tired but smiling Isiah Thomas, a bloody cut above his left eye, after Worthy did indeed miss it, and the Pistons held on to beat the Lakers, 108-105, to take a 2-0 lead in these NBA Finals. "When it rolled out, I said yeah. *YEAH!*"

Yeah. What did you expect, sympathy? Was there any sympathy when Detroit lost Thomas to injury in last year's championships? Was there any sympathy when Joe Dumars, born to be a hero, missed a shot that could have won it all last year in Game 6? None then. None now. Never mind that the Lakers showed enormous courage, hanging in despite Magic's absence (and the continued absence of their second-leading scorer, Byron Scott, also out with a hamstring injury) to nearly steal this game.

The Pistons were interested in only one type of courage: their own. So they clawed back from an early deficit, they scratched holes in the confidence of the two-time defending world champions. It was Isiah driving through the Lakers in the final moments, arching up a high toss and watching it fall. It was James Edwards rising high on Kareem Abdul-Jabbar to block his shot. It was Vinnie Johnson dashing downcourt and filling up the net with a short jumper. And it was Dumars, playing like a banshee, shooting out the lights when the Pistons needed it most — with Thomas on the bench in foul trouble. Sympathy? You must be joking.

"If we had lost this game it would have been demoralizing," said Vinnie Johnson. "We couldn't lose it, not once Magic went out (with 4:39 left in the third quarter). Maybe last year we would have lost it. But we've been there before now. We know this: You want to win this thing, you keep a team down when they're down. . . ." He sighed. "But I'll tell you man, those last

153

three minutes? I could barely breathe out there."

Isn't that right? Could you breathe watching it? All those explosions and emotions and shattered nerves? Isn't that the way you felt? The Pistons had battled back from a 10-point deficit to finally take the lead, 94-92, with 8:31 left. And from that point on, it was furious, crazy, dizzy basketball. Every shot was contested, body to body. The pressure hung like a lead amulet around the necks of every player out there, until finally, Worthy drew a foul from Dennis Rodman with two seconds left and the Pistons ahead, 106-104. Both sides were breathing heavily. "It felt good," Worthy would say of the shot.

It missed. Game 2 to the challengers.

And who knows what this might mean? NBA Finals are hard to predict, but when this one is all said and done, it might prove the critical turnaround. Oh, sure, the Pistons had proven volumes already, the best record in the NBA, the deepest bench, the tightest defensive squeeze. But the intangible the Lakers always held was attitude, championship brain cells, the kind that clicked in just in time for the desperation victory. This night, the voices were calling — *Arise, Lakers, show them who you are* — but suddenly, the Pistons were in the way.

Credit the team defense. Credit Thomas. And credit Dumars, who took over like the knight who grabbed the sword from the stone. Thomas went out less than three minutes into the game with his second foul. Up stepped Joe. Courageous? Just consider what he was up against. On offense: Michael Cooper, perhaps the best backcourt defender in the league. On defense: Magic Johnson, maybe the best player in history. No problem, right?

Dumars did not allow it to be. What a performance! During a critical stretch in the second period, when the Lakers threatened to run away, he almost single-handedly rammed the Pistons back into the game: a behind-the-back dazzle move, topped with a banker off the glass; a 15-foot jump shot; an offensive foul drawn on Mychal Thompson; a running two-hander over Tony Campbell; free throws, free throws, personal fouls, technical fouls, no problem, he'll shoot anything. And hit it. Dumars scored 26 points in the first half. Without him, the Pistons would have been long buried before Magic's hamstring gave out. Dumars finished with 33 — and so far, is the star of this series both offensively and defensively.

A word about Magic's injury: It does not cheapen the series, it is *part* of it. Certainly the Lakers are weaker without their starting backcourt. But that is not the Pistons' fault. You play the hand you were dealt. And this is where we stand. Detroit is going to LA with a 2-0 lead. Heart against heart, will against will. The Pistons are growing up before our very eyes.

Two down. Two to go. The heart of the challenger, beating louder now. We go on. ◆

NOT BAD, BOYS! PISTONS SWEEP LA FOR FIRST TITLE

June 14

INGLEWOOD, Calif. — In the end, there would be no denying them; they wanted this more than life itself. No more waiting. No more excuses. The Pistons were storming the throne room, grabbing the basketball, stealing it, owning it, banking it off glass, slamming it through the rim, counting the seconds until destiny lifted her veil and gave them that long-awaited kiss, smack on the lips.

One-two-three-four.

Champions.

"BAAAAD BOYS, BAAAAD BOYS," they sang, arm in arm on the bench, as the Pistons swept the Los Angeles Lakers in four games with a 105-97 victory to capture the NBA championship. *"WE'RE THE BAAAD BOYS!"*

Who in Detroit will ever forget? Our first NBA champions? This was the moment we had awaited forever, since the team was a laugh, since the roof collapsed on the arena, since the aura of champions used to leave them paralyzed. Not anymore.

Instead, on this magic night, against the defending world champions, it was captain Isiah Thomas down the middle like a bullet, driving, flipping, passing every Laker en route to a lay-up. And it was James Edwards, the symbol of bench strength, towering over the opponents, blocking shots, slamming in baskets so hard it brought tears to your eyes. And it was Joe Dumars, sudden hero, proving that Bad Boys can be good, shooting and driving and finally, when that buzzer sounded, finding a camera to say, "I'm going to Disney World!" although, to tell the truth, after this, Disney World will be a letdown.

One-two-three-four.

Champions.

"What did that final minute feel like?" someone asked John Salley in the champagne-soaked dressing room after the game.

"TOO ... LONG!" he said, laughing.

Doesn't that sum it all up? How long had they waited? At the buzzer, Thomas was in tears. Rick Mahorn was grabbing everybody in sight. While Forum fans watched in desperation, Pistons fans watched in unbridled glee back home, 21,000-plus filling the Palace to watch the game *on television.*

How long had we waited? That's how long, America. Television.
Champions.

"I can't describe it, I can't," said Thomas, his face dripping champagne.
"We did everything we had to do."

And how fitting an ending! Here in Game 4 was a finale that symbolized
Detroit's rise to the top — a climb from the very bottom. The Pistons were
swamped early by a tenacious Lakers team, they were scratched, clawed,
bloodied. Michael Cooper threw punches at Mahorn, Kareem Abdul-Jabbar
threw elbows at Mahorn — and suddenly the Lakers were miles ahead, a
16-point lead in the second quarter.

But live and learn. These are no longer green kids, no longer awestruck
by Lakers or Celtics. They are playoff veterans, every sweaty inch of them.
And so they came back: Thomas, little big man, rising over Abdul-Jabbar to
strip a rebound; Bill Laimbeer driving in for a breakaway lay-up; Dumars
rising like destiny, banking a shot off the glass from a ridiculous angle, in it
went, and the foul, thank you. Slowly the Lakers' lead was peeled away like
unneeded skin, the Pistons were being hatched as world beaters, one
basket, one game, one delicious moment at a time.

One-two-three-four.
Champions.

A sweep? Who would have predicted a sweep? Even the pundits who cite
the Lakers' injuries can't find fault with perfection. Play four, win four. The
Pistons survived everything the NBA could throw at them — the Central
Division, Michael Jordan, the referees, James Worthy — and finally,
wonderfully, they were hugging and crying and singing like Christmas.

"SMELLS LIKE WORLD CHAMPIONS IN HERE!" yelled Mark
Aguirre, dousing himself with the bubbly.

"BAAAAD BOYS! BAAAAAD BOYS!" came the response.

One-two-three-four.
Champions.

How wonderful, finally, for these Pistons players who, in the three-year
climb to this mountain, have endured everything from Celtic
leprechauns to Jack Nicholson. How great for the centers: Laimbeer,
everybody's villain, a guy who proved that slow and earthbound can still get
a ring, and Edwards, the oldest guy on the team, who began his career
under the tutelage of Abdul-Jabbar and won a ring in Abdul-Jabbar's farewell
performance. He played the game of his life, scoring 13 points, all in the
fourth quarter, to seal the victory. "I have never played more intense
basketball," he said, blinking champagne from his eyes. "This is so great!"

For the forwards: Mahorn, who had to watch much of last year's final
series on his stomach because of a back injury, now standing upright, waving
and slamming his big body; and Aguirre, a supposed head-case who found

that less can indeed be more, because now, as a role player, he has what he never achieved as a point-scorer in Dallas: a championship. Did you see him at the end, looking like a man who had just woke up in heaven?

For the X-factors, Salley and Dennis Rodman. Their very arrival three years ago signaled the final touches of this championship blueprint. There they were, Rodman playing through painful back spasms, Salley called upon early, responding with a slam, a jumper. How fitting that they have both matured just in time to grab the brass ring. Dennis, of course, will probably hang from it. Salley will turn it into a commercial.

And then, of course, there are the guards. Where would the Pistons be without them in this series? Thomas' gamesmanship, his direction, his confidence, coupled with Dumars' deadeye shooting, his gluey defense — and of course Vinnie Johnson's lava-flow offense. Be honest. When these three are cooking, is there a better backcourt anywhere in basketball? Anywhere in this decade?

And how fitting that, for all the years that Thomas had to carry this team, he finally reached the end of the rainbow by holding the door for Dumars, his quiet, less-noticed backcourt mate, who upped his game and collected the series MVP award. Isiah always said the team would win this title, not him. The Pistons proved it.

"What was the sweetest moment out there for you?" Thomas was asked.

"When I lost it and started crying," he smiled, almost crying again. "It was just that everything inside of me burst out. It was everything I had ever wanted."

And how about Dumars? What a series! Shooting on the run, on the jump, off the dribble, the high, delicious, arching shots that drop through like daggers. His steady hand brought the Pistons back from the pits — as it had led them, really, all series. MVP? You betcha. He had promised if the Pistons won he would finally do something crazy. "Did you do it?" he was asked.

"Nah, I just came in and lay down for a second," he answered, smiling.
Champions.

And how about the coach, Daddy Rich, Chuck Daly? How long has he waited for this? His whole life? He had never won a championship of any kind as a head coach — not in high school, college, the pros. He knew he had a first-class roster, but he remained self-effacing all season, convinced, it seemed, that if he allowed even the slightest show of optimism, God would strike him down for being cocky. When the buzzer finally sounded, the veneer finally cracked, he grinned, he smiled, he hugged.

He got soaked.

"We poured so much champagne on Chuck," gushed assistant coach Brendan Suhr, "he looks like Pat Riley now!"
Champions.

157

Nationally they will be writing about the Pistons as the New Kings in Town, but in Detroit people know this has been stewing for nearly a year. The Pistons probably deserved to win the crown last season, but life and referees and injuries are not always fair: The Pistons lost in seven games.

"Winning four," said a wizened Thomas this time, "is so much sweeter after you've lost four. Believe me."

Injuries? Forget about injuries. Asterisks? There will be none on this series. Sure, it would have been better had Magic Johnson been healthy and played in all the games. Sure, it would have been better had Byron Scott been healthy and played. Sure, sure, and so what? Wouldas and couldas are worthless now, just as they were worthless last year, when a gimpy-ankled Thomas had to struggle through Game 7 and watch his dreams dashed on the rocks.

A word here, however, for the Lakers. They played valiantly, with pride. Missing their starting backcourt, they played Game 4 like the champions they were, bursting out like wounded tigers, clawing and swiping, grabbing a 16-point lead, surrendering every ounce of desire before finally surrendering the keys to the kingdom. History will only weep that Abdul-Jabbar could not have exited in a more noble fashion than a sweep. But he is a sportsman, and all sportsmen know that time will catch you eventually. At 42, he bowed out to a younger team, and that is probably the way it should be.

On his way back from the 1,000th interview, Dumars cut through a training room, carrying his MVP trophy. There, alone, sat A.C. Green, his head in his hands.

"Hey, A.C.," Dumars said.

"Nice going, Joe. You earned it."

"Thanks, man," he said, and they shook hands.

Remember that scene. And remember these: Salley, center court, arms as high as skyscrapers. Isiah driving like a whippet. Dumars letting go a rainbow. Mahorn bumping for position, Laimbeer firing a three-pointer, Rodman up in the clouds for a rebound, Vinnie shooting in the face of countless defenders. And finally, all of them, veterans and rookies alike, in that soaking, sweet sing-song that tells the world who now sits on the throne.

Here's to a team of aggressive, sweaty, funny, spirited, driving, leaping, and finally dancing basketball heroes, who learned this night that you can't always get what you want, but if you try sometimes, you get what you deserve. Bad Boys, Best Boys, you know the rest, Boys:

One-two-three-four.

Champions. ♦

AMID THE CELEBRATION, PISTONS LOSE MAHORN

June 16

Just a moment ago, he was dancing. Just a moment ago, he was spraying champagne on his teammates, laughing with those gap-teeth, shaking his big body and singing, *"BAAAD BOYS! BAAAD BOYS!"* Just a moment ago, Rick Mahorn was the muscle around the heart of the Pistons' brand-new NBA championship team.

And now he is gone.

So much for fantasy. Welcome back to real life. On the day of their championship parade, their love dance with the city of Detroit, Pistons management rolled the dice and lost: Mahorn was left unprotected in the expansion draft — which for some ridiculous reason is held before the hangovers wear off from the NBA Finals — and the Minnesota Timberwolves, a team that doesn't even have uniforms yet, plucked the baddest of our Bad Boys right off the shelf.

"It's . . . a business deal," said a crushed Mahorn as he tried to drive away from the Palace celebration amid throngs of people who were cheering and waving banners, unaware that their hero had just been stolen.

Mahorn looked away. He had his hands on the wheel and a bag of souvenirs on the seat and he was trying not to cry in front of a TV camera and this was wrong, all wrong. It doesn't matter how mean and nasty his reputation, it doesn't matter if his back injury makes him questionable. He had just touched the end of the rainbow, the dream of every kid who ever laced up a basketball sneaker. All this — the cheers, the parade, the glory — was paradise.

And he was being thrown out.

Shouldn't there be a moratorium on this kind of news? Shouldn't we be able to celebrate for one solid day, for 24 hours, without some poke in the ribs from the real world?

Instead, this. Farewell, Rickey. He goes from the best team in basketball to surely one of the worst. Just a moment ago, he was on the podium in front of delirious fans, leading them in a Bad Boys cheer. He walked over to coach Chuck Daly, shook his hand, and said, "Thank you for having faith in me." He walked over to general manager Jack McCloskey, grabbed his hand and said, "Thanks for sticking with me through my weight problem." He was the Bad Boy turned good, the thug in the movies who, in the final scene, reveals his tender side.

And gets shot in the heart.

It's a sad, sad day," said McCloskey, backed against a wall in a Palace hallway. "We feel like we're being penalized for having depth."

He shook his head. He tried to explain. He said he had been on the phone all morning and afternoon — even on the parade float — trying to work out a deal with Minnesota to keep the Timberwolves from taking Mahorn. But it was his decision to leave Mahorn unprotected in the first place, and there is no way to minimize the impact. It was like throwing tear gas at a wedding.

Why Rickey? The starting forward? McCloskey says his bad back was part of the reason. But there is more to a player than his anatomy. What about his heart? On the court, Mahorn was the symbol of Pistons toughness. You did not mess with him and you did not mess with this team. Intimidation plays a big part in victory; the Pistons now are a lot less vicious.

Not to mention Mahorn's basketball skills. "What he does won't show up in the stat sheet," said a saddened Joe Dumars. Things like setting picks. And defense, the essence of Pistons basketball. It was Mahorn who drew assignments such as Patrick Ewing of the Knicks and James Worthy of the Lakers. Who will do that now?

The Pistons knew they'd have to leave some good player unprotected (they could protect eight), to preserve the likes of Dennis Rodman, John Salley and the starters. Vinnie Johnson's playoff performance almost guaranteed his protection. So many thought the man to go would be James Edwards, the backup center.

No knock on Edwards, who is a wonderful player and a class guy, but he is 33 years old (Mahorn is 30), he makes $800,000 a year (as opposed to Mahorn's $600,000) and he is mostly effective off the bench. An expansion team looking for starters, leaders and affordable salaries might be more likely to pass on Edwards. Hey. The whole thing is a gamble. You try to offer guys the expansion teams won't take.

But Mahorn? A veteran? A starter? An outspoken leader in the locker room?

He was gone like ice cream on a hot afternoon.

Just a moment ago he was throwing elbows, then laughing when the opponent tried to retaliate. Just a moment ago he was backing in on Kareem Abdul-Jabbar and canning a jumper. Just a moment ago he was screaming in the time-out huddle: "ONE MORE MINUTE! NO LET-UP!"

He was a symbol of what the right team can do for the wrong guy. He arrived four years ago, fat, unhappy, traded from Washington. He did not want to be here. That first season he kept to himself, and fans wondered whether the Pistons had picked up a flabby, mean-looking mistake.

But teammates. They'll get you. And the Pistons got to Mahorn, implored him to play harder, convinced him he was needed, but that he had to pull his share. He lost weight, he improved his defense, he signed on for the long haul. And he became a player.

Now, before they even put the ring on his finger, he is gone. The news jolted the Pistons in mid-celebration. They entered their locker room drunk with glee, the whole city loved them, this was the best. And they emerged, minutes later, as if there had been a death in the family.

Which, in a way, there had.

Perhaps, in time, this will be seen as an unavoidable business move. Now it just stinks. Why Rickey? Why now? Why must a harmless, wonderful day of celebration take a shot to the stomach?

It doesn't seem fair. It isn't. Just a moment ago, he was on the Palace podium, microphone in hand, leading the crowd in a chorus of *"BAAAD BOYS!"* Suddenly, to everyone's delight, he leaned over and kissed each of his teammates, one at a time, cheek to cheek. The toughest, roughest Piston? Cheek to cheek?

How sad.

He had no idea he was kissing them all good-bye. ♦

IT'S 13 THROWS TO GLORY ON TROON'S SIXTH HOLE

July 20

TROON, Scotland — Cinderella story. Former sports writer. About to become the British Open cham–.

OK. So I exaggerate. A little. But I was out there, preparing to tee off — and not just any hole, either. I was on the longest hole in the history of British Opens, the famous sixth hole at Royal Troon, a whopping 577 yards to the green. Long? Can we talk long? This thing is so long that, during World War II, they used the beach alongside it for hand-grenade practice. And I am not making this up.

Did I mention I am the world's worst golfer?

Actually, that's not true. I look up to the world's worst golfer. I'd be honored to carry his bag. I do not love to play golf. My boss loves to play golf. He sends me to these exotic golf courses, then yells at me for not appreciating them. I think it's in his contract.

Anyhow, I was determined to get the feel of this course before the Open. And the locals told me, "Go to the sixth hole." (Actually, they said, "Goo toooda sixth hooole," which is the way they talk over here. But that is another story.)

So is the way I play golf. Let me say there is no way I can play a hole 577 yards long. I have trouble with the windmills on the putt-putt course. Besides, I didn't have any clubs.

Throw it.

"Throw it?" said my colleague Jim, a writer from Florida.

"Why not?" I said. "This is such a big hole? Let's see how many throws it takes from tee to green."

"Throw it?" he said.

"Got any golf balls?"

Now I thought this was a good idea. After all, the way I play golf, my throw is my best shot. So I walked to the souvenir stand and purchased one Maxfli golf ball. Cost me four bucks. That did not include the fish and chips, which I ate, because a man should not play golf on an empty stomach. Also the baked potato. And the ice cream cone. Hey. It's a big hole.

And off we walked. And walked. And walked. Finally, we found the sixth tee.

"Where's the green?" I asked, squinting.

Jim pointed. "Straight ahead. On the horizon. See that mountain? . . ."

"All right, all right. Let's get started."

I stepped up, palmed the ball and rolled it between my fingers. I gazed at the beautiful Firth of Clyde. I gazed at the undulating hills of this famous hole. I thought of Nicklaus. I thought of Watson. I thought of Koufax.

I threw it.

"FORE!" I yelled.

(I should explain that, as this was late afternoon, few people were on the course. Just a small army of groundskeepers who looked at me, shrugged and reached in their buckets for another batch of dirt.)

And the ball landed.

And rolled into the rough.

"That's about 40 yards," Jim said, scribbling in his pad. "Only 537 to go."

"Hmmm," I said. I walked to the ball, picked it up and threw it again, a high pop-up. It bounced about 35 yards away and landed in the rough.

Another throw. Middle of the fairway. Another throw. Back in the rough. Another throw. Sand trap.

"Any sight of the green?" I asked, panting.

"Not yet."

"We still in Scotland?"

"I think so."

Now for those who appreciate the fine art of throwing the golf ball, let me assure you I mixed my tosses the way a pro would mix his clubs. I tried the famous lefty toss (27 yards), the sidearm whip (45 yards) and the ever-popular grounder to short (39 yards, four divots). Earlier, Greg Norman claimed this course was so hard and fast, "I could hit a 400-yard drive — 280 in the air and 120 on the roll."

Yeah. Maybe. But did he ever try a curveball?

"Look!" Jim said, after my 10th throw skipped through the dandelions and into the fairway and nested just above a bunker. And there it was. About 100 yards away. The flag. It was calling to me in a sweet voice. "Underhand," it cooed. "Underhand."

I whipped it underhand, the ball rolled, skipped and reached the lip of the green. Now was the time for the pitching wedge; or in my case, the pitch. I tossed meekly and watched the ball plop and roll toward the cup, toward the cup . . . past the cup, past the cup.

"How many is that?" I asked.

"Twelve," Jim said.

I dropped to my knees. I examined the lie. "It hooks a little right. This could be tricky."

I closed one eye, took a deep breath and, using only the golf tools that

God gave me, flicked my middle finger off my thumb, as if shooting a crumb off the table.

Ker-plunk.

It's in the hole.

And there you have it. Thirteen strokes — er, throws — to glory. "Nice putting," Jim said, and I accepted his congratulations. The longest hole in British Open history. We had tamed it. The groundskeepers stared at us, shrugged and threw more dirt.

We walked home. Unappreciative, boss? Ha. I might never be a great golfer. I might never even be a great golf-watcher. But for one brief and shining moment I played Troon, my way, and Greg Norman could not have done it any better.

Bo Jackson maybe, but not Greg Norman. ♦

YANKEE TOPPLES AUSSIES IN A WILD BRITISH FINISH

July 24

TROON, Scotland — All he needed was a miracle — another miracle, we should say, because he had already seen a few on this magic afternoon: a flying chip shot that landed smack in the cup, a 40-foot par putt that even he didn't dream of making. Now, here, on the 18th hole — the second time he had played it in less than an hour — Mark Calcavecchia glanced at the cloudless sky and lined up the shot: five-iron. Two-hundred and one yards to the green. Whack!

"I'll never forget it," he would recall. "I watched it rise, on a perfect line to the stick, and I said to myself, 'Well, that's it, that's the best I got, I don't even care where it lands, I can't hit it any better than that.' I mean, it was weird."

Weird? Yes. Wonderful? Absolutely. For here was a British Open finale so unusual, only an American could win it, so dramatic, only Greg Norman could lose it, so entertaining, that three men were called back for an encore: Norman, Calcavecchia and Wayne Grady, all tied at 275. Playoff time, gentlemen. Four holes. May the best golfer win.

Before it was over, each would have golden chances. There would be bunkers and rough grass and horrible luck. It would end wonderfully, historically, but even the winner will tell you it wasn't how it ended but how it got there that was the story.

And, oh, man, what a story . . .

Let us pick up on the 17th hole in regulation play, where Grady, from Australia, was walking down the fairway, clinging to a one-shot lead. A relative unknown, he had been in front since the second day of this tournament. "He'll choke," critics whispered. Indeed, Grady had finished second 26 times in his career. From inside the clubhouse, Norman studied his countryman and rubbed his chin. "You don't root for another golfer to do badly," he said later. "Well . . . yes you do."

Not that you could blame him. What a day Norman had! Came out smoking, birdied the first six holes. By the time the bookmakers finished gagging (they'd made him a 25-1 shot), he'd birdied three more, was 13 under and was inside the Royal Troon Golf Club, sipping a Coke in front of the TV set. This was the masterful golf that Norman always has been capable of — when his reputation as second banana wasn't tripping him up.

How many times had Norman just missed at majors? The PGA. The Masters. The U.S. Open. Some called him a choker; some called him the unluckiest man in golf. His fate, this time, was in Grady's hands, and Grady's hands were shaking. A two-stroke lead had shriveled to one, thanks to a bogey on the 14th, and the 17th had been his undoing all week. He glanced at the leader board. Norman. He kept seeing that name. Norman. Norman.

Poor guy. He'd been playing all day with Tom Watson, whom everyone wanted to win this tournament. Even when Watson lost his putting touch and fell hopelessly behind, the crowds cheered louder for him than for Grady. And Grady was the leader!

Still, his 15-foot putt for par looked good as it rolled toward the 17th hole. So good, in fact, that Grady began walking toward it, about to shake a fist in triumph. But the ball rolled over the hole and two feet past. "OOOH!" The gallery let out a collective groan. "I swear a ghost poked that out," Grady would say. Back in the clubhouse, Norman put down the Coke and headed for the practice green. He allowed a smile. His day was not over yet.

All this would be drama enough. But somehow lost in this Australian showdown was Calcavecchia, a freckle-faced Floridian who had never won a major in his life. At 29, he was already a reformed beer-drinker, a reformed junk-fooder and a reformed carouser. "I used to do things on a golf course that I absolutely deserved to get punched for," he would admit.

Irreverent, overweight and flaunting a self-taught golf swing that looked, well, self-taught, he lost his PGA Tour card five times from 1981 to 1985. Made little money. The top players ignored him the way you ignore the class slob.

In the last few years, however, he turned his life around. Got married. Cut down on the beer. Lost weight. Worked on his game. He and his wife, Sheryl, are expecting their first child any day. Calcavecchia (which in Italian means "old shoe") didn't want to play here, for fear of missing the birth. His wife insisted. "Something good is going to happen to you there," she told him. "I feel it."

N ow, on the 18th fairway, he was about to prove her right. Amazing. Just seven holes earlier, Calcavecchia had been hacking away, from the grass to the gallery to a thorn bush so sharp he had to wear a coat to protect his arms as he swung. Just as it seemed time to pack it up, he made the 40-footer for par on No. 11, then came to the 12th and hit his approach shot into the rough. "Great," he mumbled. From a grassy hill to the right of the green, he slapped a desperation wedge shot.

And something happened. It flew 60 feet in the air, a perfect arch, and came down in the cup like something out of a Roger Rabbit cartoon. Kerplop. Birdie. Not even a bounce. "I was more embarrassed than anything else," Calcavecchia would say. "I mean, how lucky can you get?"

Cue the music, and we'll see. He took that birdie, took another on 16, and on 18, he lofted an eight-iron as true as love itself, and it plopped down, from 161 yards away, to within four feet of the pin. "The second I saw the putt I said, 'That baby's not going anywhere but the middle of the hole,' " he said.

It did. He was tied with the Australians. To put it in American-ese, he was going to extra innings.

They have never before used a four-hole playoff in the history of the British Open. But then, what a perfect time for change. Hadn't this been Scottish golf under South American skies? Sunshine? No wind? No wonder all this strange stuff was happening.

The format was to replay Holes 1, 2, 17 and 18. Calcavecchia looked in his bag and saw he had only three balls left. "I had to borrow some from Tom Watson," he said.

Not that it seemed to matter. Norman began the way he'd left regulation — with a birdie — and Calcavecchia and Grady both made pars. On No. 2, Norman sank a 30-foot putt for another birdie — does this guy ever quit? — and surely now he had proved himself, the golf gods would let him have his major. The night before, no less than Jack Nicklaus, Ray Floyd and Tom Weiskopf had all personally urged him on. "I was," Norman would admit, "feeling pretty confident."

Calcavecchia matched Norman's birdie with one of his own, a 30-foot putt that made your heart race. Grady managed par and fell two behind. He sighed. Forget it. After leading this championship for more than two days, he was doomed, by one lousy putt, to be a footnote.

On to 17. Norman chipped to within 12 feet, and — look at this — he missed the putt! Bogey! Calcavecchia, meanwhile, rolled a 45-footer to within a half-inch of the hole. He tapped in for par.

One hole left. Tie score.

D o you feel destiny owes you one?" somebody would ask Norman when this was all over.

"Bleep," he would answer, with a look that could melt steel, "I'd say destiny owes me about four, wouldn't you?"

Hard to argue. At least if you watched the 18th. Norman, whose only major title remains the 1986 British, cracked his tee shot so hard, the ball almost split apart. It bounced in the middle of the fairway — "Great shot, Greg!" fans yelled — and then continued to roll, too fast, like a marble, and look out . . . it dropped in a bunker, 325 yards from the tee.

"The bunker!" Norman would moan, shaking his head. "I didn't even think about reaching the bunker." But there lay his ball, and there lay his chances, at the bottom of a four-foot straight drop of sand that was impossible to overcome. His heart sank. The bunker?

167

From that point, all Calcavecchia needed was to look to the heavens and wink. His final miracle came — where we began — on the approach shot to the green, a five-iron so perfect, it seemed drawn by magnetic force. It landed on the green and rolled to within seven feet of the pin as the grandstand crowd squealed with delight. Norman thrashed in the sand — a beached shark — sending the ball sailing to another bunker, then slapping it from there over the green and out of bounds. He finally surrendered. Calcavecchia stood, holding his club, in a momentary daze. "I suddenly realized I could three-putt and still win the British Open," he would say. "I was just praying I wouldn't hit the ball twice on the same stroke."

As you know by now, he needn't have worried. He dropped the putt clean and true, and captured the title that had eluded all Americans since Watson won it in 1983. "WELL DONE, MARK!" they spelled out on the scoreboard. In the press tent afterward, he sneaked a phone call to his wife back in Phoenix — "She was crying her eyes out" — and when he emerged, the new champion was crying, himself. He asked for a handkerchief and honked his nose.

"I always said if I ever got in a playoff I'd choke," he said, with refreshing candor. "To think I'm gonna have my name on this trophy . . . my god."

What else can you say? What a finish! Outside, Norman waited for his car, forcing a grin. He accepted condolences, but he is tired of condolences. He had leap-frogged 19 golfers in one day to reach that playoff, only to die in sand. Alongside him stood Grady, his fellow Aussie, who always will wonder what slipped through his fingers. They had waged a beautiful war and had lost only because someone must lose.

And someone must win. "You guys will probably think I'm crazy," said Calcavecchia, the onetime Big Mac-junkie, "but if I got the call last night that Sheryl was in labor, I'd have been on the plane home this morning."

And missed this? No way. Troon, thy name was drama. Sometime soon, a baby will be born, and Daddy will tell it one heck of a bedtime story. ♦

ON THE BUS, IF YOU CAN'T SLEEP, YOU CAN DREAM

August 18

H IGHWAY 26, South Carolina — *Dear Boss:*
I was bumping along next to Gene Roof, the lanky, curly-haired
manager of the Fayetteville Generals, and he was telling me the best
bus story he knows. Texas League. Double-A. One morning around 3, they
pulled into this motel in El Paso, and one of the players glanced out the
window and yelled, "Hey, look! That guy's got a gun!"

By the time the others looked up, the man was gone, so nobody believed
him. Heck, they'd been riding for 10 hours; everyone was punchy. Roof and
a couple of guys walked into the office.

Nobody at the desk. Cash register spilled over. Gagging sounds coming
from the back room.

"We found these two guys tied up, facedown on the carpet, just like in
the movies," Roof said, shaking his head. "They'd been held up. The
weirdest thing was, there were two cops staking out the place across the
street. But they fell asleep and missed the whole thing."

He laughed. "Needless to say, we didn't sleep too good that night."

That was 10 years ago. Since that time Roof has been up and down the
mountain, played at every level of the minors, gotten his brief and shining
moment in the Show, the big leagues, the St. Louis Cardinals and Montreal
Expos. Once, against Chicago, bottom of the eighth, bases loaded, he leapt
into the Wrigley Field ivy and caught a Bobby Bonds blast, one-handed, for
the third out.

"We were in the pennant race, so they showed it on every TV station
around the country," he said. "I shoulda taped it while I had the chance."

He sighed and watched the windshield wipers flap back and forth. The
highway rumbled beneath our feet.

I f you took all the mileage on a minor leaguer's body, you could probably
travel from here to the moon. Think of the trips! From Greensboro to
Augusta, from Little Rock to El Paso — and always, always, on the Bus. It
has become the rolling symbol of the bushes: 47 seats, eight wheels and one
bathroom. The bus is the line between the Big Time and those who still
dream of it.

Down here in A-ball, they're still dreaming. So we left early in the
morning, from the hotel parking lot, where most of the players were

swigging chocolate milk and eating Egg McMuffins. And within a half-hour of gentle highway rocking, they were asleep. Some had their mouths open. Some had Walkmans plugged in their ears, and you could hear the muffled lullaby of rock guitars and drums.

Roof couldn't sleep, and neither could I, so we sat up front and talked about the road. "Some of those trips in Texas," he said softly, "eight or nine hours, I don't know how we did it. Guys used to pass a tequila bottle and see who got stuck drinking the worm.

"For a while, I traveled with an inflatable raft, the kind they use for swimming pools. I'd blow it up and lie in the aisle and try to sleep. Then, for a while, some of us tried crawling in the luggage compartment up above. Like those."

He pointed, and I did a double take. You'd need a crowbar to get in there! "Yeah," he said, laughing, "after a few hours, you'd get a charley horse, start screaming, and it would take four guys to pull you out."

I watched Roof as he hitched his feet up on the railing and tapped on the window. He is a pleasant man from Kentucky, and by all accounts a pretty decent ballplayer. But he is 31, and to be 31 in the minors is to be resigned to the sidelines. It means you ride in the front of the bus.

And then, boss, I got to thinking. I'm 31.

We rolled through South Carolina, past gas stations and fast-food joints. This was not France. This was not countryside you brag about. This was just mileage from one stadium to the next, from one turn at the plate to another somewhere else, while you stare out the window and dream of the future. All those miles. All those nameless ballparks and gnat-filled dugouts.

"You know," Roof said, looking back on his sleeping team, "if you have any kind of heart, you have to feel for these kids. They're busting a gut trying to make it, living off no money. And nobody back where you come from even knows their name."

I nodded. And then I thought: Shoot, nobody knows Gene Roof, either. What kind of credit does he get? I thought about all those guys in the majors who take the good life for granted. And I looked again at that overhead rack that Roof once slept in. It hardly seems fair.

But that's just sentiment, I guess, and there's not a lot of time for that down here. Last night, a young prospect named Mickey Delas, a big, grinning catcher from Roseville, Mich., got called up to Lakeland. Promoted. One step closer to the Show. The last thing Roof said to him was on the bus back from the game. He pulled the mike from the mini-P.A. and said, "Mickey, don't forget to pay your clubhouse dues before you leave."

That's baseball. They come and they go. And the bus rolls on.

See ya later,

Mitch ◆

A JOURNEY TO THE BUSHES RETORES FAITH IN THE GAME

August 20

C OLUMBIA, S.C. — *Dear Guys:*
I'm leaving you. Actually, by the time you read this, I'll be on a plane back home. I appreciate your letting me wear the uniform and sit in the dugout the other night, just like a real player. And thanks for letting me hang out with you after the games at the Steak-n-Egg. Not that there was much to eat. I mean, let's face it; that steak was still moving. But, hey, $11 a day in meal money? How far does that go?

I appreciate your filling me in on the secrets of the minor leagues. Like how to chew raw tobacco. And what seat to grab on the bus. I also know never to switch bats in the middle of a hitting streak.

But I believe in luck, guys, and I think mine is working against you. In less than a week since I showed up to examine life in Class A ball, the Fayetteville Generals have lost three in a row and had one rained out. I call that bad luck, don't you?

Heck, you guys taught me about luck. DeSilva, you can't even pitch a game without first playing your lucky pinball for an hour. And Erickson? You get a hot bat, you do everything but sleep with it. Cole? You told me if you have a good night, you'll walk to the plate in the exact same steps the next night and the next, until you cool off. And Steve Carter? Weren't you the guy who told me, "The Generals are 9-0 when we visit shopping malls the day of the game"?

Until I showed up.

We went to the mall Wednesday.

You lost, 15-2.

S o it's time for me to collect my notes and my box scores and my pizza-stained T-shirts and get lost. Not that I'm crazy about leaving. Oh, it's true, I never really liked the South, and I'm not wild about hot, humid weather that makes the hair on your arms frizz. And there's not much appeal in empty ballparks and motels that smell like cleaning fluid.

And, yet, I liked my five days with your team. I can't explain why. Maybe it's the smell of pine tar and tobacco juice. Maybe it's those ballparks, hot summer nights, where they play a scratchy recording of the national anthem and everyone sings along. Maybe it's watching the manager, Gene Roof, waving his arms and yelling: "Back up, dummy! Back up!" And the rightfielder can actually hear him. Remember that, D–.

Uh, never mind.

I'll tell you this: You can have the gnats. I've never seen gnats like that. What do you have behind that dugout? A swamp? I must have smacked myself in the face a dozen times trying to kill those things. Hey, guys, ever hear of a Shell No-Pest Strip?

Gnats? They didn't show gnats in "Bull Durham." But then a lot of that movie was fantasy, wasn't it? So many people saw it and came away saying, "So that's what the minors are really like." In fact, maybe that's part of the reason I came to live with the Generals. To see whether it was true.

Here is my verdict: Bull who?

For one thing, I didn't see many groupies, and I certainly didn't see any Susan Sarandon look-alikes. Oh, you told me about a girl who hangs around Fayetteville, N.C. But you said she looked like — what was it now? — "someone tried to put a fire out on her face." Gosh. She must be swell.

As for those "Bull Durham" radio broadcasts, with the guy making sound effects in the booth — cracking wood, banging on cabinets? Come on. It's the minor leagues, not Time Tunnel. The station might broadcast only from the press box to the Dunkin' Donuts, but it's real radio.

Remember the night I asked for the biggest lie in "Bull Durham"? Mark Ettles, the relief pitcher from Australia, didn't miss a beat.

"The biggest lie in that movie is that a guy can go from A-ball to the major leagues in one step."

When he said it, you all nodded in agreement.

"Yeah, Mark."

"Amen."

It was then I realized that waiting for your chance is the hardest part of minor league baseball.

Not that you guys don't have a good time waiting. There are the pool halls. And Taco Bell. And the card games on the bus. And I'll never forget sitting with Duane Walker, the muscular outfielder from Florida, as he told me about Mudslinging.

"We only do it after it rains. We drive a Jeep back behind the stadium — there's these mud fields back there — and we start whipping around in the Jeep, bouncing all over, spitting up mud from the tires."

"This is fun?" I asked.

"Yeah. It's like a roller coaster. Or it was, until we got stuck last night. The Jeep hit a ridge, and we couldn't move it. We had to get out and push, all of us, knee deep in mud, with mosquitoes eating us alive."

"Sounds great," I said.

"Yeah," he said, laughing, "life in the minor leagues."

Life in the minor leagues. I've used that phrase a lot in the last five days.

Some people think it means the glamorous life of a pro athlete. I think it means this: Sleep till noon, watch some TV, get some lunch, wait around till 4 o'clock, bum a ride to the park, stretch, warm up, play the game, pray you get a hit, pray that somebody is watching, shower, eat some fast food before the last place closes, call home, talk to Mom and Dad, tell them that any day now you might get moved up. And go to sleep.

It is not what I call glamorous. It is not what you call glamorous. They can make all the movies they want: four men to a trailer, with pale carpeting and a overhead fan? Let's see Kevin Costner live in that for a while.

Listen, guys. I want to admit something. I collected some of your conversations. Had a few favorites, too. Like the time Mark Cole and Anthony Toney were eating Mexican food and talking about everybody's dream, getting called to the major leagues.

"When Mike Schwabe got called up? I heard it took him 20 minutes before he believed they were serious."

"Shoot, you wouldn't have to tell me but one time."

"You got that."

"I'd be gone like (clap) that!"

"Ha ha!"

"I wouldn't be sitting there goin': 'Really? Really? Are you kidding?' "

"No way."

"Be gone like (clap) that!"

"Like that."

"Yeah."

"Shoot."

"(Clap) Like that."

"You want another margarita?"

"Yep."

And then, there was the conversation on the three-hour bus ride from Fayetteville to Columbia:

"Hey, Duane, what you reading?"

"Stephen King."

"Lemme see. . . . Damn, this is big! You readin' this or just carrying it for weight?"

"I'm reading it."

"Wow! . . . You need one of them pesauras things with this, right?"

"Huh?"

"What do they call that, a pesauras? A sauras? What the hell they call that?"

"A thesaurus."

"A what?"

"A thesaurus."

173

"Yeah. One of them. Whatever. You need one?"

I've seen a lot of interesting baseball the last five days. I didn't know there were so many ways to overthrow the first baseman. And then there was the game you lost when Leo Torres threw that wild pitch with the bases loaded. Poor Leo. The look on his face when that ball sailed over the catcher's mitt.

But that's what the minor leagues are for, right? Learning. Working out the kinks. There were some good moments, too. Like when Anthony stole three bases in one game and everybody congratulated him. That kid can fly.

There was all that time between games, too, like when we bused to the bank to cash your paychecks (nobody has cars, so you ride the bus or walk). And then you persuaded the driver to take you to the local shopping mall, so you could spend some of that $225 a week. Hey, Cole. Remember when you tried on that sweat suit, then took it off, then tried it on again, then took it off and kept looking at the $100 price tag?

"Hey, Mitch," you finally asked me, "is there any way you can like, you know, put this on your expense account?"

Good try, kid.

I don't think so.

Then there was the night that a buzz went through the dugout because one of you was being moved up to the Lakeland, Fla., club. Who was it? Whom did they pick? It was Mickey Delas, the big, broad-shouldered catcher with the Cheshire-cat grin.

"Didya hear?

"Mickey's goin' up."

"Yeah. Why him, man?"

"Yeah?"

I caught up with Delas that night, as he was heading to his room. He could hardly stop smiling. "When Gene called me in, I thought I was in trouble. Then he said to me, 'You're going up.' I couldn't believe it! I'm three steps away now from the big leagues! This is what you dream about!"

It was 11 p.m. Crickets chirped. The motel was quiet. A man with a car was waiting in the parking lot, and he and Mickey would drive back to Fayetteville, get there about 3 a.m., Mickey would pack up his things, and a few hours later, fly to Florida.

The following night, he'd be with a new team, new dreamers.

And meanwhile, the Fayetteville Generals would get up in the morning and get some coffee and wonder when, if ever, their turn will come.

I'll do you all a favor when I get back, guys. I'll dispel some of the myths about the minor leagues. Such as:

1. Everyone is a bonus baby.
2. You stay in rented houses.

174

3. You all drive fancy sports cars.

4. The crowds love you.

5. You all have shoe, bat and glove deals.

Also, I will testify that, although most of you are pretty young, not all of you came straight out of high school and put on the cleats. A number went to college and are just beginning in the minor league system. Like Pat Pesavento from Notre Dame, or John DeSilva from Brigham Young, or Randy Marshall from Eastern Michigan.

Of course, some "myths" are true. Like the way you get your lucky shoes or lucky socks. Or the times you prayed for a rainout. "At this point in the season," Dan Raley, the first baseman from Triangle, Va., admitted, "you're thinking a lot about getting home." Sure. What do you guys play, 140 games in five months? And you get only four days off the whole season? That's unbelievable. A five-game series against Augusta, followed by a five-game series against Myrtle Beach, followed by a five-game series against Charleston . . .

Rain? I'd be praying for an earthquake.

Chewing tobacco.

I don't know about this one. You guys chew an awful lot for young kids. It seems as if everyone has a tin of Red Man or whatever. Still, this new guy, Kasey McKeon? He takes the cake. He arrived Thursday night, up from Bristol to replace Mickey, and I guess he was trying to make friends in the dugout, so he asked, "You wanna try some really good chew?"

He pulled out this plastic bag that contained a long, twisted tobacco plant. It looked liked a miniature tree. And he yanked about four inches off the end.

"We been curing this in my uncle's barn for about a year and a half," he drawled. "It's the real stuff. Here, try some."

Now, personally, I don't like to eat anything that looks like a tree. Not without salt, anyhow. But a couple of you tried it. Stuffed it between your gum and lower lip and let it juice up.

And then you spat it out.

Poor Kasey.

A year and a half in the barn?

Then there was the time I asked Roof, your fearless leader: "What do you tell these kids about the major leagues?"

Remember that, Gene? You've been there. You've been in the Show. Sure. Maybe it was only 48 games. But that's 48 games more than a lot of other guys get. You played at Busch Stadium. You played in Wrigley Field. You made that catch off the ivy that they showed on TV around the country. Bobby Bonds, right? Bases loaded, two out, bottom of the eighth?

I'll never forget the look in your eyes when I asked you that question.

What do you tell them about the major leagues? You sort of glazed over, you leaned back in your chair, I don't know, it was like the look you get when remembering a long-lost uncle who used to play catch with you as a kid.

"When I tell them about the major leagues," you said, your Kentucky drawl thickening your words, "I tell them to think about all good things. That's what it's like; All good things. You go up there, and, hell, there are people who cheer you during batting practice. People asking for your autograph. Nice hotels. Someone to carry your bags. Shoot, they got buses that take you right to the airplane, and when you get on that airplane, they have food for you.

"You're playing baseball in beautiful parks. You're making real money. The announcer calls your name when you come to bat and it echoes all around the stadium.

"All good things. That's what I tell 'em. Just think of all good things, and that's the major leagues."

Gene. I wish you could talk to Guillermo Hernandez.

H ere's something I'm going to remember: When I met your team's general manager, Matt Perry, his pants were dirty. Red clay. All over his shoes, too. I asked him what happened.

"Oh," he said, "I had to pull the tarp on the field."

Guys. Up in Detroit, the GM doesn't pull the tarp on the field. He also doesn't cook hot dogs and fill up the popcorn machine, and he doesn't count the money at the end of the night and put it in a little bag and have it driven to the bank. I give a lot of credit to Perry for doing that and for, in essence, saving the franchise. The guy is only 28 years old, a neat, trim, business school grad from Ohio State. But he's out there hustling, working the phones, rousing up the local businesses in Fayetteville and hiring postgame attractions such as Captain Dynamite, a nut who actually blows himself up in his "Coffin of Death."

And thanks to that, the Generals, who were on the brink of failure last November, have turned it around at the gate.

"You're sort of the Bill Veeck of the minor leagues?" I asked Perry, after noticing his calendar of Video Rental Night and Dime-A-Dog Night and Cellular-One Cushion Night and The Famous Chicken Night.

"Well," he said, grinning, "I don't think I'd bring in a midget."

Oh, good.

The Elvis sign? I have to bring that up one more time before I close this letter. Guys. I have seen a lot of things in sports. I have seen Olympic Games, I have seen Bourbon Street on the night before the Super Bowl.

I have never seen a giant billboard of Elvis Presley holding out a doughnut — like they have in the Columbia Mets' stadium. In right-centerfield. And if you hit the ball through the hole in the doughnut, what do you win?

"Five hundred dollars," one of you told me.

"A dozen jelly doughnuts," someone else said.

Too much.

Elvis, your legend lives.

You know, a lot of people asked me why I wanted to go to the minor leagues. I'm not sure. I guess it was to meet guys for whom baseball was still everything, not the money (you have none), not the fame (you have none). I want to thank you guys for restoring my faith.

Ettles, from Australia, I hope you make it to the big leagues, just so you can pay off your phone bill back home. And Erickson, Donnie, the California Kid at third base, I don't know about that tattoo you've got on your wrist. "Lucky 13"? Isn't that a contradiction in terms? I do give you credit for the best line of the week. After you popped up a few times, you sat in the Steak-n-Egg and said, "Man. If hang time were batting average, I'd be batting 1.000."

Hector Berrios, born in Puerto Rico, still goes down there for winter ball. What did you tell me? "This league is nothing compared to that. Down there, we play with some big stars. It's top-notch baseball. I'm going back to Double-A ball next year, man."

I hope you make it.

Did I mention the trainer, Steve Carter? You, Cowboy, have got to slow down. Most trainers just sort of hang around and make sure nobody's knee explodes. But you're everywhere! Doing the wash, ordering new shorts, wrapping elbows, handing out paychecks, buying aspirin, massaging arms, collecting socks, reading the road map to the bus driver. (By the way, you need to work on that part; the lost tribe of Israel had a better sense of direction.)

"I guess I end up doing a lot of odds-and-ends stuff," you told me. "One time a guy called me at 2 a.m., woke me up. I could hear music in the background. He said he had jammed his thumb, what should he do. I told him what to do and went back to sleep."

See? Smart, too.

Maybe the whole scene was summed up best by Donnie Rowland, a guy I had circled on the roster before I ever got to Fayetteville. He's from Michigan, St. Clair Shores, and I figured talking to him would be a good local story.

What I didn't know was Donnie is on his way out. At 26, he was a little too old. He had made it to Triple-A ball, Toledo; he was within a breath of the major leagues. "Then I got hurt," he told me, "and that was it. They took another guy up instead. I had to think about where I was going. They came to me and said, 'Donnie, we have to be honest with you. We don't see you playing in the big leagues.' "

I remember when you told me that story, Donnie, in the parking lot of the motel as we waited for the bus. I winced when I heard those words. "We don't see you playing in the big leagues." How many guys in the minors live in dread of that sentence?

But you know what you said? "Hey, I was lucky to get to Triple-A. I've been paid to play a game. They can't take those years away from me." I give you credit, Donnie. You took a lemon and made lemonade. You accepted their offer to be a coach, and here you are in A-ball, working with the kids. One day you might make it to the majors, as a manager.

It's the next-best thing, right?

So long, guys. I might never see many of you again. Duane, remember when you told me, "If I haven't made it by 25, I'm out of here"? And you're already 23. Nearly all of you had a similar sort of cutoff point. That's probably smart. There are few things sadder than a baseball player who stayed too long.

So if you're gone, if you never make it to Detroit, well, thanks for the week. I liked the smells and the sounds and the tastes. I liked the bus rides, and the gentle cacophony of 20 Walkmans playing simultaneously. Hey, Anthony, you sleep with your mouth open.

Ha. Just kidding.

I liked the rhythmic sound of cleats on concrete, and the pop-pop-pop of ball meeting glove. I liked the way you seemed to know what every other minor leaguer had done. ("Hey, see this guy? He stinks. He can't get around on the ball. First-round draft choice. Paid him two hundred grand. My mother swings better than him.")

I liked looking at the hotel list and seeing "Tillman Murchison" listed as "coach" and then finding out that Tillman Murchison was the bus driver. I liked walking with you from the convenience store at midnight, along some nameless southern boulevard, eating M&M's and potato chips while you asked me about Jack Morris, Lou Whitaker, what were they really like?

And what other team would let a writer put on a uniform and sit in the dugout, just to get a better feel for his story?

I liked the whole thing. The parks, the small crowds, the love of the game. Maybe I liked it because I like sports. Maybe I liked it because it was simple and young. As we grow old, those are the things we miss most.

But that's sentimental, and you have no time for that now. Take care. Best of luck. I wish you, as Gene might put it, all good things. The major leagues.

And now that I'm gone, your luck will return. Just watch.

Knock the heck out of that doughnut,

Mitch ♦

178

PETE ROSE: DENIAL, EGOISM AND THE LOOK OF A LIAR

August 25

H e left the game still kidding himself, still believing he is somehow above it, beyond the rules, too special to be caught. "I never bet on baseball," Pete Rose insisted again on the day he was banned for life, apparently for exactly that.

Thus ends the most excruciating sports story of the year. Not with a final thud of justice, but with the whoosh of verbal swords. "He did it," says Bart Giamatti, the commissioner of baseball. "No I didn't," says Rose. "Good-bye," says the commissioner. "I'll be back," says Rose.

In the final tally, all the words don't matter. Rose, the former star player and manager of the Cincinnati Reds, is out of the game, as of now, for life — the result of charges that he bet on games involving his team. He can apply for reinstatement in a year, but Giamatti is under no obligation to take him back. Not next year. Not the year after. He can say, "See ya, Pete," from now until Seattle wins a World Series.

And we are left wondering whether anyone is the better for this mess. There is no joy in expelling Rose from the only place he seemed to live an admirable life, the playing field. Yet there is no sympathy for a man who thinks the world is a little white ball that will always spin him out of trouble.

"Do you feel you'll be reinstated?" he was asked.

"Oh, absolutely," he said.

Amazing.

And sad.

A nd typical. For Rose has been, over the years, almost astonishing in his arrogance. His celebrated 44-game hitting streak came while he was being slapped with a paternity suit. His daughter, Fawn, once called him "the worst father in the world," to which he responded: "I'm a great father. I just gave her a Mercedes."

During a court hearing in late June on these same gambling charges, Pete was far away, in Atlantic City, signing autographs for $15 a pop. And on his first night without baseball, Rose was appearing, believe it or not, on one of those cable-TV home-shopping programs, chatting with callers as if nothing had happened.

The all-time hits leader? Three World Series rings? Baseball has always been his cleansing rinse. And his only concern. Three days ago, his wife gave birth to a baby girl. Yesterday, Rose said: "I've never looked forward so much to a birthday as I will to my daughter's birthday next year, because it means two days later I can apply for reinstatement to baseball."

Even children, it seems, are no more than time markers for Rose's schedule of getting what he wants.

We all knew this about Rose. We also knew he was guilty of something. He confessed in the now-celebrated report by investigator John Dowd that he bet on other sports, that he dealt with bookies. Technically, that was enough to boil the water.

But the baseball thing. That he denied, over and over, despite nine witnesses, despite the slips with his fingerprints on them, despite the handwriting analysis that said those slips, Reds games, were signed by him. Rose said, "Nuh-uh," and went on with his job, managing the skidding team and pretending, as he has done his whole life, that baseball would throw him a rope.

His lawyers, however, were scrambling. In April, they called Giamatti's office. They wanted a deal, one of those insulting verdicts in which the guilty party does a charitable act (gives money, talks to schoolkids) and all is forgiven. The commissioner said forget it.

They came back, a few months later, willing to swallow expulsion in exchange for a document that said Rose never bet on baseball. Giamatti waved his report full of evidence and said no way.

And so, in the end, the Rose army laid down its arms for a handful of words, some verbal mumbo jumbo that Rose seems to interpret one way ("I'll definitely be reinstated") and the rest of the world seems to interpret the other. Yes, it's true the signed papers do not formally say Rose gambled on baseball, but only because there was no hearing, no box score.

Make no mistake: Giamatti, the king of this court, said plain and simple he believes Rose did gamble on Reds games as a player. How ironic that the verbose Yale scholar has the cold hard facts, while Rose — a man best suited to physical force, sliding headfirst, breaking up a double play — is reduced to scrambling for words he can wave at people years from now. "Look. Nobody found me officially guilty of nuthin'."

Who believes him anymore? He has the sound of a liar, the look of a liar, he lets his lawyers step in front of him whenever the questioning gets tricky — such as when someone asked, with astonishing clarity: "If you didn't do anything, why are you accepting this punishment?"

Rose looked at his attorneys. They stepped to the microphone.

Now, whom do you believe?

OK. You might find the lifetime ban too harsh. What about all the cocaine heads who are given countless chances to rehabilitate? What about the alcoholics who surface over and over? What about the Steve Howes and the

Dwight Goodens and the Willie Wilsons? Why is Rose more guilty?

Well. It is not a question of guilt. It is a question of rules. Historically, baseball, for all its off-field trouble, has shuddered deepest at gambling. The Black Sox scandal of 1919 nearly destroyed the game. As a result, the first commissioner, Kenesaw Mountain Landis, permanently banned the eight players involved and later wrote the very rule that Giamatti cited. Anyone gambling on the sport shall be banished for one year. Anyone gambling on his own team shall be banished for life.

"I am simply citing the rules," Giamatti said more than once. "This whole episode has been about whether or not you live by the rules."

You do. Rose included.

Thus the man Mickey Mantle dubbed "Charlie Hustle," who used to count the days until spring training, who used to tell people he was born in 1941, "the year of Joe DiMaggio's 56-game hitting streak," will have new numbers to count. And a far more difficult task ahead of him. The burden is now on Rose to prove to baseball he is a reformed man, and that could take forever. The ink was not dry on the papers before he took the first step in the wrong direction.

"Do you have a gambling problem?" he was asked. "And will you seek help for it?"

"I don't have a gambling problem," he said. "And consequently, I don't plan on seeking help."

Does that sound like a man who wants to rehabilitate?

And, quite frankly, he doesn't have to. Even if he never gets back in the game, Rose can continue to profit from it. There's Japan. There's the trade-show, talk-show, lecture circuit.

And then there's his side of the story, the inevitable book, and you can figure a million-dollar advance for that baby. Considering he was making just $500,000 a year as a manager, that's not a bad wage for purgatory.

He will suffer, but he'll get by. The word out of Cincinnati is that, before Rose would accept this settlement, he had to be assured he would receive his 1990 salary. This was just a few days ago. Even to the end, he was weighing the risk and the payback. He liked the odds. He took the deal.

In months to come, when the anger subsides, there may be sympathy, and homage paid to the marvelous energy with which Rose attacked baseball: his cloud-of-dust slides, his "I-dare-you" glares at a pitcher. "The way he played the game," fans will sigh. But you know what? Any boy can play a game. You have to be a man to face yourself.

Try swinging at that one, Pete. ◆

WITH HUMOR AND GRACE, QUEEN CHRISSIE ABDICATES

September 6

NEW YORK — It was all behind her now, the last match, the last press conference, the last walk through the fans as they sang her name and reached to touch her. Chris Evert was alone with a friend in the women's locker room, dressing for the last time after 19 glorious summers of U.S. Open tennis.

"I have an idea," she suddenly said to Ana Leaird, a high school classmate who serves as public-relations director for women's tennis. "Tell Andy I fainted."

"No! Really?"

"Yeah. Tell him I fainted."

It would be a natural reaction, no? After all this? To faint? Hadn't she just said good-bye to the game she had dominated, molded, loved and honored for the last two decades? Hadn't she suffered the whole continental press corps just waiting to witness her final historical point?

Leaird burst from the locker room.

"Chrissie fainted!" she said, rushing up to Andy Mill, Chris' husband. "She fainted."

Mill moved quickly toward the locker room door . . .

And out popped Evert, all smiles.

Applause, please. The lady leaves 'em laughing. She was never much for the fires of emotion; ice was more Chris Evert's game, icy stare, ice-cold concentration.

And yet, she was the role model for a generation. She was, pardon the expression, a gentleman athlete, fusing effort and grace. Throw sneakers and Emily Post in a bag and you get Christine Marie Evert, queen of the courts, America's prom date. And there she was, taking the hard serve of young Zina Garrison and returning it into the net for her final stroke of Grand Slam tennis.

"GAME, SET, MATCH . . . " the announcer began and the crowd rose to its feet and began the farewell clap. Evert, 34, who had told the world weeks ago that this would be her last Grand Slam tournament, jogged forward and shook hands with Garrison. No tears. Not for Chris, that is.

Garrison would start crying in a minute.

"Hey, I remember going up to Chris and asking for her autograph when

I was 16," Garrison, 25, later explained. "I mean, this was really emotional."

For everyone but Evert. She kept her cool by squeezing her lips into a smile, then a grimace, then a smile again, the way she has done so many times on the court. They were hoping for a storybook ending in New York, they were hoping that the Open, her tennis cradle when she was pigtailed and 16 years old, would somehow serve as her last gold ribbon.

She got pretty far. Reached the quarterfinals. Led Garrison five games to two in the first set. And then the creak of age arrived — not in her knees but in her mind. "What happened today is the reason I'm retiring," she said in the stuffed press room, after Garrison ousted her, 7-6 (7-1), 6-2. "I play a great match two days ago, and then I come out flat for the next one. It's been happening to me all year. I can't sustain my intensity every single time out there. That's how I knew it was time to get out."

Trust her. She is showing characteristic wisdom, right to the end. How nice to see a champion leaving when she still can beat nearly everybody. What a lovely shadow that throws over her career accomplishments: 18 Grand Slam championships — seven French, six U.S. Opens, three Wimbledons and two Australians. And how many titles? One hundred and 57? More than any other player ever — male or female? You want to know how long Chris Evert has been around? At this tournament alone she has defeated 78 different opponents. Can that be right? Can you even name half that many women's tennis players?

She will be remembered, of course, for the pigtails and the kisses with Jimmy Connors and the curtsies at Wimbledon's Centre Court and the marriage to a handsome Brit and another to a handsome Olympic ski star, but, mostly, Chris Evert will be remembered for this:

"Are you glad it's over?"

"Well, I thought I would be glad when it was over, but I'm not really relieved now because of how I played two days ago. I mean, I thought I was just starting to play the kind of tennis where I could challenge anybody."

She never gave up.

She still doesn't.

As Evert left the stadium, she was spotted by young fans milling around the souvenir stands — first one, then three, then dozens. Children. In a gulp, they were all around her. Some in sweatshirts, some in dresses.

"Chrissie, over here!"

"Chrissie, we love you!"

"Chrissie! Chrissie!"

Children. Less than half her age. Less than one-third her age. Here is Chris Evert's legacy, the kids, the girls, especially, who now find it's OK to be a female athlete, it's more than OK, it's cool, it's good, it can be done without sacrificing your personality, without turning into some lead-footed monster. This is what Chris Evert leaves behind: an army in size-3 tennis dresses, whacking the ball as if it were a pinata filled with candy.

As she made her way out of the grounds, Evert passed her mother and father, Colette and Jimmy, who started her playing on the public courts of Ft. Lauderdale, Fla., back in the '60s. Players don't come up that way much anymore, the public courts. Mostly it's private lessons, live-away camps, personal masseuses. One of the few players out there today from the public courts is Garrison, the woman who sent Chris packing. There's a nice symmetry there, I think.

"Excuse me," said a heavyset blonde woman in an oversized pink sweatshirt. "Are you Mrs. Evert? I just want to say thank you."

"Oh," answered Chrissie's mom. "What for?"

"For doing such a wonderful job with your daughter. My daughter plays tennis and I always taught her to act like Chrissie on the court. I'm proud to say she had, and I just want to thank you for that."

From all of us.

For the record, the end came at 4:29 p.m. She wore a striped jersey and turquoise skirt. She had a red tennis bag. She watched films the night before and said she was going out to dinner when she got home. The trivia about Chris Evert's final Grand Slam match will go on for a long time, but not as long as our memories of her. There were a thousand quotes to mark her departure and maybe none more curiously eloquent than from 13-year-old Jennifer Capriati, the budding star from Chris' hometown, who hugged the former champion and, if she's lucky, absorbed some of those magic vibes.

"It was a bummer," Capriati said.

Yeah, it was.

Here's to her power, her style, her two-handed backhand, the way a bead of sweat seemed to dance down her temples, her victories, her defeats, her wonderful wars with Navratilova, Graf, Austin, King, Stove, Goolagong, Mandlikova, Shriver, Jaeger and Court — and the way she was able to joke when it was all, finally, over. She said good-bye, fittingly, in Louis Armstrong Stadium, named for a man who immortalized the following lyrics:

Give me
A kiss to build a dream on
Applause, please.
She gave us a lot more. ♦

THE LIONS DON'T HAVE A GHOST OF A CHANCE

September 10

H e finds me in the basement, hidden behind a stack of books.
"Go away," I say, "I'm busy."
"But it's Sunday," says the ghost in the silver and blue football jersey. "It's *Sunnnnnday . . .*"

I know it's Sunday. I know it's the first weekend of the NFL season. That is why I have surrounded myself with these fine, wonderful books. This year, I'm saying no. This year, let someone else be the sucker.

"I'm sorry," I say, leafing through the T.S. Eliot, "I just don't have time for Lions football. I have a lot of reading to do."

"First game of the season," says the ghost. "A new coach, a new offense . . ."

Ha. You think I'm falling for that again? New coach? New offense? Allow me to introduce myself. I'm the man who fell for Tommy Hudspeth. I'm the man who fell for Monte Clark. I'm the man who said, "David Lewis? He must be good. He's our first-round draft choice."

I am the man who believed it all, year after year. I have swallowed so much crow, my stomach has wings. And now you want to drag me back in front of the TV set for another 16 weeks of living hell? Ha. You have a better chance of seeing Pete Rozelle on "Love Connection."

"You better move along," I say to the ghost, flipping quickly through the Dostoyevski. "I really am busy with this book. What's it called . . . 'The Idiot'? Hmmm. Must be about a season-ticket holder."

"Kickoff in one hour," he says.

"I beg your pardon?"

A m I wrong? I am not wrong. Every man has his limits. These are my limits. Six years since a playoff game. Thirty-two years since a championship. Lousy drafts. Lousy trades. Fumbled balls. Fumbled fumbles. Darryl Rogers. Reggie Rogers. Limits.

"Besides," I say to the ghost, picking a broom from the closet and sweeping around the sump pump, "it's the same old story. Every September we think the season will be different. And by October we're mathematically eliminated. And anyhow, I have all this housework. A man's sump pump can never be too clean, you know."

"Peanuts or popcorn?" asks the ghost.

185

"What?"

"Do we start with peanuts or popcorn?"

"You're not listening."

He's not listening. He never does. I am the guy who thought Oscar Smith would be a star in our backfield. I'm the guy who thought Rick Forzano was the man for the job. I'm the guy who thought it must be the sun, or the sudden wind, or maybe an alien moonbeam, that made Mark Nichols drop all those passes.

They said it; I believed it. Every autumn I would hunker down with a bowl full of optimism, and every winter I would be left with crumbs. I was there when Mike Black missed the ball. And he was the punter. I was there when Jeff Komlo smacked a beer mug off Keith Dorney's head. I was there when they had 12 men on the field. When they had 10 men on the field. When Ed Murray missed that field goal.

"Storm windows," I say to the ghost. "What a perfect day for putting up the storm windows. Lemme see now, where did I put them? ... "

"Barry Sanders," he says.

"What?" I say.

"Barry Sanders."

Barry Sanders. Colonel Sanders. What difference does it make? Every year there is somebody new, and sooner or later he gets sucked into the quicksand. Remember how excited we were about Chuck Long? Remember the unbridled optimism when Reggie Rogers came to town? Quarterback of the future! Pass rusher for the '90s! And today we still have no quarterback and we still have no pass rush. Don't give me Barry Sanders. I mean, how much difference can Barry Sanders make? Where did I put those storm windows?

"He led the nation in rushing last year," says the ghost.

"He did?" I say.

No. Forget it. I don't want to know. This is the year I use my Sunday afternoons for culture. This is the year I put on Mozart at 1 p.m. and Paganini at 4 p.m. And when there's a Sunday night game, I'll slip on the Beethoven. Or maybe the Bach. One of those guys. Culture.

"Well, it's almost kickoff time," says the ghost. "I'm heading upstairs. I'll fluff the pillows on the couch."

"Don't bother," I say, sorting through the Stravinsky records. "I'll be down here with Concerto No. 34 in E-flat major. Or maybe No. 21 in A-sharp major. Whatever. Have a good time."

The door closes. I am flush with a wave of satisfaction. I am finally cutting my losses. I am finally getting smart. I am finally saying good-bye to Eric Hipple down on his knees, trying to remember what day it is. To Jeff Chadwick, watching the ball bounce off his fingertips. To the offensive

186

linemen yelling, "LOOK OUT!" as the Chicago Bears go plowing through them.

I am finally bidding farewell to Sunday evenings, weeping over instant replays. To a half-empty Silverdome, where opponents have more fans than we do. I have my music. I have my books. I have the sump pump. This is great.

It is quiet now.

I am alone.

I am happy.

I am content.

I am . . .

I am walking up the steps.

"Any score yet?" I ask the ghost, who has the Coke, the peanuts and the big box of hard pretzels.

He shakes his head and pats the couch, silently. I am moving closer.

"Just this one game," I say, taking a seat.

"I know," he says, turning up the volume. ♦

SANDERS' FIRST SPARK ELECTRIFIES THE CROWD

September 11

The gift wrap came off midway through the third quarter. The ribbons were cut and left on the sidelines. The crowd rose to its feet and began to scream and from that frozen moment there was one story in the Lions' opener, and only one story.

Barry.

"I was in the huddle and suddenly I heard this roar," said Bob Gagliano, the Lions' quarterback. "I didn't know what they were cheering about. And then I saw him coming."

And then he saw him going. On his first carry, Barry Sanders, the dashing rookie running back, gained 18 yards. The city fell in love. On his fourth carry, Sanders darted left into the end zone for Detroit's first touchdown. The city elected him mayor. On his fifth carry, Sanders raced around right end for 26 yards, the longest rush of the day. The city commissioned a statue.

He breezed. He flew. He knew one play. One play? Yes. The off-tackle run. He ran it nine times for 71 yards, twisted it like a pretzel, curled it like spaghetti. He bent sometimes to the left and sometimes to the right and sometimes he just said the heck with it and ran wherever the biggest hole was. The effect was undeniable. It was Christmas morning. New Year's Eve. Whenever he touched the ball it was as if 100,000 volts spit through the Silverdome seats.

"What did you say to him after that touchdown?" someone asked coach Wayne Fontes, who inherited Sanders, the No. 1 pick, just three days ago, after he agreed to a contract.

"I told him he did a super job," Fontes said. "I told him, 'Welcome to the NFL.' I told him I loved him."

"You loved him?"

"Yeah," Fontes said, sheepishly. "I was excited. I told him I loved him."

Barry. Barry.

Doesn't that sum the whole thing up? The coach said he loved him. Everybody loved him. And the Lions lost, 16-13, on a last-minute field goal by Phoenix's Al Del Greco. Here was an Oscar-winning performance in a B-movie. While Sanders was shining like new, the Lions were flubbing like old: Their new offense produced one touchdown, the team was penalized 10

188

times, Jeff Chadwick dropped four passes, Lomas Brown was benched for ineffective play. Cinderella's Opening Day carriage was turning quickly to a pumpkin — and such is the state of football around here that it almost didn't matter. People left the Silverdome talking more about the debut than the defeat. Oh, the promise.

Barry. Barry. Barry.

"Have you ever felt a surge of excitement like that in this stadium?" someone asked placekicker Ed Murray, who has been here for a decade.

"Once," he said, rolling his eyes, "when Billy Sims ran out on the field. That was my rookie year."

Here was a desert thirst being splashed by water. A grumbling hunger sat down at a buffet table. It was everything Detroit football fans have been waiting for — some excitement on offense. And while they should be reminded that not too long ago, Chuck Long debuted with a touchdown pass that made these same fans dizzy with promise, and now he's a bust, well, nobody wanted to hear that now.

What they wanted to hear was what they created themselves, a welcoming party of two-syllable celebration:

Barry. Barry. Barry. Barry.

All of which had little effect on the man himself. Sanders, only 20, began the day in a room with his parents, cutting his hair. Cutting his hair? Yes. He does that. He told his father he was a little nervous. He had been in town only three days. Was he really ready to play his first NFL game?

"I told him, 'Son, you play today you're gonna get hit, you wait until next week, you'll get hit next week,' " said William Sanders, a roofer who largely negotiated his son's five-year, $5.9 million contract. "Might as well get it over with, right?"

Right.

So the young man dressed and stood on the sidelines and did not play the first half. Then, with 5:34 left in the third quarter, on second-and-10 from the Lions' 44-yard line, Fontes took him around, said, "Relax. Be the kind of back we know you can be," and nudged him toward the field. The Silverdome erupted into a sea of "Restore the Roar" rags and the first honest-to-god cheering that has been heard in years. Such was the hysteria that Gagliano was unable to get a play called and had to waste a time-out. The players stood there, aimlessly, shaking his hand and waiting for the clock.

No matter. He served as a decoy on his first play, and the Lions picked up 27 yards on a pass-interference penalty. The next four plays were his, "36, off-tackle," the only one he really knew. And from the moment he touched the ball, he was here to stay.

Four plays later he was in the end zone.

189

I felt pretty comfortable out there," he said. "It felt good to get hit. I know that sounds weird. ..."

"What about the team?"

"It has a lot of potential."

"Were you nervous?"

"Not really."

He answered questions slowly, casually. He said the hits really didn't bother him, they weren't that much worse than college. When someone asked whether he would rate his performance a good one, he said, "We lost. So I guess it wasn't good enough."

That, of course, depends on your perspective. Fontes called him "great" and said he was the starting back as of "tomorrow." The fans swallowed him like cheesecake; he was mobbed as he tried to leave the building.

All this, and the Lions are 0-1 for 1989. So be it. The reality is that nobody stays the flavor of the month forever. And, remember, Phoenix is no great defensive team. Sanders will improve; he might well be a star. But opponents will study film and be ready for him. Injuries will be inevitable. The excitement will be there — we hope it stays forever — but no one player makes an NFL team. Detroit will get used to its newest superstar ...

"Did anything surprise you today?"

"Well," he said, shrugging, "I thought we were gonna win."

... and he will get used to Detroit. ◆

NOTRE DAME'S ROCKET SINGES MICHIGAN – TWICE

September 17

A NN ARBOR, Mich. — The kickoff came tumbling out of the wet, gray sky, and nobody could believe this. Raghib (Rocket) Ismail couldn't believe the ball was coming his way, and his coach, Lou Holtz, couldn't believe Michigan would kick it to Ismail again, and Bo Schembechler, already having a bad day, what with an injured quarterback and a sluggish offensive line, couldn't believe what had happened once would ever happen twice. A second kickoff return? For a touchdown? In Michigan Stadium? No way. There hadn't been one here against U-M since 1957.

And then there were two. The ball landed smack in the hands of Mr. Rocket, and eight seconds' and 92 yards' worth of groping defenders later, he was in the end zone, twisting the knife in what was billed as the biggest college football game of the season.

End of story.

"I told my team, 'It won't be kicked deep,' " Holtz said after Notre Dame squashed Michigan's dreams of a No. 1 ranking with a 24-19 defeat in a drizzly opener. "When they kicked it to Rocket, one of my players behind me said, 'Uh-oh, here we go again.' "

Funny. That's what Michigan fans were saying all day. What killed U-M wasn't so much that bad things were happening, but that the same bad things were happening over and over. The kicker missed an extra point, then booted an onside attempt into a teammate's leg. The running backs tried to go left, got crushed, then tried to go right and got crushed again.

And of course Ismail — who should have "See ya next week" stitched on the back of his jersey — raced through them once for 88 yards to open the third quarter, crushing the spirits of the 105,912 fans, and then, in the fourth quarter, after Michigan had rallied, he did it again for 92 yards.

End of story.

"I don't think I ever would have sat here and predicted we'd lose by 14 points' worth of kickoff returns," Schembechler said, shaking his head after the defeat, U-M's third straight to the Fighting Irish. "They beat us with a punt return last year. I mean, this is getting to be a bad habit."

And it's not the only one. In fact, it wasn't even the worst. On a day that the Wolverines couldn't kick and couldn't run, the really bad news was that they couldn't block. Their highly celebrated behemoth offensive linemen (average weight: 293) played as if all the poundage was in their feet. Where were the holes? Where was the tank-like force? Where was the traditional Michigan "three yards and a cloud of dust"? The Wolverines gained only 94 yards rushing all day. Make no mistake: That was the biggest wheel that fell off U-M's wagon.

And yet, they were still alive, they were still in it. With four minutes to go, they trailed by only five points — thanks largely to a lanky, shrugging sophomore named Elvis, who began the season as the fourth quarterback on the depth chart and finished the game as No. 1 on the hit parade. Elvis (last name Grbac) came trotting in when senior Michael Taylor took a helmet in the back. All Grbac did in his first game as a Wolverine was throw 21 passes, complete 17, two for touchdowns, and almost lead the Wolverines to a victory in a game they were seemingly not ready to win.

"With a couple minutes to go, Bo was telling us keep going, we're only a couple points down," he said. "For a little kid like me, it gave me a lot of confidence."

Not so little, either. Grbac, 19, is 6-feet-5, 220, and throws a bullet. His sudden presence — and Michigan's evolution into a passing team — might have been the day's most effective weapon against the Irish; to that point, they seemed to have the Michigan offense completely figured out. Grbac, however, was more a surprise to the media than to his teammates. Even as reporters tapped out the "star is born" stories, Schembechler admitted that Taylor, who had been hurting with a sore right arm, did not throw a pass all week in practice. "If I had it to do over again," Schembechler said, "maybe I should have started Elvis and let the chips fall where they would."

But then, he would have done a lot of things differently if he could. An onside kick with 4:08 left was botched when the new kicker, sophomore J.D. Carlson, squibbed it into the leg of a teammate well short of the needed 10 yards. It gave Notre Dame field position to run out the clock. Had he known that before, well . . .

Well, what? The point is, the game was lost a lot of ways, most of which involved the offensive line and special teams. So bad was the kicking that, when asked why Michigan didn't aim away from Ismail on the second kickoff, Schembechler half-jokingly responded: "The way we were going, I was just praying the ball stayed in bounds."

End of story.

And OK. Let's face some nasty truths here. On this day, Notre Dame was the better team. It might be because the Irish already had played one game (a victory over Virginia). It might be because Michigan, in its season opener, with new players in key positions on the special teams (and suddenly quarterback), more resembled a half-clad starlet caught with the dressing-room door open.

"Michigan is an outstanding team. If we played them tomorrow, the results might be different," Holtz said.

That is a typical response by the bespectacled coach, a man who, despite a brilliant team loaded with talent, is nonetheless full of it. Come on, Lou. You cry poor more than a room full of winos. Just once, instead of all this soft-pedaling, "We were just fortunate today to win," I'd like Holtz to say, "We have a great team, the best team, and it's up to some other team to prove it's better."

Why not? That's what everyone else is saying about Notre Dame. The Irish are No. 1 in the rankings. They stymied Michigan's rushing attack, and they won without relying too much on quarterback Tony Rice, who is usually their Mr. Everything.

So be it. Notre Dame plays for national championships. Michigan plays for its conference. That's the company line, anyhow. There were positive signs for the Wolverines — their defense looked good, Grbac and the receivers looked promising, and, besides, Schembechler has a way of turning Notre Dame losses into successful seasons. This will be a good team. It always is.

For now, Michigan's dreams will be haunted by the view of Ismail's back, racing toward the end zone in a steady drizzle, proving the theory that, while lightning never strikes twice, Lightning Irish seem to strike over and over again. End of story, for now.

The season is just beginning, isn't it? ◆

GAGLIANOS TIE THE KNOT – WITH ENGINEER'S HELP

September 27

L et me tell you about the social event of the football season, the marriage of Bob and Kim Gagliano, live, on the radio, an event that can be summed up with the following sentences:

"Are they ready yet?"

"No! Throw on another Van Halen record!"

Now. There are many ways in which a man and woman can be joined in holy matrimony. Most of them do not involve headphones. Nor do most include a disc jockey who says, "We'll be back with the wedding, right after this. . . . "

But there, in the studios of Detroit's WLLZ-FM (98.7), stood Bob Gagliano, the Lions' starting quarterback, and Kim Neumann, his fiancee and swimsuit model, before the judge, the witness, the best man — and the engineer. My eyes got all misty.

But let's back up. As some of you know, I do a talk show, with Mike Stone, on WLLZ. And a few weeks ago Gagliano was our guest. At the end of the interview, during which he was candid, pleasant and surprisingly lucid for a man who gets clobbered every Sunday, Bob asked whether he could say hi to his fiancee, Kim. The rest of the conversation went pretty much like this:

ME: When's the wedding?

BOB: We . . . don't know.

ME: Where's the wedding?

BOB: We . . . don't know that, either.

ME (joking): Well, shoot, Bob, why don't you just get married right here? Heh, heh.

Next thing I knew, the flowers were ordered.

W hich was fine by me. My biggest concern was that the wedding was the night after the Bears game. Given the Lions' pass protection, I wasn't sure whether Gagliano could stand up by then.

But not only was he standing, he looked, as Billy Crystal would say, absolutely mahvelous when he walked into the studios. He wore a black tuxedo. Kim was resplendent in a white gown. Unfortunately, they didn't arrive until 10 minutes to 7. The wedding was scheduled for 7.

"Quick, throw on another Aerosmith record!"

I should mention that the couple had wanted a small affair, just a handful of friends and a judge. They got that. And three TV stations, five photographers, reporters, disc jockeys and limo drivers. There was also enough electrical cord to wrap up Trump Tower. And me. My job was to play "Here Comes the Bride." Don't ask.

Here were the most frequently heard questions at Bob and Kim's wedding:

1. "Where's the men's room?"
2. "Testing ... one ... two ... three ... "
3. "Where's Eric Hipple?"

Bob had chosen Hipple, his backup quarterback, to be his best man. What a nice gesture. Unfortunately, Eric forgot the directions. 7:05 ... 7:10 ... 7:15 ...

"Quick, throw on another Stones record!"

Did I mention the judge? Very nice guy. And our studio? Wow! Normally it looks like a place where Keith Richards might wake up. But there were flowers and a lovely white carpet running down the hallway, which is good, because I spilled my coffee on the regular rug that morning.

And here came Hipple.

"Sorry, man," he said, "we got caught in traffic."

"Who has the rings?"

"The rings? ... "

"Throw on another Beatles record!"

What thoughts, you might ask, run though a man's mind as he is about to get married? Funny. That's just what the disc jockey asked.

"Bob, what thoughts run through your mind as you're about to get married?"

"Well, I ... "

Poor Gagliano. I think, if it were up to him, he'd have been married in his living room, then turned on "Monday Night Football." But Kim liked the radio idea; "it's fun," she said. And marriage is all about compromise, right?

By the way, as piano player, I asked Bob and Kim for their favorite song. They chose a ballad by Loggins & Messina, a lovely song, a wonderful song. Unfortunately, I had never heard of it.

"Well, what songs do you know?" Bob said.

"I know 'Love Me Tender' by Elvis," I said.

And that's what I played.

And here came the bride.

"We are gathered here today ... " began the judge, as the engineer crouched, checking the levels, "to join in holy matrimony ... "

And so it went. They looked great. They sounded great. I think. Mostly, what I remember is the sounds of the cameras:

195

"Do you, Bob (whirrrrrr), take this woman (click, click, click) to be your lawfully (squeak) wedded (hissss) wife? . . . "

The "I do's" came out clearly.

Ta-da! They kissed, we clapped and the guy in the booth reached for another Dire Straits record.

And there you have it. The first, and perhaps only, starting-quarterback, middle-of-the-season, rock-'n'-roll radio marriage. Of course, Gagliano might be replaced by Rodney Peete this weekend against Pittsburgh, making him, I think, the first player to gain a wife and lose a job in the same week.

But why worry? It's the beginning of a wonderful new life for Bob and Kim. Unfortunately, things remain the same for the Lions. As the cars left for the reception, a photographer walked up with a pad and pencil. "That best man, the blond one?" he said.

"Yeah?" I said.

"What's his name?" ♦

TIGERS' 'LES MIZ' CLOSES FITTINGLY IN NEW YORK

September 29

So tonight the Tigers begin their final series of 1989, in New York City, a perfect cemetery for a garbage season. Say good-bye to this year's model and hope we'll never see it again.

I paid my respects at the final home game. The atmosphere in the clubhouse was not morbid. It was more like a huge sigh of relief, the kind when you wipe your brow and tap your coat pocket to make sure you haven't lost your plane ticket home.

"How would you describe 1989?" I asked Alan Trammell, who was already packing for San Diego.

"A wasted year," he said. "To be honest, for me, that's all this was."

For a lot of us. About the only time the Tigers had a chance was the first day of spring training — when Sparky Anderson might have walked up to Chris Brown and Torey Lovullo and said, "Sorry, gentlemen, there must be some mistake. You're not on our team."

They've been in trouble ever since. What was once a model clubhouse has become a bus station. What was once a den of champions has become a waiting room for the next paycheck and the first week in October. Stop the season, we want to get off.

"Has this been the toughest year you've ever had in your baseball ca- ...?" I asked Mike Henneman. He didn't wait for the end of the question.

"The ultimate, the toughest, the worst," he said. "It has been a miserable season."

Miserable? That's a good word. In fact, they could subtitle all the games *"Les Miserables."* Did the Tigers really lose more than 100 games? Are they really that bad? Was it really just two years ago that we were hanging on every pitch, right to the end, watching a miracle come through on a cool October Sunday, the last game, a division championship?

It was. And now? How strange to walk around the clubhouse. Every locker tells a story. There was Doyle Alexander, as usual, a loner, reading a newspaper. He went weeks between victories this year, and who knows whether we'll see him again?

There was Matt Nokes, who went from promising to disappointing in a terribly short span, and Scott Lusader, who seems to be forever on the bubble. There was Chet Lemon, who had an awful year, culminating with a prolonged absence for a mysterious family matter in Florida. Such was the state of the Tigers that, although he was gone for several weeks, no one seemed too concerned.

"I never had a season where I went the whole year without at least one stretch where I really shined, you know?" Lemon said. "I could never get focused in this year. Never."

Focusing was his problem. Standing up straight was Trammell's. When I asked the shortstop whether he had a single day this year when his back didn't hurt, he said simply, "No, not one." And he wasn't the only one aching. Jack Morris, who missed a full six weeks with his elbow problems. Jeff Robinson — lord, how many games did he miss? And Guillermo Hernandez, who fades into the sunset with creaks and moans. Heck, even the manager was unable to perform for a while, sunk by exhaustion.

And yet, when all is said and done, the sorriest victim will be the spirit, the soul of this Tigers machine. And that, sadly, was no accident.

D o you want to know what might be the worst plays of the 1989 Tigers?
    1. Trading Tom Brookens for Charles Hudson.
2. Not bringing back Darrell Evans.
3. Allowing Chris Brown to enter the clubhouse.

Let's be honest. The Tigers of recent years — even the version that won the 1987 division — have not been rich in talent. There are no Jose Cansecos or Bo Jacksons on this roster. The Detroit secret has been chemistry, high productivity, squeezing the rag for every drop, then refolding and squeezing it again.

Darrell Evans fit that mold. Chris Brown never did. Brown was lazy, fat and uninterested, and allowing him in the door was like mixing poison in the oatmeal; hard to get out. Couple Brown and the absence of Evans with the departure of Brookens — who had always symbolized the Tigers' character, especially to his teammates — and what was once a wonderful mix of personality was now just a weave of disgruntled and dissatisfied.

And then came the season. Turning points? Yeah. Mostly they turned south. Like Robinson going down early. Like Lovullo swinging at the air. Like the four straight losses to the California Angels, all in the final inning. "That's when I knew it was over," Trammell said. "From that point on, we were just waiting for the end."

And now, the end is just about here. Tigers fans can only pray for a better next year, and looser purse strings by management, and better judgment. And the players pack up the memories. Very tightly.

"Were there any highlights?" I asked Dave Bergman. "Maybe, you know, back in April?"

He shook his head.

"April was pretty lousy, too," he said. ♦

THE END OF INNOCENCE: DEATH TAKES THREE TEENS

October 8

I ONIA, Mich. — He didn't see the bodies. Not when he arrived. Just the car, a 1972 Chevy Malibu, parked right where the phone call said it was, on a tractor path just off Frank Road. State Trooper Jim Rogers got out of his squad car and sighed. "Probably some guy fell asleep," he figured. Happens all the time. It was, after all, Saturday morning, and most people don't leave their vehicles overnight in a deserted field with the motor running.

He approached on the driver's side and peeked in the window, which, like the others, was rolled up tight. Suddenly, he felt a shiver. There was a kid slumped in the backseat and another one slumped on the front passenger side and the driver had his head back and eyes closed and, oh, god, he knew him. Danon Pierce. Football player. On the high school team. His folks had that restaurant over in . . .

"No," thought Rogers, the horror leaping into his thoughts. He grabbed for the door. It was locked. He banged on the window. No response. He shook the car, and the bodies barely budged. A crowbar, he thought. I'll get one from my trunk. As he headed back, he pulled instinctively on the Chevy's rear door and it opened. He crawled inside. The radio was playing softly. A capped bottle of Scotch was on the floor. The kids did not move. He dragged the one from the backseat out into the grass and laid him down, safe from the fumes. Then he went back for the other two.

"I need some help out here!" he barked into his police radio, but even then, it was too late. They had been there for hours, the carbon monoxide poison was inside their bodies, finished, victorious, their flesh cold to the touch. When the other officers arrived, they found Rogers — who, like the victims, grew up in Ionia and attended the high school — standing helplessly in the field, with three dead teens and a whole world of sorrow.

This is a story about growing up, which everyone in high school is in a hurry to do — but not this way, not this fast. Danon Pierce, Kevin King and Chris Sawtell were three good faces in a small-town mural who were in the wrong car at the wrong time for the wrong reasons. They had played a football game, stayed out late, drunk a little, parked the car and never woken up. And now there are empty chairs at empty lockers and a team with black arm bands and a coach who sighs and tries to find answers; there

199

are grieving parents and whispering teachers. And most of all, there are the other kids, friends who, as you might remember, are the plasma of high school. You've got to have friends; you die without your friends.

You die with them, too.

No one ever figured on that.

I keep thinking, why couldn't they have been with me? Then nothing would have happened." Bart Cunningham leans back on a steel bar and shoots a weary glance across the field, his reddish hair still sweaty from practice. It is late afternoon, and the sun is moving out of the sky.

One day earlier he had attended the funerals of his three teammates, an event so heartbreaking to this small town it closed the school and a number of area businesses. Notes were dropped in the caskets, personal messages. The families wept. The Ionia players wore their football jerseys and formed a human wall from the church to the hearses and again from the hearses to the grave sites, shoulder to shoulder, silent, big adolescent bodies, watching the coffins go past. Bart helped carry Kevin King's casket.

"The thing is," he says, almost apologetically, "normally we go to my father's house after a game. We shoot pool, play cards. It's a regular thing on Friday nights. But this time, my sister had the chicken pox, so my dad didn't want us all around.

"If they had come over to my house, they'd be alive now. If only they came over to my house. . . . "

If only. If only. What happened that night seems to be a road map of near-misses, all of which led to that empty field at 4 a.m. If only Bart's sister didn't have the chicken pox. If only the guys didn't drink that alcohol. If only they knew about the rotted exhaust system. If only it wasn't so cold outside and they didn't roll up the windows, sealing their death.

"The funerals are over," Cunningham says softly, "and I still can't believe it. I don't know how long it'll be before it hits me that . . ."

He looks up, then down.

". . . I'll never see them again."

How much do we know about our kids anymore? To ask friends about Kevin, Chris and Danon is to get a disturbing picture of teenage popularity and make-believe adulthood. On the one hand, they were good students, got A's on their report cards, belonged to the student council. They were good-looking, nicely mannered, they liked to laugh and, of course, they were football heroes. Kevin, 17, was the star fullback; Danon, 16, was the center; and Chris, 16, was the linebacker. They were leaders; on the last night of their lives the team lost, 46-0, and yet even in the fourth quarter, Chris Sawtell was urging his teammates: "Come on! We can still win this thing!"

They seemed perfect models of small-town adolescence. And yet, they also liked to drink, even at such young ages. They would cruise town and make trips to Lansing or Grand Rapids, and they never had problems getting booze — beer, wine, Jack Daniel's, Southern Comfort, you name it. Good kids. Smart kids. Drinking shots. This is a portrait of our youth.

Bill May was supposed to be with them that night. He had been with them before, on nights when they went from children to adults, nights when they drank or rumbled or raced around town in the Chevy and stayed out until sunlight. A beefy, strong-looking 16-year-old with a face that seems too old for high school, he sits now and tries to figure it out.

They came to his house after the game. There was this party, they said; these two girls were throwing it. "Come on, let's go. It'll be fun. Get some booze. Get a little buzz." Bill said his shins were really hurting him; he wanted to go but he couldn't. Thanks anyway. Next time. And they drove off in the Chevy.

It was the last time he saw them.

"I know what happened that night, because something like it happened about two months ago," he says now, his voice full of regret. "It was the time we went downtown in Danon's car. We found a buyer, got some alcohol, then we went to the back roads and mixed some drinks, did some slammers.

"Then we went back into town. Chris was the type who would get rowdy when he got buzzed, you know? He was just 150 pounds, but it didn't matter. He'd take you on, even if you weighed 350 pounds. We were on Main Street, and these guys pulled by in an IROC-Z, and he yelled something and they stopped. They got out of the car. Chris said, 'We're gonna rock 'n' roll. Come on.'

"They started slapping each other, and Chris knocked this one guy down like a ton of bricks. 'You want some?' he yelled. 'Come on!' Then another guy hit Chris and he fell into me, so I jumped in and took care of things. Chris' lips were all cut up; it looked like somebody took a razor blade to them.

"Of course, we got in trouble when we got home. We were all grounded. I think what happened Friday is that they just didn't want to go home. Not after that last time. You know how your parents are if you come home late and were drinking? So they figured they would camp out and go home in the morning. We're really into the Rambo stuff. We have this field where we stash our sleeping bags underground, and we hide food in a hollow tree."

He pauses. "I bet they wanted to camp out, but it was too cold, so they just left the car running with the heater on and you know, they fell asleep."

What makes kids act this way? What is the big hurry to be so grown up? Bill May blows a lung full of air and shakes his head. There is a sadness in his face. The whiskers seem to fall off, and the man-sized body slouches like that of a school kid on a swing.

How did it all come to this, he wonders? The driving, the drinking, the fooling around? They were just having fun.

"We're not saints," he says. "But I lost my two best friends in the whole world in one night."

The police have reconstructed the tragic night. The boys were last seen by their coach and teammates in the locker room after the game, which had been a disappointment. Kevin was ejected by an official for a skirmish, and afterward he was near tears. "It's my fault," he told his teammates. "I'm the reason we lost. I feel like crap." The others assured him he was not to blame.

After the game, the kids stopped at a house, then went to a party given by Wendy and Kathy Nobis, two girls who also attend Ionia High. They left the party and went to a friend's house, then drove around town, went to another house, then drove to the Farmers Market on Steele Street, where they were last seen talking to friends about 3:30 a.m. Somewhere along the line there was alcohol consumed. But not a lot.

After that, only heaven knows. Kevin, Chris and Danon fell asleep with the motor running, sometime after 4 a.m. on that hidden tractor path off Frank Road — which, ironically, is not far from the high school — a narrow dirt street of fields and sprawling trees that grow close to the edge and hook branches overhead, like soldiers crossing swords. It is dark there, and remote. A good place to park. A good place to sleep it off. Apparently, that's what they were doing.

"Kids had hung out around there before," said State Police detective Jack Van der Wal, who found McDonald's fast-food bags and other refuse near the scene. What the three boys didn't know, though, was that the tall weeds beneath the car served as stuffing for its faulty exhaust system, which was riddled with holes, allowing the fumes to be sucked in by the heater, through the rusted trunk and into the car.

They were sleeping in a coffin.

Had that car been registered in Detroit, it never would have passed the emissions test. But there is no such test in this part of the state. So the carbon monoxide filled the boys' lungs as they slept, attacking the blood cells, robbing the oxygen. They died with the radio on.

Chris Sawtell was wearing his high school letter jacket.

When Van der Wal inspected the car, he found a duffel bag, a portable radio, a bottle of Scotch and a bottle of Southern Comfort, still mostly full. Toxicology reports show alcohol was in the victims' systems, but not much. Danon, the driver, had the least, not even enough to fail a Breathalyzer test.

"People want to make this all about alcohol, but it isn't," Van der Wal said. "It was just a terrible accident. Had they been stone sober, they still would have died."

But would they have been there in the first place? In the days since the accident, a 21-year-old woman has been arrested and charged with providing liquor to minors at that party. She was jailed for 10 days.

Empty chairs at empty lockers.

And the kids are left to figure this all out. Dead? How could they be dead? Kevin King, the strong, tempestuous one, who would gather the team together after victories and lean in, really quiet, then explode in a yowl: "LET'S ROCK 'N' ROLL!" Dead? Chris Sawtell, the guy who made freshman girls swoon, daring, adventurous, with the easy smile of confidence. Dead? Danon Pierce, who owned the car but dreamed of motorcycles, and who was on the student council and, according to his coach, Dan Painter, "was always coming up with some idea to make the school better." Dead?

No. Can't be. They were the kinds of kids who worked at the local market or the local nursery; they waved at honking cars in this small town where everybody knows everybody else. Friday nights they carried the pride of the school, which always seems to ride on shoulder pads at that age, and they fought hard for it, football, good and real. How do kids like that die?

There is no answer. They just do. Brian Snyder knew Kevin since they were little kids. They had grown up in each other's houses, they were on the team together, Brian was an offensive lineman, and they had this special look whenever the coach would call "44 Trap." That was Kevin's play, and Brian's job was to block the safety. Do it right, and Kevin could spring for big yardage. He would come back to the huddle and high-five his buddy. Thanks for the hole. Nice play.

"It was really hard to hear that play called today and not see Kevin there," says Snyder, a husky kid with wavy brown hair and a trace of freckles. "I never played a football game without him before."

He stops and picks at the knee of his pants. His eyes are watery and he sniffs when he can't help it. "I don't know," he says. "It's not a lot of fun seeing the casket come down over your friend's face, you know? I . . . haven't really figured this all out yet. . . . "

There was a favorite photo Brian had of him, Kevin and Bart, posing like muscle men. It always made him laugh when he saw it. He doesn't have it anymore. The day before, he placed it alongside Kevin's body.

You hear that, and you see these kids, and you are overwhelmed with a sense of wrong. They are too young for this. They are too raw for tragedy. In the inner-city schools of Detroit, death has become a frequent classmate; there are, tragically, guns and knives and youths who seem anything but young. But here in Ionia, where the halls are freshly painted and the gym floor is freshly waxed and the cheerleaders practice cartwheels in empty corridors, it seems too remote. Kids here are just having fun, right? That's what everyone keeps saying.

"I know about the drinking and stuff," Snyder says. "But they weren't doing anything bad. They weren't doing anything everybody else wasn't doing. . . . "

Where do we stand on all this? The lenient will say, "We all did the same thing in high school. Alcohol didn't kill them. The car did." The more conservative will wring their hands. "What are teenagers doing out at that hour, driving around with liquor bottles, sleeping out all night? They weren't even 17 years old."

And out on Frank Road, there is now a gate across the path where the boys were found. Leaning against it is a wooden board, a tombstone of sorts, reading "RIP" and carrying a heart and a message of love from fellow students. There are roses and private notes, and most every day some girls from the school come out and tend to the site, straightening the flowers and crying in the shade of the large branches.

Empty chairs at empty lockers. Once upon a time, the three used to talk about opening their own business. Chris would be the lawyer and Danon the operator and Kevin, well, he would find something to do. Once upon a time, before they could drive, they sneaked the Chevy out and their football cleats accidentally ripped a hole in the carpet, and they had to run and get some glue and pray Danon's mom wouldn't notice. Once upon a time, they used to sleep under the stars in sleeping bags, as far back as the seventh grade, just go walking in the woods like those kids in "Stand By Me," come back into town for food and soda and then be gone again on a teenage adventure.

And once upon a time, they took the Chevy out to the gravel pits with a .22-gauge borrowed from a father and were target shooting when a bullet ricocheted off the fender and narrowly missed Danon's hip. They laughed, as kids will do. From that point, they called the car "the Gold Bullet."

Can irony get any more painful than that?

This Friday is homecoming for Ionia. It will be the first football game on the home field since the night of the accident. The players will wear black arm bands. They will dedicate the performance to their missing teammates.

And survivors such as Bill May — who could have been with them that night — will try to figure out whatever happened to simple old high school. "I tell everyone now not to drink," he says. "I'm never gonna drink again. I think we were kind of starting to have a problem, you know? We'd get a fifth of this or that and just drink it for the feeling of being drunk. Not anymore. I'm never touching a drop again."

"I just wish I could have been with them," says Brett Krause, a redheaded senior lineman who worked this summer with Chris at the tree nursery. "I wouldn't mind if they had a good time. I'd be there, sober, just to make sure they were safe. Better to be home and drunk than not to go home at all."

"I wish," Bart Cunningham says, "that my sister never had the chicken pox."

Where is the moral of this story? Where is the silver lining? These were good kids, smart kids, well-liked and healthy. Were it not for a rolled-up window or a rusty trunk they would still be alive. They were not drunkards. They were not drug addicts. It was an accident. And yet the image is haunting, our children, out there, in cars, behind bottles, acting like adults when they are really still forming, still stretching their flesh. Where is the silver lining?

There is none.

"I've been sleeping about three hours a night," says May, who never stop missing these guys. "I keep having this dream. We win the game, and we're all celebrating. Everybody's in the huddle, holding their helmets up. And then we're at my house, and Chris, Danon and Kevin are there, just like that night. I get out of the shower, and this time they talk me into going with them. We all get into the Chevy. . . .

"And as soon as the doors close, everything goes black."

He stops talking and stares at the field. A fall breeze blows his hair up, then drops it gently on his forehead. It is October now, and nobody here is as young as he used to be. Jesus. Is anybody? ♦

THESE TWO MITCHES WERE ITCHING FOR PITCHING

October 9

SAN FRANCISCO — Here I sit, brokenhearted, came for Mitch, he never got started.

It is the middle of the fourth game of the National League playoffs, and all around, Candlestick fans are going crazy. Over in Oakland, they are toasting their new champions, the Athletics. But for me, alas, the playoffs are a bust. This was to be my time. My moment in the sun. You know how some people go their whole lives and are never in fashion? They buy their first Bee Gees album the same day as "Death Before Disco" T-shirts come out? Fashion is, for such people, merely a bus that they just missed. And I am one such person. Always have been.

Until now. This was to be my time. Not because I am a Giants fan. No. Because . . . well, because of a man named Mitch.

Williams.

Wild Thing.

Surely you have heard of him? The young, semi-bearded Chicago reliever who has become the darling of Cubs fans everywhere — provided they are not within a quarter-mile of his pitches? When Mitch pitches, the ball can go right down the middle. Of the plate or the broadcast booth. On Opening Day he loaded the bases with walks, then struck out the side. And that was a well-controlled inning. Remember in "Bull Durham," when Kevin Costner, playing a catcher, grins at the batter and says, "I don't know where it's going"?

That's Mitch. My guy.

Where is he?

It is the fourth inning now. And still no sign. He hasn't played yet this series. He is the ace of the Cubs' bullpen — 36 saves, a club record for left-handers — and, to this point, all he has done is warm up and sit down. I figured by this point, everyone in America would be singing "Wild Thing" and growing stubble. I figured the whole country would be throwing baseballs as if they were trying to separate their arms from their sockets.

And, most of all, and I hate to admit this, I figured people across the nation would be . . . renaming their children with my first name.

Let me tell you something about Mitch. It is not a great name. For one thing, it rhymes with some lousy words.

For another thing, there have not been a whole lot of historic figures to honor the moniker. No King Mitch. No Saint Mitch. No famous war generals. Gen. Mitch MacArthur? Yeah. You're laughing, aren't you?

Mostly what you get when you are named Mitch as a kid is a lot of old ladies pinching your cheeks and saying, "Oooh. . . . Sing along with Mitch!" Great.

Until now. Suddenly, Mitches of the world had a whole new hero. Talented. Eccentric. Lovable? Yes. Mitch Williams is nothing if not lovable. Earlier this season, he was hit in the head by a line drive. He pitched the next day. "I've been hit in the head before," he said. "My brother used to hit me in the head all the time."

Lovable? He goes bowling after ballgames to relieve tension. Lovable? He has a tattoo — below the waist. Lovable? He was once summed up by pitcher Al Nipper: "If a bird had Mitch's brain, it would fly backwards."

Listen. I have met the man. You'd like him. He was running past the other day and I said, "Hey. Mitch. When you gonna pitch?"

And he said, "I dunno. That's what I wanna know. I'm itching. This is bad. I gotta pitch. I dunno."

A nd now we're in the sixth inning. And no Mitch. You gotta wonder about this. True. Williams is the closer. He usually only comes in late with the Cubs leading. Then again, the way the Cubs' pitchers are going in this series, if they wait for that, he might as well stay at the hotel.

Some people saw his absence as a managerial gaffe. No. I know what it is. A conspiracy. By the Williams and Roberts of the world. They've already got Will Clark and Robby Thompson. They've got Willie Mays and Bob Gibson. Let's face it. There is no shortage of Bills or Bobs or Marks or Dons or even Terrys in the sporting world. And zip for Mitches.

Oh. Yeah. In basketball there have been a few. But how many kids are on the playground, spinning to the hoop and yelling, "Mitch . . . Kupchak!"?

And then there is the famous boxer, Mitch (Blood) Green, who once called Mike Tyson a sissy and has had his license suspended 59 times. At last check, I think he moved into police headquarters, because he was there most of the time anyhow.

And now it's the eighth inning. Wait. Here he comes! Striding to the mound like a wild man. Look at that delivery! Look at that smoke! Look at him fall off the mound like somebody tied his shoes together. Finally, America is watching a Mitch in big-time action, and, and . . .

And the Cubs lose.

And he walks off the field.

Here I sit, brokenhearted. I am not sure what these playoffs will ultimately mean to the people involved. I know what they will mean to me.

My cheeks are in trouble. ♦

A FESTIVE ATMOSPHERE RIPPED APART BY QUAKE

October 18

S AN FRANCISCO — I am writing this column in the most frightening position I have ever been in, some 200 feet above the ground in Candlestick Park, which just moments ago was shaking as if the entire stadium were on a wagon being wheeled over cobblestone. An earthquake, they call it out here, with some regularity, and even as I type these words, the stadium occasionally rolls — aftershocks — with the concrete, the steel supports, everything shaking, as if suddenly there is no such thing as sturdy, not anymore.

There are people running across the field, players heading for the exits, grabbing their wives and their families, the festive atmosphere of this World Series Game 3 suddenly ripped apart. And yet, such is the nature of sports that when the initial quake hit, at 5:04 p.m., rumbling the stadium and swaying the field, some fans roared, they raised their fists, they made jokes. "It's God. He's a Giants fan!"

What do you do when the very ground beneath you begins to tremble, when you are in the upper bowl of a mammoth stadium with no hope of an exit — and suddenly there are reports of cracks in the concrete? I was on the phone with an editor in my office, discussing the night's work, when the roller-coaster feeling hit.

"Tom," I said, "the stadium is . . . moving."

"What?"

Suddenly the TV screens went out. The phones were gone. The rumbling continued for 15 seconds and, in an instant, every little tidbit of earthquake advice came splashing back. Find an open space. Get away from anything overhead. Avoid doorways.

Stay alive.

B rett Butler was running sprints in the outfield when the earth began to quiver. "I felt like I was drunk or something," he says now, holding onto a member of his family. "Then I looked up in the stands for my wife. My mother. I was screaming for them, to get out on the field. I still don't have everybody."

Suddenly there are no players here, no fans, no reporters; there are just people, and many of them are streaming down the ramps, leaping over the walls. Some are bare-chested, raising their beer cups and screaming,

"WOOH!" Others are crying, running to people with transistor radios, asking, no doubt, about the homes of their loved ones.

I have a little television plugged in my ear and the first pictures are coming across. They are, for someone who does not live with the daily threat of earthquakes, terrifying. The Bay Bridge is missing a chunk; it is dangling in the water. The Nimitz Highway that runs along the Oakland side of the bay is split in crooked lines, with cars stacked up. There are fires blazing and buildings have collapsed and they are now saying it is the worst earthquake since the big one of 1906.

On a local radio station, people are calling in, reporting the damage, defining the breadth of this disaster with every call.

"This is Sue from Oakland. We really felt it bad here. Our cable TV just blew out."

"This is Sam from Napa. I have a 55-gallon fish tank in my living room, and this quake just sent 20 gallons of water splashing all over my dang floor."

It is the kind of thing you hear about, but never envision yourself involved in. It happens elsewhere, right? You have a cousin or an aunt who told you about "the time I was in an earthquake." But it was usually a rumble of the bed, a little shake. Not a stadium rocking. Buildings don't fall down, do they?

Out on the field now, the players are collecting their loved ones, counting heads, streaming for the exits. "I've never been involved in anything like this," says Pat Sheridan, the Giants' outfielder, who once played in the friendlier confines of Tiger Stadium. "Butler said to me, 'You never been in an earthquake. You're in one now.' "

The lights went out.

The network broadcast was lost.

Players such as Jose Canseco and Carney Lansford were pointing to the sky, as if the rumble had come from the heavens, and others such as Giants manager Roger Craig and his pitcher Mike Krukow were heading for the safest ground, centerfield. In the Giants dugout a fan, reportedly suffering a heart attack, was being given oxygen by the team doctor.

Madness. The whole thing seems so crazy. An earthquake? I can only describe the feeling as the noise of a jet plane, combined with the shaking of a bumpy bus ride. That is the outside feeling. What you feel inside depends, I suppose, on your level of courage.

Darkness is beginning to fall. I suddenly realize that we are without power, without lights. A voice comes over a bullhorn.

"LADIES AND GENTLEMEN, THOSE IN THE UPPER LEVEL ARE BEING ASKED TO EVACUATE THE PREMISES IMMEDIATELY."

There is no more writing. What you are reading now, I am speaking into a telephone, one of the few that seem to be working on these suddenly crumbled streets. The game, of course, was postponed; baseball hardly matters right now. And the bus that took us from Candlestick into the gnarl of panicked traffic along Highway 101 could get us no closer than a half mile of our hotel.

On the little television screen, scenes of this suddenly ravaged city were coming fast now, one more incredible than the next. Cars crushed between levels of the collapsed Bay Bridge. A raging fire in the Marina area, which fire fighters could not contain because the water pipes beneath the ground were crushed in the quake. So fast? Can all this destruction really happen in 15 terrible seconds?

This city always has been beautiful, a favorite place to walk the streets, and yet now we are walking these streets and there is something ungodly about them, dark, eerie, no lights anywhere. People wandering with no place to go and no way of getting there.

We passed Ninth Street and it was covered in glass. Broken glass from shattered windows forming a jagged blanket that glistened in the light of street flares. We passed a tall white apartment building. "Call the police," came a woman's voice. "Call the police."

Whom could you call? What could you do? There were reports of looting and reports of people trapped in houses that were, hours ago, two stories tall and now were in the street. It was like a scene from one of those nuclear war films, people wandering aimlessly, the distant sound of alarms and sirens.

"Everybody's homeless now," mumbled a colleague.

Can it be that this night began with a baseball game? That seems so long ago.

Years from now, people will talk about where they were during this earthquake. It will become a war story, a badge of courage in the sports world, a yarn that may grow larger and more horrible with each retelling.

It is hard to imagine that now. Something harsh and terrible has happened here, smack in the center of the nation's biggest game.

I am hanging up the phone and walking to, god, I really don't know where. It is the night the earth shook, and nobody seems to know much anymore. ♦

210

SHAKEN VICTIMS WON'T FORGET EARTH'S GROWL

October 19

S AN FRANCISCO — Everything he owns is lying at his feet, a bag of clothes, a bag of cassette tapes and an electric guitar, wrapped in plastic. "How long before they get us someplace to live?" he asks. He stares at the other victims in the shelter, lying on cots and gulping Red Cross coffee.

Nobody answers.

Roman Jones, a thin young musician with wire-rim glasses, was about to step into the shower when the earth opened the day before. The floor began to rumble. The pictures began to shake. Outside on Sixth Street, a crack split the asphalt, and water began to spurt from it — like blood from an open wound.

"What the hell is going on?" Jones yelled to his roommate, Jeff Reynolds. Reynolds said, "Run!"

Suddenly, the ceiling fell in on them, they were covered with plaster and their feet were racing through the darkness — where did the lights go? Hearts beating, they heard screams in the hallway, and all they could think of was get outside, get outside. They burst through the lobby, and the ground still shook. The sidewalk was evil, it was alive, rising. They kept running. "The faster we ran," Jones says, "the worse it seemed to get."

He tugs on his shirt and sighs. An hour ago, he had sneaked into the building — under the yellow police barriers — and grabbed the remains of his life. And now he waits, in the dimly lit Moscone Center, which is usually reserved for conventions and concerts but today is swallowing the homeless, the deserted, the people whose buildings are cracked in half or have sunk into the sidewalk.

It is the morning after the night they can never forget, the earthquake, the growling of the planet. And it is not over. Here, they talk about the Anglo Hotel, their former home, which rose from the sidewalk at least six inches. Across the bay, on the Oakland side, rescuers are plowing through the concrete of I-880, which collapsed during rush hour. Dogs are sniffing for survivors. In a nearby town, six people sit holding hands, a silent vigil for a friend they believe is still alive, trapped in a building.

The horror. The survival. How can you make sense of an earthquake? What strikes you most as you travel these shaken streets is how such an

211

awesome force could be so fast and so fickle. It came during a perfectly glorious afternoon — warm sun, warm breeze — and in 15 seconds, it set this area back years, maybe longer. It razed some buildings to rubble and left others untouched. It amused some residents, like a roller-coaster ride, and forced others to drive off bridges to their death.

"I'm from Philadelphia originally, man," says Jones, as he sits down for the long wait. "I don't need this bleep. Damn. I was just getting my life together."

You live here, you take your chances. That's what they tell you. But that was when "earthquake" meant a rumble in the night and then back to sleep. We had come to cover baseball, a World Series, and suddenly, the stadium shook and the place was evacuated and here we were wandering on Market Street, after midnight, like lost children, no place to go, no lights, no food. People slept in doorways. On benches. Occasionally you heard a scream. A siren. A vendor lugged out two sacks of electric bee antennas — the kind John Belushi used to wear on "Saturday Night Live" — and because they lit up, providing two dots of green light, enough to see the face in front of you, hundreds of souls were soon walking San Francisco with little bee antennas on their heads.

Crazy. It was paradise gone mad, a lullaby of a city now covered in shattered glass.

The worst quake since 1906? Is that what they said?

The night seemed to last forever and yet, as long as it was dark, there was hope that the world would be different in the morning. That all these pictures, transmitted on battery-operated TV sets — pictures of one house leaning into the next like a drunken sailor, or a 50-foot section of the upper-level Bay Bridge collapsed through to the lower level — would somehow soften in the morning light.

Instead, the images grew starker in the daytime, more real. The body count began to swell as police and fire reports came in. At least 253 lost in the I-880 collapse. Two killed in a shopping mall crumble in Santa Cruz. One man killed on the road when horses broke free from a trailer and smacked into his car.

"I saw five bodies myself," said Ronnie McAuliffe, a bearded man with a Chicago Cubs cap who lives in the Mission District. "A wall of a building over near Townsend Street collapsed on these five cars, just buried them in a pile. I jumped in and started pulling bricks from there — you know, trying to get them out."

He sighed, then shook his head.

"They were dead, all right. Police came and took them."

California, falling down. All around the Bay Area, people were walking, no particular destination, just walking, looking, seeing cracks in the middle of a townhouse and garage doors smashed into the cars beneath them. It was arbitrary destruction, as if the devil said, "Eenie-meenie-miney . . . crunch."

Near the Marina area, streets were blocked off with yellow police barriers. It was here that the fires raged most fiercely, fires that could not be put out quickly for want of water that was lost when the quake broke the mains.

Vic Giannini, a 71-year-old retiree, was watching TV when he felt his house rumble. For some reason he went to the window and looked across North Point Street just in time to see a four-story apartment building "crumble like an accordion."

He points to it now and scratches his white hair. It is the strangest thing you ever saw. The building is collapsed and resting atop a gray Ford Tempo. It looks as if the house had been built around the crushed car. The roof is only 20 feet from the sidewalk.

"Are you saying that's actually the second floor of the building?" someone asks Giannini.

"No, no," he says, "that's the fourth floor. The other three are crushed beneath it."

There are pictures like this across the Bay Area. Houses that have simply sunk into the earth. Sidewalks that rise two feet, to a point, as if a giant arrow is sticking up from beneath the concrete. Hotel lobbies lit by candlelight; stranded guests sleeping on the couches. Cars hanging off bridges.

California, falling down.

"How bad you get it, Vic?" asks Frank Battaglia, a thick-eyebrowed plumber who, he says, has been living here for years.

"Pretty bad," comes the answer. "Everything upstairs is a wreck. Go up and see."

Battaglia goes up into the house, then emerges a few minutes later.

"Hey, Vic. My wife would give anything if our house looked as good as yours right now. She'd kiss you, she'd be so happy."

"Yeah?"

"She'd kiss you. You wanna see destroyed? My place is destroyed."

"Yeah?"

"Yeah. I'll show you destroyed. Come and see my place, you wanna see destroyed."

They turn and look at the apartments that are squashing the gray Ford. It is warm now, like the day it happened, warm and quiet. Were it not for the distant fire engines, it might be another perfect day.

"Hey, Frank," says Giannini, not taking his eye off the destruction. "I won't be needing those pipes fixed no more."

And the survival continues. Yes, there were stories of looting —
surprisingly few — but there were also sterling examples of humanity,
people opening their homes to strangers, cable cars riding through the
streets, announcing: "If anyone needs a ride somewhere, to find their
families, the transportation is free." Restaurants donated food and plates to
the Red Cross shelters. People came with blankets and blood for the
hospitals.

There is something about disaster that draws people together, and there
is something about it that makes us wonder why, what is the reason, who is
trying to tell us something? Can it really be that this stuff just happens? You
live here, you take your chances?

Outside the shelter, on Mission Street, three street people are squatting
against a building, their palms open. I drop some money in their hands and
the middle one, a big man with deep blue eyes and wild white hair, stuffs the
money in his pocket.

"Did you feel the earthquake?" he says. "I was going out to buy a jug of
wine. And the street started shaking. And I said to myself, 'Wait a minute.
I'm not loaded yet.' "

He wags a finger. "You know what I say? I say that one day, the big one
is gonna come, and this whole place will slide into the sea. We'll all meet
there, down below, no rich and no poor, just people."

I stare at him and walk away. A police car rolls past, and up ahead is
another yellow zone, another sunken building, another life to rebuild.

"We're all gonna meet there," the crazy man yells again, but by that
point I am up the street and walking fast. ◆

214

NO SENSE OF SATISFACTION AS PROBERT GOES TO JAIL

November 8

It was time to go to jail. Bob Probert, wearing jeans, a leather jacket and cowboy boots, walked slowly down the Metro Airport corridor, next to his lawyer, his mother and two friends. He chewed gum. He smiled occasionally. He looked like a big kid, which always has been part of the problem.

"Coffee, Bob?" said his lawyer.

"What's that?"

"Should we get some coffee? We have a minute."

Probert nodded. They looked around. It was early morning, still dark outside, and through the windows you saw the rain soaking the runways.

There was no place to get coffee.

"Maybe at the gate," the lawyer said.

They walked on. He was going to jail. After all the warnings, all the apologies, all the second chances and all the arrests, Probert, once a hockey player, always trouble, would pay the piper. The night before, he said farewell to his fellow patients at the rehab center and went horseback riding with several staff members. There, in the saddle, galloping away, he felt the wind at his back and the world behind him. Freedom. He felt freedo–

"Newspapers, Bob?"

"Huh?"

"Newspapers? You want something to read on the trip, don't you?"

"Yeah. Whatever."

I took a breath and approached him. It was not easy. In the past two years, I have written a string of columns about Probert — how he let down his team, broke his coach's heart, set an awful example for kids and, worst of all, never seemed to learn. He deserved what he got. Maybe more. I felt that. I wrote it. That's easy to do when you're behind a typewriter, miles away. Now we were both here, together.

"Hey," I said softly.

"Hey," he said, spotting me.

He looked at his lawyer, Harold Fried, who shrugged OK. We stepped away from his family and stood under a screen marked "departures."

"Are you scared?"

"It ... I ... it hasn't hit me yet."

"Do you think this punishment is fair?"

"Yeah. It is."

I paused. "Bob. Are you sorry?"

He nodded. "I'm sorry for a lot of things. I'm sorry for my family, for my teammates, for me. I hurt people. I messed up. Now I have to live with it." He dug his hands in his pockets, a familiar pose. I thought back on all the poses I had seen Probert in over the years: lighting a cigarette with a blowtorch; snarling at reporters; in taverns, knocking back beers like a sailor; in courtrooms, staring at the floor, after he'd drunkenly wrapped his car around a telephone pole; in handcuffs, after he'd been caught at the U.S.-Canadian border with a packet of cocaine in his underwear.

He is a criminal now, not a hockey player. He has been in a rehab center for months and reports say, for the first time, he is straightening up his act. Who knows? "I'd like to get back to hockey someday," he said. "But if I don't, I don't. I'm still a better person for being in this rehab program."

He was calm. He seemed together. Two years ago, I was the writer who discovered that Probert and several Red Wings teammates had been out drinking the night before the last playoff game against Edmonton. I wrote the story, and the team tumbled into controversy; it has never been the same. Most of those players are off the roster now. And Probert is on his way to jail. I looked at him. He looked at me. What if we never said anything about that night? What if no one found out? Where would they all be now?

B ob, let's go," said his lawyer.

"Can't be late," Probert said, grimly.

We walked together toward the gate. A TV crew approached and flicked on a hot white light. Once again Probert stopped and answered questions. Yes, he was trying to turn his life around. Yes, he understood why the judge insisted on a jail term — although the jail he'll be in the next three months is not the steel bars and handcuffs type.

"Hey, Ma, everybody, come over here," Probert said. They walked to an empty area. He lit up a cigarette and whispered a few things.

"He's a changed person,'" his lawyer said. Who knows? We write so many columns blasting athletes for acting foolishly, for breaking rules. Cocaine. Alcohol. We scream for justice. And here, in the artificial light of an airport, justice was coming to port. I waited for satisfaction. It never came.

Instead, I watched Probert hug his girlfriend and his mother and turn and walk through that jetway door. And all I felt was sorry.

Maybe I'm too soft for this business. Maybe the business is too harsh. I would like to report that Bob Probert is cured, but I can't do that, and I would like to report that he is hopeless, but I can't do that, either. I am sitting in my office now, and I guess all you really can do is watch them get on the plane and fly away. And hope that fate treats them kindly. ♦

216

NEED HOLIDAY GIFT IDEAS? THROW THE BOOKS AT 'EM

December 13

Give the gift of reading. That's what we say around here. And with only two weeks until Christmas, you'd better get moving to catch these brand new sports books, hot off the presses for the holiday season:

"BETCHA FIVE BUCKS THAT CAKE DON'T RISE" — The Pete Rose Cookbook.

"THEY SAID WHAT?" — The Jon Koncak Story.

"EVERYTHING I NEED TO KNOW, I AIN'T LEARNED IN KINDERGARTEN" — The World According to Sparky Anderson.

"THE 1989 NFL BOUNTY GUIDE," by Buddy Ryan. The Eagles coach admits there is indeed a bounty system in professional football, and lists names and prices. Biggest Catch: John Elway. "We'll pay up to $475 for knocking him out," Ryan writes. "Of course, if you break his leg, it's $500."

"NO MAS SUGAR RAY, MAS CREAM PUFF," by Roberto Duran. The former champion takes readers on a "personal journey of self-discovery" — stopping at every doughnut shop in North America.

"PETR KLIMA PACKED A POKE OF PICKLED PISTONS," by Jacques Demers. The jolly Red Wings coach writes children's stories in his unique style. Holiday favorites include "Goldiloops and Da Tree Defensemen," "Rudolph, Dat Checking Reindeer," and "Frosty Da Snow Head."

"SCRATCH 'EM IF YOU GOT 'EM" — The body language of baseball.

"YOUR KEYS, MR. JORDAN" — The private life of NBA superstar Michael Jordan, as written by the parking attendant in his apartment building. "Sometimes Michael does a 360-degree turn," says the author. "Other times, he just banks the car off the wall." 118 pages, action photos.

"HAF U SEEN MY TEEF?" by Claude (Efferdent) LeMolar. The confessions of a veteran NHL player who locked himself out of his hotel room one night and has been incomprehensible ever since.

"IT'S HARD TO BE HUMBLE WHEN YOU SPARKLE IN THE DARK," by (Neon) Deion Sanders. In this no-holds-barred autobiography, the outspoken Atlanta defender takes on the media, his teammates, and the American Jewelry Association, for not using enough rhinestones in its Zodiac pins.

"WHY MEN STINK," by Margo Adams.

"WHY WOMEN STINK," by Wade Boggs.

"THE WHINING IRISH," by Lou Holtz. The famous Notre Dame coach complains about opponents, airplane food, body odor, and the sun being in his eyes. He also writes that "SMU will be much tougher next time, and we could lose."

"I'M OK, YOU'RE LOST," by John Salley. A pictorial guide through Salley's 62-room mansion.

"TRUST ME" — An anthology of short stories by Dexter Manley, Barry Switzer, Jackie Sherrill, Roy Tarpley and Marvin Barnes.

"THE 15-MINUTE MILLIONAIRE," by Bill Lajoie. A novel about an imaginary Detroit general manager, who, after being turned down by five premier free agents, decides what the heck — he might as well keep the $16 million for himself. Foreword by Tom Monaghan, who would like to know where Lajoie is right now.

"TYSON IS A SISSY," by Salman Rushdie.

"GOT IT, GOT IT, DON'T GOT IT . . . " by Jack McKeon. The true story of the San Diego Padres general manager, who last week snapped up Joe Carter, Craig Lefferts and Fred Lynn — then went to lunch. McKeon reveals how he earned the nickname "Trader Jack" beginning with the day he traded his first baseball card and ending with the day he traded in his mother and father for a new boat. With photos, 396 pages.

"HELLO, I LOVE YOU," by Steve Garvey.

"THE CLOSING OF THE AMERICAN MIND" — Conversations with professional wrestlers.

"NOW I'M COOKIN' " — The long awaited autobiography of Vinnie (Microwave) Johnson, who reveals that, among other things, he is great with baked potatoes and bad with aluminum foil.

"THE COLLECTED MIKE DITKA, 1989" — Here, in one canvas-bound edition, are the best press conferences by the irascible coach. Read such classics as "Jim McMahon is our quarterback for now," "I'm not sure we can win another game," "We stink!" and "I blame myself." Surprise bonus: The pages are made of thin white bubble gum, which you can rip out and chew at least 14,800 times.

"DECADE OF CHUMPIONS" — A collection of raw sports stories that might have appeared in Detroit newspapers, if not for the swift eyes of the copy editors. Includes "PIBSTONS WIN THE TITEL!" "LYIN'S BEAT BEARS," and "SCHEMBECHLER TAKES A.D.'S POSITION: DANTLEY UPSET." ♦

BO SCHEMBECHLER: LAST OF THE ONE-NAME COACHES

December 14

A NN ARBOR, Mich. — He began his legacy by driving down the wrong street, getting lost and having to call the football office from a pay phone. "Uh, this is Bo Schembechler, the new coach," he said to a rather confused secretary. "Where the heck are you?"

Twenty-one years later, on a cold winter evening, he was saying goodbye. This time the room was stuffed with reporters, tight-lipped coaches, former players and a million memories. This time, he knew exactly where he was. This time, it was the university that felt lost.

"The hardest thing I've ever had to do," said Bo Schembechler, 60, choking back tears as he announced his retirement, "is give up . . . my football team . . . but I'm doing it. . . . I think I've run my luck about as far as I can take it."

There goes a legend. What will Michigan do without Bo? Who will win all those games? Who will pace the sidelines on Saturday afternoons, who will scream at the officials, who will waddle through an army of apple-cheeked freshmen every August as they squat on the playing field? "GENTLEMEN, THIS IS MICHIGAN!" he would say. "AND AT MICHIGAN WE DO THINGS ONE WAY."

His way.

It was always his way. Oh, maybe not this retirement part. He had wanted to tell his team first, but when he woke up yesterday, the story had leaked. That upset him. So did these questions about the athletic director position — a job he can't possibly keep, not if you know his personality.

Here walks the ultimate coach. On his first day of practice, 21 autumns ago, he sucked a mouthful of air and blew into a whistle — only to find the whistle was broken. So? He just screamed, "GATHER ROUND," and began a remarkable era of college football, one that would span countless big games and Big Ten titles and Rose Bowls and star players and never, never a losing season. Nor the hint of scandal. His way. Always his way. He beat Ohio State, he beat Southern California, UCLA, Notre Dame. He beat the Big Ten knotheads; he beat the doctors. He beat everything they could throw at him; he just couldn't beat himself. Finally, after a lifetime of pushing the outer envelope of his existence, he said, "All right, you win. I'll slow down. I will live."

"Something told me after the last Ohio State game I would not be back again," he said. Truth is, he knew sooner than that. The thing that was telling him was his own voice.

And there is no mistaking that voice.

This has been the greatest job I've ever had," he said. And he will miss it. Big time.

This, after all, is the last of the one-name coaches. Woody. Bear. Bo. You know how some men seem born for their occupations? Check out that walk, that frumpy coat, that crooked smile, those booming vocal cords. A football coach. "That's all I am," he would always say. As of Jan. 2 — after his final game, the Rose Bowl against Southern Cal — he will be one no more. Gary Moeller, his longtime assistant, will take over. Bo's Wolverines days, at least the active ones, will be finished.

Oh, sure, he said he "might stay on" as athletic director, the position he has held the last year. I don't buy it. Not for a second. He will be gone when the football is over. Let's face it. Bo is never one for office work. He was never one for watching. I once sat next to him in the stands, and he nearly punched a hole in my arm. And that was basketball!

No. A football coach should coach football, not play executive. Bo never really liked the role of athletic director; he really only took it because of university pressure and his desire to keep the football team away from any evil new bosses. Once he hands over the whistle Jan. 2, he will find a new challenge, something closer to home, something with fewer airplanes, something in sports. I promise you this: He will not go gentle into that good night.

He never has.

This, after all, is a man who once destroyed an office when the Big Ten sent Ohio State to the Rose Bowl instead of Michigan. A man who got so mad once at halftime, he kicked an entire tray of Coca-Colas into the air. A man who stood in the middle of practice and got blind-sided by speeding receiver, knocking him down, making his entire body throb with pain. You know what he did? He looked up, saw his team gathered in a circle and rose to his feet. "That," he said, dusting himself off, "would have killed a mortal man."

That's Bo. Ask any of his former players to tell you a story and they will inevitably launch into an impersonation, some bark, some holler, some magic words that have stayed with them years after Schembechler has forgotten them.

Think of what he has done. When he arrived, the football team was merely average, in the shadow of national champion Ohio State and his one-time mentor, Woody Hayes.

"GENTLEMEN," Bo said to his skeptical players, "THOSE WHO

STAY WILL BE CHAMPIONS!" That November, his Wolverines shocked the nation by upsetting Ohio State in the biggest game to be played in Ann Arbor this century.

He kept his word.

When he arrived at U-M, the coaches' locker room was five hooks on the wall. "GENTLEMEN," he told his staff, "THERE WILL BE SOME CHANGES AROUND HERE!" Today, they are building the Center of Champions, a state-of-the-art athletic facility that costs $12 million. Bo raised every penny from contributors and threw in a healthy chunk of his own money to boot.

He kept his word.

Throughout his time here, there were scandals across the nation, other coaches were buying players, changing grades, handing out sports cars, cheating. "GENTLEMEN," he announced. "WE WILL RUN A CLEAN PROGRAM!" They never wavered. Once, in his first year at Michigan, an overzealous booster called to complain about the use of a player. Bo ignored him.

"You don't understand," the man said. "I'm a very influential member of the M Club."

"Not anymore, you're not," Bo said. He kept his word.

So it should be no surprise that he is keeping his word now. He promised himself and his wife, Millie, who had stood there that morning two years ago as the doctors groped his chest and prepared to slice him open, that he would not push things beyond human limits. Yesterday, Millie stood in the corner of the crowded press conference, her lips tightly clenched.

"Did you cry?" someone asked her.

"All day," she confessed.

She met him on a blind date in St. Louis, back when nobody knew his name. Bo who? How do you spell that? They went for a ride in a Missouri riverboat. He played with her children. He seemed so happy. Three months later they were married.

And by the following winter, their lives had changed forever. He was suddenly coach of the Michigan Wolverines. Who knew what fame that would bring? Who could foresee the success — all those Big Ten titles, the coach-of-the-year awards, the banquets, the speeches. Who might predict that students would one day chant, "Bo is God!"

Nobody. So in the margins around football, Bo and Millie tried to build a normal life. It hasn't really been normal. "You work 14 or 15 hours a day, you get to bed late, you get up early, you eat on the run, you don't have time to exercise," said Schembechler, listing the perils of coaching. After a while you say, "It's time to stop."

The time has come.

Health concerns him now, he admits. Oh, once upon a time, he laughed at it. He suffered a heart attack the morning of his first Rose Bowl, and as they pushed him down on the operating table he said, "Hey, doc, I've got a game to coach today."

Now, health is not so funny. Despite an image to the contrary, Schembechler does not wish to be buried on the sidelines. There were moments this season when the travel left him exhausted. Another airplane. Another bus. Another press conference. Last month, when someone tried to coerce him into yet another commitment, he exploded. "I can't! I can't do it!" he yelled. "I don't want to die, OK?"

His doctors told him he was pushing his luck. Two heart attacks? Two open-heart surgeries? Sixty years old? Yeah. You could call that pushing your luck.

But what he did yesterday was not because of some X-ray or medical chart. It was not because a collapse was imminent. On the contrary. He wants to walk away while he still can.

"I'm not sick; make sure you write that," he admonished one reporter. OK. He's not sick.

B ut he is gone. This is for real. And the feeling is like losing an old friend, a favorite teacher, and, for the players — a father figure. True to form, he announced his retirement now rather than go recruiting when he knew he wouldn't coach the kids he attracted.

"That wouldn't be right," he said. And that was reason enough to say good-bye.

The man who will replace him, Moeller, his offensive coordinator, is his hand-chosen successor. Moeller not only thinks like Bo, reacts like Bo and has a rhyming nickname (Bo, Mo), he was in that car 21 years ago when Schembechler took the wrong turn and wound up cruising Ann Arbor like a general in search of his army.

"Yep, a green Toronado," Moeller said. "I can still remember that car." Good. Tradition should count for something.

It has counted for 21 years. We were lucky to have Schembechler all this time. So were his players. So were his coaches. So were the mothers and fathers whose living rooms he graced, from mansions in California to a rundown tenement in Detroit, where Bo once visited a promising player and found his mother huddled around a fire rock that was the only heat in the house.

"We've got to do something about that," he told his assistant when they left. "And we've got to get that kid into Michigan."

He came. He graduated. He is on his way to becoming a teacher.

You want to know the true Schembechler legacy? That's it right there. Kids you won't see in the NFL but who have their degree and a nice job and a family, thanks largely to the stumpy, grinning tough guy who wore the blue cap and black shoes.

There goes a legend.

"Would you like to be a sports writer next?" someone jokingly asked. Schembechler laughed. "No, because I'd be too much of a homer. I'd always come down in favor of the coach."

You know what, Bo? That hasn't been so hard to do. As Moeller spoke of the future and reporters scribbled away, someone sidled up to Schembechler and asked whether he would be available the next morning.

"Hey, man," Bo said. "I got some film to look at. I got one more game to coach here, you know."

And with that, he left his farewell party. What becomes a legend most? In this case, just being himself. Really, now. What more could you want? ♦

SANDERS LEARNED EARLY HOW TO FLY HIGH QUIETLY

December 17

First of all, Barry Sanders doesn't mind dancing. As long as someone else is doing it. Sure, when he scores a touchdown, he hands the ball to the referee like a mailman delivering a phone bill. But he isn't bothered by those who prefer a wiggle or a shake. "Hey, I used to love Billy (White Shoes) Johnson, and the Washington Smurfs and all," he says, looking down at his hands. "It's just ... not me."

Nor does he have a problem with fame. Oh, it's true, he asked whether he could skip his own Heisman award ceremony, and he passed up an invitation to the White House because he had to study. But he doesn't condemn players who search for the spotlight. "It's just," he says, "not me."

What just is Barry Sanders? Nobody seems to know. Everybody wants to. Three months after slipping on a Lions uniform, Sanders, the son of a Kansas roofer, is the most compelling figure on the Detroit sports pages. Isiah Thomas might be throwing in baskets and Steve Yzerman might be skating circles around defensemen, but, let's be honest, we have seen their magic. This is new. This is thrilling.

This is a man who takes a football, flips on his engine and leaves defenders frozen like tanks. Here comes Barry. There goes Barry. He is the best rookie in the NFL and one of the top running backs in the game. Already? Already. Walter Payton, after watching Sanders' first 10 Sundays, announced that "Barry is better than I was." Better than Payton? Who is this guy? What makes him tick?

Why is that important? Sanders wonders. Isn't it enough that I run? Don't they know what I know? A humble man can do anything without a lot of noise. When Barry was a child in Kansas, he used to pretend he was a super hero. He would enter the house and jump for the ceiling, his fingers straining for a touch, higher, high–

"Cut it out, damn it!" his father would yell. "Before I smack you!"

So he learned to fly quietly.

He has been doing it ever since.

People write that I'm this nice, shy choir boy," says Sanders, sitting by his locker at the Silverdome, a towel draped over his bare shoulders. "But that's not really true. That's just an image. They have to come up with some image for me, because plain people don't sell newspapers.

"I like to talk. I have friends. But it's hard to find someone who doesn't want to talk football these days. And football is not the most important thing in my life. Religion, my family, being at peace with myself — and then maybe football. I wonder all the time what I might be doing if not playing this game."

It is hard to imagine; his body almost screams athletics. Look at those thighs, so massive, so hard. Look at those arms, like steel cables. It is as if someone poured concrete into a 5-foot-8 flesh mold. His close-cropped hair frames a smooth face that, believe it or not, is often smiling. Really.

"Are you embarrassed by fame?" he is asked.

"No."

"Are you embarrassed by wealth?"

"No."

"What embarrasses you?"

He rubs his ear. "What embarrasses me? I guess walking in the middle of a crowd and slipping and falling on my behind. That would embarrass me."

See? A joke. Barry Sanders laughs in a gushing giggle, like he did when he was a kid back in Kansas. It was there, in that three-bedroom house in the poorer section of Wichita, he jumped for the ceiling and felt the wrath of his father. It was there he met rich kids, who would tease him about all those people living in one house. It was there he would walk with a hat pin in his teeth, like a toothpick. It looked cool, until one day he accidentally swallowed it, and from then on, never needed a prop for his ego.

It was there he watched his mother and listened to her sighs and heard his own voice. To understand Barry Sanders, you must understand his childhood. At age 21, he is still, in a way, going through it.

There were only two rules in the Sanders home. Rule No. 1: Never disobey Dad. Rule No. 2: Never forget rule No. 1. William Sanders is a stubborn, headstrong man, the father of 11, who used to race his sons backward to prove he was faster. Before Barry was born, he worked in a meat scrap company, dumping the bones of dead animals. "One day I went for a drink of water and I turned around and the boss was right there staring at me. I said, 'Hey, why don't you get off my back?' And he said, 'Hit the road.' He fired me.

"I went to the union, filed for arbitration and won. They said I could have my job back. I said, 'Give me my money. I'm not working here.'"

He turned to roofing, carpentry, home repairs. When he needed assistance, he took his three sons, William Jr., Byron and Barry, the baby. All day they would labor, with the hammers, the tar, sweating in the hot summer sun. You did not complain in the Sanders family. Not unless you wanted a good whupping. Dad said, "Get in the car." You got in the car. Dad said, "Get off that telephone and stop talking to girls." You got off the telephone and stopped talking to girls. Money? Barry was amazed that kids in school actually got an allowance "just for being alive." There were no allowances in the Sanders family. "Your pay is having a roof over your head and food to eat," said William Sanders.

Although he had eight daughters, William preferred sons. "Boys grow up to be football players," he said, as if it were their destiny. Of course, with 10 siblings, it's hard to tell if that was destiny pushing you or just someone's elbow at the dinner table. When Barry was in the fourth grade, his sister bought him an electric football set for Christmas. He spun the little men and watched them rumble along the metal field. "I identified," he admits, "with the running back."

So it begins. That same year, he signed up for football with the Beech Red Barons, a local youth team. No one figured Barry for an athlete. He was puny. On the day of Barry's first game, William Sanders went instead to watch Byron. Byron was big. Byron was strong. Byron had a chance of growing into an NFL player, who might make some big money "and get me off the damn rooftops." Go, Byron! During the game, a friend came running over, out of breath.

"Hey, Bill. You ought to see what Barry's doing down on the other field!"

"What are you talking about?"

"He scored three touchdowns already. He's running past everybody."

"Barry?" the father said. "Barry can't even play football."

Well, he said Barry couldn't fly, either.

I take after my mother," Barry Sanders says. "The only way I take after my father is that he was a great athlete. But my mother is the type who doesn't talk to hear herself talk. She would rather see other people happy than herself. I've never heard her curse. I've never seen her take a drink. She is a Christian woman. A real one."

"Do you try to live up to her standards?" he is asked.

"Yes."

"Do you fall short?"

He smiles. "Most people do."

Shirley Sanders spent nearly half her adult life pregnant or giving birth. Eleven children. She bathed them. Fed them. Took them to church. Young Barry adored her, she seemed so smart, so disciplined. But he would watch when she and her husband argued and saw how she always backed down, even when she was right. "My father is a male chauvinist," Barry says, matter-of-factly. "He always had to be right because he was the man."

Absorb and endure. That is what his mother did. And when it came time to choose between role models, Barry chose her. Thus, when the high school coach failed to start him as tailback because he claimed Barry was afraid of contact, Sanders did not argue, the way his father might. He kept his anger to himself. Absorb and endure. When he finally got to start (not until his senior year), he rushed for 274 yards and scored four touchdowns in his first game. He slipped tackles so easily, the officials checked his uniform for Vaseline.

Absorb and endure. In college, at Oklahoma State, he was given a summer job packing groceries at a supermarket. It paid $3.35 an hour. Other players on the team were given jobs paying three times that much. He knew it. He kept it inside. Four months later, he crushed the NCAA record for yards rushing in a single season (2,628, or an average of 238.9 a game). He won the Heisman Trophy. He would never need a grocery store job again.

Absorb and endure. During contract talks with the Lions, William Sanders seemed to run the show. He spoke bluntly; he called the offers insulting. As the holdout grew, he gave the impression that Barry was only interested in money. It wasn't true. Barry knew it. "People would tease me, saying, 'Your father's doing all your talking for you.' " But like his mother, he would never tell his father to be quiet. Absorb and endure.

A nd be humble. Even now, with the money he earns (a five-year, $5.9 million contract) he does not drive a Mercedes or a Porsche. His clothes are simple. There are no gold chains. Although his father nearly dragged him out of college one year early — "You go out for spring football, I'll break your legs myself," he once said — life in Wichita hasn't changed much. Barry has offered his parents whatever they want. Money is in the bank. "We're on Easy Street now," William Sanders says. "But we still live in the same house."

A good metaphor. Is it possible to be Big Time and Small Time at the Same Time? Apparently so. Sanders once told a TV reporter he hoped Rodney Peete would win the Heisman Trophy instead of him. Huh? The day he announced his NFL eligibility, he missed a plane because the clutch blew out on his rickety old car. Is he for real? People wonder.

He is for real. Give him a roof, a bed, some food and a Bible and he will want for nothing. "My mother wouldn't," he says simply. This is a guy who can count on one hand the number of parties he's been to in his life. In high school, he was nominated for homecoming king. Much to his dismay, he won.

"There's a picture I have of him and the homecoming queen that night," says Mark McCormick, his lifelong friend, a journalism student at Kansas. "You should see it. She looks so happy, all smiles — and Barry looks like he's constipated."

Well, since when is it a crime not to like the spotlight? Sanders, who says that trusting people is "harder than ever," still treats his old friends royally. Three years ago, McCormick was struggling to get by at college. Sanders took half the money he was getting on scholarship and immediately offered it to his friend. No questions asked.

When Barry signed his huge contract with the Lions, he promptly gave one-tenth of his $2.1 million signing bonus to his church in Kansas. A tenth? "Tithing. It's in the Bible," he says. End of explanation.

He gave his Heisman Trophy to the family's favorite restaurant. He gladly signs autographs for children but is wary of adults. A woman once invited him to a party. "What will we do there?" he asked. "We'll get high, have some drinks." Sanders couldn't believe it. No thanks, he said. He went back to his room and watched TV.

A nd now everybody is watching him. Usually from behind. His stop-start, dip-and-spin running makes you dizzy with excitement. The yardage meter rolls like a pinball machine. Does he really lead the NFC in rushing? Could he really win Rookie of the Year and go to the Pro Bowl?

"I *looove* blocking for that guy," says Lomas Brown, the offensive tackle. Was that a Lion talking? You bet. In three months, Sanders has helped rinse this team of a losing attitude and dipped it into the world of the possible. Hey. We can win! We got a Superstar here!

Now all they have to do is get used to that humility. In the locker room, his teammates razz him — he is, after all, a rookie — but he often ignores their teasing and they find themselves awkwardly walking away. "Yo, man, just kidding," they'll say. Is this guy for real?

He is for real, a white-hot talent in burlap wrapping. So he doesn't mind dancing — as long as you do it. And talk shows are fine — but why don't you take the microphone, OK? "People shouldn't think because I'm quiet I don't make my own decisions," he says. "I just prefer to watch people at first, to see if their walk is as big as their talk."

His is. He stretches the towel behind his neck, and every muscle in his shoulders and arms seems to pop out through the skin. Yes, it is true, he might have the world at his feet. But he probably will step over it.

The question seems to be when will Barry Sanders change? The answer seems to be, what for? ◆

THROUGH ALL THE PAIN, HE WAS HIS FATHER'S SON

Isn't life funny, Mark Messner thought. He held a spoonful of malted shake up to his father's lips, which were black and peeling, burned from the chemotherapy. "Here you go, Dad," he said. His father rolled his eyes and made a "mmm" sound, like a child. Mark smiled, pulled the spoon out and dug it back into the cup.

Isn't life funny? A few weeks ago, Messner, 22, was a rookie linebacker for the Los Angeles Rams. He was getting paid to play football. He was living in sunny Southern California. Then the phone rang. "You'd better come home," his sister said. He knew what that meant. He left the team, without pay, and boarded a plane for Detroit.

When he first saw his father, lying in the hospital bed, Mark bit his lip. Then he went out in the hall and began to sob. He showed the nurse an old photo, before the disease, and she said, "Oh, my God."

Now he sat by the bed and fed his father, the way Del Pretty had done for him when he was an infant. Of course, technically, Del was his step-father, but Mark never cared for that phrase. He figured if the man raised me, fed me, spanked me, hugged me, took me to school, wrote me poems, came to all my football games and made me feel like the most important person in the world, well, to hell with it. He is my father.

And I am his son.

"Have some more, Dad," he whispered. He looked at the blotches of red along Del's arms and legs. He saw the blood stains on the sheets where the skin had peeled away. He thought back to a year ago, when life seemed so carefree. He was heading to the Rose Bowl with the Michigan Wolverines. There would be Hawaii after that and Japan after that. And then came the NFL draft. The Rams took him with a low-round pick. Then in training camp they had him carrying the red cones up and down the field, like some equipment boy.

"Dad," Mark said one night in a phone call home. "You'd better pull my resume off my computer. I can't compete on this level."

"Just keep plugging," Del said.

"But they got me moving cones!"

"They didn't draft you to move cones."

What does he know? Mark thought. He's never been in the NFL. He owns a piano store, for Pete's sake. But eventually the Rams did come

229

around. He stopped moving cones. He played in the exhibition games. He made the team. His father had been right. Again.

Mark looked at him. The room was quiet. He dug the spoon into the melting chocolate.

Take the chemo, they had told him.
"No," he had said.
"There's no alternative."
"There's got to be an alternative."

Del Pretty had been diagnosed as having lymph node cancer in 1980. He fought the very idea, as if it had somehow insulted his pride. He spurned chemotherapy because he thought it would deteriorate him. Instead he searched for other methods. He tried special diets and experimental drugs. And eventually he beat the illness into remission. Who had time to be sick? There was the business. The family. And Mark's football games.

"He never missed one," Mark recalls. "He came to all the home games at Michigan and a lot of the road ones, too. There was this game in Indiana where the weather was horrible. He sat there in the rain the whole time."

Not that he was one of those jock-hungry fathers. On the contrary. Del Pretty was not a very athletic man. Silver-haired, dapper, with glasses and a gentle but disciplined expression, he looked more like a well-placed accountant. Which he was. But he loved his children. He would show his feelings quietly, in notes that Mark found in his college mailbox: "Dear Mark, I want you to know how proud you make me feel."

Mark's friends would tease him sometimes about how close he was with Del. It was almost corny. He had chosen Michigan over UCLA because he wanted Del to see him play. Before he left for the Rams, Mark gave his dad a record. "Wind Beneath My Wings," by Bette Midler. He told him to listen to the words, because that's how he felt.

"Did I ever tell you you're my hero.
"You're everything I wish I could be."

It was the stuff of sappy movies. Unless you know the whole story. Mark was the son of divorce, several times; his mother married and remarried. His natural father (Max Messner, a former NFL player) also remarried. The one constant in his life was Del. He was there when Mark had problems. He was there when Mark wanted to talk about life, or girls, or football. He gave honest answers. Strict, but from the heart.

When Del and Mark's mother divorced, it tore Mark apart. His Dad had to live alone in some apartment in Northville, Mich. Why? It's not fair.

And then the cancer came back.

Take the chemo, they told him.
"No," he said.
Once again he tried experimental drugs. He flew to Houston for a new

pill. He flew to California for a procedure in which animals are injected with samples from the patient's tumors, then the antibodies formed are injected into the patient.

"I'm sorry," the doctor said. "The process takes six to eight months."

"Yes?" Del said.

"Well. Quite frankly, I don't think you have that long."

What do you do when a doctor tells you that? Already the disease had changed him physically. The tumors were stealing nutrients from his food and releasing lymph fluid instead into his abdomen. He was bloated like a pregnant woman.

"He couldn't sleep in a bed anymore," Messner says. "His stomach was so large. But meanwhile, the rest of his body was suffering from malnutrition."

Alone, out of options, he went to doctors in Ann Arbor, Mich. "Chemotherapy," they said. It was early fall. Football season. Mark was in LA, getting paid. It was as if Del had held out all this time, just to make sure his son could handle adulthood.

"All right," Del said, finally. "I'll try the chemotherapy."

They put the needle in his arm.

The blotches began after the second treatment; they looked like a rash. He asked his doctors. "Must be a skin condition," they said. "Have you changed your soap recently?"

His soap?

Another round of chemo, an increased dosage. Now the skin began to puss and fester. Like a horrible sunburn, it would die and peel away. His back. His legs. Around his mouth. Without so much as a match's flame, he was burnt all over.

"It was the chemo," Mark says now. "And what was happening outside was happening inside him as well. The organs were being destroyed." How could this be? Wasn't chemo supposed to help him? You would touch his back and the skin would come off in your hands. One time, a nurse tried rubbing ointment on the sores. Del began to moan in pain. Mark came running in.

"What's wrong, what's he saying?" the nurse asked.

"He's saying don't rub, don't rub," Mark said. "It hurts too much."

This was the horrible reality: Del Pretty was dying, one layer at a time. Few of us could witness such a thing.

But the love between son and father is like God's muscle. So while his teammates worked out back in Los Angeles, Mark Messner came to Harper Grace hospital every morning, 10 a.m, two hours before visiting time, to bathe his father.

He would lift him with his powerful arms and slide him gently into the tub. Sheets of bloody skin would stick to his hands, get under his fingernails.

He did not flinch. He poured cool water over his father's body and comforted him. While Del could still speak, Mark held the phone to his ear and let him talk to the office at Hammell Music, the piano store he owned in Livonia, Mich. Together they went over the books of the church, where Del was treasurer.

When Del's vocal cords no longer worked, Mark did the talking. When Del's eyesight went, Mark would tell him what he was missing.

On Nov. 25, they put the Michigan-Ohio State game on TV. Del stayed awake for the entire thing. When the final gun sounded, Mark said, "Hey, Dad! How about that? They're going to the Rose Bowl!"

Del raised his arm and made a soft fist. He shook it once.

Two days later, he died.

Mark knew as soon as the phone rang. It was 4 a.m. His mother was crying in the other room. "Mom," he whispered, "they said Dad expired."

He paused.

"It makes him sound like a license plate."

At the funeral, Mark read a poem Del had sent him this fall. And when they closed the casket, Mark's Rose Bowl watch was around his father's wrist. Before, it was always Del taking care of business matters, but now Mark handled the arrangements. He signed the papers. He went through the bills. He re-read the old letters and thought about their final moments together in the hospital, the feeding, the bathing. The circle was complete. The child had become father to the man.

"You know," Messner says now. "I was never embarrassed in the hospital. All that blood and skin, that was just his body. It was his heart that I was dealing with. I would have done anything for him. Anything."

Today, Mark will play a football game for the Rams, the regular-season finale. When it is over he will go to call his father, as he always did. And instead, he will have to close his eyes and imagine. "I know he's watching," he says without sadness. "He used to joke about having a beer with God. I'll bet he's doing it now."

You hear about the decline of the American family, how the old are tossed aside by the young. And then you hear of a kid who left pro football to tend his dying father. These are the last words of the poem Del wrote, which Mark read at his funeral:

"If all else in a man's life added to zero, no greater success than to be counted his son's hero."

Isn't life funny? It takes us and leaves us. And love endures. Tomorrow is Christmas, and that means this: Count your blessings, everybody, count them all very carefully. One precious person at a time. ♦

IN THE DECADE, SPORTS TAUGHT TRAGIC LESSONS

December 31

N EWPORT BEACH, Calif. — I did not know what cocaine was when this decade began. I had never seen a rock of crack. Steroids were something a crazy weight lifter might try. And no one I knew had been found dead on the highway, his blood full of alcohol.

I am a sports writer. I now know all those things. I have lost count of the funerals I have covered. The arrests blur together. Today is the last day of the decade, and I have to shake my head at the candidates for "Top Sports Story of the '80s." The Miracle On Ice? Joe Montana's third Super Bowl? Jack Nicklaus' winning one more Masters?

Maybe one of those should have been the big story. This is what was: Drugs. Hands down. The biggest story, the saddest story. It dominated the decade; it took everything we thought we knew and turned it on its ear.

I can still remember when Willie Wilson and several Kansas City Royals were sentenced to three months in prison in 1983 for attempting to purchase cocaine. The judge told Wilson he was letting down millions of fans. Mothers of children spit at his name. When Wilson left the courtroom he moaned: "They're making an example out of me."

Now, six years later, Bob Probert, a Detroit hockey star with a history of arrests, is sentenced to three months in a rehab correctional facility — three months, same as Wilson — for trying to sneak 14 grams of cocaine across the U.S.-Canadian border.

And already fans are counting the days until Probert can return to the Red Wings. "Hey, he did his time," they claim.

Amazing. At the start of the decade, we were trashing anyone who even tried the stuff. By the end we are forgiving a guy who tried to sneak it into the country in his underwear.

H ave we grown so jaded? Did the names Len Bias and Ben Johnson do such irreparable damage to our hearts? Or was it just the cumulative effect of all those headlines?

Once we figured being young, rich and a terrific baseball pitcher would be enough for any red-blooded American. And then Dwight Gooden checked into a rehab clinic.

Once we figured college was full of fresh-scrubbed kids playing high on school spirit. And then Gary McLain admitted snorting cocaine the night

Villanova beat Georgetown.

Once we thought the Olympics were a safe harbor for our dreams. And then Johnson failed his steroid test, and it seemed like half the Olympic athletes fell into the pit with him.

No moment was sacred. Len Bias was chosen second overall in the NBA draft. Two days later he was dead. Stanley Wilson failed his drug test — the night before the Super Bowl. Don Rogers, a football star, died of cocaine. His younger brother, Reggie — who wept at the service — would later kill three teenagers while driving drunk.

White. Black. Old. Young. The story of the '80s had no mercy. I remember going to the airport the morning after Michigan State lost in the NCAA basketball tournament. The players sat by the gate, chewing on cupcakes. They were just kids; they were due back on campus. Except Scott Skiles. He was going to jail. I had come to interview him.

I am a sports writer, I thought.

Why do I feel like a sheriff?

And it will not go away. Who figured to write stories such as these? What happened to our sports sections? They call it reality. The rich and famous — athletes included — have always found time for substance abuse. We simply didn't always report it.

Miles Davis, the famous jazz trumpeter, who in between sets used to vomit in alleys, sick from heroin, described his addiction as "feeding the monster." We in sports had a monster of our own. We craved gods.

We kept getting human beings.

Maybe that's what the '80s were all about, this lesson: that athletes, who soar above us when the ball is in play, are no better than your next-door neighbor when it comes to normal life. They bend. They break. They fall victim to temptation. And maybe we should stop looking their way as role models for our children, and look a little harder at ourselves.

The final major headline of 1989 was the death of a man who spent much of the decade embarrassing himself in drunken stupors. When they found him Christmas Day, inside his truck, by the gate of his farm, with his neck snapped, the tributes began to pour in. What a great baseball man he had been. How sad his death. But Billy Martin wasn't buried because his baseball skills had faded. He was buried because his driver was drunk.

And another paragraph was added to the Story. We know about crack now. We know about Breathalyzers. We know about steroids and masking agents and urine tests. It is the end of the '80s, New Year's Eve, and it is astounding what the sports pages have taught us. I don't know about you. Personally, I never wanted to be this smart. ◆

1990

PERLES PUTS THE SQUEEZE ON TRUSTEES, ALMA MATER

January 24

Wait a minute. Am I missing something? Since when did George Perles become Mr. Desirable?

The way people are acting, you'd think Perles came complete with a winning lottery ticket. The New York Jets were prepared to make him a rich man, a head coach. For the life of me, I can't figure why.

But that was nothing compared to Michigan State. In a pitiful display of jockitis — the fear that losing football games will somehow affect one's self-worth — MSU chose to hand over the reins of its entire athletic department, not just football, but basketball, baseball, swimming, Ping-Pong, in exchange for Big Daddy George's agreeing not to leave us alone in the dark.

And he said, "Well . . . OK."

Can you believe this? The Board of Trustees ignored the wishes of MSU President John DiBiaggio and effectively said, "The pen is mightier than the sword — but the whistle beats them all."

And now Perles is his own boss, complete with desk, secretary and nearly free rein to conduct his football program any way he wants. Beautiful. If he asked for the English Department, would they have thrown it in as well?

Why bother? George got what he wanted. He pulled the old squeeze play as if he'd been raised in a dugout, instead of on the sidelines. Is it his cologne? Is it his witty conversation? Why on earth did anyone feel held hostage by this man? It can't be his college football record, which is a good-but-not-phenomenal 46-33-3. What's the attraction?

I can't speak for the Jets. No. Wait. I can speak for the Jets. Here is what the Jets should be saying: "Whew." They could have been stuck with a coach who has never run a team in the NFL, would have been brutalized by the New York media, and has so far proved that on defense, he is a whiz, but on offense, he is a . . . what?

MSU's trustees are not so lucky.

They can only pray their decision won't come back to haunt them.

Now before Perles boosters out there start deluging us with mail, let me ask you a question: Why is it so important for Perles to be his own athletic director? The job stinks. At least for a football man. Ask Bo

Schembechler. It's a lot of paperwork and administrative detail and frustration (or have you forgotten Penn State's being admitted into the Big Ten last month?).

Schembechler — who I don't think should have been given the job, either — turned it down twice before reluctantly agreeing to share the load with Jack Weidenbach.

And yet Perles has been jockeying for this job since it became available when Doug Weaver announced his retirement. He played the Jets' offer to the hilt, he held it out there like a mysterious other woman, until MSU, in a fit of either jealousy, panic or both, caved in and made George AD. They say it's for a "one-year trial." Yeah. And I wrote "Hamlet."

Now, unless Perles has a fondness for paper clips, the only reason he would want this job is power. Control. Not having to answer to anybody else. Given the temptations in college football — steroids, recruiting violations, academic cheating — would you want any one man so autonomous?

It's a lousy decision. In a way, it frightens me. The way I see it, you get a handful of moments in life where the naked spotlight shows your true character. Perles had such a moment a few years ago, sermonizing at the 1988 Rose Bowl how he was "a Spartan forever, I've got the best job in the world. . . . I bleed green and white. . . . " He then almost bolted to the Green Bay Packers to be their head coach. He parlayed that into a 10-year contract at Michigan State.

He had another such moment this week. Tell me something: If Perles loves MSU so much, wasn't the job of football coach good enough? Was he so afraid of a new athletic director that leaving was his only alternative?

Moments. Character. Did Perles come through this with flying colors? It seems to me, his colors kept changing.

So he may promise a "new era" in MSU athletics. But I can't say I trust George Perles anymore. A few years ago, I was in love with the guy, I bought into his humble speeches about "I'm just a former phys-ed teacher with the greatest job on earth."

The words ring hollow now. Perles may think he is honoring the tradition of Duffy Daugherty and Biggie Munn by assuming the coach and AD jobs, but that's not how you honor tradition, by holding up your alma mater.

Still, Perles is less to blame than the trustees, who showed all the conviction of a rubber band. Anytime you make a man his own boss, you are running a risk. And, no doubt, this is precisely why DiBiaggio did not want his football coach to be his athletic director.

Forgive DiBiaggio. He foolishly thought that a university president should have some authority over elements of the school. Apparently, when it comes to football, at least according to the MSU trustees, the piece is bigger than the pie.

Why did they vote to give in to Perles' power play? Who knows? Perhaps it was fear of being deserted, as happened with Darryl Rogers. Perhaps it was because recruiting is in high season. If you ask me, it was mostly a fear of losing. The Spartans have certainly improved under Perles, and with Schembechler now out of the picture, perhaps the trustees felt this was the time to strike in the Midwest, to get those recruits who used to choose Michigan automatically, gather power and — can you hear the trumpets? — become a powerhouse in the Big Ten!

You know what I say? Who cares? If that's how you get there, by your coach holding you at gunpoint, by delivering the ransom, by turning control of all the other sports on campus over to a guy who has been a gridiron man all the way, then what do you stand for? What are you winning for?

MSU better pray it never develops any scandals. It better pray that students still think of their school as a university, not a sports factory. As for Perles, I don't know what he has left to pray for. Personally, I wonder whether he has stopped laughing yet. ◆

NINERS MAKE BRONCOS' NIGHTMARES COME TRUE

January 29

N EW ORLEANS — Jerry Rice held the football high, pulled a fist and spun toward his grinning teammates. Joe Montana slapped him on the helmet and Roger Craig gave him a bear hug. They had it! Another Super Bowl! All that remained was to run out the clock, which read 10:08.

In the first quarter.

Good-bye, competition. This was so lopsided, I'm surprised the stadium didn't tip over. It was Popeye beating up on Sweet Pea. It was the Philistines against the Boy Scouts.

It was like watching a 49ers practice. No. Check that. I think the 49ers' practices are harder than this. Tell me. Was this Super Bowl ever supposed to be a game, or were we just here to sell Diet Coke? That's not a score. 55-10? That's a championship? The Bud Bowl was closer.

"To tell you the truth," fullback Tom Rathman said in the 49ers' locker room after his team successfully defended its Super Bowl title, "we began celebrating halfway into the third quarter."

It was nice of them to wait that long. And to think people said the Denver Broncos weren't good enough to beat San Francisco. How ridiculous. They weren't good enough to beat Ferris State. Obviously, after losing the 1987 Super Bowl by 19 points, and the 1988 version by 32 points, the Broncos got together and said, "Come on, guys! We can do better than that." And they did.

They lost by 45.

"We stunk the place up," said Broncos receiver Mark Jackson. Gee. That's a little harsh. Accurate. But harsh.

Let's tally up this Super Bowl XXIV, shall we? On the 49ers' side we had: points (the most ever in a Super Bowl), yardage, first downs, third downs, tackles, interceptions and time of possession. And on the Broncos' side we had: the coin flip.

S o much for statistics. Before the first dish of pretzels was gone, the only competition left in this Super Bowl was the jockeying for most valuable player. There were the usual suspects: Montana, the terrifyingly accurate quarterback, who threw five touchdowns and never dirtied his uniform; Rice, so superior to other NFL receivers that he seems to bother only with spectacular touchdown catches these days (he had three); Craig, the rock-solid running back, high-stepping and body-slamming his way for more than 100 yards of offense and a touchdown himself.

Montana got the trophy, becoming the first-ever three-time MVP winner. No surprise.

"Is this enough?" someone asked the quarterback who has the most completions, yardage and touchdown passes in Super Bowl history — and has yet to throw an interception.

"It's never enough," he said.

John Elway might disagree. You remember John Elway? Most Overwhelmed Player. Was he bad? Well. He completed some nice passes. Mostly to the 49ers, unfortunately.

Poor John. This wasn't his worst nightmare. This was his worst nightmare times 100. He must have wished he had a big orange sheet to hide under. His rifle arm was suddenly wet gunpowder. His poise was left somewhere in the Rocky Mountains. When the Broncos needed his leadership most — on the first offensive plays of each half — he threw two incompletions and an interception, respectively. All afternoon his passes hit the turf, went over his receivers' heads. He completed just 10, was intercepted twice and fumbled near his goal line.

"I wanted to have my best day," he said glumly. "I'm just trying to figure out how to win one of these things. Or at least be in one of them."

Good luck. In his three Super Bowls, Elway is now trailing, 136-40. That's a lot of catching up.

N ow, let's remember, Broncos. It is a great accomplishment just to make a Super Bowl, right? Right? Hello? Well. Never mind. It takes awhile for that shell shock to pass.

Let us focus, instead, on the 49ers, who are going to have to form their own league pretty soon, because nobody wants to play them. Can you believe these guys? They actually made sports writers look clever. We predicted a blowout. They delivered. This was their fourth Super Bowl victory in nine years and the most amazing thing is, only a few players remain from the first squad. Take your hat off to a remarkable system, an owner who isn't afraid to spend money, and an eye for talent by coaches and scouts that constructed a starting offense and defense with only three first-round picks.

What's that? A synopsis of the game?

OK. Here we go: Denver took the opening kickoff, then quickly left the stage, the way the piano tuner leaves when Billy Joel says: "I'm ready."

Out came the Maestros, a.k.a. Killer Joe and his Niners of Gold. Figuring that their first drive was important, because it was the only one the TV audience would watch before becoming totally bored and switching to the

"Wonderful World Of Disney," the 49ers did all the right things. Short passes. Quick runs. Montana found Rice over the middle, Rice bounced off perhaps Denver's best tackler, Steve Atwater, and loped into the end zone.

From then on, it was like the end of a play, where every cast member gets to take a bow. Here was Brent Jones, a youthful tight end who says, "I idolized Joe Montana and the 49ers growing up," now catching a touchdown pass from Joe to close the first quarter. Here were Craig and Tom Rathman, the old Nebraska connection, carrying the ball on 13 of 14 plays during the Niners' third touchdown drive. Here was Rice, waiting for his moment like a master thespian, streaking down the middle in the final minute of the second quarter, pulling in the Montana pass and dashing to the end zone untouched for touchdown No. 4.

And what about Montana? What more can be said? He surveyed the field like a cowboy surveys the prairie. I swear he's up there on his horse, chewing on a weed, saying to himself, "Welp, I could go there, throw it to him. Then again, I could go there, and throw it to him." Inevitably, he picks the right target. And those who criticize his short passing game got a healthy lesson in football priorities. What good is a howitzer arm — such as John Elway's — if the defense is all over you?

"Joe is the best," said Rice.

"He's incredible," admitted Dan Reeves, the Denver coach.

"Aw, it's the offensive line, really," Montana said.

Well. It's easy to be humble when you're that good. Last year, after the 49ers beat Cincinnati to win Super Bowl XXIII, Montana was the first to say to his team: "Let's repeat."

The new word is "Three-peat."

They were saying it at halftime.

G ood-bye, competition. What San Fran did to Denver, you wouldn't do to an ant. Hey, Commissioner Tagliabue. Take a hint. Maybe the NFL should realign the conferences. This was the sixth straight Super Bowl victory for the NFC, and five of those were blowouts.

It can't be good for the game. Was anybody watching at the end? Even the Denver fans were calling for the Broncos' most effective play: "AIRPORT! GO TO THE AIRPORT!"

"Someone told me you get to be AFC champions for two weeks," said Tyrone Braxton, a Denver cornerback, "but you get to be Super Bowl champions forever."

How true. Denver is already being lumped in with Minnesota, the four-time bridesmaid of this spectacle, and Elway is being compared to Fran Tarkenton. In defense of the Broncos: They have been here three times in the last four years. Even the 49ers can't say that.

They, however, can say everything else. Defense. Offense. Coaching.

They'll probably end up with the best draft pick, too. Can you believe they won back-to-back Super Bowls with different coaches? Whatever they are doing, other teams ought to steal it. Until that happens, we may be destined for Super Bowls that are over before John Madden says, "Boom!"

And what fun is that?

Good-bye, competition. The halftime featured a salute to the Peanuts cartoon gang. How fitting. The Broncos must have felt like Charlie Brown when he goes running toward that football, only to have it yanked away by Lucy at the last minute. Hey! Where did the game go?

That's what we'd like to know. ♦

JUST PLAIN JUD STANDS JUST OUTSIDE SPOTLIGHT

March 1

E AST LANSING, Mich. — So this is what Jud Heathcote does in the thick of the supposedly pressure-packed Big Ten title chase: He finds out one of his secretaries is pregnant, but she didn't want to tell him because things are so busy right now. The next day, Jud comes stalking out of his office and begins to circle the woman, sniffing like a dog.

"Does Lori smell funny to you?" he asks the other office workers.

"Huh?"

"Well, my wife said she was fragrant."

"Fragrant?"

"Yeah," he says, still sniffing, "I think that's what she said. Fragrant. Lori, is it true? Are you . . . fragrant?"

Well. What did you expect? He would walk around like a nervous wreck? Just because the big showdown with Michigan is tonight at the Breslin Center? Just because he lost arguably his best player, senior guard Kirk Manns, because of a stress fracture over the weekend? Just because, after a preseason of no expectations, people are suddenly figuring that his Spartans can and maybe should win the Big Ten basketball title?

You obviously don't know Jud Heathcote. But then, who really does? On the menu of this sports-hungry state, he is the "oh, yeah" coach. Sparky, Chuck, Jacques, Fontes, Bo, Perles, Fisher . . .

And — oh yeah — Jud Heathcote.

"I'm better off that way," he says, sitting in his half-unpacked office inside Breslin. "The less attention I get, the less mistakes they find."

Well, that's Heathcote. Always a kicker. Always a line to knock himself down a peg. Congratulate him on his longevity, and he says, "Yes, my 100th birthday is coming up." Thank him for an hour-long interview, he says, "Yeah, but I wasn't very good, was I?"

It is the mark of a man who refuses to blow himself out of proportion. You see it in the way he dresses. You see it in the way he recruits. You see it in his face when he laughs and his head shakes and his mouth curls in that funny downward smile, like the painted lips of a clown.

You see it here, in his office. Against one bare wall is a stack of boxes. Against another is a framed magazine cover of Magic Johnson — back when he was Earvin — leading Michigan State to Jud's first and only national championship. No thick leather. No rich wood paneling. No marble desk. The carpet is green, the walls are white (real surprise, huh?) and on the bookcase is giant blowup of Heathcote. It's a nice photo. Except someone has glued a yellow paper mustache and goatee over his face.

"My office staff," he says, delivering the kicker, "they keep me humble."

W ait a minute. Isn't that Michigan's job? You know. The BIG SCHOOL in Ann Arbor? So dominant have the Wolverines been in recent headlines, that Heathcote may have wondered whether anyone remembered which highway went to East Lansing.

FRIEDER QUITS U-M FOR ASU
BO NAMES FISHER U-M COACH
U-M WINS IT ALL!
Jud?

Yeah. Jud has been here the whole time. Coaching. Frieder bolts, Jud keeps coaching. Illinois gets in hot water, Jud keeps coaching. George Perles stirs up a big power struggle, Jud keeps coaching.

It's his blessing and his curse. He doesn't throw chairs. He doesn't get caught offering sports cars to recruits. On a stage full of Bobby Knights and Jim Valvanos, a guy such as Heathcote, the son of a schoolteacher, a product of the Pacific Northwest, a gritty, hardworking, poke-you-in-the-ribs-with-an-elbow kind of guy, tends to get defined only by comparisons.

And in recent years, the comparisons were almost always with Bill Frieder, the turbulent, dizzy and often controversial coach at Michigan.

"The knock was always that Bill was the recruiter and I was the coach," Heathcote says now. "It was unfair, but Bill brought it on himself. He would talk about writing letters to recruits at 4 in the morning. You know why he did that? Because he couldn't sleep at night. I can sleep at night, so I get up and write the same letter at 9 a.m. and nobody talks about it.

"Or the phone calls. They wrote how he called recruits during halftime of his games. But you know why? Because he couldn't sit still. He's always got to call somebody. I make that same phone call after the game and nobody talks about it.

"Bill created an image like he was the greatest recruiter in the world. But by doing so, he almost begged for someone to say that his coaching paled by comparison."

And that Heathcote's recruiting would never be as good. Ah, well. If he had to come down on one side of the forest, better it be the coaching side. This recruiting stuff could be nasty business. Especially because Heathcote refuses to cheat, refuses to offer a dollar, refuses to make false promises — "I can't tell five separate kids they're my No. 1 recruit, it's just too dishonest."

So be it. That's not what coaching was supposed to be about when Heathcote decided to get into it back before the war. No, not the Vietnam war. Not Korea.

Keep going. You're getting warm.

It was a town called Port Orchard, on the shore of Puget Sound, a ferry ride away from Seattle. There were mountains and cold rain. And there wasn't any money.

"My father died when I was 3 years old," Heathcote, 62, recalls. "My mother moved us to live with our grandparents. It was during the Depression. We all lived in the same house. Mostly what I remember is that I wanted to be a coach even then."

At South Kitsap High, in the 1940s, Heathcote was pure athlete. Dirty knees. Bruised elbows. He starred in baseball and football, and was the center in basketball. The center?

Yep. His coach back then was a Norwegian man named Stener Kvinsland. A driver. A disciplinarian. He's 76 years old now, long since retired and in poor health. I got his phone number and called him in Washington. When he heard Heathcote's name, his voice jumped. It's been what, nearly 50 years?

"I remember Jud as if he were alongside me right now," Kvinsland said. "Do you know, he wrote me a letter not too long ago? He told me I was his father figure when he was a boy, I guess because his father died when he was so young.

"And then, this is funny, at the end of the letter, he wrote, 'You're the reason I am a coach today. I don't know whether I should thank you or not.'"

Always a kicker.

A nd now, Heathcote is trying to deliver another kicker. A Big Ten title. This year. Can that really be the Spartans with a 22-5 record, in a virtual tie with Purdue and with a slight lead over defending national champion Michigan as they battle for the crown?

It's them. And we shouldn't be so surprised. You can take Heathcote for granted, but you can't leave him there. Sooner or later he'll come back and bite you. He did it with the 1978-79 championship team of Magic and Greg Kelser. He did it with the 1985-86 squad, where a troubled but brilliant guard named Scott Skiles took MSU to the NCAA's Sweet 16 before a mysterious time clock shot them down.

And he's doing it again. Despite losing center Mike Peplowski for a while to a knee injury. Despite the broken finger that sidelined Steve Smith. Despite Manns' sustaining that stress fracture that may cost him the rest of the regular season. "We started out with a team we thought was strong and quick offensively but very suspect on defense," Heathcote says, "and we end up with a very good defensive team that is very average on offense."

You don't make that kind of turnaround without good coaching. But then, you don't stay at one school for 14 years unless you're doing something right.

And you don't win a national championship. Remember? Before the Pistons, before Steve Fisher, it was Heathcote who brought a basketball banner to this state. Maybe he has suffered for that. Expectations soared after his Spartans beat Larry Bird and Indiana State. "People expect you," he admits, "to do it again."

So maybe that's why Heathcote seems to get publicity only when one of his players is a superstar (Magic) or in trouble (Skiles). Or maybe it's because his Spartan excellence has come in spurts: two straight winning seasons, three straight losing seasons, four straight winning, two straight losing. Or maybe it's geography. If it's not football, East Lansing may be 60 miles and 60 minutes from being the top story with the Detroit media.

So be it. Jud will be the "Oh yeah" guy. He'll joke with his office staff, he'll take the bottom bunk bed to glory. Heathcote got into this business because he likes coaching kids. He is 62 and every once in a while, those kids come back and make it worthwhile.

"Last summer, we had the 10-year reunion of the '79 championship team," he says. "Do you know that everybody showed up? Every trainer. Every equipment manager. Every player. One hundred percent attendance.

"Afterwards, in a private room, all the team members got together. And someone said, 'Hey, let's make a toast.' Well. Guys started saying things I couldn't believe. Like: 'This was the highlight of my life.' 'This was my greatest moment.'"

"Did Magic say anything?"

"Oh, yeah. It was kinda funny. Earvin toasted everybody and said, 'Man, this is the best time I've had in four years.'"

The coach smiles. He thinks for a moment.

"You know," he says, "whoever that woman was four years ago, she must have been something."

Always a kicker. ♦

SPARTANS FANS SALUTE UNFLAGGING STEVE SMITH

March 2

E AST LANSING, Mich. — The flag. He wanted the flag. Steve Smith was swimming in a sea of fans, TV cameras, beautiful noise all over the Breslin Center hardwood floor. He had done it. Pulled a dream night out of his shooting pocket and delivered the victory that people here fantasize about. Now he wanted the Spartans flag.

"Take it! Take it!" screamed a student. He grabbed hold and waved it high, a green-and-white beacon above a delirious army. What a moment! The only surprise was that he didn't heave it toward the basket. Five bucks says it would have swished.

They had done it! The Spartans had beaten Michigan, the defending national champion, their arch-rival, the monkey on their backs. And Smith was the star soldier. Did you watch him during that second half, bouncing, flopping, heaving that rock? Up and down the court he ran, as if late for his destiny, his jersey riding up his lean body, bagging around the waist, hanging wet with sweat, the way a good jersey will when you're really into the game.

And was he into the game? Hell. He *was* the game. For one glorious eight-minute stretch, Steve Smith was one with the basketball. He wanted it to go in, it went in. Sideways jumpers from ridiculous angles. Top-of-the-key bombs that could have kissed heaven. Three-pointers from across the street. Swish, baby. Don't even think about it. It was one of those rare sports moments when all the opposing players can do is stand there, earthbound, mouths hanging open.

"We tried to defend him," said a glum Steve Fisher, the U-M coach, after Smith's 36 points led the Spartans to a 78-70 victory and a solo spot atop the Big Ten. "Wilt Chamberlain could have been on him and he would have made it."

W ell. That's some compliment. But then, that was some performance. And talk about timing! Senior guard Kirk Manns was out of the lineup with a stress fracture. Rumeal Robinson, the U-M star who had beaten MSU earlier in the year with a last-second shot, was threatening to stick it to the green once more before he graduated.

Let's face it. Beating Michigan rarely meant as much as it did to MSU, if only to prove this new era — new building, good recruiting class, crack at the Big Ten title — was for real.

And Smith delivered. Man, how he delivered. The kid from Detroit's Pershing High played as if he built the court himself. Thirty-six points? Five three-pointers? Nine rebounds?

"Did you feel unstoppable tonight?" Smith was asked afterward.

"Just a little bit," he said.

Yeah. And Al Capone was just a little bit naughty. The fact is, with 13:15 left in the game, Smith began a run that would have left Isiah Thomas clapping in admiration. An 18-footer from the top of the key. Bang! A six-foot turnaround. Bang! A lay-up. A three-point bomb. Another three-point bomb. An 18-foot turnaround in which he barely looked at the rim. Bang! Bang! With each basket he pumped blood through the very aorta of Spartan Spirit. The place went nuts. Never mind the inevitable Michigan last-minute comeback. Smith had put it out of reach.

And when the buzzer sounded, he waved that flag as if he had just stormed the beach at Normandy. "Did you have a personal mission tonight?" he was asked.

"Well, I thought about something I heard, that Rumeal and Terry (Mills) had never lost to us in all their time at Michigan. That really got to me. I didn't sleep well last night thinking about it."

"Will you sleep tonight?"

He laughed. "Not too much."

He had plenty of company. Spartans fans may be too happy for slumber. After all, the team is 23-5, a lock for a good seeding in the NCAA tournament and a good bet to win the conference, something it hasn't done in more than a decade.

"For all those who say I never smile . . . " announced Jud Heathcote, the longtime Spartans coach.

And then he smiled. Five seconds' worth. I counted it.

Why not? This team continues to delight him. It continues to rise above the injuries to star players. It continues to sparkle on defense (as it did in the final minutes, making the Wolverines look as if their hands were buttered).

For such a long time, the Spartans have squirmed under the weight of U-M's excellent reputation. It had been a long time, in fact, since a Michigan-Michigan State game even meant anything.

It meant something now. And it was summed up by a local kid who couldn't miss, riding his schoolmates' shoulders, waving a flag that said you can't keep a good program down forever.

"What would you compare Steve's performance to tonight?" Heathcote was asked.

"I don't know," he said. "Maybe . . . perfection?"

And you want to hear something else? Smith is only a junior.

Now Jud is really smiling. ◆

249

TV ETHICS STAGGERED AS HANK GATHERS DIED

March 7

H e began to die in a grotesque fashion, dropping to the floor, convulsing as his teammates stared in horror. Like many people, I cannot get the image of Hank Gathers out of my head. The question is: Should it be there in the first place?

Ask television. Gathers, a powerful center for Loyola Marymount, was not the first athlete to die of heart trouble. Why, two years ago, Pete Maravich, a name more famous than Gathers', expired in a similar fashion.

But America did not buzz about Maravich the way it does this week. The reason: some 30 or 40 seconds of footage that aired on TV news across the country, showing Gathers collapsing in a heap, his mother running from the stands. The look on her face. The violent jerking of his body.

That footage did not belong on TV. Not in my opinion. The story could have been told without it. Hank Gathers was not a president. His death did not bring down a political regime. It was a tragic slice of the real world that demanded a real tug of ethics. Yet few TV stations chose not to run it.

"It's a news story," I was told when I called local channels. One weekend anchor said, "If we didn't air it, our viewers would have been cheated."

Cheated? Of what? Voyeurism? I don't buy it. There are lines in everything, including journalism. Are they not crossed when it comes to a young man's life, his dignity, the grief that a broadcast might cause his family or friends? There are only so many subjects you can hide behind the curtain of "I'm only doing my job."

Does death now fall into the category?

I think there have been more gruesome things on the air," said John Walsh, managing editor for ESPN, which brought the story nationwide. "Our policy is to warn people beforehand if something might be offensive. And we did that."

Yes. This is a tidy tradition. We warned you. But in truth, such warnings often serve to whet the appetite, to make you curious. You end up watching anyhow. Meanwhile, ESPN also had a camera at the La Salle game, when Lionel Simmons, a close friend of Gathers', was told of the death. Simmons wept. The camera whirred. News? Or staged tragedy?

Now, please. I am not placing print on some holy perch above TV. Many papers, including the two Detroit dailies, ran still photos of a dying Gathers on their sports fronts. I don't like that, either.

But in this case, the footage was incomparably more disturbing. Especially Gathers convulsing on the court and being wheeled to an ambulance. Some stations stopped the tape before that. Others did not. They ran it four and five times in the next 24 hours. Their justification was often to point to previous tragedies and say, "Well, it's not as bad as that."

That is not an answer. Nor is citing the recent footage of executed Romanian president Nicolae Ceaucescu and saying: "That was worse."

That was also different. His death signaled the end of a political era, it changed an entire nation. Ceaucescu's corpse became a national symbol.

Hank Gathers was not a symbol. His death was medical and personal. It deserved some privacy. Sure, he was a great player and a good pro prospect. But to equate his fall, news-wise, with that of a Romanian dictator, is to balloon the importance of the NBA draft shamefully out of proportion.

N ow, I know TV is a visual medium — at its best, a great one. And I know this is a hard call. But somewhere, someone has to make it. Someone has to say, "We're not going with this. It's wrong. I don't care what the other stations are showing."

That takes foresight. Courage. It also takes time. TV pictures are so powerful, they can glorify a moment or rape it. Yet the decisions to air footage are often made — as they were with Gathers — by harried young producers who have little time to catch a breath, let alone debate ethics.

And then there is the question of competition. Few stations want to be caught with their footage down. Said a candid Eli Zaret of Channel 2: "You get too esoteric in this business, you'll hurt yourself. ... Everybody this morning is talking about 'Did you see what happened?' What if the person said, 'No. I watched Channel 2 and they didn't show it'? Then you'd have made a horrible decision."

I credit Eli with honesty. But a horrible decision? I don't think so. In dilemmas such as these, maybe it's best to ask yourself a question you learned in kindergarten: Is it right or is it wrong? Somewhere inside, there should be a flame of conscience that separates the two.

That Gathers footage did little more than shock people and haunt his family. Can you imagine if you were a friend, living miles away, who flicked on the TV and watched? Sure, it brought home the tragedy of playing athletics with a heart condition. But did we really have to watch a man die to learn that? Have we grown that thick?

Or have we just grown that insensitive? There are some TV people who swear America wants to see this kind of tragedy. And others with a late-blooming conscience who now say, "Maybe we shouldn't have shown it." But the fact is, at the moment of truth, everybody did.

Sadly, that tells you all you need to know. ♦

MICHIGAN'S PROP 48 KIDS FINALLY EVEN THE SCORE

March 18

LONG BEACH, Calif. — "Are you dumb?"

Rumeal Robinson looked at the kid in disbelief. It was the summer of his freshman year, on a visit home to Boston, and this was the first time he had ever heard that question. At least to his face. It startled him, mostly because the person asking was a 9-year-old boy whose father had told him Rumeal failed a test, that's why he wasn't playing basketball anymore. "Is it true what he said, Meal?" the boy asked. "Are you dumb?"

A thousand miles away, Terry Mills walked through his old neighborhood in Romulus, Mich., hard by Metro Airport, where a year earlier he was the toast of the streets. Mr. Basketball. What a future! But then he scored a few points too low on the SAT exam. Now he heard the whispers. "He ain't going nowhere no more. He's at Michigan, but he's too stupid to make it."

Listen up, everybody. It's time to finish the story. Langston Hughes, the poet, once asked: "What happens to a dream deferred?" Four years ago, Robinson and Mills, one the shy adopted son of a Boston postal worker, the other a lanky, smiling but naive local hero, were held out of basketball, their dreams deferred. They were part of an experiment called Proposition 48. If your memory is good, you can still hear the outrage: "Kids like that don't belong at Michigan. . . . They're nothing but dumb jocks. . . . They'll never make it. . . . "

Where are the critics now? Robinson and Mills, who today lead U-M into the second round of the NCAA tournament against Loyola Marymount, have become not only the stars they were projected to be on the court, but young men, mature students. One will own a bachelor's degree this summer; the other needs just a semester's worth of credits. So where are those reporters who, during Mills' and Robinson's freshman year, banged on their door at 2 a.m., looking for a scoop? Where are the writers who tried to sneak into their classes and the photographers who stalked them like wild game? Where are the "fans" who talked behind their backs, or the critics who held up posters during games: "REMEDIAL ROBINSON." "TERRY: CAN YOU READ THIS?"

This is a story about two kids who had their lives changed forever because of a test score. They were tossed together like lab rats. They got insulted, depressed, dejected. Finally, they got even. They hung from heaven as the Wolverines captured the national championship last April. Now, as they wind down their careers, they are here to tell you they also got an education.

Man, what an education.

T hat first year, it seemed like every reporter in the world was after us," Mills said a few days ago, sitting in an empty Crisler Arena. "They'd call at all hours and say, 'Is Rumeal or Terry there?' and I'd have to say, 'Naw, they went out.' 'Well, who's this?' 'This is a friend of theirs. I'm just answering their phone.' . . .

"Sometimes they would come to our room and start banging the door. We had nothing to say. After a while, we just went out the window."

He laughed. "I guess it's a good thing we were on the ground floor."

Out the window? College freshmen shouldn't have to live like that. But there was little normal about these particular freshmen. From the moment they arrived on campus in Ann Arbor, Mills and Robinson ceased to be two of the finest high school players in the country. They were suddenly "The Prop 48 Kids," star recruits of coach Bill Frieder who had failed to meet the new standards of at least 700 on the SAT test and a C average in a core curriculum of high school classes. Both made the grades. Both missed on the test. Not by much, maybe 30 or 40 points. But under the new Prop 48 rule, they could be admitted only if they forfeited their freshman year of eligibility.

On the one hand, that made life easier. They could focus on college, the work, the new environment. On the other hand, here were two kids who had played basketball all their lives, it was the thing they did best, they were quite likely one day to be professionals (and both are projected first-rounders in the NBA draft). Yet if they came to practice, they could only sit and watch.

"One time during a break I stepped out on the court just to mess around one-on-one with Glen Rice," Mills recalled. "I knew Glen from high school. We were just playing, you know? But I could feel everyone looking at me, like, 'You better not do that, Terry. You're not supposed to even be on the court with us.' "

Soon, he and Robinson stopped going to practice. After a while they even stopped attending games. It was easier to watch on TV than to sit in the arena and feel the sweat, hear the crowd, your skin starts tingling, then you look down and realize you're wearing boots instead of sneakers.

They took to playing one-on-one together, Mills versus Robinson, countless games in late-night gyms. But after a while the contests grew old. "Rumeal would go right past me five straight times," Mills said, "then I'd back in on him and dunk."

They stopped playing. They grew sluggish; they put on weight. For the first time in their young adult lives, they were working without a net.

Still, somewhere between the reporters and the lonely gymnasiums, between the whispers of "there go the dumb kids" and "they don't deserve to be here," a special friendship began to evolve. Mills and Robinson shared pizzas and late-night bull sessions. They had a fish tank in their room in West Quad, loaded with Oscars and piranhas, a good conversation-breaker with girls. "Watch. Now we'll feed him a goldfish." They both liked music, Marvin Gaye and Dream Boys and rap and soul. Rumeal, a quiet, talented artist, would sometimes ask Terry to pose so he could sketch him. Terry did it for a while, then balked: "People get paid to do this kind of thing, right?" he told his roommate.

They shared meals and walks to class. They shared turns hiding from reporters. And they shared something else: depression.

"We would get down about the whole situation," Robinson admitted, sitting alongside the empty court. "I was really homesick and sometimes I'd say, 'I want to go back to Boston.' But Terry knew how to get me out of it. Other times, it would be his turn to go to class and he'd say, 'Forget it. It don't make no difference anyhow.' And I knew what to do."

He laughed. "Just pull the sheets off him and turn on all the lights."

Together, they dragged and cajoled each other through that first semester. And the second semester. They took a class called "History of the Black Athlete" where the professor, Jon Lockard, encouraged them to talk about their situation. "I tried to show them that fate had dealt them a favor allowing them to spend a year totally on themselves," said Lockard, who has been teaching at U-M for 21 years. "They could get into the rhythm of school, discover the joy of learning. . . . Both did very well in class. And I can promise you, no tutors wrote their papers for them. They did it themselves. . . .

"As far as I'm concerned, Terry and Rumeal have shown themselves more than worthy of being college students. Their Prop 48 problems have less to do with ability than with circumstances."

And circumstances, sadly, are one thing SAT tests fail to measure. Mills, remember, endured adults hovering around him since the eighth grade, when he sprouted six inches and became a playground legend. He would recognize college scouts in his high school hallway. He would get letters and phone calls from potential suitors. What was he, 14 years old?

That's bound to affect a kid — no matter what books he reads. And yet it's mild compared to the Rumeal Robinson Story. Born in Jamaica, never met his father, abandoned by his mother years later in the United States. Found wandering the halls of a Cambridge, Mass., apartment building, taken in by a volunteer social worker named Helen Ford, who along with husband Louis and a houseful of kids provide Rumeal with a daily shower of love and warmth. There isn't always time in a young life like that to learn the relationship between "PARSIMONIOUS" and "PRECIPITATION." But there is time for character. Time for dreams.

"You know, it's funny," Robinson said, looking down at his blue jeans. "When I was maybe 13, not long after I moved in with the Fords, I had a dream about playing football — and I was wearing a Michigan helmet. I never watched Michigan games, but there I was, in a Michigan helmet. That's weird, isn't it?"

No weirder than this: He winds up at Michigan and one day, as a freshman, he turns to Mills and says: "How are we ever gonna get back to where we were as seniors in high school? We only have three years here. . . . Terry, the only way is the national championship. We got to win that thing before we finish."

A dream deferred? Last April, on a drizzly night in Seattle, the whole world watched as Mills hit an overtime basket to pull U-M within one point of Seton Hall. Then, with three seconds left, Robinson stood at the free throw line, his heart thumping but his hands steady. . . .

He did it. Champions! Moments later, Rumeal was in the arms of his old roommate, hugging in a way only the two of them could understand.

You can argue that Mills and Robinson succeeded despite Proposition 48, or because of it. Both admit the year off and the adjustment process were invaluable to their success in college. But the criticism and the bubble-like existence also made life hard and ridiculous. "Even now, if I pass a class, they say, 'Well, how hard a class was that?' " Mills said. "They think I'm taking bowling or something."

No bowling. No basket weaving. The two have succeeded — and, it is worth noting, with nary a whisper of trouble or off-court controversy. Mills is just one semester shy of his degree in sports management and communication. Robinson will earn his diploma on time; he will wear the cap and gown this spring.

Maybe the lesson is that all freshmen should be made ineligible, given a year to adjust. But this lesson is also obvious: You cannot always measure potential with a No. 2 pencil. The people in Princeton who make up the tests may themselves need a course in human environment.

Robinson said it best: "In the neighborhood where I grew up, sports was stressed more than academics. They kept telling me, 'Make yourself better; play more basketball.' So I did. When they said, 'Go home and read for an hour,' I said, 'Yeah, right.' Nobody else did that.

"But that's why it's wrong to judge someone based on his high school experience. Once you get to college everybody's studying. It makes you study more — you have to jump or you get left behind. If back in my old neighborhood, one friend said, 'I'm going to study,' and another friend said, 'I'm going to study,' then I'd probably have said, 'Well, I'm studying also.' But where I came from, everybody said, 'I'm playing basketball.' That's the only real difference between there and here."

They ought to print that paragraph on every loose-leaf notebook in America.

So "The Prop 48 Kids" have shed the label; they take the court today as seniors, co-captains, students, men.

"Do I feel educated?" Robinson said. "Yes. I do. I feel like I can do anything now."

Mills nodded. "But my story won't be complete without that diploma." When asked whether he were the type to hang the sheepskin on his wall, the guy they once called "stupid" had to laugh. "Me? I'm liable to carry it around in my pocket!"

So be it. A brain that is challenged and a pocket full of dreams. Isn't that what college is supposed to be about? ♦

WHEN I HEARD THE VOICE, IT WAS FLORIDA CALLING

March 30

L AKELAND, Fla. — So there I am standing in my cornfield when this voice comes out of nowhere.

"If you go there," it whispers, "they will play."

"I beg your pardon?" I say.

"If you go there ... they will play."

I poke my hoe in the ground. I look at my dog. I check to see whether I left the transistor radio on. I look at my dog again.

"If you go there ..." the voice of baseball repeats, "they will play."

I cock my head. "You gotta be kidding me."

They gotta be kidding me. First of all, the voice sounds like Vin Scully's. Secondly, I promised to have nothing to do with baseball this year. That's right. I promised to boycott the game after watching the owners and the players behave like 4-year-olds during contract talks, acting as if $200 million wasn't enough to buy a can of soup.

Enough, I said. Every few years we endure this ridiculous process and then, like lambs, we come back to the ballpark. Not this time. Not me. Baseball, I decided, is a greedy, cold-blooded business, and if I wanted to watch that, I could go to Wall Street.

"Whoever you are, you're barking up the wrong tree," I say to the voice, as I enter the house and wash up. "Or should I say whispering? You're whispering up the wrong tree. Either way, you're in the wrong tree. I'm finished with baseball."

"If you go there ... they will play."

I'm not going anywhere. Where are my car keys?

N ot that I didn't once love the game. Not that I didn't once love to stand behind the batting cage, my fingers curled around the links, feeling the warm Florida sun on my back and hearing a strapping young ballplayer say to me, "Move your damn hand before you lose it."

Not that I didn't love that. But that was a long time ago. I have new things to do now. I have developed a life without the National Pastime. I have books. I have the corn. I have the dog.

"If you go there ... Sparky will ramble."

"Hah! That's a good one," I say, driving to the airport. "I've heard Sparky ramble enough for two lifetimes. I've heard Whitey grumble about baserunners and Roger pontificate on the split-finger fastball. Believe me, I've had baseball talk up to my ears. You know what? It's just talk. Who needs to talk baseball anymore?"

"If you go there . . . Sparky will ramble."

Unbelievable.

Why should I go there? Isn't this spring training the very residue of greed? A shortened, non-traditional version of what was once a great tradition? Six weeks to three weeks? Pitchers way behind hitters? Or is it hitters way behind pitchers? Whatever. Why should I go there?

Besides, I have a very full schedule these days. A stack of books to be read. A new show on the Arts & Entertainment channel, Swedish opera, I believe. And if I get so desperate for sports, there is always Red Wing hock–

Well. OK. Forget that last part.

"You're still wasting your time," I say, as I purchase a ticket. "I told you: not interested. Baseball? I would sooner spend an evening with Donald Trump. And I really wish you'd stop interrupting me. People are staring."

"If you go there . . . Trammell will double."

"Oh, now stop that," I say.

Once I might have fallen for this stuff. Once the lure of green grass and a warm breeze and the sight of nine men scattering across the field, slapping their gloves . . . well, once I might have been tempted. But who can remember that stuff anymore? My mind is too cluttered with arbitration and Jose Canseco's driving and Pete Rose's gambling, and Donald Fehr looking like he needs a barber and a shower, not necessarily in that order.

"You're not dealing with a softie," I say, as I pick up my Florida rent-a-car. "We're talking principle here. The public trust. You can abuse the public trust only so often before the public fights back."

"If you go there–"

"Don't start," I say. "Remember Steinbrenner? Umpires on strike?"

"If you go there–"

"Matt Nokes' arbitration? Chuck O'Connor's speeches? Ron Darling calling $5,000-a-month strike pay 'horse track money'?"

"If you go there–"

"I'm not going anywhere. I am not going anywhere. I'm telling you for the very last time, I am . . ."

I am standing outside the stadium.

I hear the national anthem. I hear a muffled roar of a crowd. I hear the announcer bellow, "NOW BATTING, PLAYING SECOND BASE . . . "

I will hold my ground. I will not move. I will remember all the times my trust has been smashed, the greed, the wealth, the disappointments.

"If you go in . . . ," says the voice, "they have hot dogs."

"Who's pitching?" I ask. ◆

258

ERNIE HARWELL: A STEADY VOICE IN A SEA OF CHANGE

April 9

L AKELAND, Fla. — Year after year, winter after winter, the voice stirs from under the snow. It heats up, it melts free, it crosses your lawn and taps the frost from your window. "Time to wake up," it seems to say. "It's spring. I'm back."

You yawn. You smile. It is a voice you trust, an easy pitch, not too shrill, not too deep, a sprinkle of Southern accent — genteel, that's probably a good word, a voice that would sing you a lullaby or tell you bedtime stories. It asks for nothing, this voice. It never scolds. It never whines. It wants only to live inside your transistor radio, to narrate from your car speakers as you drive on a summer night. It is the human lyric of the double play and the single up the middle. It is the call of a rookie with a smoking fastball. It is the game the way the game would sound if only the game could talk. It is the voice of baseball.

It belongs to Ernie Harwell.

"He's the best," people say, as if stating a law of nature. And he is still here, behind the mike in that little booth at Tiger Stadium. Amid all the turmoil, all the change, all the money and lawyers and lockouts and strikes, Ernie's voice remains as much real baseball as green grass and orange dirt. He has outlasted owners and outlasted managers and watched rookies turn to old-timers and old-timers turn to the grave. He was speaking into that microphone before his new boss was in high school. He sold his first story to The Sporting News the year Sparky Anderson was born. He used to shag fly balls with Jackie Robinson and ride the train with Gil Hodges. He had a fight with Leo Durocher and called Denny McLain's 30th victory. You name it, he has seen it. And he is still here.

That voice. On your worst days, it can make you feel good. On your good days, it can make you feel better. Bag of potato chips, Ernie on the radio. Window rolled down, Ernie on the radio. Suntan oil, Ernie on the radio. A Tigers game without him would be like playing with a purple baseball. In 30 years with the Detroit club, this is how many broadcasts he has missed: two. One in 1968, for his brother's funeral. One last year, to receive a major award. Oh, yeah. There was this night in the mid-'70s, at Tiger Stadium, against the California Angels, when it began to rain. After a while, an announcement came to the broadcast booth: "Game canceled, doubleheader tomorrow." Harwell, as he had been doing for years, relayed the message over the air — never knowing it was a practical joke. Then he packed up and left.

Ten minutes later, on the freeway, he turned on the radio to hear the postgame program. "Wait a minute, folks," said Ray Lane, "apparently, the game has not been canceled. They're going to start back up. . . .

"Ernie! Ernie! Wherever you are! Come back!"

Harwell got off at the next exit, returned to the park and finished the broadcast.

See? Even when he tries to leave, the game calls him home.

D *ing how!"*

The cook looks at him. He doesn't understand.

"*Ding how?"* Harwell repeats.

"Oh, meestah. You speak Chinese?"

"Well, ha ha . . . just that word. I learned it when I was over there."

He smiles. The cook smiles. Everybody smiles. We are in a Chinese restaurant, where baseball is hardly a dominant subject, but people still react to Harwell as if he is an honored guest. His voice does it. It sings of hospitality.

He takes a seat next to his wife, Lulu, whom he met almost 50 years ago at a fraternity dance at Emory College. They talked about books. She thought he was "cute." He proposed in a letter. They still hold hands today.

At 72, Harwell seems more frail now. His face shows the lines of experience, his hair is whitish-blond and often tucked under a beret. He wears glasses; he has for years. Now and then he will dig his fists into his pockets and stiffen while he sucks in a deep breath, as if trying to realign his bones. Breathing is important for the voice, he will tell you, and to this day, he takes a morning walk and holds in air for 10 paces and lets it out for 10 more, a trick he was shown by a Russian violinist back in the 1940s, at his first job, WSB in Atlanta, "The Voice of the South." Those were the days when radio stations used orchestras, not compact disc players.

Ernie Harwell does not have a compact disc player. He does not have an answering machine. He has radios. One in the living room, one in the kitchen, one in the office, one in the family room, one in every bedroom and one little portable that Lulu takes on her nightly walk around the neighborhood, so she can listen to her husband broadcast the games.

He seems as dedicated to radios as he is to his subject, which has always been baseball, as long as we can remember. Oh, he broadcast some football, some golf, some tennis, some bowling. He wrote articles for Esquire, Collier's and The Saturday Evening Post. He covered the Japanese surrender at Wake Island. While in the Marines, as a correspondent, he had this idea for a story about the president's mail — how much he gets, how much he answers. He contacted the White House. They set up an appointment. Eleanor Roosevelt met him in the Green Room. Alone. They talked for 90 minutes. "She was very accommodating," he says. Eleanor Roosevelt?

Still, the ballpark is Harwell's natural stage. It has been since his first major league season in 1948, working for the Brooklyn Dodgers. His first road game was at Braves Field in Boston. They didn't have a booth. So he and his engineer sat in the rightfield stands with their equipment on their laps. Can you picture that? "The fans were all around us," Harwell recalls. "Looking over our shoulder, looking over our heads. You had to try to block them out."

You need a hell of a focus. But then, that always has been the strength of a Harwell broadcast. Focus. Oh, he can tell you almost anything about baseball history. He just won't. Not unless it's pertinent. He does not chew the fat. He does not drop names. He will talk about the rookie left-hander, tell you which way the wind is blowing, set the bases, shift the outfield, call the pitch, bring you right in — and let you float above the action.

Silence. The magic is in the pauses. Dizzy Gillespie, the famous jazz trumpeter, once said: "It took me my whole life to learn what *not* to play." So, too, does Harwell know when to leave it alone, when to let the crowd noise or the beer man or your own imagination take the mike from his hands. This is radio. This is play-by-play artistry. What separates him from those other pretenders trying to become famous with their mouths is this: Ernie Harwell respects the game.

Sure, there are flashier names in media. Guys such as Harry Caray, who scream "HOLY COW!" every five minutes. Guys such as Al Michaels, who give sports a slick, corporate feel. Guys such as John Madden, who are hired to go "BOOM!"

Somewhere along the line, something was lost. Except at Tiger Stadium. Except in that little booth. Baseball nuts in Pennsylvania and Virginia and Indiana still sit in their cars, late at night, fiddling with the knobs, until the signal from WJR wafts in across the skies, and they can hear that voice with the touch of Georgia accent. ("Hello evrahbody, welcome to Tigah baseball. . . .") Make us young again, Ernie. Make it fun again, Ernie. Year after year, in the first game of spring, he opens with the same sentence: "For lo, the winter is past, and the song of the turtle is heard across the land. . . ."

He's quoting the Bible. Song of Solomon.

That's Ernie's idea of flash.

Y ou know, the game hasn't changed all that much," Harwell says now, after returning from the restaurant and taking a chair in his hotel room. "A lot of people think the players are more money-minded than before.

261

They say, 'This guy is making $3 million so he won't hustle.'

"But it's all relative. I read a book not too long ago that went back to the 1934 season. It reprinted baseball stories from the top sports writers of the day. And one of those guys wrote, 'It's no wonder the players of today don't hustle! They're making $3,000 a year and have two-year contracts!' "

Harwell laughs, perhaps for the irony, perhaps because he can still remember 1934. And 1944. And 1954. Those were the days you rode trains with the players, you played cards, you passed beer. You glorified their heroics and shut your eyes to their antics. Harwell was with the Brooklyn Dodgers for much of that time. He rode the trains. He shagged fly balls in the outfield, right alongside the players. He was not afraid to call men such as Robinson, Hodges and Campanella his friends — a *faux pas* among today's more hard-bitten journalists.

"I guess I've never really gotten comfortable with the whole antagonistic relationship, especially the drugs and alcohol thing," he says. "You know, I've never seen a person use drugs. I never have. In the old days, you might see a player get on the train a little tipsy from too many drinks after the game. But things were a lot different. The feeling was much more paternalistic between the reporters and the players — and between the owners and the players. Back then, the owners were former baseball men themselves, or baseball families. If a guy got drunk, the owner would bail him out of jail, give him an advance, never say anything about it.

"Nowadays, they don't do that. They're at odds with each other. And besides, the owners aren't the same kind of people. They're corporations, guys who made a lot of money and want to buy into the game."

Harwell has endured his share of owners. And general managers. He has worked for the Dodgers, the Giants, the Orioles. He has done more than 4,500 Tigers games. He has witnessed the strikes and lockouts and walkouts and players coming from jail and players going to rehab centers.

He is asked whether the participants could ever do something so terrible, so revolting, that the fans would give up on the game.

"I honestly don't think so," he says. "They've gone through just about everything there is. To me, baseball is sort of like the church. The church has always taken all kinds of abuse. People in it have made terrible mistakes in the name of religion. And yet it survives.

"Besides, I really believe if a guy is a jerk, but he gets up there in the bottom of the ninth and hits a three-run homer, the fans are going to cheer, no matter what. That's baseball. It goes on and on."

A nd so does Harwell. Once upon a time, he dreamed of the cheers himself. As a child in Georgia, he spent hours on the sandlots. Second base. Fielding grounders. Broadcasting was probably the last career anyone would have predicted; after all, young Harwell's tongue did not move properly when he spoke — they call it tongue-tied — and for years, everything came out with an "f." The word sister, he pronounced "fifter." Christmas was "fifmaf." Once a month, in school, he would have to stand and "debate or declare." The other kids would laugh. *"Ernie can't talk right. Ha ha ha. . . . "*

That he survived that trauma and prospered from it (with the help of an elocution teacher) is credit to his quiet strength. And the fact that he had bigger things to worry about. When Ernie was 6, his father, Gray, who owned a furniture store, was afflicted with multiple sclerosis. Paralyzed and homebound, he would live another 36 years and never move his limbs. The store was lost. Money was scarce.

In the mornings, Ernie and his two brothers would lift their father from the bed to the wheelchair. Then they would gather up cakes and sandwiches their mother had been making since 4 a.m. and deliver them via streetcar to drugstores and society functions. It was the Depression. A nickel here. A dime there.

He wrote. He loved writing. He even considered music (and has written nearly 50 songs that have been recorded). But, in time, he fell in love with radio. His first broadcasting job was in 1946, with the Atlanta Crackers of the Southern League. When they played at home, he called it all. When they went on the road, he recreated the game in a studio. A telegrapher would send the play-by-play by Morse code, and Harwell, in a small, smoky room with another telegrapher, would take the message and let his imagination take over:

"Let's say the Morse code read: 'Jones grounds out to short.' I'd say, *'Smith on the mound, the infield in a bit, wind blowing out to right, Smith looks in to his catcher, Brown, he's got his sign, here's the windup, here's the pitch . . . ground ball to short, Morton over to Morgan, he's out, one away.* . . . '

"Then I'd go on to the next batter. I'd have a little piece of wood that I banged on the table whenever the batter was supposed to hit the ball.

"Sometimes, the telegraph machines would break down for 20 or 30 minutes. Then you'd really have to stretch. You'd have the guy foul off about 25 pitches, go in for a new bat, get in an argument with the umpire, anything you could think of."

Harwell laughs at the fuss people make over those old days. Re-create? Twenty minutes of make-believe? He shrugs and says that "anyone with a voice could do it." Sure. And Picasso painted by numbers.

Harwell did, however, learn two golden rules of radio on those long, black-coffee nights. One was that — no matter what your imagination — you must be true to the box score. People will check. This was the other:

"On radio, nothing happens," he says, smiling like a leprechaun, "until the announcer says it does."

A nd what a fitting way to end the story, because many people already believe that about Harwell and the Tigers. Nothing happens until he says it does. It seems remarkable that in 30 years, he has never had a run-in with a Detroit player. Or that his longtime partner, Paul Carey, cannot remember a single cross word between them. "I guess I run away and hide if there's trouble," Harwell demurs. A better explanation is what Susan Sarandon says at the start of the baseball film "Bull Durham": It's a long season. You've got to trust it.

So today, in Boston — the same city where 42 years ago he broadcast from the rightfield bleachers — Ernie Harwell kicks off another season. The voice will carry the familiar drawl ("Thank-ya, Mistah Carey," "Here come the Tigahs," or his first line today, as always on Opening Day, "Happa New Year!"), and those listening in offices and cars and on transistor radios will instantly be transformed, shaken from hibernation.

If the game is great, his voice will rise with excitement. ("High and outside, that's my pitch," he jokes of his tone.) And if the game is a downer, if the month is a loser, even if the whole season goes south — well, you won't know it from Harwell. It is a lesson he learned from his father.

"After he got sick, he couldn't read. The disease affected his eyesight. But he loved to listen to baseball games. Sometimes it was all he had. We forget that when the team is in last place, not going anywhere. We tend to say, 'Aw, what's the difference?' But there are a lot of people out there who still really care about it, kids, older people, shut-ins like my dad. It means something to them."

And so it means something to Harwell. His father never heard him do a Tigers game. He died in 1960, the year Ernie got the job. He missed the magic. For 30 years, we have not. It doesn't seem fair. It probably isn't.

What was it Ray Lane yelled over the air that night? "Come back, Ernie! Wherever you are!" The mikes are on. The snow has melted. And today, shortly after lunchtime, which is when all baseball games should be played, you will hear that familiar tap on your now frost-free windows. The voice is back. Spring has come again. ◆

JOHN SALLEY LEAVES 'EM LAUGHING IN THE BIG APPLE

April 11

N EW YORK — So there we were with nothing to do in Boston except maybe eat another lobster and talk about Bill Buckner's spring training when I suddenly turned to Mary Schroeder, our ace photographer, and said, "Say, Mary. I've got a smashing idea. Let's jet on down to the Big Apple for the premiere of that hot new comic sensation that everyone is talking about. Won't that be a stitch?"

And Mary said: "Spiffy!"

And I said: "James, call the limo!"

Actually, we didn't say any of that, but I figured that's what you're supposed to sound like when you go from sports writer to theater critic, which is what I did for one night in New York, sort of, if you think about it. Actually, I was reviewing the stand-up comedy debut of a 6-foot-11 basketball player, which is kind of redundant because, if John Salley stood up any more ... *he'd need an elevator to tie his shoes!*

Ba-*dum*-bump!

Thank you.

Now, right off the bat, let me say that Salley was funny, even if he kept adjusting the microphone, and all the other comics who followed him ... *had to bring boots and a rope!*

Ba-*dum*-bump!

Thank you.

This was a pleasant surprise because, personally, I was a little worried about Salley when, after flying down from the Tigers' opener at Boston, hopping in a cab, racing to the club, pushing past the crowd of people and working my way inside, I finally found Salley pacing nervously near the stage, and he looked at me and this is the first thing he said:

"Yo, you know any good jokes?"

B ut hey, maybe that's how Billy Crystal warms up. Of course, Billy doesn't often pepper the audience with giant people such as Dennis Rodman, David Greenwood, Scott Hastings and William Bedford. And they all sat together near the stage. When people yelled, "Down in front!" ... *they turned and said, "WE ARE!"*

Ba-*dum*-bump!

Thank you.

But this was an unusual night. For one thing, Spike Lee, the famous director, was in the audience. His advice to Salley before the show was memorable, and every comedian should remember it.

Spike said: "Be funny, man."

This was also an unusual night because all the money was going to benefit David Auponte, a 12-year-old boy from Brooklyn who was severely burned by drug users when he refused to smoke crack cocaine. Salley had visited Auponte at a hospital during the day. That was the hard part.

This was the easy part.

Wasn't it?

"I've always wanted to do this," Salley said before the show, as people filed in, and he greeted every one. "Comedians are my favorite entertainers. I've wanted to try this since I was 16 years old. But I'm nervous, man. Look at my leg. It's *shaking*.

"I've been worrying all day long about how I should open the show. They had this program on Showtime with all these young comedians, right? And I was thinking what if I just used one of their jokes? But then someone in the audience might yell out, 'Hey! I heard that joke on Showtime!' And I'd have to say, 'Yeah! So did I! That's why I'm using it!' "

He looked at me. "What do you think?"

I told Salley not to worry, he could read the menu and it probably would come out funny.

See, I know what some people do not: that Salley, 25, has had to do this his whole life. Stand up. Be entertaining. Critics say he does more of that than basketball.

But hey, when you grow up that big and gangly, you *better* learn to make the jokes first. Besides, by the time Salley was 10 he was going door-to-door in Brooklyn for the Jehovah's Witnesses, which matured him in a hurry.

"I'd knock on the door — this 6-foot, 6-inch black kid, right, ringing your doorbell — and I'd say, 'Hello, my name is John Salley and I'd like to –'

"WHUMP! Right in my face."

So he was prepared for a rough crowd. And remember, he plays for Chuck Daly, who cracks a smile during a basketball game as often as Dan Quayle gets a standing ovation. The other afternoon, Daly and Salley got into a shouting match that was captured on network TV.

"Socks," Salley said now. "We were arguing about . . . his socks. Yeah. That's it. I said you can't wear pink with green, Chuck. Get with it."

A good comedian can think on his feet.

Back to the show. More people filed in. Salley seemed to know every one of them. Or he did by the time they sat down. ("Hello, how are you; you gonna laugh at my jokes tonight or what?") When Rodman walked past, Rodman asked whether it was OK to use his video camera.

"You're DENNIS RODMAN!" Salley bellowed. "You're an ALL-STAR! You can do ANYTHING YOU WANT!"

"So it's OK then?" Rodman said.

Stricken with a sudden fear that no one would get his jokes, Salley rushed over to Spike Lee, who hadn't moved from his place at the center table.

"Spike, man, what should I do?"

Spike said: "Do the funny thing."

But enough of my blabbering. On with the review. Salley took the stage at the Stand-up NY Comedy Club to great applause. He waved and yelled, "WHAT'S UP?" And then he said . . .

Well, I can't print that.

After that he began to talk about his friends in the audience, especially this one who –

Um, I can't print that.

He did introduce Scott Hastings. I can't print what he said. Oh. He did ask one guy with big ears to stand up, and Salley said, "I just wanted to show Dennis Rodman he wasn't the only one with ears like that."

Everybody laughed, except Rodman, who was still trying to figure whether it was OK to use the camera.

Ba-*dum*-bump.

That's a joke.

And then Salley said –

Oops, can't print that either.

Anyhow, as the evening progressed, he got more comfortable and after a while he was ad-libbing, which has always been his best sport. Personally, I liked it when he announced that Magic Johnson was getting married, and some woman let out an "Awwwwwwww," and Salley glanced at her and said, "Yeah, like *you* had a chance." Also there was the time he identified a Detroit News sports writer in the crowd and said, "You gotta learn to stop writing in crayon, man."

In between Salley's bits, the real comics came up and did routines that included a lot of basketball humor. One said that the New Jersey Nets "are really making progress on that 25-year plan, huh?" He added that the sign in New Jersey where the team plays now reads: "Interstate 95, Nets 91."

I thought that was good.

But then, I laugh pretty easily.

And then Salley did his closing monologue.

But I can't print any of it.

And so it's time for our four-star review: I give John Salley . . . three stars! Run and see it!

(By the way, it's not that the routine was dirty, it's just, well, think about

Eddie Murphy or Robin Williams or Richard Pryor in concert — think about printing some of that in a family publication. It's damn — uh — darn tough.)

For his part, Salley seemed relieved it was over. He said he might try again sometime, but not for a while. Too taxing. "It's like being at the free throw line all by yourself, down two points with one second on the clock. I'd rather be laughing with my teammates," he said.

And thus, as theater critic, I cannot recommend you buy tickets to this show, because it was a onetime-only performance. But you can go see the Pistons play at the Palace. Maybe Daly will wear the pink socks again.

By the way, after the show, I asked the club owner, a bearded man named Cary Hoffman, what he thought of the Pistons' power forward as a comic.

"He was great," Hoffman said. "He's a natural. I'd give him 20 minutes any night."

Hmm. That's about what he's getting from Daly. ♦

AT THE END OF THE BENCH, YOU PLAY AT NOT PLAYING

April 18

E*verything we do is insane. It keeps us sane."*
— **Scott Hastings, philosopher**

"So where's the popcorn?"

"Huh?"

"The popcorn. Don't you know the rules?"

"Yeah. Any fan sitting in that seat has to buy us popcorn. And beer."

"But . . . the game is going on!"

"We know that."

"Wait a minute. . . . You guys eat during a game?"

"Of course."

"When else?"

"Are you serious?"

"We're serious."

"And we're hungry. Get going."

Grab a sleeping bag. Fill the canteen. We are heading for The End Of The Bench. Which isn't exactly The End Of The World. It's worse. Even Columbus never looked for The End Of The Bench. If he did, this is what he would have found: Scott Hastings and David Greenwood, ordering popcorn.

Not that they eat it. Oh, once, against the Knicks, Hastings, after countless nights of sitting, shoes tied, jacket on, and never playing, finally decided to sneak a handful. "And a minute later," he says, "when the kernels were still back in my wisdom teeth, and I'm trying to pick them out with my tongue, I hear Chuck Daly yell, 'SCOTT! SCOTT! GET BILL. GO GUARD PATRICK!' "

"You must have panicked," I say.

"No, I was happy to get in. And athletes are pretty superstitious. So we figure from now on, we should eat popcorn every game."

"Right," Greenwood says. "Popcorn. Good idea."

W elcome to The End Of The Bench. Scott Hastings and David Greenwood. They come out with the Pistons, night after night, race through lay-up lines . . . and sit. And sit. And sit. Occasionally, they get into the action, for a pass, or a free throw, or three minutes' worth of garbage time. "But basically," they say, "our job is to get stiff for two hours." They squirm, they scream at refs, they make up jokes, they check out the fan in the fourth row. They order popcorn.

"Does it ever get so boring you run out of ideas?" I ask.

"The last Charlotte game," Hastings says.

"Yeah," Greenwood says, "I looked over and you were all foggy eyed. I yelled, 'SCOTTIE! SNAP OUT OF IT!' "

"Thanks, man," Hastings says. "I almost lost it that night."

This is the story of two men who have decided if you can't join 'em, joke 'em. Other stories have been written about the last guys on the bench. Usually, they carry quotes such as: "I'm ready if the coach needs me. I don't mind waiting." Very nice. Very sweet. Complete bull. This is the real story. A world where boredom is the enemy, where humor is essential, where a "hello" from the head coach is a special occasion. A world where you rush to catch the bus because it might leave without you. Sitting? Watching? Night after night, without breaking a sweat? Who in his right mind wants to be one of the last two players off the NBA bench? It's grueling. It's frustrating.

And after careful study, Hastings and Greenwood have concluded there is only one way to avoid going nuts.

Go nuts.

DAVE & SCOTTIE'S HOW TO AVOID BOREDOM, IDEA NO. 87: TAKE A LAP

HASTINGS: We got the 20-second time-out down to a science.

GREENWOOD: Yeah. As soon as it's called, we get up and try to circle the team while patting each of the guys on the butt –

HASTINGS: – and get back to our seats before the buzzer sounds.

GREENWOOD: One lap.

HASTINGS: One lap.

GREENWOOD: You can make it in just under 20 seconds.

HASTINGS: Of course if you stop to say something, it takes longer.

GREENWOOD: Yeah. Usually you can only say, "Good job," and move on.

Now, let's get something straight right from the start: Nothing Hastings and Greenwood do is meant to take away from the team. They root. They holler. They want to win just like the other guys. Why else would they go through all this sitting?

But, yes, there are times they scream obscenities at the ref for a bad call, and then, the instant the ref turns their way, they spin their heads toward the stands and go, "Who said that?"

And, yes, there are times when, for want of something better to do during the game, they check what their wives are wearing:

"Say, Dave, Joyce looks really good tonight."

"Purple skirt. Got it for her last year."

There is the little dance they do to the warm-up song "You Can Call Me

270

Al" by Paul Simon. ("Sort of a Temptations thing," Hastings says.) And there are the discussions they get into with the fans, who often sit inches from their end of the bench.

"This one time in Dallas, a woman got all upset over one of our players cursing," Greenwood says. "So Scottie decided to talk to her."

"Yeah," Hastings says, "I asked, 'What is a dirty word really? I mean, aren't all words basically clean?' "

"After a while, he convinced her."

"Maybe I just confused her."

Maybe these two should go on the road. Live from Detroit, it's . . . ScottieWood! You ask how these guys can get away with all this stuff? Have you ever tried reaching the top of your profession — and then just watching? The distance between stardom and trivia is just a few yards on the NBA bench, but those few yards can feel like a black hole. It was into this breach that Greenwood, 32, and Hastings, 29, tumbled this season, one a former first-round draft pick with a long career on losing teams, the other a stringy-haired veteran with a lanky body and Jay Leno's sense of humor. Unlike many 11th and 12th men, they were not rookies, they were not kids all starry-eyed and "happy to be here." No. They were veterans who knew better. They grew friendly. Close.

Now they are Martin and Lewis.

DAVE AND SCOTTIE TALK ABOUT FEAR

GREENWOOD: Unlike some other bench guys, we never root for the starters to get in foul trouble.

HASTINGS: Yeah, because our biggest fear is that the starters will all foul out and they'll actually use Vinnie Johnson at power forward before they use us.

GREENWOOD: Who needs that kind of embarrassment?

HASTINGS: Really.

O f course, we might have seen this coming with Hastings. Wasn't he the Atlanta Hawk who once slapped high-fives with owner Ted Turner after sinking a three-pointer? Wasn't he the guy who wrote a column for the Miami Herald last year as a player for the expansion Heat? Didn't he once suggest the Heat's losing streak could be solved with three easy steps? 1) Keep working hard. 2) Pick a fight with every opponent averaging more than 20 points. 3) Trade for Magic Johnson, Michael Jordan and Karl Malone.

Hastings, 6-feet-10, is a Huck Finn face stuck on a giant scarecrow body. If he can't make you laugh, you're medically dead. You could picture him in overalls, steering a raft down the Mississippi. Of course, he'd be playing Nintendo at the same time. What do you expect from a man who comes from Independence, Kan.?

They call guys like Hastings "free spirits" — usually right before they call them "free agents." That's what he was last July. After stints with New York, Atlanta and Miami, he signed with the Pistons.

Greenwood came a few months later. He, too, was a free agent and was coveted by several teams. But, at 32, a new team wasn't enough. He wanted a ring. Coming out of college, he was a star, the second player taken in the entire 1979 draft. Unfortunately, the first was Magic Johnson, who went to Greenwood's desired team, the Lakers. Greenwood went to Chicago. He suffered there until the arrival of a kid named Michael Jordan — then the Bulls traded him to San Antonio. He suffered there waiting for a kid named David Robinson — then the Spurs traded him to Denver. Timing? You want to talk timing? David Greenwood had the timing of the coyote in the Road Runner cartoons.

"I figured Detroit could use me, since they had just lost Rick Mahorn," he says. So he signed in October. A one-year deal. A slow training camp hampered him. Then the improved play of James Edwards, John Salley and Dennis Rodman left little room for his 6-foot-10 presence.

Suddenly, the former hero of UCLA found himself in the last seat on the Detroit bench. What? "I said to Scottie, 'I'm not used to this, man. If you ever look over at me and see me losing it, you gotta help me, OK?'"

Scottie nodded OK. He knew just what to do.

DAVE AND SCOTTIE'S HOW TO FIGHT BOREDOM, IDEA NO. 128: CHEW A TOWEL

GREENWOOD: Scottie has this thing during the game where he just chews the end of a towel until he can pull a string out between his teeth.

HASTINGS: I used to leave it hanging there, just to hear people yell, "Hey, you got a string hanging from your mouth!"

GREENWOOD: Then one day he started blowing them onto people.

HASTINGS: They're just little threads. Sometimes James Edwards will come over, and he'll be all sweaty. I'll blow one at him.

GREENWOOD: And it sticks.

HASTINGS: Yeah. It's pretty cool.

Now, I know what you're thinking. Goodness. All that money and so little work and these fellows are having . . . fun? Well, before you condemn it, remember that these fellows, despite their spots on the bench, are still better than 97 percent of the basketball players on this planet. That's the crazy thing about the NBA. You take a guy who was king of his high school, prince of his college and suddenly, in the pros, he's the mop-up man. "I don't care if you're Mr. Optimist of the world," Hastings says, in a rare serious moment. "Nobody can sit there and watch his job being done by someone else and feel like he's contributing."

"I never used to think about bench guys when I was a starter,"

Greenwood adds. "I've gained new respect. It's one of the hardest things to do. I really believe guys sitting would give up some money for the chance to play.

"And garbage time doesn't cut it. I'll be honest with you. Going into a game with 30 seconds left and a 35-point lead — that's not playing basketball. It's almost like an insult. That's like saying the guy ahead of you can't last another 30 seconds, so *you* get in there. Heck. *We* have a better chance of getting injured coming in cold than the guys who were already playing.

"Garbage time is a lose-lose situation. If you play well, they say, 'Aw, it was just against the other team's scrubs.' If you make a mistake, they say, 'See? That's why we can't play him.' "

Hastings listens. He nods. "Last month, I went into a game with 12.8 seconds left and came out with 11.6 left." "Amazing," Greenwood says.

"Yeah. I got what we call a trillion."

A trillion? "Yeah. That's when the box score reads: 1 minute played, followed by a row of 0-0 0-0 0-0 0 0 0. I got lots of those."

DAVE AND SCOTTIE ANSWER THE QUESTION: WHO ARE WE?

GREENWOOD: Honest now, Scottie, when was the last time a coach came up and said, "Hey, how you doing? How's your wife and kids?"

HASTINGS: Never!

GREENWOOD: See? We do not exist.

HASTINGS: Right. We are like the twins that the family hides in the basement.

GREENWOOD: We are like professional blackboards; there's nothing there.

HASTINGS: We are like the insurance policy that you get when you're first married –

GREENWOOD: – and then you stick it in the attic –

HASTINGS: – and 40 years later you dust it off and say, "HEY, HONEY, LOOK WHAT I FOUND! IT'S DAVE AND SCOTT!"

Which is not to say they are bitter. Oh, sure, they want to play. And maybe they wish the coach would feel what they feel. But their enthusiasm for teammates is almost legendary. Joe Dumars, during his recent injury, spent the first few games sitting amid the Hastings-Greenwood show. "You guys are too into it for me, man," he said finally, moving back uptown. "I can't believe how much you yell!"

Often times, when a Piston is having a bad stretch, he will come to the bench and get an earful from Daly. Then he'll wander to Hastings and Greenwood, who he knows have been watching. "James, you drove the baseline the last five times. Go to the middle next time," they'll whisper.

"Salley, stop thinking so much and just go up with it. . . . "

Often, the advice is good. And when the guy goes out and sinks a basket, he turns to Greenwood and Hastings and smiles. Let's face it. Sitting on the bench makes you a keen observer.

But, mostly, sitting on the bench just leaves you sitting on the bench. Sometimes, even the jokes can be painful. There was the time when Hastings and Greenwood were giving a verbal lashing to referee Darell Garretson. Finally, Garretson turned and said, "Hey, you getting in the game tonight, Greenwood?"

Ouch.

There was the time when Hastings was a few seconds late getting back to the locker room. The Pistons have a tradition after every game of huddling together, putting their hands in, and giving a word of togetherness. By the time Hastings opened the door, it was finished. They had forgotten him.

"That must have hurt," I say.

"Yeah," Hastings admits. "But me and Dave just put our hands together and went 'YeeeaaaAAAH!' You know, our own thing."

The truth is, it's not easy, this life of understudy. It's dull and it's agonizing and you always feel you should be doing more. Especially when you've put in your time in the league. But you can swallow life's lemons or you can turn them into lemonade. Hastings and Greenwood go for the laughs.

"Guys on the team ask us why we're cheering so much," Greenwood says. "But I say, 'Wait a minute. I didn't sit on this bench all year so we can *lose* the championship! Are you kidding? Are you crazy? I WANT A RING!'"

He turns to Hastings. "And he wants a Porsche 928."

And on they go. If the Pistons do indeed repeat as NBA champions, their pine ride will have been worthwhile. If not, about all they have to show for this most unusual season — besides a lot of "trillions" — is their friendship. Actually, it's one of the nicest things about the NBA.

"We have grown pretty close, haven't we?" Greenwood says.

"Yeah," Hastings echoes. "Of course, 10 years from now when Dave is living on the street somewhere in a cardboard box and I'm living in Buckhead, Ga., I don't know if we'll still reach out and touch each other. . . ."

If you can't join 'em, joke 'em. Live from Detroit, it's ScottieWood! By the way, should you go to a Pistons game and sit alongside these two and they turn and ask you for the popcorn, you can take it from me. They're only kidding.

Now, about the beer . . . ♦

CHUCK LONG GETS HIS WISH AND HE WON'T LOOK BACK

May 3

H ell is over for Chuck Long. He goes free now. The golden boy with the quarterback savvy who four years ago was supposed to save this franchise is being sent to California for a third-round draft pick — the football equivalent of selling a Pinto through the Tradin' Times — and the Lions are happy to get that much. And Long? Long is so thrilled he's running around the house like Sally Field at the Oscars. "They like me!" he keeps yelling at his wife, Lisa. "The Rams really like me!"

This is the guy who finished second to Bo Jackson in the Heisman Trophy voting. The guy who was hailed in Detroit headlines the day he was drafted: "THE LONG ERA BEGINS." Yeah. Nobody knew how long. Took four years. Felt like forever. He leaves now, like a forgotten soldier, hearing the echo of cheers for a new savior, Andre Ware, another guy who has used that little Heisman statue to get everybody all excited. People are saying Ware is the future. Chuck Long, 27, must be laughing his head off.

"If I learned one thing in my time here it's that there is no future in the NFL," he says. "Teams can't really wait four or five years. If you don't win in two years, three tops, heads will roll. I'm just glad this whole thing is behind me."

Why not? He had become cancer in the Silverdome. He got booed. Fans and coaches gave up on him. The Lions tried desperately to deal him, and he worked out for the Rams as if his life depended on it. But know this, even as we say good-bye: Chuck Long never did anything wrong here. He was a victim of timing, a victim of coaching, a victim of injury. But how a man goes from first-round draft pick to clipboard holder in four years may have more to do with lousy management than lousy athlete.

And Chuck Long might get the last laugh after all.

H ere is Long's Detroit career: 1) We love you! 2) Where have you been? 3) Have a seat. He came late to training camp his first season, contract holdout, and that tripped him up. He had a shining moment that November when his first NFL pass landed in Leonard Thompson's hands for a touchdown. "I should have retired right then," Long jokes.

Because the rest was a steady slide into the mud. The Lions got worse, not better, and people questioned Long's arm, his feet, his leadership. After hurting his elbow in the 1988 preseason, he was rushed back too soon by

Darryl Rogers, who was desperate at that point to save his job. Didn't work. Rogers got canned anyhow. Long went on the injured list. The new coach, Wayne Fontes, was never much for the slower, drop-back style. He switched to the run 'n' shoot, and as soon as a new kid named Rodney Peete showed some promise, Fontes threw his arm around him and said, "You're my guy." Long was treated as if he had bad breath.

Things deteriorated. Normally an upbeat guy, he began to gripe. We did a TV interview together once and Long asked me beforehand to "please mention I want to be traded." When injuries to the other quarterbacks forced the coaches to look his way, Long, hurt and embarrassed by his status, foolishly demanded a promise: If he starts the game, he finishes the game. It was over right then.

"You get thrown on a shelf, after being the No. 1 quarterback, and that's really hard," he says. "It got so bad, I didn't even want to go to work. I had to drag myself out of bed each morning."

I ask whether he is already packed for LA.

"Not yet, but soon. Let's just say we're moving out of town . . . and I don't plan on being back in the near future."

He goes free now. He started all of 21 games here. Was he any good? How can you tell? In 21 games? Maybe he was a bad pick. Maybe he had bad coaching. Maybe he was hurt too much. Whatever. The irony is that in LA, Long, now healthy, will be backing up Jim Everett, the former Purdue star who got less acclaim than Chuck in college at Iowa. And Long's happy about it. He can't wait to go. Let's face it. His chances of a Super Bowl are a lot better out there, where the team doesn't practice in the parking lot.

The Lions? Here they sit, with a new hero. Ware. A nice kid with a ton of statistics and that little bronze Heisman thing. Will he be the answer? You tell me. Every coach wants to draft his own quarterback, build his own system. Rogers tried it with Long. Now Fontes tries it with Ware.

And the fans sit and wait. Amid the hoopla on draft day, few mentioned that this is the second time in four years the Lions spent the big pick on a quarterback. Good teams don't do that. They say this is a new regime? It was a new regime with Rogers and Long. The fact is, Detroit has a stack of passers, and you wonder whether this organization knows what it's doing.

Long doesn't wonder. Not anymore. I can still see him the day he arrived in Detroit, all golden locks and youthful promise. Someone asked about the Lions' losing ways and he shrugged as if it were a mosquito bite.

"I've won everywhere I've played," he said with youthful bravado. "In high school. In college. I believe I can win here."

Now he leaves, quietly. It's not even a big story. Today's savior is tomorrow's want ad. And the Lions know it better than anyone else.

You listening, Andre? ◆

PISTONS SET TO DEPLOY SECRET-WEAPON MOM

May 8

Forget it. This series is over. I don't mean to sound cocky, but the Pistons can't lose, not now, not since the plane arrived from Seattle and a certain woman got off and gave her son a hug.

Give it up, Knicks.

James Edwards' mom is in town.

"Oh, now, don't jinx it," she said, laughing.

OK. We won't. We will simply say that Popeye had his spinach and Superman had his phone booth and James Edwards has his mom, so Patrick Ewing can stay home. Not that Edwards needs his mother to play well. As any Detroit fan will tell you, Edwards — also known as "Buddha" — has been having a great season as Detroit's power forward.

It's just that when his mom visits, James, a confirmed bachelor, sees his game elevate, which is impressive, because he is already 7-feet-1.

Maybe it's the pot roast.

I must confess, I was unaware of the Secret Mom Weapon until Scott Hastings and David Greenwood, the "Weekend Update" staff of the Pistons, told me of her earlier visit, around Christmas, which inspired James to new heights.

"She was here for a few weeks, and James played great," Greenwood explained.

"Yeah, and the day after she left," Hastings added, "he scored nine points."

Convinced that this was no coincidence, the two of them put a charity dish on the locker room table, under a sign that said, "BRING BUDDHA'S MOM BACK TO TOWN." They collected, Hastings said, $2.30.

"Did James accept it?" I asked.

"Nah," Hastings said. "He got embarrassed and took the dish away. I guess he figured if we couldn't raise the whole $200, it wasn't worth it."

Now before Edwards turns completely red, let's remember that mothers have a good NBA tradition. Magic Johnson's mom cooks for the Lakers when they visit Detroit. And Mary Thomas, Isiah's mother, has become such a celebrity they made a TV movie about her.

So it seems only fitting that Nan Edwards, a charming woman who drove her only son to his high school practices and waits for his phone call after each Pistons game, should receive some credit, too.

After all, she does the cooking.

"Oh, I guess I eat a little better when she stays with me," said Edwards, who, like any good son, makes up the guest room when Mother comes to town. The two of them share meals together, talk after the games. Edwards says they were always close, ever since he was a kid in Seattle.

Of course, Hastings won't leave it at that. He has this whole thing figured out: "He eats better! He's home early! Heck, he's in the house watching TV with her at 9:30 at night! What's James, 34 years old? He's 22 now. His mom comes into town, he's 22 years old.

"If teams were smart, they'd fly all moms in for the playoffs. Are you kidding? We'd be awesome."

Now, maybe Hastings is crazy. Or maybe he has something here. I checked. Lo and behold: During the Christmas stretch from Dec. 16 to Jan. 6, when Mrs. Edwards came to visit, Buddha was indeed at his best. He averaged nearly 18 points and shot 57 percent. He was the leading scorer twice, and the Pistons were hot.

And as soon as she left, James shot 3-for-10 against Chicago.

Must be a hell of a pot roast.

Anyhow, Mrs. Edwards' arrival should be inspiring news to the Pistons, considering that Edwards will be one of several big men trying to stop Ewing, who is so hot he doesn't need relatives.

In the first round of the playoffs, Ewing destroyed the Boston frontline of Robert Parish, Kevin McHale and Larry Bird, all of whom are old enough to be his grandfather. And now he threatens Detroit. Normally, you might worry about such a thing.

Not with the Mom Factor.

"Goodness, I don't know if I have that much influence," said Nan Edwards, who describes herself as "of retirement age," stands 5-feet-11, and, in her day, might have been a pretty good player.

"The facts don't lie," I said. "How do you explain your influence?"

"Well, James knows I want to see him win," she said. "And we have always done things to please one another. Maybe that's it."

Sounds good to me. Mrs. Edwards was here during last season's championship run. And she might stay through this season's finals, which should make Chuck Daly happy. I don't want to say the Pistons could sweep this series in four games. I will say that Sunday, Game 4, is Mother's Day.

Sorry, Knicks. Maybe next year, you can bring your mothers in to visit. I'm sure they'd love to see New York City and pay $17 for a hamburger. For now, the Pistons have the secret weapon, and, if I were you, I wouldn't fool with it. After all, you know the old saying:

It's not nice to fool Mother Edwards. ◆

THE FUTURE? HOW DOES FIELDER FIELD SOUND?

May 25

TIGER STADIUM, Sept. 1, 1990 — Ever since Cecil Fielder hit his 62nd home run of the season last week, things have been pretty crazy around here. You can't get near the stadium. The line forms before dawn — reporters, mostly. From New York, London, Moscow. About 900 reporters are here from Japan, and all they want to know is how many yen it would take to get Cecil back there for another season.

Of course, Cecil has had some pretty interesting offers since last Tuesday, when he smacked that Guillermo Hernandez hanging curveball into the cheap seats for home run No. 62, breaking the all-time single-season record with more than a month to play. People were surprised. Not that Hernandez threw a hanging curveball; they pretty much expected that. But they were surprised Cecil hit it out, because he'd already banged three home runs in that game. Geez. Does the guy ever get tired?

One thing is for sure. Old Cec' really messed up baseball's publicity people, who figured he wouldn't get No. 62 until the weekend. That's when they had Bruce Springsteen coming in for the national anthem, along with the 300 dancing girls, choreographed by Paula Abdul, and the giant ice cream sculpture. Instead, after Cecil hit Nos. 59, 60 and 61 with three swings — and it was only the sixth inning — the commissioner yelled, "Rain delay!" even though there wasn't any rain, and the game was suspended until President Bush could fly in from Washington, D.C., and Roger Maris' grandchildren could be rushed in from Ohio. Both arrived in their pajamas. The president, a tad confused, began his speech saying, "Mr. Shevardnadze, let me say I am delighted to be in your country. . . ."

Naturally, all three networks were broadcasting live. Ted Koppel did "Nightline" from home plate. Oprah Winfrey walked among the crowd, asking, "Do home run hitters make better lovers?" Mike Wallace tried to sneak into the dugout, but Sparky Anderson said: "You ain't no ballplayer. Hey. Bo!"

And Bo Schembechler tackled him.

After a while, the sellout crowd began to chant, "CEEE-CIL! CEEE-CIL!" Finally, the big man himself came out of the dugout, put his hands on his hips and replied: "CEH-CIL! HOW MANY TIMES DO I HAVE TO TELL YOU? IT'S PRONOUNCED CEH-CIL!"

It was quite a moment.

Of course, by now it has been replayed on most every TV show in America, including "Good Morning America," "Good Afternoon Dallas," "Good Evening Seattle" and "The Prudential Halftime Report." I suppose you also saw the 15-page photo story in Life magazine, and the Newsweek, Time, Forbes, GQ and Field & Stream cover stories. By the way, that last magazine has changed its name to Fielder & Stream. And Cecil doesn't even fish.

He doesn't watch Barbara Walters, either. But that didn't stop her from doing a special, in which she asked the slugger, "Cecil, if you could be a twee, any twee . . . " Quite frankly, Cecil doesn't understand what all this fuss is about, even if he is hitting .391. He also doesn't know what a twee is.

Cecil keeps saying the same thing. "I'm just looking for good pitches to hit." He says that to everybody. Except the Japanese reporters. When he sees them coming, he runs, because they keep throwing money at him. One time, they dumped a barrel of yen on his head. Yesterday, one of them drove up in a truck. Cecil hid in the shower.

Sparky has been having a good time with this. He keeps smoking that pipe and saying, "Boys. I told you before the season, Cecil would hit 30 home runs. I just didn't say how many times he would hit 30."

Meanwhile, the rest of the Tigers have begun touching Cecil's bat before each game, for good luck. The team batting average has soared to .314. The players have also thrown out their protein juices and nutrition shakes and adopted Cecil's diet, which, as near as anyone can tell, is pretty much anything he wants, whenever he wants, especially pizza.

Did I mention the movie?

Yes. It stars Kevin Costner and James Earl Jones. It's called "Fielder of Dreams." A voice comes to a Toronto baseball player and whispers, "If you swing, it's outta here! . . ." It's in development.

And to think, nobody thought Cecil could do it. Back in May, when he had 17, they kept waiting for him to fade. But by June he was calling 'em, upper deck or lower deck. By July, he was calling the row number. In August, Cecil's relatives were sitting in the bleachers, and before he swung, he yelled, "Hey, Uncle Mel! Heads up!"

So now the crowds come out every morning. Traffic is backed up to the SouthFielder Expressway, and also on GreenFielder Road. Mayor Coleman (Cecil) Young has declared the slugger's bat a historic monument and plans to hang it next to the Joe Louis fist. A bat and a fist ought to convince visitors that this is not a town to be messed with.

Like I said, this sure has become a crazy place. I guess the really crazy thing is that it's liable to get worse next week.

That's when Dan Petry goes for his 40th victory. ♦

WHEN WILL THE PISTONS HEAR FROM THEIR FANS?

May 30

I am about to say something that needs to be said, and I hope you forgive me if it sounds a little blunt:

We stink.

I am talking about fans at the Palace. I am talking about their attitude and their volume. I am saying it now, because if this city really wants the Pistons to get serious against the Bulls, well, we ought to heed our own advice.

Let's be honest: The atmosphere at the Palace in Auburn Hills, Mich., is no better than mediocre compared to other NBA arenas. Compared to a place such as Chicago Stadium, where your bones rattle on every basket, the Palace is comatose. It needs a transfusion. For this, I blame the Pistons' front office, which has turned the building into one endless commercial; and I blame the fans, many of whom seem to think making noise doesn't go with comparing Calvin Klein sweaters. Hey. You in the ninth row. The game is out here. On the big wooden floor, remember?

People from out of town laugh at what goes on inside this arena. Here we are, with the best basketball team in the country, and we act as though we're watching MTV — when we're not playing trivia quizzes or leaving early to beat the traffic. Personally, I would like to line up a few thousand real fans outside the Palace, and every time someone leaves early, one of those people gets to take the empty seat and keep it for the rest of the playoffs. And that's just one idea. . . .

1.Shut Off The Big Screen. The biggest problem with the Palace is that monstrosity hanging from the rafters. It's like being hypnotized. Every time there's a break in the action, the giant screen takes over: "And now, for tonight's Comedy Clips!" Boom. Two minutes of John Belushi or Steve Martin. "And now for tonight's Nestle's Crunch Time Moment!" Boom. Two minutes of highlights. There are quizzes, games, electronic ball races. I swear, the biggest cheers are for those three stupid balls.

It's ridiculous. Since when does an NBA game need more commercials? It has gotten so that as soon as there's a time-out, everybody looks up, including, sometimes, the players. It's surreal. You become so passive watching that scoreboard you barely notice the game has resumed.

If they shut that thing off, people would naturally be more eager to get back to the action. They'd count the seconds. They'd stir and rumble. And

281

when play finally resumed, they'd be ready to roar. Hey. You want to watch Belushi? Rent a videocassette. Give your ticket to a real fan.

2. Leave The Court To The Players. Once upon a time, the court was a holy place. But at the Palace, during time-outs, we have children and teenagers and bankers and advertising execs running all over it, shooting baskets for prizes. There's the "Michigan State Lottery Three-Point Shootout," where some bozo gets escorted out by two scantily clad tuxedo girls and inevitably throws up a whiff. There's the "Dunham's Fast Break Contest," a shameless exploitation of two children who race up the floor trying to sink a basket first. For heaven's sake, they're just kids. The loser always looks as if he's going to cry.

I lose count of all the different shooting promotions. One time, a guy almost bumped into Joe Dumars trying to throw up an extra shot as he walked off the court. What, Michael Jordan is not enough? We have to see "Ralph, from Novi" make an ass of himself?

3. Thank You, Mr. Announcer. Although Ken Calvert is a nice guy and does a credible job in calling players' names, someone apparently has told him this is the Comedy Castle, particularly at halftime. He kibitzes and wisecracks about shooters in these goofy promotions, which only makes the Palace seem like Amateur Night. Enough. Give it a rest.

N ow, please. I am not trying to be a party poop. What I want is to enhance the party. This is a basketball game, not a sideshow. You want fancy clothes and elegant behavior, try the Whitney.

But to inspire pro ballplayers, to make them go for that rebound when their chests are heaving, to make them dive for the ball when their legs are heavy, you need noise, not electronic dots. I promise you, the Bulls could not have done what they have done to the Pistons without that thunderous crowd. The Pistons deserve an equal weapon. And they shouldn't have to provide a dog and pony show.

As evidence, I point to Madison Square Garden, where there is absolutely nothing going on during time-outs. No jokes. No contests. And the place is LOUD, the fans go BERSERK. Remember, these are hardened New Yorkers, who must worry each time they stand up that someone will steal their wallet. If they can do it, we can.

And don't tell me about rich people not cheering. Palace tickets are less expensive than those at the Forum, and about the same as Chicago, Boston, Portland and New York — and you can't hear yourself think in those arenas. Besides, since when does your income affect your vocal cords?

No. It's about attitude, same as it is for the Pistons right now. If the front office really wanted to help, it would forsake a few advertising dollars and turn off the Big Screen. And fans, simply stated, it's stand up or shut up. Unfortunately, we already know you can do the latter. ◆

AN UNTIMELY FAREWELL FOR THE HERO'S HERO

June 11

PORTLAND, Ore. — He had been braced for this death for weeks now, calling the hospital, hoping against hope, even instructing his wife, Debbie, "If Dad dies during a game, I want you to promise me you'll be the one to tell me, OK? And not until after the game is over. Just you, OK?"

She promised. Now the game was over. Sweat was pouring off his arms and face. Joe Dumars took a last look at the scoreboard and walked off the court, happy the Pistons were back in this championship hunt. He could hardly wait to call home and tell them — and then his coach, Chuck Daly, pulled him aside.

His wife was on the phone.

This is a story about courage and effort and life and death — and perspective. Yes, Joe's dad was always big on perspective. He had no legs, no mobility, but he had a heart as big as Louisiana, where he lived, and he passed it on to his son, and his son has been passing it on to Detroit every day he pulls on a uniform. Once, early in his career, Dumars called home after a Pistons game and his father got on the phone. "I saw you today on the TV, son. You played good. And they pay you for that?"

"Yeah, Dad," Joe said, laughing, "they do."

"That's a good job you got there. Hang on to it."

"OK, Dad. I will."

It was that kind of love, one of those quiet relationships where you go right from childhood to adulthood and you never stop thinking your dad is the smartest man on earth. Joe Dumars thought that. Every day of his life. He thought it before he went out for the game and showed the country how great he plays basketball, and no doubt he is thinking it as he sits in his hotel room, his mind a million miles from the NBA Finals.

"This hurts so much because we all know how tight they were," said John Salley, shaking his head, after the 121-106 Detroit victory in Game 3, which went from very important to not important at all. The players had been slapping each other's backs, proud of the spirit they had shown in this raucous, foreign arena, and suddenly the word spread and the room went quiet and nobody was slapping each other anymore.

Could there be a more poignant afternoon? Can fate really be this . . .

ironic? Here was Dumars, playing the hottest game of these NBA Finals, scoring 33 points, leading the Pistons from the depths of their despair to a victory that puts them right back on the track for a championship. He was making shots from the floor and from midair and from ridiculous angles — he was amazing — and all afternoon, the whole time, he never knew. His father. Joe Dumars II, 65, had died just hours before the game, from congestive heart failure. The Pistons had gotten the phone call; Daly, the assistant coaches and Isiah Thomas had been informed. No one else. And not Joe. They kept Debbie's promise. They said nothing.

Now here was Thomas running the floor with his teammate, trying not to look at him too often, as if his face might give it away. How tough was this? "I knew something that would shatter his world," Thomas said afterward, shaking his head. He sat in the office where Dumars got the phone call. Already now, Dumars was gone, whisked away so he would not have to deal with reporters prying into his private tragedy. Thomas got up, and carried his teammate's No. 4 jersey, still soaked with the afternoon's sweat. He folded it neatly and walked down the corridor.

"It really puts everything in perspective," he said.

Perspective. There was the time Joe Dumars went riding with his father on the produce truck, convinced, as children often are, that Dad's job was nothing but fun. Nine hours later, his arms dead tired from lifting crates, he trudged back into the house. "You do this every day?" Dumars asked. His father just smiled.

Perspective. There was the time when the diabetes first struck, and the first leg had to be amputated, and the father lay in the hospital bed, a sheet pulled over his tragedy. Joe stood in the doorway, not sure what to do, but his father beckoned him and spoke in a sure and steady voice. "Son, I want you to look at this," he said, and he pulled back the sheets. "Take a good look. This is what it is now. We go on from here. I don't ever want you feeling sorry for me, all right?"

Perspective. There were all those nights Joe would call home after an exhausting road trip, or 100 straight interviews, and his dad would get on the phone, his dad, who had spent all day in bed, smoking cigarettes, robbed of what you or I might think is a normal life, and yet he was the upbeat one, cheering up his rich and famous son.

"I'd say, 'Dad, how can you be so positive with all the things that have happened to you?'" Dumars once recalled. "He would answer me, 'Son, I got everything I need.'"

Perspective. So it was no surprise that last June, when the Pistons realized their dream of the NBA title, when the champagne was poured over their heads and they were dancing and singing, it was no surprise that Dumars told a reporter that "this ring goes to my dad." The greatest thing he had accomplished should, naturally, go to the greatest man he knew, right?

Perspective.

Suddenly, this whole championship is cast in that light, this whole crazy series that had people so up in arms about who had the better city and who got the bad foul calls and who pushed off when he shot — suddenly all that is very small, and it can never be that big again. Sometime soon, Dumars will be back in the house where his father constructed his first basketball hoop — a sawed-off door and a bicycle rim — and you can bet he won't be thinking about his 33 points, or the fact that the Pistons are on the verge of another championship.

Why? That's what you ask yourself. Why do these things happen, why now, why to him? The truth, of course, is that they happen every day, to one of us, to someone, and only the chosen few have it trumpeted across the newspapers. It doesn't make it easier to swallow.

After the game, the other Pistons were noticeably upset by the news. Vinnie Johnson, who had his best game of the playoffs, who snapped out of his slump for 21 points, who should have wanted to be interviewed more than anyone else in the building, stood before an army of reporters and said, "I don't want to talk now, OK?"

Brendan Suhr, who lost his father to the same killing disease last summer, stood out on the court, wiping tears from his eyes. "We talked about the disease a lot, we compared stories," Suhr said. "I told him how much it hurt when my father died, but how you draw strength from it in the end."

In the end, that is the best any of us can hope for Dumars. That he draws comfort and strength. Whether he comes back to play in this series is really unimportant, and to talk about it at this moment is to insult his father's memory.

And you would never do that. Not to this man, who, were this not the day he was called to heaven, would have liked nothing better than to sit at home, watching the television his son bought him, and see little Joe light up the game.

"There was this one shot today," Thomas said, allowing a small smile, "where Joe came down the lane, and he threw it up, real high, and it went way up and fell through. I looked at him and I said to myself, 'Your father put that one in, Joe.' "

Amen. ◆

285

SWEET REPEAT! PISTONS WIN BACK-TO-BACK TITLES

June 15

PORTLAND, Ore. — The shot went up, the shot swished through, and suddenly the Pistons were dancing off the court and into the castle on the clouds, carrying the scars and lumps and exhausted smiles that told you the journey was tough, the journey was costly, but the journey, finally, was over.

Twice is nice.

"BACK TO BACK, BABY!" they sang in their champagne locker room, dancing and wiggling literally back to back, after beating Portland, 92-90, with a last-minute flourish — and a last-second miracle jump shot by Vinnie Johnson — to capture their second straight NBA championship. "We win! We won! BACK TO BACK, BABY!"

Back to back, indeed. Back to glory. Back to the throne room. Back-to-back crowns on their heads, something only two other franchises have accomplished in NBA history, and that's a long time. They did it with stamina, perseverance, desire, and, ho-ho, just a little drama. You weren't scared when they trailed by seven points with two minutes to go in a foreign arena, were you? Hey. This team thrives on that stuff.

So it was that Johnson got that look in his eye and locked his radar on the basket, jumper, jumper, nothing but net. And Bill Laimbeer got that tight jaw, and rose above the Portland players and grabbed rebound after rebound, his 16th, his 17th. And Isiah Thomas threw a prayer into the air and the prayer was answered, good! Tie game!

The crowd was swallowing its tongue now. The Pistons' bench was hollering encouragement. John Salley hid his head in a towel — "I couldn't watch" — and Chuck Daly felt his stomach flip over. The clock ticked down, destiny hung in the balance — " . . . four, three, two . . ." — and finally, Johnson, 33, one of the guys who can still remember when this team couldn't give away a ticket, left the floor and let it fly and you knew it was over, they knew it here, and they knew it in the sold-out Palace back in Auburn Hills, Mich., where 21,500 were watching on a giant TV screen.

Swish!

Twice is nice.

"Vinnie said, 'Gimme the rock,' " Salley recalled, wiping champagne from his eyes in the locker room. "And we said, 'Oh, you want it? OK.' "

Johnson laughed and doused himself again. "It's the biggest shot of my life!" he exclaimed.

"WHERE'S VINNIE AT?" screamed Mark Aguirre, wielding another bottle of bubbly. "I WANNA GET HIM!"

Go ahead. Splash Vinnie. Splash Buddha. Splash Zeke. Splash Chuck, who may have ended his career on the highest note. Splash them all. But know this: It was damn tough to get here. These are not the smooth young colts who galloped to the title last year without missing a beat. These were tired warriors now, wearing the strain of all those nights during the endless season when the opposing team wanted a piece of the champions. These Pistons were hobbled. They were cut, bleeding. Dennis Rodman was rolling on a bum ankle. Isiah Thomas was swallowing blood from a blow to the nose. James Edwards was taped above the eye. Joe Dumars was playing with the memory of his father, who passed away, still tugging at his insides.

But here was the heart of a champion shining through. The last nine points of the game? On a foreign court? What do you call that?

Call it another championship.

Twice is nice.

W as this sweeter than last time?" someone asked Thomas, who scored 29 points and was easily voted MVP of the NBA Finals.

"It was, because people doubted we could do it this time," he said, tugging on a brand new cap that read, "Back to back NBA champions." "We're not as physically talented as last year. But we're smarter."

And they're in the history books. Remember, not only have they won successive NBA titles, but in doing so they have lost *just one game in the Finals,* and — almost incredibly — have not dropped *a single Finals game on the road.* In two years? They really won three straight in Portland? It takes a full team to do that.

How fitting then, that they were all dancing back to back, all these players, subs and starters, relieved, overjoyed, exhausted. And how fitting that each of them had at least one moment in this postseason run, even from the farthest end of the bench. William Bedford? He was in there against Chicago. Gerald Henderson? He scored maybe the weirdest basket of these Finals — the almost disastrous lay-up to end Game 4.

David Greenwood and Scott Hastings? Here were two veterans who had turned to eating popcorn during regular-season games, so useless did they feel. And yet in the Finals, where the big horses run, suddenly, they were out there together — not in garbage time, mind you, but in critical junctures of the game.

"What will you do with your ring?" someone asked Greenwood, who had waited 11 NBA seasons.

"Safety deposit box," he said.

Smart. As for the others, well, call them the Starting Eight, for at any given moment, any one was the star. How many games did Detroit win thanks to James (Buddha) Edwards — "We're riding the Buddha Train!" they used to sing in the locker room — and how many nights did Mark Aguirre pull their bacon from the fire with a sudden explosion of inside and outside shooting?

Vinnie Johnson? Critics had him buried after Game 2 — "too old, he's done" — and yet out came the Microwave and scorched the Blazers in Games 3 and 4, and he makes the biggest shot of the year to end the season?

Amazing. And what about John Salley, the only member of this team to do a nightclub comedy routine? Wasn't it delightful to see him get serious once the whistle blew, rising on his jets, blocking Patrick Ewing, blocking Michael Jordan, blocking Clyde Drexler? The Joker is growing up, folks. "I want to announce if Chuck Daly leaves, I'll take the coaching job!" he yelled at a TV camera.

Well, not completely grown up.

Bill Laimbeer? He deserves some kind of award for these Finals, maybe the Joyce Brothers Award, for crawling into the heads of the Trail Blazers and screwing them all up. He kneaded them, nudged them, outrebounded them, outglared them. By the end, they were so irritated by his presence, they were like a man destroying his house trying to kill a fly. And after every victory, Laimbeer, who still can't run or jump worth a nickel, smirked and said, "Whatever it takes."

Aren't you glad he's on our side?

And wouldn't you say that about Dennis Rodman, who drove himself to tears during these Finals battling his bones, fighting to play on that bum ankle, jumping on a trampoline during games to stay warm?

And for all Rodman was unable to do, Thomas seemed doubly capable. His shooting this series seemed to come from the gods — they kissed each ball in midair and, swish, it fell through the nets. "We tried everything," moaned Portland's Terry Porter after Game 4, Isiah's finest moment. "We got a hand in his face. We jumped with him. What can you do?" Nothing. This was his series, his ball, his net, his time.

His magnificence was matched only by the courage of his backcourt mate, Dumars, who will never forget these Finals; he can't. His father died just hours before his best game, Game 3, and that long walk to the office where the phone call awaited will forever be etched in his brain. "It was awful hard," he finally admitted, talking for the first time after the game. "Sometimes I was dying out there."

Yet this is the character of the man: He did not ask for sympathy. His father had taught him endless lessons from the bed where he spent his final years, among them, "Do your job and see it through." Joe stayed just long enough to do that. He will be on his way home by the time you read this, tending to more important matters now. His teammates understand.

"When my shot went in I grabbed Joe and said, that was for our dads," Johnson said. "My father passed away in October. He used to let me stay up late and watch the Knicks on TV. Now we're here and . . . well . . . I just told Joe, this is for our pops, man."

What can you say after that?

Nothing. Just as there was nothing for the Trail Blazers to say. They gave a good effort, but they crumbled at the end, as inexperienced teams will do. Even the normally crazed Portland fans seemed to sense it. Finally, they could only stand and applaud the Detroit conquerors as they ran off the court. Nice.

And why not, when you consider this list: Boston, Milwaukee, Chicago, Los Angeles, Indiana, New York, Chicago and, now, Portland. The Pistons have, in order, chopped them all down over the last two postseasons. That's serious stuff.

A word here about Chuck Daly. Seven years ago, he took a franchise that never had back-to-back winning seasons, and in his time, he has never had a losing one. He is a master motivator and people manager, and he has succeeded in bringing out the part inside players that makes them want to win rather than argue. With that magic, he has built a team.

And in the end, it's those team scenes that stay with you: Salley palming Thomas' head and rubbing it joyously. Rodman hurling himself into the arms of a startled Aguirre. Laimbeer punching Edwards in the arm, then grinning. Hastings and Greenwood kissing each other for the cameras. And finally, all of them, dousing each other with champagne and wiggling in unbridled joy for all they've done, all they've endured, all they've accomplished. "BACK TO BACK, BABY!"

Twice is nice.

Anybody for three? ◆

FINALLY, THE SPOTLIGHT BELONGS TO NAVRATILOVA

July 8

W IMBLEDON, England — In a good play, the secondary characters peel away, one at a time, taking their bows, until the star is left alone in the applause. This is how it should be. This is how it was under warm and cloudy skies at Centre Court, Wimbledon. Martina Navratilova shook hands with history, solo at last, and took her bows.

This time there was no Chris Evert, whose white hat had always made Martina seem dastardly. Gone, too, was Helen Wills Moody, whose record of eight Wimbledon singles titles had been such a dangling carrot all these years. Navratilova looked toward heaven. She began to cry. The day before, with her nerves jangling, she was reminded of the words of her new mentor, Billie Jean King, who said: "Don't get caught up in all this other stuff. All you have to do tomorrow is hit the ball." And so she grabbed a tennis ball off the TV set, put it in her pocket and walked around with it all day, taking it out, squeezing it, feeling its simplicity.

And on this day, after 75 minutes of simple tennis mastery, she watched her opponent's ball fly long over her head — "Out!" called the linesman — and she raised her hands in the air. She had done it. After spending half her life making annual pilgrimages to this royal playground, she owned it. All alone. It was her stage. And, apparently, her seats, too, for she jumped into the stands and scurried upward, stepping over startled people's heads until she reached the family box, where she hugged members of her entourage and said thanks.

You can do that when you've won nine Wimbledon titles — more than anyone before you. Even so, Navratilova later admitted with a laugh, "I scanned the climb first, to be sure I could make it." They call this the wisdom of age. At 33, it is just one of the things Navratilova has mastered.

It is time we gave her credit for the rest.

H ere we have a champion who has waited half her life to be accepted. She is a victim of the American hero system the same way Vanna White is a ridiculous beneficiary of it. There was warm applause finally for Navratilova in American living rooms — but she had to do something extraordinary to earn it. Nine titles? Geez. How many athletes win nine of anything? Does anyone have nine Kentucky Derbies, nine Masters, nine World Series rings, nine boxing championship belts?

"Did it make it sweeter because you played so well?" someone asked Navratilova after she conquered first-time finalist Zina Garrison to win Wimbledon, which, by the way, is her first Grand Slam title since the U.S. Open in 1987.

"Well, it didn't have to be a thing of beauty," Martina answered, honest as always. "I mean, as long as you win, they don't put an asterisk next to it saying, 'She won, but she didn't play so hot.'"

On this day, however, she was hot. On this day, she was as young as she wanted to be. Against Garrison, 26, who defeated the mighty Steffi Graf to earn the final, Navratilova was a tennis textbook. She put magic on her topspin. She hit volleys from all angles. She defended the net the way a Mississippi grandpa defends his porch. Tennis is more than hitting, it is thinking ahead, two and three shots, moving your body like a chess piece in anticipation. To win the last point of the next-to-last game, Navratilova covered more ground than a lawn mower, racing to retrieve all of Garrison's angled volleys, sprint, whack, sprint, whack — yet, at the same time, she forced Garrison into position as if she were a puppet, until, finally, Zina's angle was more difficult; she hit into the net. This was beautiful tennis. Even the British TV announcers were left to invoke a most American cliche: "She can do no wrong."

Funny, isn't it? That was not always the case. For a while, she could do no right, at least as far as her adopted country was concerned. No matter what Navratilova, a Czech defector, accomplished on the court, she could not get America to unfold its arms and embrace her. She was too robotic. Too distant. Her private life too weird. Not coincidentally, Ivan Lendl, also Czech born, has suffered these same slings and arrows.

Evert once explained it this way: "I'm American. And as much as she wants to be 100 percent American, Martina is Eastern European and a lot of Eastern Europeans are like her on the court. . . . She's sensitive, vulnerable, she has a good sense of humor, but on the court you only see the aggressive, confident player."

Ironic that such words should come from Evert, who, image to the contrary, was truly the more ruthless of the two. To win a match, Chris would slice your arm off. Not so Martina, who was much more insecure, more prone to cry, more jittery. And yet the public perception was exactly the opposite. Martina looked so muscular, she spoke with an accent, she wore glasses. Chris wore earrings and lip gloss. Because America usually picks heroes on skin-deep characteristics, it was a pretty easy choice.

And so for all those years, even when she was winning all the titles, and was ranked No. 1 in the world, and was miles ahead of her peers in terms of training, health, mental fitness, Navratilova was defined by Evert. She was Chrissie's foil, the ying to Evert's yang, the dark hat to the white hat, the ugly duckling to the swan. Even toward the end, when Evert was not much of a Grand Slam threat and the two admitted they actually liked one another, Martina was defined by that friendship. It was Chrissie saying she liked her that gave her the OK.

How fitting then, that in her finest hour — and say what you will, Wimbledon is still the measure of any tennis player's legacy — Navratilova was at last a flock of one. Alone at Centre Court. All the others have gone, Evert, Mandlikova, Austin, the names that once made up the notches in her gun, a gun that often backfired.

Good, because Navratilova should never have needed other names to be defined. She is more than somebody's rival; she is, arguably, the finest woman athlete of our time. She has been on or near the top of her profession for twice as long as most of her peers. She has more singles championships than we could go into. She is the most decorated doubles player ever. She is a pioneer in training, adapting much of her schemes from the likes of the Dallas Cowboys and the Edmonton Oilers. She is the biggest sports fan on the tour, and that includes the men.

She is also a forthright, courageous woman who has had her birthright, sexuality, femininity and finances raked over by the press. Once, she complained that lower-level players at the Australian Open weren't getting enough prize money to pay their way. The next day's headlines had her complaining about her prize money and calling her "Money Bags Martina."

When she had the brashness to bring her lover, Judy Nelson, to Wimbledon — and mind you, neither has ever behaved in anything less than a dignified fashion — the London tabloids had a field day. They still snicker.

Tough. Their loss. Martina Navratilova has come a long way from the scared, junk-food-loving teenager who sneaked away from her home country for the love of freedom, and could not return until a few years ago, in an emotional reunion. It is doubtful many of us would have had the courage to do much of what she has already done, let alone the talent. To have done it while being unappreciated much of the time is even more remarkable.

So, happily, she has her own perch now. And yet, to her credit, she seems to have grown more humble over the years. Someone asked her whether she would contact Wills Moody, 84, who lives a quiet life in Carmel, Calif.

"No," she answered softly, "I mean, I wouldn't want it to seem like I broke her record and now I want to meet her. I've wanted to meet her for years. I once was in Carmel and I thought about driving past where she lived, but I didn't want to disturb her privacy. If she would agree to meet me, I would love to meet her."

"When did her historic record become your goal?" she was asked.

"History never really was. It was just to win one more Wimbledon. I just felt I could do it. If I had won just four, I would have kept trying for a fifth. The history part just makes it nicer. I'm glad people who didn't get a chance to see Helen play can one day say they saw me."

We should consider ourselves lucky.

Maybe now we will, at least whenever we recall this final scene: Navratilova, wiping a tear from her eye, taking congratulations from the Duchess of Kent, who, in a fitting show of appreciation, gave the new Queen of Wimbledon a kiss. Let the others be defined by her now. They have peeled off, moved to the side, they are clapping in the wings. It has been a hell of a show, and Martina finally has the good light now, all to herself. She has earned every dot of it. ♦

DEMERS, LOYAL TO THE END, DESERVED A BETTER FATE

July 16

MALTA — So it turns out, I am the last to learn that Jacques Demers was fired. That'll teach me to go on vacation. The news, it seems, never stops, no matter where you hide, at least not the bad news. And while I would like to ignore it, to tell myself that coaches get fired all the time, I tried. I can't.

In the last four years, I've come to know this guy, this hopeless optimist with the mustache and the bad accent, and I once felt as if he would be around forever. Maybe I just wished it. Here was such a rarity in pro sports — a man with a heart. And last week he was summoned to Mike Ilitch's house to have that heart squished. Sit down. You're fired.

So I called him, from over here. Which, it turns out, is more than some people have done since he was dumped, including his captain, Steve Yzerman, who is on vacation, I guess someplace where they haven't invented the telephone. My friends, I know you've heard a crater's worth of talk on this subject, but I feel, even from this far away, that I must say this: The Red Wings should be ashamed of themselves. They have stripped Detroit of one of its most admirable heroes, and it's damned unfair, because he was buried by some of the very people he most trusted. And while I'm sure those people would like to wipe their hands of his dust and get on with the new guy, Bryan Murray, who arrives today as coach and general manager, there are a few things about Demers the. man that maybe they and you should know.

And I'm gonna say them, like it or not.

First of all, no one fretted over the team's recent slide more than Demers. I know this, because now and then, over the past year, he would call me at home, usually early in the morning, asking to talk privately about his team and his coaching. Why, he wondered, weren't things as they were three years ago, when his young players captured the hearts of this hockey-hungry city?

Most people have too much of an ego for this. They talk to the media only to rag on some teammate or owner. Not Demers. If he respected you, he'd ask your opinion. And he respected a lot of people. In all the times we spoke — on the record, off the record — not once did he knock his star players, his general manager, his assistant coaches or his front-office people.

Not once. If there was a problem, he blamed himself. I want this known, because, obviously, some of those same people didn't return the favor. If they did, he'd still be coaching today.

Even when we spoke now, Demers refused to point fingers. "Maybe I'm an idiot," he said, "but I just don't want to believe that people would go behind my back. That would hurt more than losing my job." This, despite the fact that every rumor mill has some players and even assistant coaches bad-mouthing Demers in private, including Yzerman. This, despite the fact that Ilitch himself told Demers that a few key players informed him that Jacques couldn't motivate the team anymore.

Yes. Well. Let's talk about motivating a team where players are handed $5,000 checks for winning a few midseason games. Let's talk about motivating a team where, by simply making the third round of the playoffs, each player winds up with more loot from the owner than he'd get if his team won the Stanley Cup. Let's talk about motivating a team where players who were fined $16,000 by Demers for their parts in the demoralizing Goose Loonies incident in Edmonton eventually got that money back from the owner anyhow — without the coach even knowing it.

Let's talk about motivating a team where Bob Probert and Petr Klima were permitted to make a mockery of the very word. Team? Did you know that at one point, when Demers — who made mistakes in cushioning those two, mostly because his own father died an alcoholic — finally reached his boiling point and told the higher-ups, "Let's get rid of them. Whatever it takes. They're destroying the team," did you know that he was told the following? "You're the coach. We pay you to coach them. That's all."

Um-hmm. Let's talk about motivation and how it all must be Jacques' fault.

Or let's talk about a fellow named Jimmy Devellano, who was also conveniently out of town, in Lake Placid, N.Y., a most interesting name given these tumultuous events. I have one question: Why is Devellano still employed? Why is he not guilty for the Wings' recent failures? He has been here eight years and only once did the Wings finish above .500. A coach can only work with the players provided. Where were they? Sure, people will point to the Adam Oates-for-Bernie Federko trade and say, "Wasn't that Jacques' doing?" In fact, the resentment over this trade prompted several players to turn on Demers, to whine and mope. One actually accused Demers to his face of "trading for your buddy Bernie Federko." Demers had to explain that he and Federko were not buddies, simply a former coach and player being reunited. What he should have said was, "Grow up and play hockey." He also should have said that Devellano had a major role in that trade, too.

And yet, instead of a departure, Devellano simply abdicates his GM duties to Murray and slips into a new office upstairs, safe from the flood.

Beautiful. Typical sports world justice. Devellano, who didn't do his job, survives this thing. And Probert, who did nothing to deserve his job, is still on the team. And Klima, who was never more than a selfish boy on fast skates, winds up with his name on the Stanley Cup as part of the Edmonton Oilers.

And Demers is fired.

Sure. Makes sense, right?

B ut let me get back to what makes Demers unique, and why, in some ways, he may be too good for this organization. Over the years, I've seen him in a lot of situations. I've seen him scolding players; I've seen him talk to them like a father. I watched at a charity roast when a blind woman rose to sing a version of the national anthem and Demers began to cry. I saw his face when I informed him that Klima and Probert had been out drinking that night in Edmonton. It turned white. And yet, he refused to duck my questions.

I saw him that night at Joe Louis Arena in 1987, his finest hour, when the Wings fought back from a 3-1 series deficit and beat Toronto in seven games to capture the Norris Division playoffs crown. He waddled onto the ice and tossed a puck to his wife, Debbie. And I saw him this spring, his lowest moment, the night the Wings were eliminated from making the playoffs; he was hoarse, bloated, red-eyed. He looked like a man who had tried to suck in all the bad air in the locker room, so his boys could go out and win one more game.

In every pose, I saw the same thing: Heart. Passion. Commitment. And now, I listened to Demers talk, that same rollicking voice, but tinged with sadness: "I woke up this morning and I felt like the loneliest man in the world," he said. "I've gone my whole hockey career and never got fired. I was proud of that. Suddenly, after all this time, I don't have a team to go to. No practice, no office. . . ."

He sighed. "And the thing is, we were ready to jell. Jimmy Carson was healthy. Probert was finally back and straight. We made some good pickups. We're ready to go. . . ."

Listen to him. He's still talking as if he's coaching the team. And he refuses to bad-mouth the very people who did him in. For this type of loyalty, the Wings waited to fire Demers until mid-July, when there is almost no chance of him finding a job for next season.

Class move.

S ometime in the near future, the truth about all this will come out. Did Yzerman have a role in the firing? Why did Devellano tell Demers he knew nothing about his dismissal — come on, the man is in the organization, isn't he? Ah. Whatever. By that point, people will already be putting mothballs on the Demers Era, typing it into the record books as four seasons, two coach-of-the-year awards, one never-ending controversy and no Stanley Cups.

Those on the inside will never dismiss it so easily. Yes, it is true, Demers, like all fired coaches, will continue to be paid for the three years on his contract. No one is painting him as broke. But it won't be money that will be missed. There was some magic here once, in the shape of this pudgy pied piper who, for nearly two years, had a bunch of hungry kids believing that effort was enough, that sweat was an elixir, that anything was possible. We fans believed it, too.

Gone now. Maybe the new guy will do well. Maybe he'll be lucky enough to avoid a season-long injury to Carson, a lame goalie, a Probert-Klima fiasco that poisons the soul of the team. "Bryan Murray is a good man; he'll do well," Demers told me over the phone. Typical. It was like listening to your grandfather tell you everything will be all right, even as he lies in a hospital bed.

Maybe all sports organizations are this callous. Maybe winning is not only the bottom line, it's the only line. If Jacques Demers was fired, after all he did and all he tried to do, then there can be no other conclusion.

But that doesn't make it right. I don't care how many players or front-office people hide behind that excuse. At some point, you make an allowance for character. You see the man behind the suit. Since his firing, at least four players have been to Demers' house to express their sorrow, and many more have called him. So he must have gotten through to some of them, right?

He got through to me. He got through to a lot of us. You have this feeling now not unlike the end of that film, "Dead Poets Society," where a teacher with character is fired by his employers, but his disciples — most of them, anyhow — stand up on their desks to salute as he leaves.

I'm standing now, even 4,000 miles away. *A bientot,* Jacques Demers. You deserved better. ◆

HOW I TOOK THE LOW ROAD TO HISTORIC ST. ANDREWS

July 19

S T. ANDREWS, Scotland — Before I get to my newest favorite athlete and my personal choice to win this year's British Open, a golfer who is allergic to grass, I want to tell you about an exciting new travel experience: sitting on a highway, waiting for a Scottish tow truck!

Sounds great, huh? This is how I spent much of my first day here, after my rent-a-car broke down somewhere between the Firth of Forth and the Fifth of Schnapps.

This, I should add, was a car I did not want to rent in the first place, except that when I landed at the airport, I realized — and here's where the story gets interesting — that I was on the WRONG SIDE OF THE COUNTRY! Oops. Well, now. That could be a problem. I was pretty sure I had asked my travel agent to book me into the nearest airport to St. Andrews — merely the most famous and history-laden golf course in the world. But maybe she thought I said, "Book me near St. Andrews Tool & Die Shop," which is probably in Glasgow, the city where I landed, which is only about two hours west of the golf course, give or take a few sheep.

This, by the way, is how I learned I was on THE WRONG SIDE OF THE COUNTRY: I stepped up to the rent-a-car counter and asked the young Scottish woman how far the airport was from St. Andrews.

She said: "Ooooh, fir!"

And I said: "Fir?"

And she said: "It's queet fir, yees!"

And I said: "Fir?"

She then made a face that, had she spoken English, or at least English that I could understand, would roughly translate to: "This idiot is on the wrong side of the country, and he's making fun of me? What a dork."

And then she rented me a car that broke down.

O f course, the first thing you must do when your car breaks down in a foreign country, a good 25 miles from the airport, is NOT PANIC. So I got out and began to stroll along the highway with my hands in my pockets, as if I suddenly decided a walk through exhaust fumes would be a lovely way to spend the afternoon.

And eventually I spotted a car dealership, and I went in and explained my problem to two men who were sitting behind a desk, smoking cigars. They were very nice, and they let me use the phone, which was great, until the woman from the Scottish AAA started talking on the other end.

This, as near as I can tell, is what she said:

"Whysee deery oot me root?"

What do you say to that? Yes? No? Sorry, I'm married? Eventually, I had no choice but to put on one of the salesmen, who told her: "Looook, grayne see hees to aulto fellaw query ooly beens o'laly, OK?"

He hung up and said: "Forty-five minutes."

Which was more like two hours.

But let's get back to Bernhard Langer.

Yes. Bernhard Langer, that serious-looking golfer from West Germany, and my newest choice for Athlete We Should Root For From Now On. Hey. You thought I had problems, sitting there on the highway? Wait. We now learn that Langer, 32, who has made more than $3 million on the tour and has even won the Masters, is, and I am not making this up, allergic to grass. That's right. And trees. Serious allergy. Has had it for years!

In fact, the doctor who discovered the problem reportedly told him: "I find it unbelievable that you can go out to work on golf courses every day. To me, it is amazing that you can live."

Well, now. That's sort of a downer, isn't it? That's like telling Chuck Daly that silk makes him break out in a rash. And wait. The doctor wasn't finished. He also told Langer, "I have never seen a sportsman with such a high level of muscle tension, not only in your back, but in your entire body."

Hmm. You know, I've often watched Langer play, and I always thought he looked a little stiff. Now I realize his back was screaming, "Get me a heating pad!" And his nose was going "aahhhh . . . ahhhahhhh . . . ahhhhhhhchhhoooo."

Which may explain the yips.

Yep. Yips. Langer suffers from them, too. This means, at the drop of a hat — or, in his case, a tissue — he can lose his putting touch. It has already happened three times and has cost him numerous tournaments.

Now I don't know about you, but a bad back, shaky wrists and drippy sinuses are an awful lot to heap on one golfer.

I think it's even worse than all those second places Greg Norman has to put up with, or all the short jokes Ian Woosnam has to tolerate. (Wee Ian, they call him over here. I think in the States they call him Dudley Moore.)

So I am going to make Bernhard my new favorite, and pick him to win the British, for all the hay fever sufferers of the world. Also, I promise never to complain about a lousy rent-a-car, now that I see how bravely Langer suffers his woes. When asked how long he could take it, Langer said: "I'll just carry on as long I can. Right now, I don't feel like a wreck."

If he wants one, he can have mine. It's on the highway, not fir away. ◆

THE U-M MAN WHO BROKE SHOAL CREEK'S BARRIER

August 2

W hen Louis Willie was 13 years old, he boarded a Dallas streetcar and made his way to the back, past the "Colored" sign, where it was safe for him to sit. It was a September morning, during the Depression years, and he was on his way to school.

Soon the car was filled. A middle-aged white man lumbered down the aisle. Seeing no empty seats, he looked at Willie and said, "Get up, boy."

"No," Louis said.

The man glared. "I said get up, boy."

Now Louis' heart began to race. He looked for help. He saw a black man sitting across the aisle. "Mister, I'm in the colored section. Do I still have to get up?" Louis asked.

"Son," the man answered, softly, "yes, you do."

The shame. The helplessness. He never forgot those feelings. He remembered them through high school, through college, through graduate school up North, at the Univeristy of Michigan, where he was the only black in his class to earn a master of business administration degree. "It still burns in my heart," he says.

And now, more than 50 years later, Louis Willie, a successful Alabama businessman, has been asked once again by white men to stand up. This time, however, they said please. This time, they were almost desperate; they needed a black to break the color barrier at Shoal Creek Golf Club near Birmingham, Ala., where the PGA Championship had become a tinderbox set to explode in their faces.

And because this is important, and because he is that rare type of individual who has absorbed hatred yet has never taken to hating, Louis Willie said yes. He would join. He can't really golf too well, but he would join. He would be the first. That sound you hear is a mountain being moved, by a gentle, 66-year-old businessman.

"I guess I better take some practice swings somewhere," he said, laughing. "My handicap is a little embarrassing, you know."

B ut then, this thing has never been about handicaps. Not the golf kind, anyhow. Ever since Hall Thompson, 67, the founder of the club, announced that the Shoal Creek members "have a right to associate with whomever we chose. . . . We will not be pressured into accepting blacks," the pressure has been on to do exactly that. Sponsors dropped out. Protesters gathered. This is the kind of club hosting the PGA Championship? The story grew from local sidelight to national front page. It crawled inside our consciences, an ugly worm that reminded us that, for all our supposed progress in racial relations, we still have a lot of locks on the doors.

"To be honest, before this incident, everybody took the all-white policy for granted," Willie said. "After all, Shoal Creek was not alone."

All too true. In fact, it is fairly standard for country clubs across the United States to segregate according to race, religion or national origin. The "official" policy, of course, is open admission. This is the reality: Only someone sponsored by a member will be considered, and then, he must be voted in by a committee of members. It's like a tree house. Like a high school clique. Peer pressure builds the wall, and it is strong and impenetrable. We don't want any of them in our club.

So prevalent is this attitude that a large number of tournaments on the professional golf tour — which are telecast to millions of homes each weekend — are hosted by whites-only clubs, including the Masters. And until now, almost nobody complained.

Aren't we past this? Doesn't it sound like Jim Crow, like something out of the '50s? It does. But then racism never had an overdue date. It eats time; it falls by inches. Finally, if we are lucky, it gives.

So now Louis Willie, the son of a Pullman porter and a schoolteacher, will golf at Shoal Creek. His membership, offered by Thompson himself, waives the $35,000 entry fee and includes full privileges, including sponsoring other members. This, no doubt, has quietly enraged many white members, who still carry several clubs of prejudice in their bags. They probably wish the PGA never dropped in on their precious real estate.

Willie anticipates them. He knows they will smile, shake his hand, then grumble after he walks away. "I am not naive," he says. "I know about two-facedness. I know about tokenism. But the welfare of our community is the most important thing. A divided community is never good. If suffering a little two-facedness is the only sacrifice I have to make to bring harmony back to our city, I will gladly do it."

You wonder how one man gets to be so wise. But then, you wonder a lot of things with this story. How many Americans — although they would never say it out loud — feel that Shoal Creek had the right to close its doors, that people who pay money ought to be allowed to set the rules? For all the colors that have melted together in our country, there is still a sense of "us and them" — between whites and blacks, Christians and Jews, rich and poor. It is historic, perhaps even rooted in human nature. It is one door you can't just kick in. You chop at it, you whittle, you slap, you bang.

You play golf. Louis Willie says he has been inside Shoal Creek only once, to watch the 1984 PGA — which was held without protest — but he intends to go there now, beginning with a dinner at the restaurant with his wife. Then, he says, he has a lot of friends "who are chomping at the bit to play that course."

And he laughs. He is amused at any suggestion that he is somehow a hero. He says he is merely a concerned citizen of Birmingham, president of the Booker T. Washington Insurance Co., which also owns construction and cemetery concerns. He notes that in years past, Alabama had "white cemeteries and black cemeteries," but now blacks are being buried in white cemeteries, whereas whites still refuse to be interred alongside blacks. Some prejudices, obviously, die more slowly than others.

But they do die, and one stupid prejudice dies today. Shoal Creek should force other country clubs to follow suit, to establish truly open membership. And Louis Willie, who once surrendered his seat to hatred, will now, half a century later, have the chair pulled out for him. True, his putting may be suspect, but he knows this much: You aim for the green. And green, after all, is the only color that should matter in golf. ◆

Etc.

THE REEBOK PUMP? IT'S TRULY INFLATED FOOTWEAR

January 7, 1990

A friend of mine recently walked into my house and began strutting around the living room.

"Well?" he said.

"The bathroom is over there."

"No. Didn't you notice? I got the Pump."

"That's great. Did you have a flat?"

"No, stupid. The Reebok Pump. The shoes. Look at my shoes!"

I did. They looked like most of the athletic shoes kids wear today. But these had a little rubber basketball popping out of the tongue.

"That's the Pump!" he said. "It's great. You pump it, and it fills the shoe with air until it's perfectly contoured to your foot."

Well, now, shoot, I thought. Here it is, only one week into the '90s, and already I am hopelessly behind.

"You should get some," he said, leaping around the couch. "They're the most comfortable shoes in the world. Whee!"

"How much did they cost?"

"One hundred and seventy dollars."

I looked at him. "You bought five pair?"

"Come on. These are special. Haven't you seen the hip TV ads with Dominique Wilkins, Dennis Johnson and Pat Riley?"

"Sure," I said. "What do those guys care? They haven't paid for their own shoes since they were in high school. I'm not sure Pat Riley even wears athletic shoes. Unless they have some Italian designer on the heel."

He smiled. "The Pump, Pump, pump it up, pump it up, pump-pump-PUMP-PUMP–."

And he flew out the window.

Now, I was never one for fashion footwear. I ignored the Earth Shoe, the Moon Boot, the Disco Heel. Besides, I have trouble with the idea of inflatable sneakers. I mean, what if you get a flat? Do you call AAA? ("Help! Corner of Main Street. Size 9. And bring some laces.")

But because everyone says the Pump is revolutionary, and because I know kids are already nagging their poor mothers and fathers ("It's just $170, Dad! You're so cheap.") and because I know that pretty soon, dope fiends in New York will stab an innocent teen for his Pump shoes, and a new

305

crime category will be introduced, I figured I should go see for myself.

I went to a shopping mall and there it was. In among the running shoes, tennis shoes, bicycle shoes, weight lifting shoes and walking shoes (walking shoes?). The Pump.

"I'd like to try a pair," I said to the salespeople, most of whom looked as if they were still in high school themselves.

"Pump it up!" they said gleefully.

I pulled one on — it looks like the shoe Neil Armstrong wore when he walked on the moon — and began to squeeze the little rubber basketball. It felt like a nurse was taking my blood pressure through my foot.

"It's a little tight," I said.

"Let some air out," they said. "Press the button on the back."

I did, and heard a soft *wssshhh* of air. Several heads turned.

"It wasn't me," I wanted to say, "it was the dog." Unfortunately, my dog has the good sense to go barefoot.

This is not the way I remember shopping for sneakers. (We called them "sneakers" before we were enlightened by major corporations such as Nike and adidas that there is a big difference between sneakers and "running shoes." About 80 bucks, I'd say.)

There were two kinds of sneakers back then: Pro Keds or Converse. Black or white. And they didn't cost $170. For that much money, you could have had the whole store.

This is how you shopped for sneakers: You put them on, and the salesman pressed his finger on the rubber tip. If you didn't say "Oww!" your mom said, "We'll take them." Then you went shopping for underwear.

How do they feel?" I was asked.

"Where do I get my skis and poles?"

"Ha-ha. Really. The Pump is very special, you know. It has little air bags, and layers of polyurethane, and a unique heel design, and a little window so you can see inside. . . . "

I tried to imagine a pickup basketball game in these shoes. Would I have to stop in the middle and yell, "Time out! My shoe's deflated"? What if we suddenly heard a *wssshhh* sound? Was it the wind, or one of us?

I am told Nike makes a version that comes with a small pump you must carry with you. What if I forgot it? Does someone have to get on the floor and blow into my foot? Could I stop at a gas station?

As I bounced around the store, I noticed a pair of black Converse sneakers. The kind with the rubber tips. "How much for those?" I asked.

"Oh, those are $26."

And that's what I purchased. Who needs the Pump? With the money I saved, I bought two new snow tires. Maybe Pat Riley doesn't wear those.

But at least when I get a flat, I don't get shorter. ♦

LAWRENCE DELISLE'S QUIET DESPERATION

January 14, 1990

I never got much out of reading Thoreau. Maybe because I read him in high school. An urban teenager doesn't exactly fall for a guy who moves to the woods and talks to squirrels.

I do, however, remember one line he wrote. It struck me when I read it and it has stayed with me all these years: "The mass of men lead lives of quiet desperation."

What did he mean by that, I wondered? Did grown-ups really have it so tough? Quiet desperation? Such contrasting words. Like "dying hope." Or "deafening silence."

Or "I didn't mean to hurt my babies."

That last sentence has been in my brain since I read it in the police statement of a 29-year-old tire store manager named Lawrence DeLisle. Five months ago, on a warm summer night, DeLisle allegedly slammed his foot on the gas pedal and drove his station wagon — with his wife and four children inside — smack into the Detroit River. The adults escaped; they swam to the surface, gasping for air. The children drowned.

It was originally deemed a tragic accident. But a week later, in a rambling and confused conversation with a police investigator, DeLisle suggested he might have been trying to kill everyone in that car — including himself. The reasons he gave were 1) the suicide of his father, something few of us have had to endure, and 2) the pressure from work, bills, children and a wife — things many of us endure every day.

It is the latter that haunts me. Could life become so intolerable that you might think of ending it like that, in a river, the water rising, no way out?

"I didn't mean to hurt my babies."

Quiet desperation.

Chances are you read the transcriptions of the DeLisle tapes. Were you shocked? How could you not be? The horror. The senseless death. Here were four beautiful kids — they had just stopped at McDonald's — and now they were at the bottom of a river.

We may never know the true story. Even DeLisle's statements — in which he said, "I don't even want to go to trial. Just lock me away" — were ruled inadmissible in his trial because of the interrogation methods used by police. (That ruling has been appealed.) Just the same, what disturbed me most was not DeLisle's gruesome account of the incident, or his alleged attempt to kill his family by leaving a candle near a leaking gas pipe.

What got me were exchanges such as these:

Police: What were you thinking about?

DeLisle: Peace. . . .

Police: What were you thinking about?

DeLisle: Not having to pay bills every week. . . .

Police: At the time you wanted to be rid of everybody, didn't you?

DeLisle: I just want it to be over . . . the constant repetition. Same thing day after day.

Is it possible that everyday pressures — a thankless job, credit card debts, sexual friction with a spouse — could push a man to such an unforgivable act? Can "normal" life be so awful? We distance ourselves from killers by believing they are sick creatures, out of the ordinary. What frightens me is how ordinary some of DeLisle's pressures were.

And not just him. We read today of how a man in Boston may have murdered his pregnant wife, in part because the baby would have interfered with his career. We hear of children murdering parents for inheritance money, because their jobs don't pay their bills. Horrifying. DeLisle said he loved his wife, he loved his children. He also said he sometimes wanted to escape them all.

Quiet desperation.

How many more Lawrence DeLisles are out there? Who knows? He could be a lone troubled man or one of an army of walking time bombs. In eight years of reporting, I have learned this much: We never know what is going on inside the heads of the people next to us. Not even if we live with them, eat with them, work with them.

We never know. People bury their darkest thoughts; they appear perfectly normal. But inside, private demons — such as DeLisle's memory of his suicidal father — can chew at the heart, making the most simple parts of life seem too burdensome, and the most unthinkable solutions somehow appealing.

So we have men driving into rivers and parents selling babies and husbands injecting wives with poison to rid themselves of things such as debt or marital problems.

And we can only draw this conclusion: Perhaps surviving everyday life is more noble than we think. Perhaps we should ignore sports stars and actors and celebrate instead the husband or wife with two jobs and no bank account who still has time to hug the kids.

God knows not everyone is making out that well. "The mass of men lead lives of quiet desperation." OK, Thoreau. I get it now.

It scares the hell out of me. ♦

AN AWARD-WINNING QUERY: WHY WATCH THE OSCARS?

March 25, 1990

W ell, once again, movie fans, it's Mr. Oscar here to answer your Academy Award questions.

Let me start by saying there are three things you can count on in this year's broadcast: 1) You will not win. 2) You will not be nominated. 3) You will fall asleep before the good awards are given out.

Well, I can see you're excited already. Let's begin, shall we?

Q. Can you explain the purpose of the Academy Awards?

A. Certainly. The basic purpose of the Academy Awards is to get you to pay for a movie you otherwise wouldn't drive across the street to see by sticking a little naked statue in the advertisement that reads, in BIG letters, "ACADEMY AWARD WINNER" and, in little letters, "best sound editing by a foreign mutant in a documentary about baked goods."

Q. How are the nominees selected?

A. Easy. They are the same every year:

BEST ACTOR: One foreigner you never heard of, one guy who should have gotten the thing 20 years ago, Dustin Hoffman, anybody in a Vietnam movie, and Let's Just Give Away This Last Nomination To Some Idiot From "Saturday Night Live" Who Doesn't Stand A Chance And Watch Him Spend $900 On A Tuxedo. HAHAHAHA.

BEST ACTRESS: Meryl Streep.

Q. What is the order of the Oscar show?

1. Boring dance number. 2. Best Lighting Award. 3. Boring Explanation of the Rules. 4. Two-hour tribute to Lassie. 5. Diet Coke commercial. 6. Cher in a jockstrap. 7. Oops, we're out of time.

Q. What's the difference between a Documentary Short and a Documentary Feature?

A. About an hour's worth of sleep.

Q. Who is the Best Boy?

A. Why, you are, son.

Q. Mr. Oscar, every year the acceptance speeches get longer and longer. Can't something be done?

A. Yes. This year, the Academy has inserted a small nuclear device inside the statuette, which must be disarmed within 30 seconds or else KAPOW! Try thanking your fifth-grade music teacher now.

Q. I am an Academy Award nominee but cannot attend the ceremonies. Who should I send in my place?

A. First of all, you are assuming you will win. HAHAHAHA. Fat chance. However, this raises an important issue: The substitute. Most people feel it should be someone you know, like and trust. Come off it! This is Hollywood! The substitute should be a migrant worker from Central America who has not showered in a week and whose acceptance speech goes, "DEATH TO THE CAPITALIST MOVIE EXECUTIVE! ALSO, I WANT TO THANK MY MOTHER."

Q. Hey, Mr. Oscar, I can't stand it when those damned foreigners win. Why don't they get their own awards show?

A. *Je ne sais pas, vous ete une fleur.*

Q. What are this year's animal awards?

A. 1. Best Performance By A Dog Who Sleeps With A Police Officer. 2. Best Performance By A Fish Not Named Wanda. 3. Best Gorilla (male). 4. Best Gorilla (female). 5. Best Performance By Snake Not Currently Working As A Lawyer. 6. Best Aardvark.

Q. What is an Adapted Screenplay?

A. A screenplay that was loved very much by its real mommy but had to be raised by someone else who also loved it very much.

Q. Mr. Oscar, I watch your show every year. Why must these talented actors and actresses read those foolish cue cards when they present the awards?

A. Why, I don't know what you're talking about. Let's replay a segment from last year's show:

MAN: You know, the role of Special Effects cannot be underplayed.

WOMAN: Honey, I Shrunk The Laundry.

MAN: And then he said, "Burritos? I thought this was Italian food."

WOMAN: But seriously, folks.

Hohoho. That's great stuff. It's killing me.

Q. I am nominated for a major award but don't think I will win. How should I react if the scum who does win is sitting next me?

A. That depends. If the TV camera is on you, nod quickly as if to say, "Smashing job, chap, well done." As soon as the camera is off, pull a knife and recite the following: "You die. You dead. You history. And the guy holding your award has a social disease."

Q. What is the Key Grip?

A. Wrap your palm over your thumb, then putt the ball toward the hole.

Q. Is it true Woody Allen never comes to the Oscars because he plays clarinet at a New York City nightclub every Monday?

A. Yes. However, the audience at that nightclub never hears him play. They are all gathered around the TV set by the bar, fast asleep, still waiting for Best Costume Design. ◆

IS ONE DOLLAR A WEEK TOO HIGH FOR JUSTICE?

April 8, 1990

It was a New Year's Eve party. She was a high school senior. She left in her car. Three minutes later, she was dead.

A drunk driver killed her, just a mile from her home. She never saw him coming. He was not even injured. When he crawled out through his window and saw the wreckage, according to a witness, he said, "Boy, am I in trouble now."

The girl's parents were called. They came quickly. On the way, they prayed it was a mistake. When they saw her blue Volkswagen, crushed like paper, they stopped praying.

They wanted justice. They went to court. They could have sought millions in damages; at first they did. Then they changed their minds. This was all they asked: The young man who killed their child must write a check for $1 a week in her name. Do it every Friday, because that was the day she died. For 18 years, because that was how long she lived.

One dollar a week. Mail it to their house. The driver readily agreed.

This happened eight years ago in Fairfax, Va. It made news last month because the man has stopped making payments. It is not the first time. In fact, he began missing them within two years of the crash. For a while he sent his father's checks. For a while he sent nothing. For a while he sent dollar bills.

Last year, the checks began to bounce.

Then they stopped coming altogether.

The girl is still dead.

All we wanted was a visible sign that he remembered what he had done," says Patricia Herzog, whose daughter, Susan, was killed that night. "When we first suggested the payments, he was very quick to accept the idea. It was better than a million-dollar lawsuit. But since then, well, it seems like he just doesn't want to do it. To put it bluntly, he keeps forgetting."

So the Herzogs took him back to court. This time the man, Kevin Tunell, 26, arrived with his lawyer and two boxes of signed checks, which extended to the year 2001 — or one year more than what was agreed to. "Here," he said. He offered them as a compromise. The Herzogs refused. The point, they said, was to write Susan's name every week, to remember the crime, just as they must remember it every day.

So Tunell took the witness stand, before a judge. He began to cry. He said he was not trying to hurt anyone, but that he was still haunted by the crash and the weekly payments were such painful reminders. That, the Herzogs figured, was the point. But the judge, Jack Stevens, turned to the parents and questioned "the wisdom" of their persistence. "To err is human, to forgive divine," he said.

They should have knocked over his chair.

Why is it always the victims who are asked to adjust? What did they do to deserve their fate? In ancient societies, if a man was caught stealing, they cut off his hand. Accused of blasphemy, they cut out his tongue.

Now for taking the life of an innocent girl, Kevin Tunell — who, because he was convicted as a juvenile and a first-time offender, never spent a day in jail — was asked to pay $936. Over 18 years.

That was too much?

In a film called "Crimes and Misdemeanors," a man is haunted after having his lover murdered. For weeks he cannot sleep. He is on the verge of confessing. Then one night, he does sleep. And the next morning he wakes up, and the birds are singing, the sun is shining. Suddenly, it doesn't hurt so much. He is safe. He is free. He goes on as if nothing ever happened.

Could we really forget a life so easily? Could one dollar a week become an annoyance? "He never knew Susan; he was drunk when it happened," says Mrs. Herzog. "It's hard for him to feel bad about a stranger.

"People ask us how we felt when we got his checks. The truth is, we didn't feel anything new. Our pain never went away. If he only endured his once a week, he's lucky."

Let it be known that Tunell was seriously drunk at the time of the crash (.17 on the Breathalyzer). Let it also be known that the Herzogs are not teetotalers. They simply do not drink and drive. They have another daughter who was hit by a drunk driver and spent nine months in a wheelchair and on crutches. The man who hit her had no insurance. He has since disappeared.

All they want is some justice for their child, a little piece of soul for one that was lost. Judge Stevens — who said, "I take no joy in this" — sentenced Tunell to 30 days in prison for missing his payments, but suspended it pending an appeal. And now they wait.

The irony, as Patricia Herzog says, "is that this man never went to jail for killing our daughter. But he might end up there for forgetting her."

Then again, which is the greater crime? ◆

A PAMPERED BACHELOR LEARNS ABOUT BABIES

April 22, 1990

S AN FRANCISCO — Today we are going to talk about babies, because I have been out here all week waiting for a baby, and when the little bugger finally arrived I felt like cradling him in my arms, and whispering softly in his tiny little ear, "HEY! WHAT'S YOUR PROBLEM? DON'T THEY HAVE CLOCKS WHERE YOU COME FROM?"

But let me explain.

Being a normal, healthy, American bachelor, I have always based my knowledge of childbirth on a most reliable source, namely the "I Love Lucy" show. And I think most guys will back me up on this. We believe that childbirth is something that happens in the middle of the night, when Lucy, lying in bed after a rough day of getting stuck inside a washing machine at the laundromat, turns on the light and says, "Uh-oh!" and Ricky says, "Wha? Luzeee, wha's wrong?" and Lucy says, "Ricky! Don't get nervous, honey. I'm having the baby," and Ricky goes, "WAAAAA!" and runs out the door in his slippers.

And two hours later the baby is born.

From this we learn the man's role in childbirth is 1) make sure you have your slippers and 2) act like a complete idiot. And I can handle this. Which is why, eight months ago, when my only sister told me she was pregnant with the first new child in our family since my brother — who is 29 years old, so he can't really be considered new anymore — I said to her, my voice full of pride, "Sister, I shall be there when the infant is born."

Just call me Ethel.

T here was, of course, one glitch: I live in Detroit. My sister lives in San Francisco. That could be tough. After all, Lucy did the whole baby thing in one 30-minute show. And that was after spinning around the laundromat.

So I would have to be swift. I made my brother-in-law promise to call as soon as my sister went into labor. Finally, Monday, the phone rang.

He said: "It's started."

I said: "WAAAAA!"

And I raced to the airport.

I called before I got on the plane: "How far apart are the convulsions?"

"You mean the contractions?"

"Whatever."

"About 15 minutes."

Oh my god. This would never do. The kid would be playing Nintendo by the time I arrived. I got the first seat on the plane, closest to the door. When we landed, I dashed outside. My father was there waiting.

"Boy or girl?" I said.

"Relax. She hasn't had it yet."

Wow. This was a long one. We reached the house. We entered the house. There was my sister, who looked like, well, the house.

"Hi," she panted, in between convulsions. I mean, contractions.

And we waited.

And we waited. Two hours. Four hours. Past midnight. Past 2 a.m. This was not at all what I expected. "Why aren't we rushing out the door?" I asked. "Why aren't we jumping in a taxicab?" I looked at my brother-in-law. "Where are your slippers?"

"The doctor says not even to come in until the contractions are five minutes apart."

"But when Lucy had her —"

They looked at me. I stopped.

We waited some more — 6 a.m., 8 a.m. My sister actually was going backwards, her contractions further apart. Finally, she rose and said: "I'm hungry. Let's go for breakfast."

"Breakfast?" I screamed. "You can't eat! You'll explode! You —"

We went to breakfast. A few hours later, we went for lunch.

Pretty soon, it was Wednesday.

"Labor can take several days," my sister said calmly, even though, now and then, she would suck air like a fish. "Or it could be false labor. Or they might even induce labor." I couldn't believe what she was saying. But then, being a normal brother, I couldn't believe she had found a husband, either.

Anyhow, with my concept of childbirth shattered, I decided to go to a basketball game. This is a bachelor thing to do. At halftime, I found a phone. I called. No answer. "Must be snack time," I figured.

I tried the hospital. Lo and behold, she had been admitted. I asked for the room. My brother-in-law picked up the phone.

"Lu'zee?" I said.

"It's a boy!" he said.

"WAAAAAA!" I said.

And that was it. I missed the whole thing.

So here I sit, with my first nephew. When he is old enough, I will teach him the most important lesson in life. I will sit him down. I will turn on "I Love Lucy." And I will tell him not to believe anything he sees, none of it, not one single moment.

Except the laundromat part. ◆

GOOD-BYE TO SAX PLAYER GORDON, AND ALL THAT JAZZ

April 29, 1990

W e have lost a great man. He died in a hospital bed in Philadelphia. Few people noticed, because he didn't have a hit TV show or a People magazine cover. You make your living playing jazz saxophone in America, you don't expect a big funeral.

Dexter Gordon should have had one anyhow. He played jazz sax all right, some say he helped mold it, wailing, crying, deep, throaty ballads and hard-bopping solos that left you breathless, teary-eyed; if you ever heard him play, you know this is true. The sad part is, you probably never heard him play, not if you are the typical American music listener. There may be a Madonna or Van Halen album in your collection should you be in your teens, or a Sinatra and Mathis LP should you be in your 50s, but albums by Dexter Gordon, Bud Powell, Chet Baker, Coleman Hawkins — they call you a jazz "nut" if you have these, as if there were something crazy about falling in love with brilliance.

Crazy? Why? Did you know these men had to leave their own country to hear real applause? They played to wild crowds in Europe during the '50s and '60s. Some stayed there. Some died there. Some, like Gordon, went and came back and probably wondered why. His gift was be-bop, dancing notes around the melody of standards, sometimes erupting fast like a volcano, sometimes playing slow as a kiss at midnight, but always sweet, elegant, original, and here he was, scraping by, night after night, while four idiots named Kiss were painting their faces and wearing spandex and yanking in millions.

Now, who's crazy?

A fter Gordon died — kidney failure killed him — I pulled his albums out from my collection. Inside one is a lovely story about the week he returned to New York after 14 years of living abroad. He was sitting in the club one afternoon when the phone rang. No bartenders were around, so he picked it up.

"Hello, Village Vanguard," he said, like an employee, "uh-huh . . . yes, on Tuesday night, Dexter Gordon plays here . . . uh-huh. . . . Who's this? This is Dexter Gordon. . . . Yes. . . . Why, thank you, sweetheart. . . . "

I smiled. Jazz men. When I started in this business, I did a magazine story on a be-bop pianist named Red Garland. Like Gordon, Red was now an old, slow-talking, bespectacled man. I introduced myself at a New York club one night, and asked whether he would let me interview him.

"Only if you buy the beer," he whispered.

Deal. For two hours he filled my ears with countless tales of smoky nights and hot music, famous names, famous tunes. What a rich life! This man had played with legends, Coltrane, Miles, he'd made dozens of records, and here he was, just grateful for a drink. Toward the end of our talk, he told me about the night in Boston when he was supposed to play with Charlie (Bird) Parker, whom most consider the greatest jazz saxophonist ever. But Bird never showed up. The next morning, Garland bought a paper and saw the headline: "Jazz Star Dies From Drug Addiction."

"I cried," he said.

And he wiped his eyes again. A few years later, I picked up a paper and saw that Garland, too, had passed away.

And now, another newspaper, and Dexter Gordon, 67, is gone. Sarah Vaughn, the great jazz vocalist, said good-bye a few weeks ago. We never appreciate artists such as these. Not while they're living. Not once they're dead. It's crazy. Here is one form of music that America can claim as its own — not classical, not opera, they belong to other countries — but jazz, it was born on this soil in cities such as New Orleans, Kansas City, St. Louis, it is as rich as gravy and as original as clouds, and yet you want to know what got Gordon the most attention in his long career? A movie.

They called it "Round Midnight." Came out a few years ago. Dexter played himself, basically, an old tenor sax man, plagued by alcohol, who goes to Paris and meets a Frenchman who tries to save his life. In one scene, Dexter is arrested and taken to a mental hospital. He slumps in the chair and answers a doctor's questions.

"You know," he rasps, in a gravel voice, "there are some nights where I'm playing . . . and playing . . . and at the end of the night, I look at my saxophone and the mouthpiece is all bloody. Full of blood. But I hadn't felt anything. Do you understand, doctor?"

We have never understood. And now Dexter is dead. His obituary got less ink than a story about New Kids On The Block. It is crazy and unfair — these jazz players are American treasures — and what can you do? I suppose if you love the music, if it speaks to you the way it did to these artists — then you only can put on their albums and close your eyes. There's magic on that vinyl, magic and blood. Neither, it seems, will ever dry up. ♦

HE TRIED TO BE HERCULES; STEROIDS SHATTERED LIFE

August 12, 1990

Twice a week, in the early morning, he takes his cane and tries to walk around the block. His steps are labored, his movements stiff and exaggerated, like a puppet yanked by strings. He passes the red brick house and the one with aluminum siding. Cane. Step. Cane. Step. *You can do it,* he's thinking. But by the time he turns the corner, he is sweating. Soon he is short of breath. Past the silver fence now. Around the next corner. Cane. Step. "You're dragging your foot, Sam," his therapist tells him. Sam grits his teeth. He is thinking "walk" but the message does not reach his legs. This is what happens when you have a stroke. It's like someone snipped the phone lines from your brain.

Past another porch now. Another driveway. Past the house with the American flag. The third corner is in sight, but his foot is shaking, it is turning inward, against his will. Cane. Step. *Come on . . .*

"OK, good job, Sam, that's enough for today," the therapist finally says, and Sam stops, sweating hard. His wife, Laura, pulls up in the car. He rides the rest of the way home, cane on his lap. He went 500 yards. It took 40 minutes. A good day. Very good.

This is a story about a man and his muscle, and the pills and injections that made those muscles grow into his enemy. Back when Sam Virgo was turning heads with his physique, it was easy to get steroids. Doctors prescribed them. Weight lifters sold them. They were available at just about any gym, places you or your kids could enter today. Some came with a label on the bottle; some you took on faith. They are so common, these steroids, that once, Sam saw a guy shoot up, then walk around the gym with the syringe hanging from his butt.

"Crazy," he says now, shaking his head. Crazy, yes, like those photos from five years ago, in which Sam's leg muscles bulge, his waist is narrow as a basketball hoop, his lats form a V under his arms so thick he looks like a bat spreading its wings. Back then, as a bodybuilder, the mirror was his lover; he sculpted himself the way an artist sculpts clay. But now he looks in the mirror and sees the flabby stomach and the sunken flesh and the left side that feels as if it's always asleep. Once in a while, he will try to flex a bicep and he will feel, he says, "like crying."

Have you ever wanted to look big, to feel tough, to be noticed in a crowd?

317

Have you ever wondered what you'd sacrifice for that? This is not the story of some fallen NFL superstar. This is about one of us, a guy next door. All across America this month, kids return to high school football practice, college students are working out, adult males meet their lifting partners at the gym after work. And the little pills are there. Always have been. And everyone thinks he knows his limits. Which, of course, is what Sam Virgo thought. In 11 years of steroid use, he studied all he could about chemicals, proteins, hormones. He read books. He read medical journals. He thought he had learned it all. But it wasn't until after the stroke, which hit him when he was 32 years old — "I tell people I had a stroke and they say, 'A stroke? My *grandfather* had a stroke,' and I say, 'Did he recover?'" and they say, 'He's dead.' " — it wasn't until after this that Sam learned courage. The kind it takes to say, "Help me. I want to live."

Listen up, dumbbells. You might want to hear this.

W hen I was a kid, you know who my heroes were?" says Virgo, 36, his speech still slow and soft from the stroke four years ago. "Superman. Hercules. I loved the way they were drawn. I wanted to look like that. And the closest I could come was bodybuilding."

In this way, he was not alone. How many million Americans want a shape they can show off? Sam Virgo, understand, was not some crazy psychopath; he was a normal guy, a college student with a good head for business who, when he was 21, walked into a Vic Tanny's, like a lot of us, and began working out. And he talked to other lifters. And he heard about these pills. And eventually, in the mid-1970s, he went to this doctor who ran a diet center and who asked Sam what he wanted. Sam said he wanted to get big. The doctor, Sam says, then prescribed steroids, Dianabol, in pill form, and DecaDurabolin, which he injected into Sam's hip every other month. Just like that. A doctor did this?

"He told me about how big all his other weight lifter patients had gotten with this stuff," Virgo says. "He bragged about it."

The doctor still practices today and has several offices. He wouldn't discuss Virgo's comments.

S am saw the results of the steroids immediately. He arms grew thicker, his recovery time shorter. He could lift now with the big boys, hundreds of pounds in squats, bench presses, leg presses. For a year or two, he kept going to that doctor and another for pills and injections. Then he began buying at the gym. This is how it works: You see a guy. You ask what he's using. You ask where you can get some. Maybe he sells it to you.

Now Sam was big. He could feel his bulk against the cotton of his T-shirts. When he walked, he felt power, and he thought people would find this attractive. "Actually," he says now, "they were just scared. I looked like a brute." He began to act like one, too. He grew moody. Aggressive. Steroids do this. One time, in the gym, some teenagers were watching him lift. He glared at them, picked up a bench and threw it across the room. "How about working out someplace else?" he barked. They scattered.

He was sweating constantly. At night, he could barely sleep. He would rise and do hundreds of push-ups and sit-ups, just to burn off this energy. His sex drive was heightened. His anger was ever-boiling. He fell into a state of constant anxiety, a feeling, he says, "like you have to go somewhere, even when you have no place to go."

In 1982, he quit his job as a buyer for an aircraft parts manufacturer. He couldn't get along with the people anymore. The gym. Only the gym was his sanctuary. He began working out all the time, six hours a day; he could bench-press 375 pounds and leg-press 860. He increased his steroids. He used multiple combinations. He began to think about bodybuilding competitions. He read the books. Studied the poses. In the spring of 1985, he entered a local contest called Mr. Highland. During the competition, he began to feel weak. He had to lie down backstage. "I must have overtrained," he thought. He finished sixth.

Two weeks later, at an Ironman competition, the same thing happened. He was dizzy, short of breath. Deep down, he suspected the steroids were hurting him. But he kept swallowing them. Kept sticking himself with a needle in the mornings. "I once read a survey of bodybuilders that asked, 'If you could take a pill that would guarantee you first place but would kill you in six months, would you do it?' " Sam says. "And 90 percent said they would."

He pauses. "And I would have, too."

The first stroke came a year later. Sam was living in an apartment with Laura, then his girlfriend. He woke up and the room was spinning. He stumbled into the bathroom, suffering diarrhea and vomiting at the same time. "The tops of his *feet* were sweating," Laura recalls.

She phoned the doctor, who said it was probably food poisoning. When they finally went to the hospital, 12 hours later — Sam didn't want to go because "I wanted to work out the next day" — the people there didn't know what to make of him. Tests, for some reason, revealed nothing. Only months later would a neurologist determine it had been a stroke. At the time, one nurse thought he was a drug addict. A week later he was discharged.

From that point, Sam felt "a constant sense of doom." He never wanted to be alone. In August of that year, during a workout at the gym, he was talking to some other lifters, and his speech began to slur. They laughed. "Am I talking funny?" he said. They said yeah. He panicked. He had read about this in the journals. A stroke. "I gotta get some air," he said.

It was too late. He collapsed in the doorway. His eyes rolled back. The ambulance came. His left side went numb. In the hospital, he kept

319

mumbling, "Where's my arm?" even though it was resting on his stomach. He couldn't collect his thoughts. He was there, but not there. At one point, he tried to get out of bed and tumbled to the floor. His sister rushed to help him. "Get off of me!" he yelled. "Let me up! Get off me!" But she was nowhere near him. What he felt was his own dead weight, on top of him like a corpse.

There are stories about professional wrestlers who took steroids for years and now have failing livers and crumbling bones. There is the story of Steve Courson, a former NFL lineman who took steroids since college and now has cardiomyopathy — same as Sam — and needs a new heart. There are stories everywhere about what the little pills can do to you, and yet people keep taking them and medicine just doesn't know the limits. Every day it's a new horror. One doctor told Sam Virgo he would not live without a heart transplant. Another told him his heart "was the size of a basketball," and the steroids could have done that, since the heart is a muscle, too. Maybe that led to the blood clots that led to the stroke.

All Sam knew was that he wished he were dead. He asked his mother where she had put his gun. "I couldn't even wipe myself in the bathroom," he says, softly. "Can you imagine the shame of that?"

With his left side paralyzed, Sam came home from the hospital in a wheelchair. Laura quit her job to take care of him. Within a short time, almost unbelievably, she became pregnant. Her first reaction was shock. "God, we didn't want a baby," she says. "We thought it would be born deformed, sick." She considered an abortion.

Instead, she and Sam chose to marry. It was a quick and simple ceremony. The families squeezed into the front room of Sam's parents' house in Dearborn, Mich. — the same house where he grew up fantasizing about Superman, the house where he and Laura now lived. A judge read the vows. Sam slumped in a chair. When the part came to kiss the bride, Laura leaned over and found her husband's lips. His face was half-stiff. It was not a fairy tale. It was not the way they dreamed it would be. Even today, strangers ask Laura, a very attractive woman, why she did it.

"Sometimes," she says, "all you have in life is to say you love somebody."

And sometimes, that is enough. The baby was born, a beautiful healthy girl named Kimbra. And suddenly, Sam Virgo had a reason to live. He stopped thinking about guns. He signed up for rehab treatment. He regained some feeling on his left side; he got out of the wheelchair and began to walk with a cane, first a few steps, then a few more. His doctors were surprised. "Sam is very smart and extremely motivated," says his therapist, Dan Geer, from the New Life Rehabilitation Center, who makes that walk with him in the mornings. "He says to me all the time, did you read this article where thousands of high school kids are taking steroids now? They don't know what they're doing. Look at me, Dan. Look at me!"

Yes. Look at him. A nice guy. A smart guy. Maybe like a lot of guys you know. Sam has friends out there, pushing barbells over their heads even as you read this. They never call him. They pretend he doesn't exist. "We used to say, 'Let's live dynamically until we're 50, and then we won't care,'" Sam says. He looks at his body, twisted and soft. "I didn't quite make it. I lasted to 32."

There is no happy ending to this story. There is only hope, the hope that someone hears it and throws the pills away, the hope that people stop thinking strength and looks are so damn important. The hope that Sam Virgo can one day go the full distance on those sunny mornings, without a cane. "Crazy, no?" he says, sighing. Crazy, yes. But when it comes to steroids, going around the block is easy. It's trying to get back that can break your heart. ◆